J. H. Bernard, R. Atkinson

The Irish Liber hymnorum

Vol. II

J. H. Bernard, R. Atkinson

The Irish Liber hymnorum
Vol. II

ISBN/EAN: 9783741179044

Manufactured in Europe, USA, Canada, Australia, Japa

Cover: Foto ©Angelika Wolter / pixelio.de

Manufactured and distributed by brebook publishing software (www.brebook.com)

J. H. Bernard, R. Atkinson

The Irish Liber hymnorum

THE IRISH LIBER HYMNORUM

EDITED FROM THE MSS. WITH TRANSLATIONS, NOTES, AND GLOSSARY

BY

J. H. BERNARD D.D.,

Fellow of Trinity College, and Archbishop King's Lecturer in Divinity in the University of Dublin

AND

R. ATKINSON, LL.D.,

Professor of Sanskrit in the University of Dublin.

VOL. II. TRANSLATIONS AND NOTES.

London.
1898.

LONDON:
HARRISON AND SONS, PRINTERS IN ORDINARY TO HER MAJESTY,
ST. MARTIN'S LANE.

CONTENTS OF VOL. II.

PAGE.

INTRODUCTION.
 § 1. The Metrical Systems of the Latin Hymns   ix
 § 2. The Metrical Systems of the Irish Hymns   xxxi

TRANSLATIONS OF THE IRISH PREFACES AND HYMNS.
 Preface to the Hymn *Audite omnes* (No. 1)   3
  ,, ,, ,, *Christus in nostra insula* (No. 2)   8
  ,, ,, ,, *Celebra Iuda* (No. 3)   9
  ,, ,, ,, *Parce Domine* (No. 4)   11
  ,, ,, ,, *Sen Dé* (No. 5)   12
 The Hymn *Sen Dé* (No. 5)   14
 Preface to the Hymn *Cantemus in omni die* (No. 6)   17
  ,, ,, ,, *Hymnum dicas* (No. 7)   18
  ,, ,, ,, *In trinitate spes mea* (No. 8)   19
  ,, ,, ,, *Martine te deprecor* (No. 9)   20
  ,, ,, ,, *Gloria in Excelsis* (No. 10)   21
  ,, ,, ,, *Magnificat* (No. 11)   22
  ,, ,, ,, *Te Deum* (No. 13)   22
  ,, ,, ,, *Altus Prosator* (No. 14)   23
  ,, ,, ,, *In te Christe* (No. 15)   27
  ,, ,, ,, *Noli Pater* (No. 16)   28
  ,, ,, Prayer of St. John (No. 17)   29
  ,, ,, Epistle of Christ to Abgar (No. 18)   30
  ,, ,, Hymn *Genair Patraic* (No. 19)   31
 The Hymn *Genair Patraic* (No. 19)   32
 Ninine's Prayer (No. 20)   36
 Preface to the Hymn *Brigit be bithmaith* (No. 21)   37
 The Hymn *Brigit be bithmaith* (No. 21)   39
  ,, *Ni car Brigit* (No. 22) and Preface   40
 St. Sanctan's Hymn (No. 23) and Preface   47
 The Lorica of St. Patrick (No. 24) and Preface   49
 The Hymn of Máel-Ísu (No. 29)   52
 The Names of the Apostles (No. 30)   52
 Preface to the Amra of St. Columba (No. 33)   53
 The Amra of St. Columba (No. 33)   55
 St. Adamnan's Prayer (No. 34)   81
 Pedigree of St. Mobi (No. 35)   82
 The Hymn of St. Philip (No. 36)   83
 Miscellanea (No. 37)   84
 The Release of Scandlan Mor (No. 38)   85
 The Death of St. Columba (No. 39)   87

CONTENTS.

TRANSLATIONS OF THE IRISH PREFACES AND HYMNS—*continued*.

	PAGE
The Five Divisions of Munster (No. 40)	88
In Praise of Hymnody (No. 41)	89
The Three Kings (No. 42)	90
Preface to *Benedicite* (No. 43)	91
,, *Christe qui lux es* (No. 44)	92
,, *Quicunque Vult* (No. 47)	92

NOTES AND TRANSLATIONS OF THE IRISH GLOSSES.

	PAGE
The Irish Prefaces	95
The Hymn *Audite omnes* (No. 1)	96
,, *Christus in nostra* (No. 2)	106
,, *Celebra Iuda* (No. 3)	108
,, *Parce domine* (No. 4)	112
,, *Sén Dé* (No. 5)	113
,, *Cantemus in omni die* (No. 6)	123
,, *Hymnum dicat* (No. 7)	125
,, *In trinitate spes mea* (No. 8)	132
,, *Martine te deprecor* (No. 9)	134
,, *Gloria in Excelsis* (No. 10)	135
,, *Magnificat and Benedictus* (Nos. 11 and 12)	137
,, *Te Deum* (No. 13)	138
,, *Altus Prosator* (No. 14)	140
,, *In te Christe* (No. 15)	169
,, *Noli Pater* (No. 16)	171
The Prayer of St. John (No. 17)	172
The Epistle of Christ to Abgar (No. 18)	173
The Hymn *Genair Patraic* (No. 19)	175
The Prayer of Ninine (No. 20)	187
The Hymn *Brigit be bithmaith* (No. 21)	187
,, *Ni car Brigit* (No. 22)	189
,, *Ateoch rig* (No. 23)	206
The Lorica of St. Patrick (No. 24)	208
The Lamentation of St. Ambrose (No. 25)	212
An Abridgement of the Psalter (No. 26)	216
The Hymn *Alto et ineffabili* (No. 27)	218
,, *Abbas probatus omnino* (No. 28)	220
,, *Inspirut noeb* (No. 29)	221
The Names of the Apostles (No. 30)	222
The Hymn *Ecce fulget* (No. 31)	222
,, Phoebi diem (No. 32)	223
The Amra of St. Columba (No. 33)	223
The Prayer of St. Adamnan (No. 34)	235
The Pedigree of St. Mobi (No. 35)	235
The Hymn *Pilip apstail* (No. 36)	236
Miscellanea (No. 37)	236
The Release of Scandlan Mor (No. 38)	236
The Death of St. Columba (No. 39)	238
The Five Divisions of Munster (No. 40)	238

NOTES AND TRANSLATIONS OF THE IRISH GLOSSES—*continued.*

	PAGE
In Praise of Hymnody (No. 41)	239
Hymn on the Three Kings (No. 42)	239
Benedicite (No. 43)	239
The Hymn *Christe qui lux es* (No. 44)	240
,, *Christi patris in dextera* (No. 45)	241
Cantemus domino gloriose (No. 46)	241
Quicunque Vult (No. 47)	242
The Lorica of Gildas (No. 48)	242

INDICES.

I. Of Personal Names	246
II. Of Places and Tribes	256

The Metrical Systems of the *Liber Hymnorum*.

§ 1. The Latin Hymns.

ADMITTING that a certain importance may be naturally assigned to the question of the origin of the metres in these hymns, I have yet thought it better to set forth simply the facts ascertainable from the investigation of the texts themselves, without entering upon the difficult problem of their possible relations to continental writings of the early period. Whatever theory be held as to the original forms of Irish Metric, it must necessarily take into account the facts thus ascertained.

The hymns that are the subject of this section are numbered in our collection 1, 2, 3, 6, 7, 8, 9; 14, 15, 16; 27, 28, 31, 32; 44, 45; 48. With one exception, they are the work of Irish poets, according to the undisputed tradition of native writers, but the internal evidence for this belief is not equally strong in the case of the several poems. The one admittedly foreign element is the hymn of St. Hilary of Poitiers, *Ymnum dicat*, which, as we shall see, bears the unmistakeable stamp of a totally different system of metrical structure and consequently of treatment of the language. This is a classic poem; the others are vulgar Latin.

The Prefaces do not add much to our knowledge. When, *e.g.*, on *Martine te deprecor* (No. 9), the scholiast says that it is made in rhythm and that there are six capitula, each of two lines, he states, no doubt, what is sufficiently obvious; but when he adds *non æqualem numerum syllabarum singulæ lineæ seruant*, it is equally obvious that he had not rightly conceived the metrical system. That the poet did not construct the hymn in any irregular manner may be taken as certain; he knew well what rules he intended to follow, and these rules were never so elastic as the Preface would lead us to infer. That the metrical laws were duly observed by the writers of our hymns cannot be doubted; but to an ear accustomed to the rhythm of classic verses, the effect must be very unharmonious and disconcerting. We can hardly think that the writers were familiar with Latin classical poetry. But to anyone familiar with their laws of versification, there is no lack of dexterity in the structure of these verses. Interpolations demonstrate themselves as such, by exhibiting the incapacity of the later versifiers to comprehend or imitate the earlier style (as in l. 25 of Hilary's Hymn), or by the thoughtlessness that introduced an incongruous construction into a complex clause (as in l. 33 of the hymn *Celebra Iuda*), or by the use of wrong metres, as will appear in the sequel.

It is not necessary to determine what the poets regarded as a 'line,' in every case; but as the long line always has a cæsura, it may be laid down that the unit is *seven- or eight-syllabled*. How many times this unit is repeated before the stanza is complete, is left to the poets' choice. Taking this seven- or eight-syllabled structure as the *unit*, and assuming two of these units as the *line*, the following synopsis may be given of all the varieties of metre found in the hymns :—

    A.   *unrhymed*.
        a,   2 (8 + 7)   = Hymn No. 7.
        b,   4 (8 + 7)   =   „   „ 1.
    B.   *line-rhymes*.
        a,   2 (8 + 7)   =   „   „ 6, 8.
        b,   2 (7 + 7)   =   „   „ 9.
        c,   2 (5 + 7)   =   „   „ 3.
        d,   2 (6 + 5)   =   „   , 48.

C. *unit-rhymes.*
   a, 2 (8 + 8)   = Hymn No. 15, 16, 31, 32, 45.
   b, 4 (8 + 8)   =   „   „ 2, 27, 44.
   c, 6 (8 + 8)   =   „   „ 14.
   d, n (8 + 8)   =   „   „ 28.

We must now go through these in order.

A. *Unrhymed Hymns.*

Aa. The unrhymed hymns may be considered first, as being probably the least influenced by native tendencies. Hymn No. 7 (that of St. Hilary) is distinguished from all the rest by the circumstance that it observes both *quantity* and *elision*. It is, in short, a regular trochaic tetrameter catalectic (*quod a poetis Græcis et Latinis frequentissime ponitur*, according to the F Preface), divided by a cæsura after the eighth syllable:

ȳmnūm | dĭcāt | tŭrbă | frătrŭm,
ȳmnūm | căntūs | pĕrsŏ|nĕt.

The rule set forth in the Prefaces that a spondee should not occur in the third place is fairly adhered to; but the Prefaces note its infraction in ll. 9, 24 (see also 29, 34, 38, 60, 67). In other respects the *quantity* of the Latin vowels is observed (note scandĕrē crucem in 39). Also, *elision* is regularly carried out, as in 9, 14, 20, 23, 29, 32, 49, and 72, 73,[2] 74.

Now this strict observance of quantity and elision throughout makes it highly probable that ll. 25, 26 are spurious:

uinum | quod de|erat | idris   motar|i a quam iu|bet
nupti|is me|ro re|tentis   propin|nando | pocu|lo

Here (*a*) *dēĕrat* is impossible; (*β*) *motari* could not have escaped elision; (*γ*) *idris* should have been *ydriis* (trisyll.), like *nuptiis* in the following line; (*δ*) *prŏpinnando* could not have begun a trochaic measure; (*ε*) *uinum* has to be taken as dependent on *motari*, 'to be changed *into* wine,' for *quod* is never used as = 'because,' but only as the neuter relative;

and (ζ) no definite meaning can be elicited from either *mero propinnando* or *nuptiis retentis*. Under these circumstances (to which may be added that it was found necessary to signify in one MS. the *ordo uerborum*), we cannot doubt that this stanza is an interpolation, although it is found in all the MSS.

Some points are to be noticed in the concurrence of vowels. The semi-vocalic nature of *i* and *u* often constituted a difficulty to the transcribers, who have variously modified the text in consequence. Thus 8 *ante | sæcŭlă tŭa fŭisti* is impossible, for *-la* in *saecula* could not be long, *tui* could not be monosyllabic, and *fuisti* could not be dissyllabic, for *u* before a vowel does not coalesce therewith. A gives us the true text, viz., *antĕ | sæclă | tŭ fŭĭsti*. The usage is for non-initial *u* to be pronounced separately; thus we have 6 *iannŭā*, 13 *pŭĕrperam*, 18 *flŭĭt*, 24 *mortŭŏs*, 32 *instrŭŭntur*, 45 *affŭĭt*, 55 *mortŭĭs*, 58 *iānŭĭs*. An exception is found in 30 *duodecim*, which must be scanned 'without the *u*,' as the marginal gloss says; *i.e.*, it is pronounced *dwodecim* (cf. Italian *due*, but *dodici*).

Similarly with non-initial *i*. We have 10, 40, *omnĭŭm*, 11 *Gabriēlis nuntĭō*, 16 *nuntĭātum*, *potentĭæ*, 19 *nutrĭendus*, (26 *nuptĭīs*), 27 *milĭă*, 34 *Pontĭō*, 38 *implĭs*, 39 *noxĭīs*, 56 *tertĭă*,¹ 62 *filĭŭm*, 64 *filĭōs*, 65 *glorĭăm*. But initial *i* has the consonantal value; cf. 4 *Iesse*, 10 *iubet*, 31 *Iudas*, 36 *Iudaeorum*, 45 *Ioseph*. In l. 58 the metre demands *clausis ianuis*, although all the MSS. have *ianuis clausis*.

It seems probable that the hymn originally ended with l. 66. Not only does *turba fratrum concinemus* of l. 65 furnish a fitting ending to a piece beginning *ymnum dicat turba fratrum;* but metrical changes appear in the stanzas which follow. Apart from the repetition 67 *galli cantus, galli plausus*, we have the rhyme 68 *nos cantantes et præcantes*, which is out of keeping

---

¹ In 56 *nuntiat* is wrong. The meaning is that the women are first warned (53), and then they announce to the Apostles; so that *nuntiant* which preserves the metre also keeps closer to the narrative (Lc. xxiv. 9). CG read *nuntians*, but that, while restoring the metre, does not remove the awkwardness of construction.

se. must refer to the nom. of nuntiat
  the last night

with the unrhymed character of the poem.[1] Stanza 69, 70 is anomalous, because 69 *quæ* is unelided and made long before *immensam*. It is also difficult to explain *maiestatem* or to connect it with the previous stanza. Lines 71, 72 are also incorrect, for each has a spondee in the third foot; *qui* is unelided in 72; and we have 71 *dŏmino* and 72 *cŭm eo*. The last stanza is still worse; it has 73 *glŏrĭā*, *ingĕnĭto* and *unigĕnĭto*, 74 *sĭmul* and *spĭrĭtu*. These are possible in Irish *cantica*, but inconceivable in this Hilarian poem.

The result of this analysis goes to show that the hymn ended with l. 66; probably the rest was suggested by *ante lucem* of l. 65. It will be remembered that the Preface knows nothing of *ymnum dicat* as a *morning* hymn; its statement is "sic nobis conuenit canere *post prandium*."

Ab. The other unrhymed poem to be considered is the Hymn of St. Sechnall (our No. 1).

Here we are on totally different ground, for *quantity* and *elision* (save in the penult) are completely ignored. Thus while Hilary's line-endings all have the antepenult (correctly) long, Sechnall's line-endings exhibit the following: 1 *mĕrita* 6 *hŏmines* 8 *dŏminum* 16 *æthĕriam* 17 *euangĕlica* 19 *prĕtium* &c. And in like manner no account is taken of elision, e.g., 1 *audi|tĕ om|nĕs*, 2 *uĭri | ĭn Chri|stŏ*, 8 *ŭnde | ĕt in | cælis*, 9 *fĭ|dĕ im|mŏbĭ|lis*.

The rhythm of the verses is given by the obviously intended *cretic* ending of each line, where, it will be observed, the natural accent of the voice in pronouncing the word is secured by the short penult, e.g., *mĕrita, epĭscopi, ángelis, apóstolis*.[2] Hence the

---

[1] This stanza is, indeed, hardly capable of translation. "The song of the cock, the wing-clapping of the cock feels the approaching day, we singing and beseeching (the things) which we believe are about to be." The gl. explains *futura* as *praemia caelestia*; but if *praecantes* is to be taken as governing *futura*, we have a double awkwardness of structure to be added to the unsatisfactory disconnectedness of the two lines.

[2] Todd remarked that 66 *indutus* is the only case where the second syllable of the seventh foot is not short. This is quite correct, if we read in 70 *-uĭdet* instead of *-uĭdit*.

line rarely ends with a dissyllable; this only happens indeed in ll. 22, 23, 24, 28, 32, 46, 72, 85, forms of *bonus* and *deus* being the dissyllables chiefly found, and nearly all being preceded immediately by a verb.[1] On the other hand, Hilary has no objection to the dissyllabic ending (cf. ll. 5, 9, 10, 18); but save with *iubet* in ll. 10, 25, and *diem* in l. 67 (two of which are probably spurious on other grounds), the dissyllable with him is preceded by a monosyllable.

In the case of *i* before vowels (save before another *i*), there is always separate enunciation: thus we have 49 *annuntìat*, 50 *grátiàm*. But wherever *ii* occur together, they are read as one vowel, e.g., 2 *Patricí*, 19 *nauigí*.

In the case of *u* there is also separate enunciation; hence *siiam trádit ánimam* is the true text of 60 and *spìritáli pòculo* of 68, as Todd saw. After *q*, *u* is not a vowel; *quem*, *quo*, &c., are monosyllables. Todd held that 36 *cuius* was to be read as a trisyllable; but this is out of the question. It is always dissyllabic, as is also *huius* in 19, 55.

In the two poems just examined, of Hilary and Sechnall, we have typical examples of the classic and of the mediæval style. The latter is the natural outcome of the old rhythms in the poetry of the people at large, as distinguished from the elaborated structure of the scholars, who obeyed the sterner stress of the classic method.

But this unrhymed poetry, even with the adornment of acrostic arrangement, of definite 'numbers,' and recurring beat of accent, did not satisfy the æsthetic longings of poets and people. The poets in Ireland were not content to secure the charms of rhyme at definite intervals, but have superadded a luxury of harmonies of assonance and alliteration, which could hardly fail in the long run to limit the available vocabulary, but which at any rate mark these verses with the stamp of a special class that is not found elsewhere, and should secure to the poets a fitting niche in the world's anthology.

[1] In l. 32 *in cruce* practically counts as a single word.

B. *Line-rhymes.*

Ba. The first to be considered is St. Colman Mac Murchon's hymn in praise of St. Michael (our No. 8). The metre is, as in St. Sechnall's hymn, 2(8+7); but the new feature is unmistakeable. The *rhyme* is thoroughly Irish rhyme, and all the stanzas are perfect in this respect.

Rich trisyllabic rhymes occur throughout as follows: *omine, nomine; doctore, corpore; inergiae, superbiae; archangeli, angeli; species, requies; probabilis, fragilis; uiribus, milibus; aulia, gaudia; filio, consilio.* The full rhyming accent is, of course, on the antepenult; but all the three vowels are in exact correspondence, as are also the consonants which separate them. Thus in *doctore, corpore*, the group of consonants *ct* corresponds to *rp*, just as in ll. 11, 12, *noctibus, sortibus, ct* corresponds to *rt*.

In the last stanza but one, the poet seems to have been inspired to a final effort of technical skill, which it will not be easy to parallel for the richness of its rhymes, assonances, alliterations and harmonies:—

| æterna possint præstare | regis regni aulia |
| ut possideam cum Christo | paradisi gaudia. |

Here note (1), the rich trisyllabic rhymes; (2), the two *p*-alliterations in each line; (3), the harmonies *reg*is *reg*ni, and (4), the correspondences *possi*nt, *possi*deam, as also *prest*are and *Christ*o.

The poet was obviously quite conscious of his aim and of its success: he immediately adds his *Gloria Patri*, which in this case is quite in harmony with the metre, and may probably be genuine. The subsequent lines *adiuuet nos*, &c., have nothing to do with the Hymn itself, but are merely a later addition for liturgical purposes.

It is astonishing how little of the technical structure of this poem seems to have been perceived by those who have handled it. It is hard to say what was in the mind of the writer of the T preface in setting down his last sentence; but he was writing carelessly, for he has put .xi. before the *dæc* in line 11, and he says that there are *sixteen* syllables in each line. The F preface is correct in both items, but it does not contribute much to our knowledge of the real nature of the rhythm. It is evident that Todd had no clear conception of the metrical laws when he suggested[1] that "*adiutorium* (l. 7) seems to have been pronounced in four syllables." This would simply ruin the line, for the suggestion ignores the syllabification of -*īum* and the necessity of an eight-syllabled unit before the cæsura, thereby producing an eight-syllabled unit after the cæsura. The *et* of T in the line should of course be omitted with FR, and *Michaelis* should be written *Michælis*, as F gives *Michæl* in 11, 13, 15, where T has simply *Michel*.

A second hymn of exactly the same metre and style is Cuchuimne's hymn to the Virgin (our No. 6). Todd again failed to understand the metrical law. He says (l.c. p. 138): "the classical reader will not form a high idea of our author's skill in Latin prosody." But Latin prosody has absolutely nothing to do with the matter. These pieces are poems in Latin written in popular metre by Irish poets; the prosody of the classical language is replaced by accent and by rhyme, and the rhymes in this case are rich and perfect:—

cànte|mùs in | òmni | dìe | cònci|nèntes | vàri|è
còncla|màntes | dèo | dìgnum | ỳmnum | sànctæ | Màri|æ̀

Here we note that (1) every line ends in a tri- [or poly-] syllable, rhyming richly: *variè, Mariæ; Mariam, ui-cariam; domini, homini; pătĕrno, mătĕrno; uener-abilis, stabilis; similis, or-iginis; pĕriit, rĕdiit; edidit, credidit; somnia, omnia; fecerat, stĕterat; galiam, Mariam; pu-erperæ, decerpere* [T is of course wrong]; *testibus, cel-estibus.*

[1] *Liber Hymnorum*, p. 168.

THE HYMN OF ST. CUCHUIMNE.

(2) In the 'even' lines, the assonances are equally perfect:—
Here we have 2 di*gnum*, *ymn*um 2 ;

    4 *au*rem, *lau*dem ; 6 oport-*unam*, *cura*m ;
    8 con-*ceptum*, sus-*ceptum* ; 10 re-*cèsit*, ex-*stètit* ;
    12 *plane*, hum-*anæ* ; 14 uirt-*utem*, sal-*utem* ;
    16 lo*tus*, to*tus* ; 18 s*ani*, Christi-*ani* ;
    20 m*orte*, s*orte* ; 22 per-*fecti*, sus-*cepti* ;
    24 pi*ræ*, di*ræ* ; 26 fru-*amur*, scrip-*amur*.

Nothing can be more certain than the *intention* in these cases: the poet regarded the assonance in the 'even' line as an indispensable condition of the poem.

(3) One alliteration at least occurs in every stanza:—

    2 *d*eo, *d*ignum ; 7 *p*rius, *p*aterno ; 9 *v*irgo, *v*enerabilis ;
    10 ex-*st*etit, *st*abilis ; 12 *p*role, *p*lane ; 13 *p*rius, periit ;
    15 *M*aria, *m*ater, *m*iranda ; 16 *l*ate, *l*otus ;
    19 *t*onicam, *t*otum, *t*extam ; 20 *st*atim, *st*eterat ;
    21 *l*ucis, *l*oricam ; 24 *d*iræ, *d*ecerpere.

Here, also, the deliberate purpose of the poet is undeniable

And probably we shall not be far wrong in holding that, as the hymn was sung *varie*, i.e., *inter duos choros* (gl.), or as the text again says, bis per chorum *hinc* et *inde*, the last verse was sung in unison by both as a general 'invocation' to Christ, after the antiphonal rendering of the hymn to the B.V.M.

Bb. These two masterly specimens of the Latin Hymns under the hands of Irish poets are unfortunately the only ones that are left us of the kind. In the poem now to be considered, *Martine te deprecor* (our No. 9), we have a very different metre; the formula being $2(7+7)$ with line-rhymes *dissyllabic*.

Nothing definite is known about the poet Oengus, but the metre deserves close investigation. The principles of its structure are evidently quite different from those with which we are now familiar, because not only is *Christum* to be elided before *ac* in l. 2, but we find 2 Mar*iam*, 8 mort*uis*, 12 uolunta*rie*, where the two vowels are monophthongal. But the important element is the dissyllabic rhyme, which proves that the rhythm must be *iambic*.

I should not be hard to persuade that this poem of Oengus was somewhat of an experiment. The preface says: *et ostendit hymnum suum, et laudauit Adamnan hymnum;* perhaps there was an element that struck Adamnan as being unwonted.

Taking the fifth stanza of this hymn, viz. :—

    uerbum dei locutus   secutus in mandatis
    uirtutibus impletis   mortuis resuscitatis,

if we read the verses simply, making *ui* monophthongal (or perhaps = *vi*), it is almost impossible to avoid the conclusion that loc*ùtus* and sec*ùtus* were intended to rhyme, and that mand*àtis* and resuscit*atis* are also dissyllabic rhymes.

If then, on the basis of this verse-ictus, we assume that *dissyllables* are oxytone, and *trisyllables* paroxytone, we shall accent the above stanza as follows :—

    uerbùm dei locùtus   secùtus in mandàtis
    uirtùtibùs implètis   · mortvìs resùscitàtis

Examining then each word on this assumption we find the most definite usage of words as to their accent :—

- (I) Every trisyllable is paroxytone. Thus, 1 *martìne, deprècor, rogàris;* 2 *spirìtum, habèntem;* 3 *martìnus, laudàuit;* 4 *cantàuit, amàuit;* 5 *elèctus, salùtis;* 6 *donàuit, uirtùtis;* 7 *locùtus, secùtus, mandatis;* 8 *implètis;* 9 *homìnes, duplìce;* 11 *domìnum;* 12 *Martìne.*
- (II) Words of four syllables have accents on ultimate and antepenult. Thus 8 *virtùtibùs* 12 *volùntariè, deprècarè.*
- (III) Words of five syllables are accented paroxytone and on the fourth last syllable. Thus 8 *resùscitàtis* 11 *magnitudìne, egrètudìne.*
- (IV) Dissyllables are dependent for their accent on the

ictus. (a) If they follow an atonic syllable, they are paroxytone; otherwise (b) they are oxytone:—

Thus, (a) 2 *Chrìstùm* 3 *orè* 4 *puró, cordè, atquè* 5 *signà, sibì* 6 *magnǽ, atquè* 7 *verbùm, deì* 8 *mortuìs* 9 *Sanàns, curà* 10 *màla, dìra* 11 *Deùm, passùm* 12 *proptèr* And (b) 1 *pàtrem* 2 *sànctum, Màriam, màtrem* 3 *mèrus, mòre, dèum* 4 *èum* 5 *dèi, vìvi* 6 *dèus, pàcis* 9 *lèpra, mìra* 11 *nòstrum, nòbis, mìre.*

In these verses the beat being iambic, and every trisyllabic paroxytone, a trisyllabic word can only stand with its initial syllable in the odd places. The formula is:—

$$\smile - | \smile - | \smile - | \smile -$$

Thus *te Martine* could not occur with *te* in either 1st, 3rd, or 5th syllable; the trisyllabic word must begin at one of these points. Obviously also two trisyllables cannot stand together; hence any such combination as *propter nos laudauit* at the beginning of a line is impossible, because *proptèr nos* would not leave the right beat for *laudàuit*. For this reason *Christùm ac* must undergo elision in l. 2, being followed by *spirìtum* (cf. Fr. *esprit*); and similarly *Mariam* could not be a trisyllable; in 8 *mortuis* must be a dissyllable, and in 12 *uoluntarie* must have only four syllables.

The verses are not all easy to construe; and possibly the limitations of the metric may have contributed to the awkwardness of construction in some of the lines. In the third stanza, what can be the grammatical relation of *electus* and *deus*? If *electus* be taken as agreeing with *Martinus* in the same way as the words *locutus* in the fourth, and *sanans* in the fifth stanza, then the line *donauit deus* 6, has no place in the sequence at all. Stanzas one and six are addressed to Martin, but the four inner stanzas are apparently *one* narrative sentence.

Bc. The hymn of St. Cummain the Tall (our No. 3) exhibits a variation in the number of syllables preceding the caesura.

This has a thoroughly Irish structure, on the basis of the system, 2 (5 + 7), with end rhymes :—

    Cèlebrá Iudà   fèsta Christi gaùdià
    àpostùlorùm   èxultàns memòrià

Here we have genuine Irish rhymes in which not only the rhyming syllable final but the preceding letters are harmonised. Thus *gaudia, memoria* is a rich rhyme of three syllables, in which the intervening consonants are of the same (Irish) class. Note also the rich rhyme of *pàstoris, càptoris*, in the second stanza. In the stanzas which follow, the triple rhyme occurs pretty frequently, showing that it was sought for, though it was not absolutely indispensable. We have 5, 6, præ*ceptoris*, *seminis*; 7, 8 egreg-*ia*, aduocam-*ina*; 9, 10, dom*ini*, sæc-*uli*; infant-*ia*, ub-*era*; 13, 14 P-*ilipi*, peru-*igili*; 15, 16, *nutibus*, *nubibus*; 17, 18, Par-*thiæ*, scien-*tiæ*; 19, 20, mu-*nere*, pro-*pere*; 21, 22, co-*minus*, alte-*rius*; 23, 24 tell-*ura*, epist-*ola*; 25, 26 Cannan-*ei*, sangu-*ine* [here it is not impossible that *dei* should be the last word of the line]; 27, 28 m-*eritis, editis*; 29, 30 justit-*iæ*, Alaxandr-*iæ*; 31, 32 euangelist-*æ*, honor-*e*; 33, 34 merit-*a*, oper-*a*; 35, 36 mart-*iris*, susp-*iris*; 37, 38 u*alida*, suffr-*agia*; 39, 40 I-*acula*, propugn-*acula*; 41, 42 pect-*ora*, sæc-*ula*; 43, 44 gen-*ito*, ag-*io*.

There are no assonances nor alliterations sought for, nor are other harmonies introduced save incidentally. No attention is paid to quantity, for here, too, the short penult of the verse ignores the classical quantity, as in *præceptŏris*, &c., and even *suspĭrĭs* (36). Elision is not permitted, so that in 11 the reading of F *lecti* is correct, against the *electi* of T, which would need its final *i* to be elided before *ab*, for the metre. Again, in 27, the reading of F *prelecti* is correct.

The treatment of initial *i* before vowels is not quite uniform, for we have 1 *iùda*, 11 *iòhannis*, 24 *iesu*, but in the two cases of *iacobi*, 9 and 21, the two vowels are sounded separately, just as in Mad*i*ani (27), and *i*acula (39), invit*i*ata (41). The case of *i*acula, not *j*acula, is very noteworthy, as it is quite foreign to the general usage, by which initial *i* before a vowel is consonantal; cf. *jacula* in *Altus Prosator*, l. 96. As usual *ii* is a monophthong; e.g. *euangelt* (4).

The verse 45, 46 though ending with *alleluia*, like the preceding stanzas, has nothing to do with the poem, as the measure is totally different.

The Lorica of Gildas.

Bd. We have now to consider the *Lorica of Gildas* (No. 48), which is most instructive in respect of the treatment of Latin words by this class of writers. As in the other Latin hymns of this Irish family, no elision is observed, and quantity is often ignored; the whole attention is concentrated on the number of syllables, and on the rhyme correspondences. The metre is trochaic trimeter catalectic, and the formula is $2(6 + 5)$. In every pair of lines there is a cretic jingle of assonance (trisyllabic).

The last three syllables exhibit these following principles :—

(1) The last vowel always rhymes exactly, and a succeeding consonant, if present, is always the same; thus we have as the rhyming finals, *a, e, i, o ; as, es, is, us ; am, em, um ; at.*

(2) This final vowel may be preceded immediately, (a) by another rhyming vowel, or (b) be separated from it by a single consonant, *b, c, t ; l, m, n, r*, or in four cases by the combined consonants 83 *ll*, 23 *mn*, 45 *rm*, 85 *nt*.

In case of (a) we have the combinations, *i-a, i-am, i-as, i-at ; i-e, i-es ;* but *i-am* rhymes with *e-am, i-at* with *e-at, i-a* with *e-la* and *u-a*, and *i-as* with *u-mas*.

In case of (b), we have the liquids 'rhyming' with each other: *m, r ; n, r ; n, l ;* but we have *l* rhyming with *c* and with *t ; r* with *c :* in other words, the single consonants that are used as 'interveners,' were apparently allowed as equivalents, except *b* which is only used with itself.

There are also the four cases of double consonants rhyming with single, in these harmonies: *mn* = *r*, *nt* = *n*, *rm* = *r*, and *ll* = *n*, where also the double consonant does not lengthen the preceding vowel.

The vowel remains in general the same, but these varieties are observable: *ima, era; antes, ines; era, ula; onas, enas; one, ine; ormi, ori; otem, icem; ici, uri; ulum, icum; ere, ore; ine, ere; itu, ulo; i-a, ela; i-as, umas; u-a, ela;* i.e., it is obvious that *any short vowel* satisfied the conditions of the verse. Thus we find: *a*, with *i; e*, with *i, o, u; i*, with *e, o, u; o*, with *e, i;* and *u*, with *e, i*, &c.

(3) The antepenult has a long vowel (not always correctly), which is so frequently the same as to show that the writer must have sought identity as far as obtainable; and the separating consonant was no doubt made to harmonise to the utmost extent possible under the conditions.

This 'lorica' is of great importance, because it shows the pronunciation with the strong stress of voice producing the effect of a long vowel. For it is plain that only thus could the effect of the poem have been realised. It demands a little effort, no doubt, to accept the possibility of such a rhyming equation, for instance, as *tùtela* = po-*tèntia* in l. 32, but until this be accepted, there would be little use in presenting *virgin-ès omnes* as a rhyme for *conf-ès-ores* in 24, which it assuredly was intended by the poet to be. And the horror to a Latinist will not be diminished by the presentation of *gùturi* = *cèrvìci* as a satisfactory specimen of the possibilities of the verse.

In the text of B, are several minor errors; thus 8 should have *militiæ;* 18 *ualeam;* in 19 the last word is of course wrong, but whether we read *agonthĕtas* or agonŏthĕtas as the rhyme to *prŏfĕtas* will depend on the determination of the number of syllables in *deinde*, which I think is trisyllabic; in 20 quatvor has probably to be read as a dissyllable; in 21 *prŏrĕtas* is an extraordinary transformation of πρῳράτης, to rhyme with *athlĕtas* (ἀθλήτης); in 42 *atque* has probably to be deleted; in 46 facie, in 47 supercilĭs should be read; in 49 there is a syllable too many, which is probably to be secured by emending the first word into *puplis;* in 52 *uvae* is evidently to be omitted, because it is the same as *linguae* 51, and even so gurgulĭoni has to be read with synizesis of *io*, or more probably as *lyo;* in 57 *dom'ne* has to be read, or *deînde* of the other MSS.; in 64 *unguibus* is necessary; in 66 *que* must be added to *nervos* with ΔΨ: in 72 *tibĭs* et *calcibus* are the right readings; in 80 there are two syllables extra in the line, but emendation would be mere guessing here, (perhaps *renes* for *reniculos* or should we omit *fitrem* as a gloss?); in 81 whatever *toliam* may mean, it exemplifies the use of *lyo* in 52, for it must be *tolyam*, dissyllabic; in 88 read præter-ii, in 91 utĭ; in 95 either *iam* is to be read, or there is a syllable wanting; in 97 delete *factis* with CNΔ.

C. *Unit-rhymes.*

We now enter upon the consideration of the poems in which the vowel at the cæsura rhymes with the final vowel of the line. The stanzas may include two, four, or six lines; but the principle is the same. In all cases the second hemistich is *octosyllabic*, which at once distinguishes this section from those which have gone before. This, indeed, is the normal measure for hymns, being that in which most of the verses in our collection are written.

Ca. The commonest form is the two-line stanza, 2 (8 + 8), exemplified in our No. 15, the hymn ascribed to Columba, beginning:

In tè Christè credèntiùm
misèreàris omniùm.

The rhyme bears only on the last syllable, though the preceding syllable usually has the same or a kindred vowel. But there is nothing Irish in this stanza, metrically, and most probably the real Irish poets, such as Colman and Cuchuimne, would not have regarded this hymn as deserving a high place for its artistic structure. The rhymes are poor, and largely made up of mere grammatical identities: *credentium, viventium; ascenderat, salvaverat,* &c. These do not merit much applause. The alliterations are mere repetitions: *uita uiuentium; uirtus uirtutum, iudex iudicum; princeps principum,* &c. In fact the hymn has every appearance of being a mere hasty after-thought, as indeed the Preface leads us to infer.

It naturally falls into two divisions, the first (ll. 1–16) addressed to the Trinity, and the second (ll. 16—end) addressed to Christ. In both sections there are irregularities of all sorts. L. 10 is wrong, for

> deus rex regni in gloria
> deus ipse uiuentium

does not furnish rhyme at all, and *regni* suffers elision before *in*, which is not permissible. In l. 14, "*omnia* noua *cuncta* et uetera" is very poor. The stanza which begins with l. 19 is incomplete. l. 23 is intolerable, for *redemeret* cannot rhyme with *passus est*. In l. 24 *penetrat* is poor rhyme for *ascenderat*, apart from the tense of the latter. In l. 26 *gloria* has its final vowel elided, although *patri* does not suffer elision before *ingenito*.

There is nothing to be said in favour of this hymn; it is quite unworthy of being placed in juxtaposition with Columba's great poem, the *Altus Prosator*.

The next poem, *Noli pater* (our No. 16), is written in the same measure, 2 (8 + 8); but it produces a totally different effect, because the rhymes are rich. Here too we are face to face with a mere fragment of three stanzas. Thus we have: ind*ulgere, fulgore;* form*idine,* ur*idine;* terr*ibilem, similem; carm*ina, agm*ina; culm*ina, fulm*ina;* amant*issime,* rect*issime;*

i.e., in the first three stanzas the cæsura- and end-rhymes are trisyllabic rich rhymes in absolute correctness, where both vowels and consonants have the requisite harmonies. But the fourth stanza is not quite so good; the fifth has no harmony and is incomplete; and the remaining pair of stanzas have nothing to do with this poem at all.

The first three stanzas have the real Irish rhyme (although it may fairly be doubted whether even line 6 is genuine), which at once brings the poet into line with Colman and Cuchuimne. But *sæcula* and *regimina* would not have been approved of by these past masters in the art of 'harmony,' while *gratia* and *sicera* would have been certainly rejected. They belong to the style of which we have another example in *ecce fulget clarissima* (our No. 31) which is now to be examined.

Here at the outset we meet a difficulty, for how can clarissim*a* be held to rhyme with sollempnit*as*? That it is not an error is clear from l. 13, where the same occurs, gentilit*as* with monit*a*; so 16 astuti*a* with fuer*at*, and 17 dilectissim*i* with presul*is*. These bad rhymes at once disclose a totally different theory of versification.

The two hymns (31 and 32) to Patrick and Brigid, probably belong to the same period, though the latter does not furnish an example of the bad rhyme referred to, and with the exception of l. 2 (where gaudi*a* would remove the objectionable want of rhyme), has at least its final vowel correct.

The same measure, 2(8+8) is found in the hymn *Christi patris in dextera* (our No. 45), which was evidently written by a late imitator of the early hymns (see below, p. 241).

So in the alphabetical hymn *Abbas probatus omnino* (our No. 28), we have the similar system n(8+8). Here there is no further requirement of harmony than the final vowel (and consonant); the vowels *ie* may be monophthong, as in 15 *probátus sápiēns péritus*, or be sounded separately as in 17 *requiēscit post óbitum*. Note also—*lasriūs* in 12, and the monstrosity in 9, *ieiunus* as a word of *four* syllables.

The late hymn No. 44, does not even rhyme accurately, and is of no importance here. It comes under the head Cb. This is also the metre of the hymn in praise of St. Ciaran (our No. 27), upon which something must be said. The MSS. YZ preserve the metre better than T, e.g., 1 *ineffabili*, *cetui* 2 *specule*; l. 4 is given more accurately in the former MSS. The lines (9–12) *Rogamus deum* have nothing to do with the poem itself, for l. 9 is not in rhyme and has a syllable too many. The same is true of l. 10, in which also *Ciàrani* has to be read as four syllables, although in the poem itself we have *Querànus* with three.

It is possible that the lines should be arranged differently, and that we should print one stanza of the pattern Cc, 6(8+8), followed by two supplementary lines. Certainly lines 4 and 5 run together, *Quiaranus . . . inaltatus est;* and the phrase *nouissimis temporibus* recalls the words of the antiphon appended to the *Altus Prosator* (vol. i. p. 81), *nouissimo in tempore*. *Rogamus deum*, &c., of our hymn in praise of St. Ciaran, would then correspond to the invocation *Deum patrem . . . inuoco* which follows the antiphon at the end of the *Altus*. See below, p. 218, where Colgan is quoted as giving a line very like l. 7 as the beginning of a hymn of Columba in praise of Ciaran.

Cc. We now proceed to consider the *Altus Prosator* of St. Columba (our No. 14). Its metre is 6(8+8), with cæsura- and end-rhymes. No attention is paid to quantity, for even in the penult syllable of the line, which must always be *short*, we find such cases as 10 *majĕstas;* 20 *antĭquus;* 74 *infĕrnum;* 103 *cupīdo;* 108 *erumpĕmus;* 123 *vexīllum;* 135 *venīsse*. The stress of the voice on the accented syllable for the beats was quite sufficient for the measure.

But in order to read the verses properly, attention has to be paid to the treatment of concurrent vowels. Here the modern habit of printing *u* and *v* indiscriminately by *u*, and *i* and *j* by *i*, has introduced a needless difficulty. These letters *i* and *u* are always consonants when they are *initial* or come *between two vowels*, hence 96 *jacula* ; 97 *judicem* ; 103 *hujus* ; 45. 88. 89. 90. 91 *cujus* ; 10 *majestas* ; 44 *dejectus*. This is carried out so that in compounds the initial preserves its rights even after a consonant; hence 18 per-*v*icacis; 18 in-*v*idia; 24 di-*v*ersorum. But then, even this does not explain all, because we have 7 sal*v*a ; 66 fer*v*entibus; 82 re-*v*olvere.

Omitting then the cases of *consonant vowel*, there remain to be considered the numerous cases of the concurrence of two vowels. These are treated in the following table.

The following combinations are possible:—

Initials	Finals.				
	a	e	i	o	u
a	—	ae	ai	—	au
e	ea	—	ei	eo	eu
i	ia	ie	ii	io	iu
o	—	(o-e)	(oy)	—	—
u	ua	ue	u	uo	uu

They occur as follows:—

[1]AË: 45 aëris ; (97 Isra*h*el ;)
AÏ: 92 sinaï.
[*au* is always a monophthong, 18. 33. 35. 54. 111. 133.]
EA: 125 ficulnea.
EÏ: 52 ceruleïs ; [53 *vineis* F ;] 57 deï, 68, 70, 132 ; 114 eïsdem ;
EŎ: 6 deos ; 17 eodem ; 135 deo.
EU: 6 deum ; 71 eundem ; 114 obeuntibus ; 115 redeuntibus.

---

[1] Of course *æ* is read as *e*, and *y* = *i*. It is to be observed that in the combination *qu*, *u* is always treated as a consonant ; hence we have the monosyllabic *qua*, 27, 64, 67, 84 ; *quæ*, 81 and *passim* ; *qui*, 12, 21, 58 ; *quo*, 28, 40.

ĬA: 5 glorĭa; 12 celestĭa, prĕvilegia; 23 tertĭam, &c., cf.
26. 29. 30². 50². 51. 56. 57. 67. 68. 85. 88. 93. 95. 96.
109². 111². 112. 136. 139. [It is plain therefore that
in 30 *bestias* is trisyllabic and that *et* should be
omitted as in all MSS. save T; also that *etralibus*
should be read (with EI) in 114, as *ethrialibus* has
five syllables.]

ĬE [Ĭæ]: 1 dierum; 5 dietatis; 16 superbiendo; 18 cenodoxiæ,
&c., cf. 21. 48. 67. 75. 91. 98. 99. 100. 101². 107². 118,
120². 129. [Hence in 102 *mulierum* is to be read
mulyerum, where *li* merely represents the liquid *l*.]

ĬI: always = ĭ, cf. 22 bestiis; 63 obĭcibus; 72 promontoriis
[Hence in 53, we have to read *vinĕīs*, with all MSS.
save T.]

ĬO: 7 gloriosus; 10 otiosa; 14 stationis, &c., cf. 21. 22. 35.
36. 37². 44. 51. 59². 64. 81. 86. 87. 89. 103. 105. 115.
116. 128. 131. 134. 138.

ĬU: 9² sedium, virtutium; 24 infernalium, &c., cf. 34. 40.
45. 46. 49. 65. 74. 76. 77. 100². 102. 120. 126². 127.

[OĔ: 5 co-æternus.]

[OY: a monophthong: 97 Móysen.]

ŬA: 5 perpetua; 55 evacuant; 93 tonitrua. [In 89 T has
et tua, which gives no meaning, though it preserves
the measure; but the reading of MEIII *etiam* which
was no doubt intended to mend the sense, unfortunately ruins the measure, because *iam* is *jam*, so
that *etiam* is only a dissyllable; and in any case
etiam never occurs in these hymns. I have little
doubt that the word should be *eternæ*, eĭnæ.]

ŬE: 16 ruerat; 42 intueri; 46 perduellium.

ŬI: 4 cui; 19 suis; 21 fuit; 39² ruit, suis; 85 sui; 138
perpetuis.

ŬO: 38 duobus, 124; 100 tonitruorum; 88. 130. 131.
quatuor.

ŬU: 40 vultuum; 67 influunt.

With respect to the rhymes, the chief rhyming syllable is *us*[32] of the *nom. sg.* or the *dat.-ab. -ibus*; with *us* we have the rhyme *os* twice, 108 and 134, just as the rhyme *is* = *es* occurs 25 and 49; but *as* only rhymes with itself. With other consonants final, of *t* we have only *-erat* 16, 27, 84; *-am* occurs once 26 ; *-(i)um* is pretty frequent. The remaining rhymes all bear on the vowel final a^{22}, e^{14}, i^3, and o^{12}.

But there is no rhyme ending in *-nt* or in *r*, so that common terminations are conspicuously absent: we have no ending like præval*ent*, deficia*nt*, vocabi*tur*, pati*tur* found, e.g., in Sechnall's hymn.

The rhymes occur therefore as follows, ranged in the order of their frequency:—

us ; is, as, es, os ;
um ; am ;
erat[1] ;
a, e, o, i.

No special attempt is made to secure alliteration or assonance, which occur only incidentally and not in obedience to any rule.

Cb. The last hymn to be considered is Ultan's alphabetical quatrains in honour of Brigid. The metre is similar to the last allowing four lines instead of six to the stanza, 4 (8 + 8).

But it is to be observed that the poem consists only of three stanzas, beginning with X, Y and Z respectively, for the last four lines beginning *audite uirginis laudes*, do not form a quatrain of either this or any other metre: certainly not *this* metre, because the 'units' do not rhyme; certainly not any other, because the first three lines are (8 + 7), while the fourth is (7 + 7) measure, with rhymed 'units.' In addition, the second line has nine syllables, for perfect*i*onem has five syllables, so that it is wholly impossible to regard *any one* of these four lines as forming any portion of the original poem of Ultan.

---

[1] In 27 rhyme is absent, for *fecerat* does not rhyme with *condidit* ; and the reading *considerat* of E involves the omission of *et* before *aquas*, which breaks the symmetry of the line.

The three lines at the end, *Brigita sancta sedulo*, are really written in this metre, but they could not have formed portion of the alphabetical hymn, because they do not form a quatrain, and they end with *in sæcula sæculorum*, the whole being an invocation which could hardly have stood *second* [B] in an alphabetical poem.

The only difficulty in the three genuine verses of the hymn is the syllabification of the word *consueuit*, in l. 10; for *-sue-* must be dissyllabic, and then *u* between vowels must be consonantal, so thàt we can only have *con-su-e-uit* of four syllables and this does not satisfy the measure. The other MSS., unfortunately, do not enable us to put the matter right, but the insertion of *et* before *diurno* is a reasonable conjecture. In other respects, the rhymes and the numbers are all correct.

But I cannot think it probable that this hymn of Ultan originally contained a whole alphabet of quatrains. In the first place, it is quite certain that the Preface when speaking of 'the *first* capitulum, and the *last three* capitula causa brevitatis,' is thoroughly wrong in its statement about the *first* capitulum, which is not present. Further, I doubt whether it be possible to consider the lines, *Christus in nostra insula quas vocatur Hibernia*, &c., in any other light than as an *introductory* stanza, for a specification of this kind would be quite out of place in the antepenultimate stanza of a lay poem. The poem referred to in the Preface as beginning with *Audite virginis laudes*, is categorically declared to contain the enumeration of Brigid's miracles, and that could not have been effected in the twenty stanzas remaining of an alphabetical poem. And, in fact, the uncertain manner in which the Preface (T) speaks of the author of this Hymn, shows that little was known about it; the words *dicunt alii*, &c., make it probable that the final clause was itself merely an inference from the presence of *Audite virginis laudes* in sequence to our Hymn.

The Metrical Systems of the *Liber Hymnorum*.

§ 2. The Irish Hymns.

In an attempt to investigate the metre of the Irish hymns contained in this book, we are confronted with the problem of the relations of Irish metric to Latin metric. It is possible that Irish verses with a *definite* number of syllables were unknown in Ireland before the introduction of Latin. In what form the early pagan poets set forth their passions and their dreams we have no knowledge; but in a language of strong word-accent, such as Irish is proved by its morphology to have been from the earliest times, the native speech must have run together the unaccented short syllables, much after the fashion that still prevails,[1] so that it is not improbable that the limitation of a line of verse to a definite number of syllables became a rule in Ireland only through foreign influence. It is not without significance that the names used in reference to metrical matters are borrowed; thus we have *rithim*, *line* &c.

The word 'rhyme' is of unknown origin, the Romanic languages have transmitted it to the Germanic, but they did not get it from Celtic, where it does not exist. The Old Irish *rím* refers to 'number' as does the OHG *rím*, but the notion of 'rhyme' as we understand it was not expressed thereby. There are abundant examples in our poems of perfect rhymes, but the essentials of Irish rhyme involved *harmony* rather than *identity* of the consonants. The expression of the native metricists is *comharda*,

---

[1] Thus, *e.g.*, the dissyllabic sound *hyúló* is nearly all that the ear can hear of the word which is spelt *shiubhaileoghaidh*.

which denotes a definite 'correspondence' of a particular kind in the last words of lines; *e.g. oi + r* is a good *comharda* with *oi + g*, or *all* with *am*. To this end the later metricists, following without doubt an immemorial tradition, divided the consonants into classes that contained such as were held to be capable of forming 'harmonies' with each other, viz.:

p,	k,	t						
b,	g,	d						
f,	x,		h,					
v,	γ̇,			y,	l',	n'	r'	
					˚l	˚n	˚rr	˚m ˚ng

The last row embraces the *l* &c. of hard 'timbre', denoted by the vague half-utterance of *u* [ö] before the consonant.

This very excellent classification is amply justified by the results so far as sound is concerned; and it may be noted that it must have been constructed by *native* writers, because some of the sounds were not extant in the classic languages. But whoever first elaborated it, the practice must have been early; and we can have no reason for doubting that the Irish poets of two thousand years ago were experimentally acquainted with its meaning and value as one of the implements of their art. Other names are used, such as *amus*, inner rhyme, or 'assonance,' and *uaim*, 'alliteration,' but it is unnecessary to dwell upon these here. No difficulty can arise from the use of familiar terms such as *rhyme, assonance* &c.; and it is convenient to use the term 'assonance' to denote the Irish rhyme in the case of *non-final* words, leaving 'rhyme' for *final* words. The term 'alliteration' can be held to denote in general the identity of the consonantal initial, or the occurrence of two words with any vowel initial.

Early Irish poetry then must undoubtedly have been characterised by the presence of these two fundamental conditions: (1) strongly-accentuated utterance, and (2) harmonies of words. The number of syllables employed was not an original feature; and it is not unlikely that the *Rhetorics* which we find in the early stories were typical of the prose-poetry that preceded the syllable-counting of post-Christian days.

The uncertainty which envelops thes Irishe hymns[1] (for the Prefaces add little of a positive kind to our knowledge), makes it unfortunately necessary to have recourse to inferences, and that on very limited data. All that we know is that about the year 1100, (when a perfectly definite system of metric was understood, as is plain ex. gr. in the *Saltair na Rann*,) we find in two MSS. these Irish Hymns, written in a manner that showed the respect in which they were held, and accompanied by Prefaces declaring their great antiquity. But the prefaces are quite unhistorical, and the verses contain abundant proofs of middle Irish forms, so that they are assuredly not to be taken as mere copies of *Old Irish* poems. They no doubt contain fragments or even sections, handed down by long tradition from older times, but they present too many dubious elements to admit of their being regarded as genuine poems by the authors named in the Prefaces, handed down by transcribers liable to err but not desirous of altering.

As there is no ground for inferring the priority in time of one of these poems over the other, so far as the MSS. are concerned, I begin with the analysis of the one perfect poem in our collection, so as to show what the possibilities of the case were, to a poet.

The Hymn Brigit be bithmaith.

This poem, in praise of Brigid (our No. 21), is variously ascribed in the Preface to Colum Cille and to Ultan. Whoever may have been the author, he was an excellent artist, and the existence of this poem shows that (1) metrical laws had been thoroughly elaborated when it was composed, and (2) that the natural accent of the words was preserved in the verse-ictus.

I have transcribed it, marking this natural accent, to show

---

[1] The hymns considered in the following pages are numbered in our collection 5, 12-24, and 29.

that Irish poets did as a matter of fact write rhythmical verses
with a definite number of syllables:—

Brígit be bíthmaith	breo órda óiblech
donfé don bíth-laith	ingrían tind táidlech.
ronsóera Brígit	sech drùngu dèmna
roróena rèunn	càtha cach thèdma.
doródba innunn	ar còlla cìsu
in chróeb co mblàthaib	in màthair Ísu.
ind fír-og ínmain	co n-órddain àdbail
biam sóer cech inbaid	la'm nòeb do Làignib
leth-chòlba flàtha	la Pàtraic prìmda
in tlàcht uas lígdaib	ind rìgan rìgda.
robbèt iar sínit	ar cùirp hic cìlicc.
dia ràth ronbróena	ronsòera Brígit.

On examining these verses it is plain that the beat is absolutely *iambic*, but that the natural accent of the words has its full play; yet every metrical requisite is also present:—

[a] The measure is 2 (5 + 5).
[b] The rhymes are dissyllabic, and perfect.
[c] Alliteration is always observed in the latter half of each first line, o = o; d = d; c = c; o = a; p = p; c = c; (vowels alternating with each other).
[d] Assonances knitting up the half-lines in some form or other, occur in every stanza: bith-maith, bithlaith; ronsoera, roroena; blàthaib, màthair; inmain, inbaid; ligaib, rigan (or ligdaib, rigda); sinit, cilicc; broena, soera.

This is what the true poets composed: these verses are stamped with the hall-mark of artistic perfection, and they teach us what opinion is to be held on the other verses in our collection. The Latin Hymns of Mac Murchon and Cuchuimne, and this Irish Hymn of Colum Cille or of Ultan prove that the so-called Hymns of Colman and Fiacc and Broccan are merely products of pious zeal, which the *poets* would not have deigned to acknowledge as poetry.

The Hymn Sén Dé.

We may take the other poems in the order of their occurrence, for, as far as poetry or metric is concerned, they are much on a level. They represent very distinctly the mood of the early Irish church: a general invocation, referring to the Old Testament worthies, two hymns specially referring to Patrick and Brigit, and a hymn of Sanctan which is a kind of 'lorica', followed by the well-known Lorica of Patrick.

Beginning then with the *Sén Dé* (our No. 5), we feel at once the wide difference between these verses and the poem of Ultan just examined: everywhere there are irregularities of measure, of rhyme, of ictus, and neither assonance nor alliteration is regarded as an essential element in the stanza. But the word *do·n·fe* of Ultan is just as old as the same word in Colman; nor is there any reason for maintaining that Ultan's poem is of later date than Colman's, save just this irregularity. Obviously, it would be merely begging the question to assert that Colman's must be older *because* of the irregularities. *Prima facie*, the probability is the other way, for we have seen the like careful workmanship in the Latin poems, so that it is more probable that the early Christian poets would, in their native poems, strive after the perfection which they had attained in their Latin poems, than that they would be content with such poor specimens as the kind we have here, after their success in the foreign language.

The truth is that *these* Irish poems have all the appearance of being a sort of *versus memoriales* badly put together.

The *Sén Dé*, for example, cannot be regarded as a *popular* poem, intended for the instruction of the people, on account of the Latin phrases which are interspersed; but one does not see either how it could have been read with any effect even by students of theology after the fashion of *versus memoriales*, owing to the marked difference of structure in the beats of the verse. In each of the following lines, e.g., we have only *two* clearly marked beats: 21, *in nòstris sermònibus*; 22, *dilùus tempòribus*; 23, *incèrto de sèmine*; 24, *ab òmni formìdine*; whereas in others we have *three* beats: 32, *ùlli leònum òri*; 21, *règem règum rogàmus*.

Be that as it may, however, an investigation discloses the following facts: First, *elision is not practised*. Thus: 2, *for a oessam*, [brought about by the deletion of the initial *f*]; 3, *no utmaille*; 5, *itge Abeil*; *Heli, Enoc*; 7, *Noe ocus*; 8, *tairle adamna*; 9, *ailme athair*; 12, *Iesu Aaron*; 16, [a] *apstalaib*; 17, *Maire Ioseph*; 18, *anma Ignati*; 19, *robai hi*; 22, *Noe a*; 24, *a airnigthe*; 25, *sæcla habetur*; 29, *ruri anacht*; 35, *nostro opere*; 36, *occa i*; 43, *la haingliu i*.

It will be seen that in the Latin as in the Irish, hiatus is permitted. Thus in 35 whether the pronunciation was *nostrò opère digno* (for the verse-ictus), or followed the normal pronunciation *nòstro òpere dìgno*, in neither case is there possibility of elision.

When we ask if the exact number of syllables in each line was always strictly maintained, we come upon our second observation, viz.: *Vowels coming together are monophthong, whether the vowels be long or short.*[1]

Thus:—
- *ai*: 1 Maire; 2 cain: 3 utmaille; 5 Adaim, cobair; 6 fogair; 1 tedmaim, 'tairle; 9 ailme, athair; 10 ernaigthi, ainglech; 11 snaidsium, 'snaid, maire [Lat. *mare*]; 14 fiadat; 15 baptaist; 16 apstalaib, cobair, &c.
- *ei*: 5 Abeil; 25 tein; 32 leic; 33 slabreid; 34 reid, amreid.
- *eo*: 15 eoin [pron. *yo-in*, or perhaps *Ow-en*, as now].
- *ia*: 2 cia, tiasam; 6 dian; 11 tria; 16 diar, 20, 31, 34, 45; 20 sciath; 45 liar, ria.
- *ie*: 12 Iesu, 16.
- *io*: 9 Ioseph, 17; 37 Ionas; [but 13 Iob].
- *iu*: 11 snaidsium: 15 dítiu; 27 snaidsiunn, 38; 43 aingliu.
- [*o·ä*: *ro·*anacht, 30, but *ro·* is separated from the *a*.]
- *oe*: 2 foessam, 51; 6 soerat, 10, 24, 25, &c.; 19 noeb, 46, 51; 33 foedes; 52 broena; [but 7 *Noè*, 22].

---

[1] But in 32 the Latin *suum* is dissyllabic, and *leonum* is trisyllabic.

oi : 11 Moisi ; 31 'roigse ; 34 doroiter ; 37 móir.
ua : 9 uas(er) ; 10 uasal ; 20 huan ; 29 ruadi.
ui : 3 suide ; 4 ruire ; 11 tuisech ; 15 adsluinnem ; 39 guidi ; 41 huili ; 50 huile.

There is one example of the union of three vowels, in the interpolated lines, 40, timch*uai*rt, but it is also monophthong. Thus, whatever vowels come together they are pronounced together. To this the only exceptions are in the proper names *Iob*, *Noë*, and *Eoīn*, as dissyllables.

On examining the poem, it appears that all the half lines contain seven syllables, with these exceptions :—

16 *Iesu con apstalaib* (S.T., but F has con*a*).

25 *qui per sæcula habetur* (but here *sæcla* must be read).

It seems therefore that the writer intended that his poem should follow these laws :—

1. Each stanza to consist of two lines rhyming dissyllabically.
2. Each line to have a cæsura after the seventh syllable and to end with the fourteenth.
3. All vowels coming together in the same word to be pronounced in one syllable, but not so when coming together in separate words.[1]
4. With the exception of the last ictus on the penultimate syllable of the line, the place of the ictus was not fixed, but the number of syllables in the line naturally limited the number of beats, to *two* or *three* in each half-line.

The law of the stanza may be exhibited, thus :—

```
      First half-line              Second half-line
     two or three beats           two or three beats
   ⌒⎴⎴⎴⎴⎴⎴⎴⌒              ⌒⎴⎴⎴⎴⎴⎴⌒
   1  2  3  4  5  6  7  |  8  9  10  11  12  |  13  14
   1  2  3  4  5  6  7  |  8  9  10  11  12  |  13  14
                                                Rhyming.
```

[1] The compound *diar* ' to our ' is one word, as is 45 *liar*.

The following will exemplify the nature of the accentuation and the place of occurrence of the beats, in the body of the hymn:

sen Dè donfè fordontè	macc Màire ronfèladar
for a òessam dun innòcht	cia tlasam caintèmadar
itir fòss no ùtmaille	itir sùide no sèssam
ruire nìme fri cech trèss	issed àttach adèssam
itge Àbeil macc Àdaim	Hèli, Ènoc diar còbair
ronsòerat ar diangàlar	seciplèth fon mbith fògair
Nòë ocus Àbraham	Ìsac in màcc àdamra
immuntìsat ar tèdmaim	nachantàirle a dàmna

The irregularity in the number of the beats, cannot be always stated with certainty, for though it may be possible to assert a secondary accent in 15, ropdìtiu *dùn*, rop snàdud, this is hardly possible in 16, *rop diar còbair fri gàbud*, for none of the words will bear any stress beyond the two marked; I have not therefore enumerated all the individual cases.

The first stanza is remarkable for its ending, as the lines must rhyme on the antepenult, *fèladar-tèmadar*. But with this exception, and the Latin half-lines 21, 22, 23, 24, the accent is on the penult, until we come to the last line, 38, where we have the stress on the ultimate. It might seem here indeed, that, as it was apparently *de rigueur* that the writer should finish with the first half-line, which ended *fordontè*, he had to introduce the monosyllable. This repetition is just as disconnected from the rest of the stanza as is the similar repetition in Broccan's Hymn, l. 188.

The foregoing observations on metre only relate to ll. 1–38, where the poem was shown to end by the very form, but even this first division is itself composite, and ll. 1–20 may be clearly distinguished from ll. 21–38. There is a double list of saints and martyrs invoked, and some names occur in both lists. Thus in ll. 1–20 we have the historical sequence: Abel, [Elijah], Enoch, *Noah*, *Abraham*, Isaac, Jacob, Joseph, Moses, Joshua,

Aaron, *David*, Job, the prophets, the Maccabees, John the Baptist, Jesus, the Apostles, Mary, Joseph, Stephen, Ignatius, martyrs, hermits and virgins.[1] Then in ll. 21-38 we begin again, with *Noah*, Melchisedech, Lot, *Abraham*, the Three Children, *David*, Daniel, Peter, Jonah, the italicised names being common to both series.

This repetition plainly denotes the use of an additional document, from which the writer was making excerpts. In this case the addition was characterised by the quite peculiar introduction of Latin rhyming lines or half-lines, as shown here :—

21	regem regum rogamus	in nostris sermonibus
22	....	diluui temporibus.
23	Melchisedech rex Salem	incerto de semine
24	....	ab omni formidine.
25	....	qui per secla habetur
26	ut nos omnes precamur	liberare dignetur.
28	....	limpa fontis in gaba.
30	....	Dauid de manu Golai.
32	suum profetam	ulli leonum ori.
35	....	nostro opere digno
36	....	in paradisi regno.

The last stanza of the second section (ll. 37, 38), has plainly been added to round off the piece. *Jonah* does not come naturally into the series after *Peter*. When the writer had got as far as l. 36, where the (assumed) Latin original probably ended with *in paradisi regno*, he too sought to bring his work to an end, and so the repetition of *Sen dé donfe fordonte* demanding a monosyllable to rhyme with *te*, the familiar stop-gap *monar ngle* was suggested, and Jonah and his whale suited this well enough.

In the lines next following, the metre is different, for lines 39, 40 make a stanza with rhyming trisyllables at the end, *guide-se, scule-se*, while lines 41-43 have a wholly incongruous

---

[1] The whole Litany may be compared with the litany given in *Saltair na Rann* (poem cxxxviii. p. 107, l. 7297 ff.), which follows a similar *Biblical* list, though Stokes has obscured this by not perceiving that *Oeth* mentioned in it is not the Odyssean Οὖτις, but *Ehud*.

metre, of rhymes at middle and end; the caesural *fír* in 41 rhymes with the final *ríg*, and the caesural *·issam* in 42 with the final *·rissam*, while 43 has a trisyllabic rhyme *hil-lethu, bith-bethu*. Then ll. 44, 45 return to the metre of the original poem; and this stanza may have been its conclusion as first written. Lines 47-54 are also in the original metre, but they can hardly be regarded in any other light than as a later appendix.[1]

These considerations lead to the following analysis of the poem. *The Introduction* (ll. 1-4); *The Litany* (ll. 5-20); *The Supplementary Litany* (ll. 21-36); *The Jonah finale* (ll. 37, 38); *The Supplementary lines*, 39, 40; 41, 42; 43; *The original conclusion* after l. 20 (ll. 44, 45); *later invocation to Irish Saints* (ll. 47-54).

The Hymn Genair Patraic.

We now come to the hymn of St. Fiacc in praise of St. Patrick (our No. 19); the Preface is quite unhistorical, and it is impossible to regard the hymn as of the age there assigned to it. It will be convenient to begin the metrical investigation by giving an analysis of the piece, accompanied by an indication of the nature of the rhymes in several stanzas:

Stanza.	Subject.	Rhyme.
(ll. 1-2)	Patrick's birthplace, and age in captivity	dissyllabic.
ii[1] (ll. 3-4)	His name and parentage	,,
iii (ll. 5-6, &c.)	His captivity	,,
iv	Victor bids him escape	,,
v	and sends him to Germanus to Italy	,,
vi	He studies with Germanus	,,
vii	'Angels were bringing him back'	trisyllabic.
viii	The call from Fochlad's Wood,	dissyllabic.

[1] The fact that neither the words 'around this school' in l. 40 nor 'on this monastery' in l. 47 have any glossarial note perhaps suggest that these later verses were written in the monastery where the notes were added. See p. 117 below.

Stanza.	Subject.	Rhyme.
ix	for the conversion of the tribes	dissyllabic.
x	The tribes prophesy his coming	,,
xi	Loegaire's druids do not hide it	,,
xii	Patrick's crusade against idolatry	,,
xiii	His devotional and ministerial life	,,
xiv	His asceticism	,,
xv	His recitation of the Psalter	,,
xvi	His couch a stone	,,
xvii	His miracles	,,
xviii	His preaching	,,
xix	The perdition of the Sons of Emer	,,
xx	Patrick's preaching for sixty years	,,
xxi	Darkness of Paganism over Ireland	,,
xxii	Armagh a Kingdom; Tara desolate	,,
xxiii	Patrick's wish to go to Armagh	,,
xxiv	Victor and the Burning Bush	polysyllabic.
xxv	His dignity to Armagh; himself to heaven	dissyllabic.
xxvi	Privileges of his hymn, &c.	monosyllabic.
xxvii	Tassach gives him his last Communion	,,
xxviii	Light for a year after Patrick's death	dissyllabic.
xxix	The sun stood still for Joshua;	monosyllabic.
xxx	more fitly for the saints	,,
xxxi	Patrick's requiem	,,
xxxii	Angels take part in it	dissyllabic.
xxxiii	He ascended with 'the other Patrick'	,,
xxxiv	The humility of his service	,,

Of the two rules observed in the case of the *Sén Dé*, viz.: (i) *Elision is not practised.* (ii) *Vowels coming together are monophthong, whether the vowels be long or short*, it is to be noted:—

(i.) This rule is fairly well observed in the piece *Genair Patraic;* but there are six clear instances of elision, viz.: 14 *atchithi hi fisib* [F *itchithe*]; 20 *co de a iartaige* [F *co ti an*]; 28 *consena a rige*; 33 *morferta il-lethu*; 52 *il-laithiu in messa* (F om *in*); 65 *adella in Patraicc*.

Now the early Latin poems do not tolerate elision;[2] nor do

---
[1] The proper name *Odissi* probably accounts for the trisyllable in l. 4.
[2] See above p. xi.

the hymns *Brigit be bith-maith* and *Sén Dé*. On the other hand the later poem *Saltair na Rann* supplies several examples of elision.[1] It thus appears that the progress is from non-elision towards elision, and therefore that, other things agreeing, the date of the *Genair Patraic* (or at all events of the lines containing the elisions), is later than *Sén Dé*.

The combinations of monophthong concurrent vowels in the same word in *Genair Patraic*, are as follows:—

> *ae* : only one instance, 2 *dæc*, which must be regarded as a dissyllable, or the line would be too short ; but the symbol is that constantly given as *æ*, and not *ea*.
> *ai* : nearly 100 instances, but all monosyllabic.
> [*ea* : 42 déacht, dissyll.]
> *ei* : meicc, leicc, deis-, ceilltis, asbeirtis, lēir, feiss, creitset, adfēit, éitsecht, beith, gēillius.
> *eo* : 4 deochain.
> *ia* : bliadna &c., dia, Torrian, cian, iarum, cian, briathar grian, ciasu, iar.
>   [But there are four cases of exception, viz., *līa* 29 ; *gniad* 7, 30 ; (frī-a, 62)].
> *iu* : 10 -ciurt ; 30 fliuch ; 34 fiuscad ; (51 biu).
> [*oä* : 4 *hoä* ; and 31 *fo'aid*, dissyll.]
> *oe* : noeb, cloen, Loegaire, dorroega.
> *oi* : dōine, toimled, chois, canōin, cōicat, coirthe, croich, Trinōite, soillse, assoith.
> *uä* : tuatha, tuargaib, suas, uacht, tuataib, uadib, conhualai, uabar ; [but 12 *nuä*, 20 *tuä*].
> *ui* : forruib, huile, ymmuin, luim, cuilche, luid, muine, buide duit, Nūin contuil ; [but 21 druīd (?) dissyll.].
> [*uai* : tuaith, 29, 41, 57, but *huäir* 59, dissyll.]

The exceptions to the rule are the dissyllables: 2 *dæc* ; 42 *deacht* ; 29 *lia*, 7, 30 *gniad* ; 62 *fria* ; 4 *hoa*, 31 *foaid* ; 19 *nua*, 20 *tua* ; 21 *druid* ; 59 *huair*.[2]

Now of these words none occurs in the *Sén Dé*, unless perhaps we regard the compound *fria* as on a par with *li-ar*, *di-ar*, in l. 45. Perhaps *biu* in l. 51 might be taken as a dissyl-

---

[1] E.g. 59 *in buidi in derg*; 77 *grainne a nguir*; 105 *rigin in bla*; 121 tri *chulrumma intsain*; 135 *isse in met sain*; 156 *ua huarda im da*.

[2] The dissyllable *huair* seems extraordinary, for the *i* cannot be regarded as forming a separate syllable, so that perhaps the writer intended *huaire*.

lable, in which case there would be an additional example of elision.

We have, therefore, no material in this respect on which to base a judgement as to the respective dates of the two poems.

On examining the rhymes, it will be perceived that the verses do not all follow the same metrical system.

The abnormal stanzas are vii, xxiv, xxvi, xxvii, xxix–xxxi; and these must now receive special examination as regards their subject matter.

vii (ll. 13, 14). This stanza plainly interrupts the course of the story. Stanza vi tells of Patrick's education, stanza viii of the call from Fochlad; how then could stanza vii say, "the angels were bringing him"?[1] And this becomes even more unmeaning, when l. 14 is considered; for the visions are apparently seen by Patrick.[2]

xxiv. (ll. 47, 48). Stanza xxiii tells that when Patrick was sick he desired to go to Armagh, but an angel came to meet him and (stanza xxv) said to him, 'Dignity to Armagh,' &c. This is quite consecutive, but stanza xxiv drags in the name of Victor and the allusion to the miraculous Bush, and omits all mention of the angel's orders, "Revertere ad locum unde uenis," as given in the original source.[3] It almost seems as if this stanza had been substituted for an earlier one, which told what the angel said in forbidding Patrick to go to Armagh. Other difficulties which it presents, are the meaning of *dofaith*, and of *aridralastar*, and the subject of *adglastar* (F *adgalastar*). Taking these things in connexion with the unusualness of the rhymes, I am led to the conclusion that the stanza has been interpolated.

---

[1] Apparently *do·d·fetis* is to be used in the same sense as *do·n·fe*, 'May He bring us.'

[2] Cf. Muirchu's note in *Book of Armagh* (fol. 2 a 1) 'eum crebris uissionibus uissitauit dicens ei adesse tempus ut ueniret' &c.

[3] Muirchu's narrative (*Book of Armagh*, fol. 8 a 1). But if the writer of the original poem had really had Muirchu's notes before him, he could not have inserted this item so baldly.

xxvi (ll. 51, 52). We now get into a fresh metric system with monosyllabic rhymes, and these stanzas (xxvi, xxvii, xxix-xxxi), seem to me to follow a tradition distinct from that of Muirchu. In stanza xxvi the two *priuilegia* mentioned are different from the corresponding *petitiones* which were granted by the angel according to Muirchu. In the *Book of Armagh* (fol. 8 a 2), the *secunda petitio* is "ut quicumque ymnum qui de te compossitus est in die exitus de corpore cantauerit, tu iudicabis poenitentiam eius de suis peccatis." *This* would seem to allude to the hymn of St. Sechnall, but the stanza under consideration speaks of "A hymn which thou hast chosen in thy lifetime,' language quite inappropriate to that hymn. Is it not plain that the Lorica of Patrick is intended by these words? The Preface to the Lorica shows exactly this promise, using indeed the same words; cf. vol. i. 133, 7 *bid dítiu do*, and 8 *bid lúrech di-a anmain*, with the expression in the hymn, l. 51 *bid lúrech díten do cach*, 'a lorica of protection.' Again, according to Muirchu, the *quarta petitio* was that "Hibernenses omnes in die iudicii a te iudicentur"; but how can this be represented by the Irish words *immut... regat... do brath*, 'Around thee .. they will go to Dobm'? Indeed this *quarta petitio* has already been alluded to in the dissyllabic stanza xviii, which renders doubtful any second allusion such as we have here.

xxvii. Here the introduction of the name of Tassach without explanation, is curious and anomalous; these monosyllabic stanzas must have belonged to a different narrative in which reference had already been made to Tassach.

xxix-xxxi. With stanza xxviii we again take up the Muirchu tradition, for the words in l. 55, "to set a boundary against night," are exactly Muirchu's "contra noctem terminum pones." But the monosyllabic stanzas xxix and xxx do not at all follow out the comparison of Muirchu, which refers to Isaiah's prayer for a sign to be sent to Hezekiah (2 Kings xx, 11). Then, again, in stanza xxxi we have "Ireland's clerics went to keep watch over Patrick"; this is the common tradition referred to by the Four Masters (*sub ann.* 493), "During the twelve nights that the religious seniors were watching the body with psalms and hymns, it was not night, &c." But the stanza is plainly interpolated, and that wrongly, for "the sound of the singing" which "prostrated" the clerics of Ireland is not mentioned in the *previous* stanzas, although it *is* referred to in that which follows. In the dissyllabic stanza xxxii we have "God's angels on the first night kept watch unceasingly," which is Muirchu's order. His words are " In prima nocte exequiarum eius, angueli uigilias . . fecerunt . . . omnibus quicumque ad uigilias in illa prima nocte ueniebant dormientibus." "The angels sang, and everyone fell asleep thereat," would have been the natural way of placing stanzas xxxi and xxxii.

There is, therefore, something abnormal in everyone of the cases in which the regular dissyllabic rhyme is broken in upon. The impression made on my mind is that of a late compilation, in which the narrative of Muirchu plays, directly or indirectly, a considerable part, though there may have been other accounts current at the time. I think that the five monosyllabic stanzas were borrowed from another poem having a different account from that of Muirchu. To these considerations adduced above may be added the facts that the monosyllabic rhymes give us 58 *adfeit* contrasted with 12 *adfiadat* for 3 pl. pres.; that they give 62 *fosrolaich* (F *fosrolaic*), compared with *fosrolaic* in l. 38, where the F glossator evidently felt a difference and probably a difficulty; and that they give 53 *anais* contrasted with 11 *ainis* (if the latter be taken to mean "he stayed");—facts, which of themselves might be unimportant, yet when falling in with other differences, are not to be left out of account.

Now if we accept the above argument so far as to admit the possibility of this poem's being a patch-work from two or more poems of different rhyming systems, the destructive criticism will have to be carried farther. For there are not wanting other considerations based on the course of the narrative, which seem to show that even the dissyllabic rhymes are not wholly free from interpolations.

I. Even in the first line we meet a difficulty, for *is ed atfet hi scelaib*, which the F gl. 'periti' evidently takes to mean, 'this is what the well-informed *tell* in stories,' can hardly bear that meaning. The word is common enough in this kind of *cheville*[1]. If therefore *atfet* were to be accepted as the plural on the strength of *periti* (and in fact even if we accept *adfeit littri* of 58), we should have a strange use in a short poem of an extraordinary form *adfeit* [atfet] along with *adfiadat*. But if *atfet*[2] be singular, (which it certainly is in *S. na Rann*), then it would seem that the only subject it can refer to is Patrick himself. Here however we meet with another difficulty, for *hi scelaib* would be an astonishing expression for 'in his biography.' In FM 594 *atfet* is found with *scela* as its subject, but it is difficult to believe that this can be other than a misunderstanding[3] of the normal *adfet scel*, 'the story tells.' But the assertion for which this guarantee is given is, that St. Patrick was born *in Nemthur*, and this name is not found in the Saint's own writings. It certainly seems more reasonable to take *hi scelaib* to mean 'in stories,' and to regard this as proof of other early narratives, which may very well have included poems from which our compiler may have made excerpts, or of which he may have made use without paying much heed to minor incongruities.

It seems natural in the second line to come to the conclusion that *dæc* was taken as a dissyllable.[4] But it is to be noticed

---

[1] Cf. *Saltair na Rann*. 2249 *adfet in scriptuir*, 2518 *adfiad in scriptuir*, 2526 *adfet scribenn*, 2530 *adfet in scr.*, 4203 *adfet scel*, &c., the plural being *adfiadat* 862, as here 12.

[2] In the Index to the *Felire of Oengus*, the Editor gives *atfet* = *narrabat*, and *atfet* = *narratus est*, as occurring at Mar. 23 and April 18, but it is pretty certain that neither one nor the other is correct, and that *ar'roet*, 'he received', or something of the kind is meant.

[3] Cf. Todd's *Nennius*, p. 34, 6, where it should be noted that instead of *adfet* (translated, 'it was told'), the other MSS. have *innister*, the normal passive present.

[4] As for example in Saltair na Rann 6822, though perhaps mainly (or only) to get a rhyme, for it is *dée* monosyllabic in 85, 3076; but no rhyme is wanted here, and F has only *dée*.

that the clause *maccan sé mbliadan dæc* is left without a verb, and though that is not unusual where the subsequent clause may be regarded as relative, as in the next line, "Succat his name (was) what he was called," yet there is something abnormal in such omission when the following clause is, as here, a temporal clause introduced by a conjunction, "[he was] a youth of 16. when he was captured."

ix. This stanza exhibits the children of Fochlad's wood praying that Patrick would come to convert from impiety the tribes of Ireland, while stanza x narrates that these very tribes were prophesying the advent of a new Prince of Peace, and the desertion of Tara. But if the tribes of Ireland were prophesying —and it was a curious prophecy for pagan folk to make—where was the need of saying in stanza xi that Loegaire's druids did not conceal Patrick's coming? Stanza ix is probably an interpolation. L. 17 is wrong measure; the half line *gadatar co tissad in noeb* has *eight* syllables, not one of which can be left out, because *gadatar tissad* would be a monstrosity, while the omission of the article before *noeb* would be intolerable, and *gadtar* is out of the region of possibility. Besides what is *lethu* in the second half line? The same writer could scarcely have used this rhyme *lethu* with *bethu* here, and then used it again twice, in two consecutive stanzas xvii and xviii, in such utter vagueness of meaning; it seems to mean only 'broadly,' which can hardly be tolerated here. But the use of it as = 'apud eos,' would be a new feature in the poem, and certainly suggests a different hand.

There is a manifest break between lines 22 and 23, and this latter is particularly noticeable for its assonances, *beba, eua,*[1] *treba,* on a different system of metric.

xiv, xv. Stanzas xiv and xv have also the cæsural assonance *sine* (F) = *rige, Bairche* = *aidche,* which does not occur anywhere else. In l. 30, if the correct analysis of the final rhyme

---

[1] The word *eua* can hardly be anything else than *feba,* but why so written?

be *fo gnia*, as seems unavoidable, it is curious that the form *fo* [= *ba*] occurs nowhere else in these hymns. Besides *feiss* of 27 is practically the same as *foaid* at 31, inasmuch as it is the *cold* that is spoken of, so that *uacht sine* 27 of the cæsural-assonance stanza, has very much the same reference as *ni leice a chorp a timmi* 32, where there is no assonance. In this later stanza we have all the appearances of a glossatorial verse, with its *iarum*, and the expressions *cuilche fliuch* and *ba coirthe a·adart*.[1]

xvii. In this stanza, we come upon several peculiarities, which seem to argue that it was a late interpolation, for the sake of inserting some notice of the miracles performed by the Saint: namely, (1) the repetition of *pridchad*, which is mentioned in the next stanza, *pridchais;* (2) the use of *soscelad*, not found anywhere else in these hymns; (3) the elision of the final in *ferta;* (4) the curious word *luscu* (a word glossed by both T and F as *bacuchu*, but which seems not really known from any other source with the meaning alleged); (5) the use of *mairb* in this manner, as a *nom. pendens;* (6) the identity of rhyming words *il-lethu* and *do bethu*, and (7) the somewhat similar letters in the words *dosfiuscad* 33 and *dosfuc* 35. It seems to me almost impossible to regard this stanza as an original part of the poem.

xix. Here, after Patrick's miracles have been mentioned in xvii, xviii, we suddenly are jerked back again to the pagan Irish! The reference in l. 39 to his *coming* is surely out of place, as is the mention in l. 41 of the pagan Irish worshipping idols.

xx. The abruptness of the change between xxi and xxii makes it almost certain that there is an interpolation in l. 44, with its personal reference in ni-*m* dil; this stanza again is suddenly followed by an account of Patrick's illness.

xxxiii. I have only further to point out that stanza xxxiii,

Cf. LB notes to *Felire*, Mar. 5 (towards end), and see LB 33*β*55.

with its vague *conhualai* in l. 65, its elision in the case of adell*a*, its reference to "the other Patrick" (where did the visit take place?), lead me to infer here also interpolation, in spite of the rhyme in this case being the normal dissyllabic. This last stanza is the more probably genuine that it does not attempt to establish itself as such by the repetition of all the half line.

Admitting, as I do without reserve, the uncertainty of subjective criticism, I have not deemed it right to pass by in silence the objections that are to be urged against the genuineness of the poem in the form in which we have it. Many of these objections would be still valid, even though the metrical system was uniform throughout; but the presence of the metrical variations seems to me to suggest strongly the relatively late 'compilation' of the poem; the neglect which it exhibits of poetical and metrical considerations can only be attributed to a period of decline and decay.

Ninine's Prayer.

The *Oratio Ninini* (our No. 20), shows no appearance of a regularly constructed poem, though there seems to have been an initial effort in that direction, for the first lines present the formula $2(7+5)$; but all throughout there is a rhythmic tendency that is unmistakeable. It may be mere accident, but it is at all events noteworthy that an alphabetic order is observed in the lines:—*a*irdirc, *b*res, *c*athaigestar, *d*edaig, *f*onenaig, *g*uidmit; and that all throughout also the alliterative element is strongly marked, as in these words in order:—a p p; a a a b b; c d d c d d; f f f f; g g; pp; b b; d d d; p p. But it adds nothing definite to our knowledge of the metric system.

It is styled in the preface an *ortha*, 'prayer,' a word used in the *S. na Rann* in connexion with other words that seem to infer for it something of a *musical* element, viz. l. 4321 co *cetlaib, cliaraib, airfitiud, orthonaib,* córaib, *molbthogaib;* but of

THE METRICAL SYSTEMS OF THE IRISH HYMNS.

course this is too vague to admit of anything but speculative inference.

The Hymn Ni car Brigit.

In the hymn of St. Broccan (our No. 22) the difficulties are far more numerous than in the hymns already discussed. The language, in many of the stanzas, does not admit of grammatical analysis, and in some of them, metre and logic are set at defiance. It is impossible to handle the question of the metric without taking into consideration other questions also.

I begin by giving a table in which are set out the subject matter and the rhyming system of the several stanzas. The order of incidents is nearly the same as in the *Vita Brigidae* by Cogitosus, and in the fourth column the numbers of the corresponding chapters in Cogitosus are given.[1]

Stanza.	Subject.	Rhyme.	Parallel Chapter in Cogitosus' *Vita*.
i	Brigid a recluse	monosyllabic, $2 = 4$.	
ii	Her virtues	dissyllabic, $2 = 4$.	
iii	,, ,, ...	,, ,,	
iv	,, ,, ...	,, $1 = 3, \& 2 = 4$.	
v	,, ,, ...	,, ,,	
vi	,, ,, ...	,, $2 = 4$.	
vii	Her congregation at Plea	wrong dissyllabic, $3 = 4$.	
viii	Her veiling by Mac Caille	dissyllabic, $2 = 4$ ...	3
ix	An invocation to God ...	monosyllabic, $2 = 4$.	
x	St. Kevin and Glendalough ...	,, $1 = 3, 2 = 4$.	
xi	Her virtues (continued) ...	,, $2 = 4$.	
xii	Her innumerable miracles ...	?	1
xiii	The multiplication of the butter	dissyllabic & trisyllabic, $1 = 3 \& 2 = 4$ ...	2
xiv	The multiplication of the bacon	dissyllabic, $2 = 4$ ...	4

[1] Cogitosus has some additional incidents in his *Vita* which are not reproduced in our hymn; he ends (c. 36) with a chapter on the impossibility of telling all the miracles of Brigid.

THE HYMN NI CAR BRIGIT.

Stanza.	Subject.	Rhyme.	Parallel Chapter in Cogitosus' Vita.
xv	Her fair harvest weather	dissyllabic, 1 = 3, 2 = 4(?)	5
xvi	The triple milking of her cows	monosyllabic, 2 = 4 (?)	6
xvii	She hangs her cloak on a sunbeam	dissyllabic, 2 = 4	7
xviii	The undiminished flock	monosyllabic, 2 = 4	8
xix	The bath of ale	,, ,,	9
xx	The healing of the nun; the stone made salt.	dissyllabic, 2 = 4	10, 11
xxi	The giving of eyes to the flat-faced man	monosyllabic, 2 = 4	12
xxii	The dumb girl	dissyllabic, 2 = 4	13
xxiii	The bacon untouched by the dog	trisyllabic, 2 = 4	14
xxiv	The boiled meat did not stain her robe	monosyllabic, 2 = 4	15
xxv	The leper and the calf	,, ,,	16
xxvi	,, ,, ,,	,, ,,	,,
xxvii	Her oxen return home	,, ,,	17
xxviii	The run-away horse	,, ,,	18
xxix	The blessing of the wild boar	,, ,,	19
xxx	The wild dogs hunt a pig for her	dissyllabic, 2 = 4	20
xxxi	The escape of the wild fox	monosyllabic, 2 = 4	21
xxxii	The tamed bird	,, ,,	22
xxxiii	The nine outlaws and their harmless weapons.	,, ,,	23
xxxiv	The champion Lugaid	,, ,,	24
xxxv	The removal of the oak	,, ,,	25
xxxvi	The bangle found in the salmon	dissyllabic, 2 = 4	26
xxxvii	The loom and the cooking of the calf	monosyllabic, 2 = 4	27
xxxviii	,, ,, ,, ,, ,, ,,	,, ,,	,,
xxxix	The breaking of the trinket	,, ,,	28
xl	into three equal parts	dissyllabic, 2 = 4	,,
xli	The blessing of Condlaed's garment	,, ,,	29
xlii	,, ,, ,, ,, ,,	? ...	,,
xliii	The honey in the wall	dissyllabic, 2 = 4	30
xliv	The miracle of the mead	monosyllabic, 2 = 4.	
xlv	Invocation of Brigid	,, 2 = 4.	
xlvi	,, ,,	dissyllabic, 2 = 4.	
xlvii	,, ,,	monosyllabic, 1 = 3, 2 = 4.	
xlviii	,, ,,	dissyllabic, 2 = 4.	
xlix	,, ,,	,, ,,	
l	,, ,,	,, ,,	
li	Privilege of praise	,, ,,	
lii	,, ,, ,,	,, 3 = 4 ?	
liii	Invocation of Mary and Brigid	,, 2 = 4 ?	

The variations of metre are very striking. We must either suppose that all these licences were tolerated by the original composer, or that the irregularities have been imported by subsequent admixture. How the former theory can be upheld with any show of argument, I am unable to imagine, but it will be maintained, I daresay.

The repetition of the opening words *Ni car Brigit* after l. 188 denotes that the poem proper ended at that point, and suggests therefore that the last six stanzas are a later addition. In the body of the piece the general principle is that the quatrain has four heptasyllabic lines, the 2nd and 4th of which rhyme. The laws laid down above (p. xxxvi) are generally obeyed, viz.: *There is no elision*, and *In the same word concurrent vowels are monophthong, so far as the measure is concerned.* But even the stanzas i–xlvii show many incongruities, which indicate that the piece is made up of elements derived from different sources.

Stanza i forms the Introduction and is in monosyllabic rhyme; we then pass to stanzas ii–vi in dissyllabic rhyme recounting the virtues of the saint. Of these, stanzas iv and v rhyme their first and third lines as well as their second and fourth.[1]

Stanza vii at once arrests the attention. The rhyme *dama, gaba* of the 3rd and 4th lines is quite anomalous; and further the stanza has no imaginable connexion with the verses between which it is placed. Nobody knows exactly what it means, for the word *plea* in l. 26 resists all analysis; but in any case it has nothing to do with the veiling of Brigid in the next stanza.

Stanza viii contains a story told by Cogitosus, but (as will be seen from the table) the regular Cogitosus series does not begin till Stanza xii, and then it proceeds in order, so that the incident here recorded seems out of its place. The identity of l. 31 with l. 125 *ba menn inn-a himthechtaib* is also a suspicious circumstance.

---

[1] The rhymes are perfect in v; in iv *santach* is probably intended to rhyme with the trisyllabic *cessachtach*, as well as *mathim* with *cathim*.

Stanza ix in monosyllabic rhyme consists of a general invocation to God which would be almost equally relevant anywhere else, although no doubt it is intended to describe the "prayer" of l. 32.

Stanza x is an unintelligible verse, in which St. Kevin and Glendalough are introduced without any justification. No doubt the glossators have explanations to offer, but they are quite inadequate. This and stanza xlvii furnish the only instances of monosyllabic endings with alternate rhymes, 1 = 3 and 2 = 4.

At stanza xi we revert to the virtues of the saint, in sequence of ii-vi; but stanza xii presents us with many problems. Its metre has a strongly marked trochaic beat, as in the line,

cāirm i cḣala clìas nach bì,

which shows a system of *ictus* quite different from (say) stanza v. But the metre of it is undefinable, for it is uncertain which of the lines were intended to rhyme. *Brigti* seems to have been written thus, with *ti* instead of *te*, to get a rhyme, but whether with *rí* or *bí* it is impossible to say; and as *dune* is (with just as much or as little reason) written *duni* in F, we have the four lines ending *ri*, *Brigti*, *duni* (F), and *bi* in an undeterminable mixture. It is with this curious stanza that the Cogitosus series begins.

In the next stanza (xiii) we have an absolutely different order of rhyme, viz., dissyllabic in 1st and 3rd lines, trisyllabic in 2nd and 4th. And the excellence of these rhymes *foided, hoeged*; *fenamain, lenamain*, is noteworthy; the poet who made them could not have been guilty of stanza xii.

In stanza xv we have *crabdig* (F) = *anmach*, and (possibly) *mad-bocht* = *a gort*, the alternate lines rhyming.

Stanza xix. Here (l. 74) as at l. 45 we have the verbal form *dorigenai* used as a quadrisyllable, whereas at ll. 133, 161. we find the trisyllable *dorigne*.[1]

---

[1] This is the normal form in the *Saltair na Rann* where the older *dorigenai* does not appear.

Stanza xxi. We have here (l. 82) the quadrisyllable *dorigenai* which necessitates elision; and yet elision is the later custom, while the spelling *dorigenai* is the earlier form. (In l. 45 it is not elided). Further in l. 81 there is a difficulty about the scansion. The missing syllable cannot be got out of *ruirmiu* any more than out of *airmiu*,[1] from the readings of F *rurmo* and *airmo*; and indeed we have the subjunctival *dorurnne* in l. 134.[2] And again the last line of the stanza (l. 84) comdar forreil a *di suil*, is identical in construction with the last line (88) of the following stanza (xxiv) comtar forreil a *comlabra*, where the measure is wrong. It will hardly be maintained that two stanzas of this kind could have been written by the same poet in one poem. And even if we emend into *labra* in l. 88, what is the meaning? To translate 'till her speech was clear' is impossible with the plural *comtar*; and there would be no meaning in 'till her *speeches* were clear' when we are talking of the recovery of speech by a dumb girl. A further anomaly in stanza xxii is the form 86 *Brigta* (so also at l. 71); cf. *Brigte* in l. 139 and the unintelligible *Brigi* of the additional stanzas at ll. 196, 197.

The metre of stanza xlii is hardly determinable.

Stanzas xlv, xlvi, xlvii may possibly have been taken from some poem quite distinct from the main body of the piece, and added here to wind up the Cogitosus narrative. In xlv we have the extraordinary *for don . . . bet*; the *sí* (F *sith*) in l. 178 is unaccountable, and the other two lines of the stanza are nearly

---

[1] This was evidently a recognised formula as *e.g.* in the verse FM 919,

ni *ruirmiu* ni *airema*
fo·bith is-am triamain-si
a tainic de ancessaib
Ereann isin mbliadain-se.

The spelling here is of course the later spelling of the Four Masters, who felt that *airema* would have to be made a trisyllable.

[2] This also is a line which shows a common formula of the time. Cf. *Saltair na Rann* 788 ni fail ro·airme a n·árim, with our line 134 ni fail do·rurme co cert. Cf. also the subjunctive in l. 162 ni fail dune do·da·decha, where F reads do·decha, which is correct so far as the number of syllables is concerned, but does not help to explain the word.

unintelligible. Then in l. 181 the reference to the *claidib tened* is very curious, and quite inapplicable to Brigid.

Stanza xlvii (as pointed out above) is in a metre of which the anomalous stanza x furnishes the only other example in the poem. It is impossible to trace any connexion between its first three lines and the fourth.

The last six stanzas (xlix–liii) are apparently of the nature of an appendix to the poem; but it will be observed that while five of them exhibit perfect dissyllabic metre (2 = 4), stanza lii is quite irregular. In this we have the third and fourth line rhyming, $Dé = immalle$, against all analogy.

In the last stanza we have a line (212):

<blockquote>for a fóessam dun *dib-linaib*,</blockquote>

which recalls a similar line in the *Sén Dé* (l. 2), viz.:

<blockquote>for a oessam dún *innocht*.</blockquote>

But the number of syllables cannot be made to tally, and Broccan's l. 212 is obviously wrong. All the lines in the stanza are made to end in words with long *i* penult; but it is probable that *Brigit* was meant to rhyme with *línib* and *riched* with *dichill*, and in that case we have again a complete change of metre.

The syncretism and composite character of the piece seem to be established by the foregoing analysis. There is no *a priori* impossibility in the hypothesis that a school of writers[1] are responsible for the construction of the verses, whether as a set task and as a translation of Cogitosus, or whether as a gradual growth in imitation of other extant poems which followed the lines of Cogitosus' narrative. It is of course impossible to assign either date place or person; and it is alike impossible to divide the verses so as to group together the writers of each, though the table given above will suggest tentative arrangements.

If indeed it were a matter of certainty that these verses had been put together thus as one poem, at a very early date, a fact of the kind would simply have to be accepted and the result

---

[1] See the gloss on l. 43 of the *Sén Dé*.

regarded as a proof of the undeveloped state of Irish poetry and of Irish narrative excellence. The difficulty is to see when these verses could have been put together save at a period of absolute decay,—an epoch of metrical, poetical and intellectual poverty.

It was assuredly not at anything near the period when a Columba, an Adamnan, or a Secundinus flourished; it bears all the marks of the terrible era of the Danish viking scourge, wherein the arts and learning of the Irish came nigh to utter destruction. These relics of Irish poetry are probably the early attempts of the clergy to put into metric form the memories of the past that had escaped destruction, but they exhibit the utter dislocation of studies that followed upon the invasions of the Northmen. The Hymn of Ultan represents the early traditions of excellent workmanship, the Hymn of Broccan has no excellence of any kind either as verse or as poetry.

The Hymn of St. Sanctan.

This poem (No. 23) is ascribed by the Preface to a Welshman styled Bishop Sanctan. The time of its composition is admitted to be uncertain, and the poet is credited with a miraculously conferred knowledge of the Irish tongue which he had not before possessed. There are some unusual phrases common to this and to the Lorica of Patrick, e.g., l. 5 *togairm* and l. 7 *issum* are found at l. 2 and l. 62 of the *Lorica*.

The metre of the original poem (ll. 1-40) is heptasyllabic iambic measure, rhyming in dissyllables at the even lines (2 = 4). There is, however, evidence of another strain of metric throughout, the last three lines of each quatrain tending to rhyme; thus in stanza i we have *am, um, am;* in ii, *sim, sum, sum;* in iii, *le, me, re;* in iv, *locht, locht, locht;* in v, *sta, sat, sta;* in vi, *lar, mor, lor;* in vii, *dros, bas, bas;* in viii, *thaib, tha, thaib;* in x, *thrach, thach, thach.*

There are difficulties, however, in most of the stanzas, In i we have as a dissyllable the word *tǘus*, with possibly a Welsh predilection (cf. *tywys*). In ii, the rhyme is not perfect, for *guasim* is not a good rhyme to *uasum*, whatever meaning is assigned to *no·d·guasim*. In vi, *amor* of the third line is a far better rhyme with *galor* than is *celar*. Stanza ix seems anomalous; in it alone the harmony of the last syllables in the last three lines of the quatrain is not observed, l. 35 is short by a syllable, and the rhyme *finna*, *thenga* (F *thinga*) in l. 36 is not very satisfactory, and lastly, we do not really know the meaning of the words. In stanza x (l. 40) the rhyme ·*ethach*[1] is of itself sufficient for the corresponding *sethrach* (l. 38),[2] and the particle *ro* seems to form a syllable too many; probably ·*roethach* is to be read, which would correspond with ·*sæthrach* of F in l. 38.

The first two supplemental stanzas (xi and xii) do not belong to the metre of the original poem, but are in *setna*-metre, the formula of which is $2(8 + 7)$. In xi we should certainly read *sruthib* in l. 41 and *glan gel* in l. 42, with F. The last stanza of all, reverts to the heptasyllabic lines with rhyming dissyllables ($2 = 4$), and may possibly have belonged to the original poem; it also has the final harmonies *im*, *ib*, *il*.

The linguistic difficulties throughout make a reader wish that the 'donation' mentioned in the penultimate clause of the Preface had not been *tam cito*.

The Lorica of St. Patrick.

This piece is not in metre, but it is evidently constructed with an eye to proportion, the phrase *Atomriug indiu* which recurs five times being followed by invocations of much the same structure in each case, concluding with nine rhythmically turned lines in invocation of Christ. Perhaps the piece was originally written in a particular shape, in imitation of some form of material breastplate.

---

[1] Cf. *Saltair na Rann* 817 *at·ethach*.
[2] Or *sethach* according to the T gloss.

It is probably a genuine relic of St. Patrick. Its uncouthness of grammatical forms is in favour of its antiquity. We know that Patrick used very strange Irish, some of which has been preserved; and the historians who handed down *mudebroth* (see p. 178 below) as an ejaculation of his would probably take care to copy as faithfully as they could the other curious Irish forms which the saint had consecrated by his use.

The Hymn of Mael Isu.

There is nothing to observe on this short poem (No. 29) save that the quatrains consist of four lines of six syllables, ending in dissyllables rhyming on the even lines (2 = 4).

ROBERT ATKINSON.

LIBER HYMNORUM

TRANSLATIONS

OF THE

IRISH PREFACES AND HYMNS.

Preface to the Hymn of St. Sechnall.

F] *Audite omnes*, &c. Sechnall *filius Restituti* of the Lombards of Letha, and of Darerca sister of Patrick made *hunc hymnum*, and Secundinus was *Romanum nomen eius*; but the Gaels made Sechnall of it. The place (of its composition was) Domnach Sechnaill; the time, that of Aed mac Néill, or of Loegaire; (as to its cause, it was) for the praise of Patrick it was made; *uel causa pacis fecit, quia nocuit quod dixit Secundinus*: "a good man (were) Patrick, were it not for one thing, viz., *nisi quod minime praedicaret caritatem*." *Et iratus est ei Patricius et dixit:* "*propter caritatem non praedico, quia alii sancti post me uenient in insulam et indigebunt obsequio hominum (et ideo) relinquo caritatem praedi-*

B] *Audite omnes. Locus huius hymni* Domnach Sechnaill: it is that Sechnall who made *hunc hymnum* for Patrick.

As to Patrick, his origin was of the Britons of Her-cluaide; Calpurn was his father's name, Fotaid his grandfather's, who was a deacon. Conchess further, was his mother; Lupait and Tigris were his two sisters.

Now Patrick had four *nomina*, viz. Succat, his name with his parents; Cothraige, his name when he was in service to four persons; Magonius, his name from Germanus; Patricius, from Pope Celestine.

But as to the cause of Patrick's coming into Ireland, it happened in this wise, viz., seven sons of Sechtmaide, a king of the Britons, were in exile, and they plundered Armorica of Letha. There chanced upon them at that time in Armorica a body of Britons of Hercluaide: here Calpurn mac Fotaid, Patrick's father, was slain, and Patrick and his two sisters were there taken prisoners afterwards. The sons of Sechtmaide then went over-sea to Ireland, where Lupait was subsequently sold, viz. in Conalle Muirthemne; Patrick was sold in Dal Araide to Miliuc mac Ua Buain, and to his three brothers; and they sold his two sisters in Conalle Muirthemne, but they knew not each other's lot.

Well, four persons, one of them being Miliuc, bought Patrick, and hence he got the name "Cothraige," from the circumstance that he was servant to a household of four. But when Miliuc saw that he was a faithful slave, he bought him from the other three, so that he served only Miliuc, for seven years after the fashion of the Hebrews; and he suffered great tribulation in the wilds of Slemish in Dal Araide, while herding Miliuc's swine. It chanced now that Miliuc

F] *care"; et ideo fecit Secundinus hunc hymnum causa pacis. Fecerunt pacem Patricius et Secundinus.* It is the first hymn that was made in Ireland. *Secundum ordinem alphabeti factus est;* twenty-three capitula in it, four lines to each capitulum and fifteen syllables in each line. There are further three places in it in which there is found 'in' *sine sensu causa rhythmi.* Now when Sechnall had finished making this eulogy, he went to show it to Patrick, to whom

B] saw a vision of the night, viz. he thought he saw Cothraige coming to him into the house where he was, having a flame of fire over his head and out of his nostrils and ears; and it seemed to him that the fire played threateningly over him to burn him, but he drove it from him and it did him no harm; but his son and his daughter who were in the same bed with him, these the fire burnt to ashes, and the wind scattered those ashes all over Ireland. Thereupon Cothraige was summoned before Miliuc, who told him his vision; and Cothraige gave judgement on it as follows: " The fire thou sawest in me is the faith of the Trinity which glows in me; it is that faith I shall preach to thee in after time, and thou wilt not believe; but thy son and thy daughter will believe, and the fire of grace will burn them." Now when St. Patrick was born, he was brought to the blind flat-faced youth to baptize him: the priest's name was Gorianas. As he had no water with which to perform the baptism, he made the sign of the cross over the ground with the babe's hand, and water came out, *et lauauit Gorianas faciem suam,* and after that his eyes were opened, and he, a person who had not learnt letters before, read out the baptismal office.

Tempus autem, that of Loegaire mac Neill, king of Ireland; *causa,* in order to praise Patrick. For Sechnall had said to Patrick, " when shall I make a eulogy for thee?" Patrick replied, " I wish to have no eulogy of me in my lifetime." *Dixit* Sechnall, " *non interrogaui utrum faciam, sed quando faciam." Dixit Patricius,* " *si facias, uenit tempus,"* for Patrick knew that the time of his death was near at hand. Sechnall, son of Restitutus, made *hunc hymnum* for Patrick, for he was a pupil of Patrick's, and also *filius sororis* of Patrick; he was descended from the Lombards of Letha, *ut dixit* Eochaid Ua Flannucáin:

> Sechnall mac Ui Bard, of the victory,
> victory of world's men,
> of seed pure-fierce, whiteness of colour,
> Lombards of Letha.

Longobardi dicti sunt eo quod habent longam barbam. Secundinus 'secans delicta' aliorum, uel 'secedens ipse a delictis' interpretatur.

Now when Sechnall was making this hymn, there happened to be a fair held near Domnach Sechnaill, and a message went from Sechnall to forbid it, and went unheeded. Thereafter Sechnall went back,

PREFACE TO THE HYMN OF ST. SECHNALL.

F] he said, "I have made a eulogy for a certain son of life, and I should like thee to hear it." "My welcome to a eulogy (of any) of the household of God," said Patrick. But Sechnall began his hymn at *Beata Christi*, that Patrick should not hear for whom it was made till the whole should have been recited. However, when Sechnall uttered *Maximus in regno caelorum*, *dixit Patricius*, "How could *homo* be *maximus in caelo?*" *Dixit Secundinus: "pro positiuo positus est hic superlatiuus."* On the conclusion of the recital, "(Give) me the reward for it," said Sechnall. "Thou shalt have it,"

B] and raised his hands to God, and the earth swallowed thirteen chariots of them *cum suis equitibus, et ceteri in fugam exierunt*.

Uel haec est causa, viz. because of the annoyance Sechnall gave Patrick, in saying, "a good man were Patrick were it not for one thing, viz. the small extent to which he preaches charity." When Patrick heard it, he went to Sechnall in great anger. Sechnall had just finished mass except going to Christ's body, when it was told him that Patrick was coming to the place in great anger against Sechnall. The latter thereupon left the oblation on the altar, and bowed down to Patrick, who drove the chariot over him; but God raised the ground around him *hinc et inde* so that it did not harm him. "What has happened to me?" asked Sechnall. Patrick replied, "What is that one thing *dixisti*, that I did not fulfil? For if I do not fulfil charity, I am guilty in respect of God's commandment. God knows that it is for charity that I do not preach it; for there shall come *post me in hanc insulam* 'sons of life' who shall stand in need of being served *ab hominibus*." "I did not know," said Sechnall, "that it was not through remissness thou didst so." Then said the angel to Patrick, "All that shall be thine." So they made peace then, Patrick and Sechnall. And whilst they were going round the cemetery, they heard a choir of angels singing around the oblation in the church; and what they sang was the hymn beginning, "*Sancti uenite Christi corpus*," etc.; hence this hymn is sung in Ireland when one goes to the body of Christ, from that time onward.

And after that, Patrick sent Sechnall to Rome, for some of the relics of Paul and Peter and other martyrs, (as amends) for the blame he had laid upon him: those are the relics that are in Armagh in the shrine of Paul and Peter.

Now when Sechnall had finished the composition of his eulogy, he went to show it to Patrick, and when he had come to Patrick, he said to him, "A eulogy that I have made for a certain 'son of life'; I want you to hear it." Patrick replied, "I welcome a eulogy of any man of God's household." But Sechnall began his hymn at "*beata Christi custodit*," that Patrick should not perceive for whom the hymn was made till it had been all recited. But when Sechnall recited "*Maximus namque in regno caelorum*," Patrick

F] said Patrick, " the number of hairs that are on thy cloak, i.e. on thy hood, the like number of sinners (shall go) to heaven, for the hymn." " I will not take that," said Sechnall. " Thou shalt have," said Patrick, " this boon : everyone who shall recite it at lying down and rising up shall go to heaven." " I accept that," said Sechnall, " but the hymn is long, and not everyone will be able to commit it to memory." " Its grace," said Patrick, " shall be on the last three capitula." " *Deo gratias*," said Sechnall.

B] shifted about from place to place, *et dixit*, " How can a human being be '*maximus*' in *regno caelorum*?" *Dixit Sechnall*, "*Pro positiuo est hic*; or, it is many of his own race that he excels." " Good is the answer," said Patrick. Now when Sechnall had finished reciting the hymn, there came up a man and a woman having food with them for Patrick, viz. curds and butter: *Bera nomen uiri et Brig nomen mulieris*. Said Patrick, " A house in which this hymn shall be recited before dinner, shall never have scarcity of food ; and further a new house in which it shall be recited *prius*, shall have around it a watch (consisting) of Patrick with Ireland's saints." As it was made manifest to Colman Ela *et aliis cum eo ;* and as it was made manifest to Kevin *cum suis*, when he came out of the church one Sunday into the refectory. *At hymnum hunc cantauit, Patricius cum multis patribus apparuit ei ; et ter cantauit, et tunc quidam stultus dixit*, "*cur canimus hunc hymnum sic?*" *et dixit* Kevin, " that is not good," said he, " *quia apparuit nobis Patricius cum suis discipulis quamdiu cantabamus hymnum*."

When the recitation of the hymn was complete, Sechnall said, " (Grant) its reward to me." " Thou shalt have it," said Patrick, the number of days that there are *in anno*, the like number *de animabus peccatorum* (shall be permitted) to go to heaven for the making of the hymn." " I shall not accept that," said Sechnall, " for I deem it little, and the eulogy is good." " Thou shalt have," said Patrick, "(granted to thee that) as many as are the threads in the cloak of thy cowl, so many sinners shall go to heaven, for the sake of the hymn." " I shall not accept (that either)," said Sechnall, " for what believer is there that will not take with him as many as that to heaven, without his praising a man like thee at all ?" " Thou shalt have (this)," said Patrick, " of Ireland's sinners seven every Thursday, and twelve every Saturday (admitted) into heaven." " It is (too) little," said Sechnall. " Heaven for everyone who shall recite it at lying down and at rising up, shall be thy boon," said Patrick. " I shall not accept (even) that," said Sechnall, " for the hymn is long, and not everybody will be able to remember it." " All its grace," said Patrick, " on its last three capitula." " *Deo gratias*," said Sechnall.

F] *Longobardus genere, ut dixit* Eochaid ua Flannucáin:

> Sechnall, son of Ua Baird,
> victory of the world,
> of seed pure-fierce, whiteness of colour,
> Lombards of Italy.

Longbardi dicti sunt eo quod barbam longam habent.

As to Succat, (it was) Patrick's name *apud parentes eius*; Cothraige, *nomen eius apud Miliuc; Magonius, apud Germanum; Patricius, a papa Celestino.*

B] The angel promised the same thing to Patrick on the Cruach, viz., heaven to the person who shall recite at lying down and at rising up its last three capitula, *ut est*:

> "A hymn thou hast chosen in thy life
> Will be a Lorica of protection for everyone."[1]

This is the first hymn that was made in Ireland. It is in alphabetical order *more Hebraeorum sed non per omnia*. There are in it twenty-three capitula, four lines in each, and fifteen syllables in each line; *et si quis inuenerit plus minusue, in eo error est.* There are two or three places in which there is 'in' *sine sensu sed causa rhythmi* &c. (The opening words are) *similitudine Moysis dicentis,* "*Audite caeli quae loquar,*"[2] *et Dauid dicentis,* "*Audite haec omnes gentes.*"[3]

---

[1] *Hymn of St. Fiacc*, l. 31.   [2] Deut. xxxii. 1.   [3] Ps. xlvii. 1.

Preface to the Hymn *Christus in nostra*.

T] *Christus in nostra.* Ninnid Pure-hand mac Echach, made *hunc hymnum* for Brigid.

Or, it is Fiacc of Sletty that made it.

Dicunt alii that it was Ultan of Ardbreccan that made it, for it is he who collected Brigid's miracles into one book, beginning *Audite uirginis laudes*. It is in alphabetical order, and was made in rhythm. It contains three capitula, each of four lines with sixteen syllables to each line.

Dicunt alii that this was a long hymn, but here there are only four capitula of it, viz. the first and the last three capitula *causa breuitatis*.

F] *Christus in nostra.* Ninnid Pure-hand mac Echach, made *hunc hymnum* to praise Brigid.

Or Fiacc of Sletty; its beginning is *audite uirginis laudes*.

Or it was Ultan of Ardbreccan that made it, to praise Brigid; for it was he who collected Brigid's miracles into one book. It is in alphabetical order, and was made in a well-known rhythm. It has four capitula, with four lines in each, and sixteen syllables in each line.

Preface to the Hymn of St. Cummain the Tall.

TF] *Celebra Iuda.* Cummain the Tall mac Fiachna, king of West Munster, *ille fecit hunc hymnum.* And as to that Cummain, it was by a daughter that Fiachna begot him, in intoxication. *Et interrogauit Flann,* "of whom hast thou him?" *et dixit,* "*tui*"; *et dixit pater,* "*oportet mori*"; "*ita fiat,*" said the daughter. *Sed quando natus est,* to Ita's Cell *ductus est et ibi relictus est* on the top of a cross in a little basket [*cummain*]; *inde dictus est* Cummain. *Et ibidem nutritus ac doctus est,* and it was not known whence he was *tamdiu donec uenit mater eius ad uisitandum eum ad domum abbatis Itæ,* for she often used to come to him. And she came one day to the house, and Ita's coarb was not at home, *et potum postulauit, et mater sua dedit ei sinum abbatissae* to drink a drink out of it; so he drank a drink out of it, but Ita's coarb rebuked her for giving the vessel to him; and then she said:

> "notice not
> though I give a drink to my brother;
> he is Fiachna's son, he is Fiachna's grandson,
> Fiachna's daughter is his mother."

After that he studied in Cork till he became a sage; *uenit autem postea ad patrem et ad patriam,* viz. to the Eoganacht of Loch Lein. Now everybody says that Cummain resembled Fiachna, *inde dixit:*

> " No falsehood to me, though I say
> 'near is our relationship (in) us three,'
> (for) it is my grandfather (that is) my father,
> (and as to) my mother, she is my sister.
>
> if (ever) good sprang out of evil,
> it is I that have the great preeminence;
> (for as to) my sister, she is my mother,
> (and as to) my father, he is my grandfather.
>
> near is the appellation:
> I am grandson of thy mother;
> even my mother is laid as an accusation
> upon the brother of thy brother.

i.e. upon thee, O Fiachna, for thou thyself art thy brother's brother.

TF]   there comes to me friendly tie doubly
      with the seed of Fiachra Gairrine :
      inasmuch as he is a grandson and a son to him,
      the person Cummain to Fiachna."

Tunc Fiachna intellexit filium suum Cummaine esse, and it is he who made this hymn. The reason of its composition is : Cummain went in reliance on the apostles, that Domnall son of Aed mac Ainmerech should be able to weep, in order to ask forgiveness for his crimes, for he was quite unable to do so before through the hardness of his heart. Now his soul-friend was Cummain, for a message had gone from Domnall to Colum Cille to ask him whom he should accept as soul-friend, or whether he himself should go eastward to him. *Unde dixit* Colum Cille :

"The sage whom he will choose from the south,
it is with him he shall get his need :
he will bring 'cummain' to his house,
to the fair grandson of Ainmere."

and it is Cummain that was foretold therein. When, however Cummain, after composing the hymn, went to ask about Domnall's state, Domnall was in the house at the time, weeping for his crimes. *Tunc dixit* Cummain, "Now" &c. ; and then he flung from him the purple cloak that was on his back, viz. a cloak his mother [F]lann had made for him. *Tunc dixit* Cummain :

"O king, a sign (?)
that thou permittest me not according to my will,
Domnall refuses it, so that he takes not (?)
the little cloak of fair [F]lann upon him."

Therefore he went in reliance on the apostles, and Domnall wept for his crimes thereafter, so that Cummain said :

"Now
Domnall recognises a King above him (viz. God over him);
his good is the good in the next world ;
this (earthly) good is not his good."

In tempore autem of Domnall son of Aed mac Ainmerech was it made ; in rhythm *uero fecit*, two lines in each capitulum, with twelve syllables in each line ; it was based on a prophet's rule,[1] *Celebra Iuda festivitates tuas*. This hymn was composed in Daire Calcaig.

[1] Nahum i. 15.

Preface to the Hymn of St. Mugint.

TF] *Parce domine. Mugint fecit hunc hymnum* in Futerna. *Causa i.e.* Finnian of Moville *exiit* to learn with Mugint and Rioc and Talmach *et ceteri alii secum.* Drust *rex* of Britain *tunc et habuit filiam i.c. Drusticc nomen eius, et dedit eam legendo* with Mugint. *Et amauit illa Rioc, et dixit Finniano: tribuam tibi omnes libros quos habet Mugint scribendum si Rioc dedisses mihi in matrimonium. Et misit* Finnen Talmach *ad se illa nocte in formam Rioc ; et cognouit eam, et inde conceptus ac natus est* Lonan of Treoit. *Sed Drusticc estimauit quod Rioc eam cognouit, et dixit quod Rioc pater esset filii ; sed falsum est, quia Rioc uirgo fuit. Iratus est Mugint tunc et misit quendam puerum in templum, et dixit ei : si quis prius in hac nocte ueniat ad te in templum, percute eum securi. Ideo dixit quia prius Finnianus pergebat ad templum. Sed tamen illa nocte domino instigante ipse Mugint prius ecclesiæ peruenit ; et percussit eum puer, propheta dicente* " *conuertetur dolor eius in caput eius, et in uerticem ipsius iniquitas eius descendet.*"[1] *Et tunc dixit Mugint* "*Parce*" *quia putauit inimicos populum populari.*

Or, it might be on this account he made this hymn, that his crime might not be visited on the people.

Uel Ambrosius fecit, when he was in disease.

Uel Dauid fecit, ut alii dicunt, sed non uerum ; but it is from him are taken [the words], "*dic angelo tuo percutienti*" *usque* "*populo tuo.*"

F adds] And there came great trouble on him at last, for there appeared to him foes attacking the people, so that he went in reliance on the Lord to free the people from their foes, and there he made "*Parce domine.*"

Or perhaps it was for this reason that he made this hymn, *ut diximus*, that his crime should not be visited on the people.

---

[1] Ps. vii. 17.

Preface to the Hymn of St. Colman.

T] 'God's blessing.' Colman mac Ui Cluasaig, a scholar from Cork, made this hymn to save himself from the Yellow Plague that occurred in the time of the sons of Aed Slane. For there were many people in Ireland at that time, and their multitude was such that they got only thrice nine ridges for each man in Ireland, viz. nine of bog, and nine of grass-land and nine of forest, so that the nobles of Ireland's men fasted along with the sons of Aed Slane, and with Fechin of Fore, and with Aileran, and with Manchan of Liath and many others, to get the population reduced, for there had come a scarcity of food owing to their numbers; and therefore the Yellow Plague was inflicted on them, so that there died of it in that year the sons of Aed Slane and the elders we have mentioned *et alii multi*.

Dicunt alii that it was Colman who composed it all, but others say that he composed only two quatrains of it, and the school the rest of it, viz. each man of them a half-quatrain. It was composed in Cork, in the time of the two sons of Aed Slane, viz. Blaithmac and Diarmait. Now the cause of its composition was this. A great pestilence was sent upon Ireland's men, viz. the Buide Connaill; it ransacked all Ireland, and left alive only every third man in Ireland; and so it was to protect them and also his school that Colman composed this hymn against that pestilence. And it befel him to be composing it just at the time when he began a journey to a certain island of Ireland's sea outside, in flight from this

F] 'God's blessing.' Colman mac Ui Cluasaig, a Cork scholar, made this hymn, in collaboration with his school, and it was probably a half-quatrain each man composed; or else, he made the hymn all by himself. As to the place, it was from the island at Cork up to the island towards which they went in their flight from the pestilence. It was made in the time of the two sons of Aed Slane, viz. Blathmac and Diarmait. The cause of its composition was that a great pestilence had been sent upon Ireland's men, viz. the Buide Connaill, and it attacked all Ireland, so that it left alive in Ireland only every third person; of it died the sons of Aed Slane, and Fechin of Fore, *et alii multi clerici et reges in eodem anno perierunt*. And it was to save himself and his school that Colman

T] pestilence, so that there might be nine waves between them and land, for pestilence does not come across beyond (that distance), *ut ferunt periti*. And a certain person of Colman's school asked, "What was the blessing, in which going on a journey befel them?" Then spake Colman, "What blessing is that?" said he, "why, what but God's blessing?" For this is what they sought after, to go forth on islands of the sea, on flight before the disease.

F] composed this hymn against that pestilence, and he chanced to be composing it just when he began a journey to a certain island in the sea, that there might be nine waves between them and land, for pestilence does not come over nine waves, *ut ferunt periti*. And a certain person of his school asked Colman, "What was the blessing, in which going on a journey befel them?" Then spake Colman, "What blessing is that?" said he, "why, what but God's blessing?"

The Hymn of St. Colman mac Ui Cluasaigh.

TF] God's blessing bear us, succour us! may Mary's son protect us!
Under His protection may we be to-night! whithersoever we go, may He well protect!

In rest or in activity, seated or standing,
Heaven's King, against every battle; this is the supplication we shall make.

5 A supplication of Abel, Adam's son, of Eli, of Enoch, for our help!
May they save us from swift disease, wherever throughout the world it threatens!

Noah and Abraham, Isaac the wondrous son,
May they come around us against pestilence, neither let famine visit us!

We beseech the father of the twelve, and Joseph their younger [brother],
10 May their prayers save us to a King of many angels, noble!

May Moses, good leader, protect me, who protected through *Rubrum Mare*;
Joshua, Aaron son of Amra, David the daring youth!

Job with the tribulations, may he protect us past the poisons;
May God's prophets guard us, with Machabæus' seven sons!

15 John Baptist we invoke, may he be a shelter to us, be a protection;
Jesus with His apostles be for our help against danger!

May Mary, Joseph, watch over us, *et spiritus Stephani*,
From every strait release us remembrance of *Ignatius'* name!

Every martyr, every hermit, every saint who lived in chastity,
20 Be a shield to us for our defence, be an arrow (sent) from us against demons!

Regem regum rogamus in nostris sermonibus,
Who saved Noah [and] his crew *diluuii temporibus*.

TF] *Melchisedec rex Salem incerto de semine,*
   May his prayers free us *ab omni formidine!*

25 The Saviour, who freed Lot from fire *qui per saecula habetur,*
   Ut nos omnes precamur liberare dignetur.

   Abraham of Ur of the Chaldees, may the King protect us, may He protect us!
   May He free me, He who freed the people *lympha fontis in Gaba!*

   The King, who saved three children from a furnace of fire with redness,
30 May He save us, as He saved David *de manu Goliath.*

   May the Ruler of lamp-lit heaven have mercy on us, for our wretchedness!
   He who left not *suum prophetam ulli leonum ori.*

   As He sent the angel who loosened Peter from his fetter,
   May he be sent to us for our assistance, may every rough thing be smooth before us!

35 To our God may we render ourselves pleasing, *nostro opere digno,*
   May we be with Him in eternal life *in paradisi regno.*

   As He freed Jonas Prophet from a whale's belly, bright deed,
   May the good King, threatening, mighty, protect us! God's blessing bear us, come upon us!

   Truly, O God, in very truth, be granted this prayer:
40 May there be infants of God's Kingdom all around this school!

   In very truth, O God, be it true! let us all attain the peace of the King!
   If one might attain, may we attain, into heaven's Kingdom may we win!

   May we be without age, in (endless) space, with angels in eternal life!

   Great Kings, prophets without death, angels, apostles—a noble sight!
45 May they arrive with our heavenly Father to bless us before a devil host (can reach us)!

                                   God's blessing.

TF] Benediction on patron Patrick with Ireland's saints around him,
Benediction on this monastery and on every one therein!

Benediction on patron Brigid, with Ireland's virgins around her,
50 Give all ye fair testimony, benediction on Brigid's dignity!

Benediction on Colum Cille with Scotland's saints o'er yonder!
On the soul of noble Adamnan who passed a Law upon the clans!

(May we be ever) in the shelter of the King of the elements!
His protection may He take not from us!
May the Holy Spirit sprinkle us! may Christ free us, bless us!
55   God's blessing.

Orent pro nobis sancti illi in caelis, quorum memoriam facimus in terris, ut deleantur delicta nostra per inuocationem sancti nominis tui Iesu; et miserere qui regnas in sæcula sæculorum. Amen.

Preface to the Hymn of St. Cuchuimne.

TF] *Cantemus in omni die:* Cuchuimne *fecit hunc hymnum* to praise the Virgin Mary; and in the time of Loingsech mac Oengusa and of Adamnan *factus est; incertum est uero in quo loco eum fecit.* The cause of its composition was to free him from the evil life in which he lived, *quia coniugem habuit et in mala uita cum illa fuit.*

Or maybe it was to get made smooth before him the part of his reading he had not yet attained to, that he made this eulogy for Mary. *Ut Adamnanus dixit:*

> Cuchuimne
> read science up to [the] ridge;
> the other half that is over
> he left for his hags.

Cuchuimne *dixit:*

> Cuchuimne
> read science up to [the] ridge;
> the other half that is over
> he will read, he will leave [his] hags.

or,

> the other half of his allotted path (?)
> he will read all, till he become a sage.

In rhythm now he made it; and fourteen capitula therein, with two lines in each capitulum and twelve syllables in each line.

Preface to the Hymn of St. Hilary.

T] *Hymnum dicat.* *Hilarius episcopus et princeps ciuitatis quæ dicitur Pictauis fecit hunc hymnum Christo, in monte Gargani,* after eating the dinner *illic* in the house of the robber. And after giving thanks to God, the sons of life faded *post,* till they were no bigger *quam infantes,* as it seemed to a priest who was with them. An angel came and said to them, "*nisi penitentiam egeritis, in infernum ibitis.*" *Egerunt ergo penitentiam, et dedit deus indulgentiam eis per istam laudem: sic nobis connenit canere post prandium.*

Aliter: locus i.e. specus in pectore montis Iouis inter Alpes in qua philosophi ante fuerunt. Tempus, Ualentiniani et Ualentis. Persona, Hilarius. Causa, i.e. angelus postulauit quando uenit ad Susannam urbem cum tricentis uiris, i.e. c. de clericis et cc. de laicis. Unus uero de clericis mortuus est pro frigore hiemis et Hilarius orauit pro suo monacho. Illa autem nocte angelus dixit ad eum, "debet te scrutari scripturas et hymnum facere deo." Ille ergo fecit iuxta imperium angeli et mortuum suscitauit per gratiam dei.

Metrum trochaicum tetrametrum est; hic recipit spondeum omnibus locis practer tertium locum et trochaea omnibus locis; in quo aliquando tertio loco prioris uersiculi spondeum reperies ut "factor caeli et terrae factor," et "uerbis purgat leprae morbum." Currit autem alternis uersibus, ita ut prior uersus habeat pedes quatuor, posterior uero tres et syllabam.[1]

Hymnus Graece, 'laus' interpretatur Latine; uel hymnus 'memoria' dicitur, sicut in psalterio Graeco 'ymnos testmon,' hoc est *'memor fuit nostri';* and it is for the praise of God especially that *hymnus* is due; and it is sung to a melody, *ut Augustinus dicit* in the Decades. *Hymnos primum Dauid propheta in laudem dei composuisse manifestum est.*[2]

---

[1] Cf. Baeda *de arte metrica* c. 21.   [2] Cf. Isid. *De Off.* l. vi. 1.

Preface to the Hymn of St. Colman Mac Murchon.

T] *In trinitate spes mea.* Three sons of Murchu of Connaught made this eulogy for Michael; Colman, the eldest of them, was a bishop, while the other two were priests. *Causa*, viz. on their pilgrimage they went and a great storm befel them on the Ictian sea; so they went to a certain island, and a great famine befel them; so that it was to free themselves from that famine they made this eulogy.

Or, it was to free Rodan's island from demons; for there was a certain transgressing bishop in (it) before that, and it is in France. *Et postea ad Hiberniam uenerunt. Incertum est autem in quo tempore factus est.* Now it was made in rhythm, and it has eleven capitula with two lines in each, and sixteen syllables in each (line). The rhythm is...according to the presence there of *omine*.

F] *In trinitate spes mea et reliqua.* Sons of Murchu of Connaught made this hymn for Michael, to free themselves from a tempest of the Ictian Sea, or to free themselves *de fame in insula maris Tyrrh·ni*. Maybe also it was Colman alone that made it, for he was the eldest of them, and further he was a bishop, while the other two were priests; *uel inter se fecerunt. In quo tempore uero factus est incertum est.* Now it was made in rhythm with eleven capitula in it, with two lines and fifteen syllables to each. The rhythm is... according to the presence there of *omine*.

PREFACE TO THE HYMN OF ST. OENGUS MAC TIPRAITE.

TF] *Martine.* Oengus mac Tipraite, priest of Cluain Fota Baitan Aba, composed *hunc hymnum. In Cluain Fota factus est. Causa autem :* Adamnan was on circuit of the churches of Colum Cille in Ireland, and he got as far as Uisnech in Meath, where there was summoned to him every man in orders against whom there was an accusation in the land; and the summons reached Oengus on the night of Martin's feast, *et timuit ualde ut fecit hunc hymnum in honorem Martini* to free himself. *Uenit* then Oengus to the tryst on the morrow, with his hymn ready by him, and there was shown to Adamnan, Martin on the right hand of Oengus; so then Adamnan rose up before him, *et honorificauit eum cum osculo, et omnes mirabantur causam honoris; et dixit Adamnan ut uidit Martinum secum,* so that it is on account of Martin's being along with him that he paid him honour. Thus then Oengus was freed; *et ostendit hymnum suum et laudauit Adamnan hymnum, et dixit,* "personal reverence (shall be) for him who recites it on going to meeting or court," and that it would be a protection against every disease; and heaven for reciting it on lying down and on rising up.

In rhythm also it was made; six capitula in it with two lines in each; correspondences also there are in it, *et non æqualem numerum syllabarum singulæ lineæ seruant.*

Preface to *Gloria in Excelsis*.

TF] *Gloria in excelsis. Angeli dei cecinerunt primum uersum huius hymni in nocte dominicæ natiuitatis.* They composed it at the Tower of Gabder, *i.e.* a mile east of Jerusalem; and they composed it to show that the person who was born there was the Son of God. In the time of Octavianus Augustus it was composed. *Ambrosius autem fecit hunc hymnum a secundo uersu usque ad finem hymni.*

B] *Gloria in excelsis deo.* Angels composed the introductory verse of this hymn, on the night of the Nativity; and at the Tower of Ader they composed it, a mile east of Jerusalem. To show that he who was born there was the Son of God they composed it. Further in the time of Octavianus it was composed. But Ambrose composed the remainder, viz., *a secundo uersu usque in finem laudis*, &c. *Ambrosius*, sage and bishop, composed *hunc hymnum* to praise Jesus; and at night it is due to be sung.

It was composed also in rhythm; seven capitula in it, with seven lines to each, and seven syllables in each line.

Preface to *Magnificat*.

TFB] *Magnificat. Maria mater Domini fecit hunc hymnum. In tempore uero Octauiani Augusti fecit in quadragesimo enim secundo anno imperii eius Christus natus est.* It was made in a certain mountain-city in the tribe of Judah, near Jerusalem, in Zacharias' own city; *ibi Iohannes Baptista natus est.* And it is to that city Mary came to enquire about Elizabeth, when she heard of her being pregnant, viz. in the sixth month. And it is in it that speech was given to Zacharias, and in it Zacharias composed the *Benedictus*, and in it the *Magnificat* was made. Now the cause is this, viz. Mary came to enquire about Elizabeth, wife of Zacharias, for she had heard of her being pregnant *post longissimam sterilitatem. Omnes enim cognati eius eam uisitabant. Intrans ergo Maria ostium domus suæ, Elizabeth dixit cum motatione infantis in utero suo,* " *En mater domini uenit ad me*"; *et ob id dicunt Iohannem prophetasse antequam natus esset; et tunc Maria dixit* " *Magnificat,*" *et in hoc tempore filium suum Maria concepit.*

Preface to *Te Deum Laudamus*.

T] *Haec est laus sanctæ Trinitatis quam Augustinus sanctus et Ambrosius composuerunt.*

F] Niceta, coarb of Peter, made this canticle. And in Rome it was made. *Incertum autem quo tempore et ob quam causam factum, nisi Nicetam deum laudare uoluisse diceremus, dicens,* " *Laudate pueri dominum, Laudate nomen domini, Te deum laudamus etc.*"

Preface to the Hymn *Altus Prosator.*

TF] *Locus huius hymmi* Hi. *Tempus* of Aedan mac Gabrain, King of Scotland, and of Aed mac Ainmerech, King of Ireland; *Mauritius autem uel Phocas* was King of Romans *tunc.* The person was Colum Cille *de nobili genere Scotorum,* 'Columba' *dicitur ut "estote prudentes sicut serpentes et simplices sicut columbae." Causa, quia uoluit Deum laudare. Per septem annos hunc hymmum scrutans in nigra cellula sine lumine, i.e.* to beg forgiveness on account of gaining the battle of Cuil Dremne over Diarmait mac Cerbaill, and the other battles that were gained because of him.

Uel ut alii dicunt, it was suddenly made, viz. one day Colum Cille was in Hi, and nobody was with him but Baithin, and they had no food except a sieve of oats. Then said Colum Cille to Baithin, "Nobler guests (than usual) are coming to us to-day, O Baithin"; viz. folk of Gregory, who came with presents to him. And he said to Baithin, "Stay at home in attendance on the guests, that I may go to the mill." He takes upon him his burden from a certain stone that was in the church, *i.e.* Blathnat its name, and it still exists, and

B] *Altus prosator.* Colum Cille *fecit hunc hymnum Trinitati per septem annos in Cellula Nigra, i.e.* in Colum Cille's Black Church in Derry; or it was composed quite on the spur of the moment, *ut alii dicunt,* viz. when Colum Cille was in Hi alone, save for the presence of Baithin only. Now it was then revealed to Colum Cille that guests were coming to him, viz. seven of Gregory's people came to him from Rome having presents for him, namely, the Great Gem of Colum Cille—and that is a cross extant to-day—and the Hymn of the Week, a hymn for every night in the week, *et alia dona.* So Colum Cille enquired of Baithin what there was of food in the common stock. Said Baithin, "There is a sieve of oats." "Attend thou on the guests, O Baithin," said Colum Cille, "that I may go to the mill." Thereupon Colum Cille takes on his shoulders the sack from the stone that is in the refectory in Hi; and the name of that stone is Moel-blatha, and luck was left on all food that is put thereon. After that, as he was going to the mill, Colum Cille composed this little hymn *Adiutor laborantium*; and it is in alphabetical order.

TF] upon it there is made division in the refectory. But his burden felt heavy to him, so he composed this hymn in alphabetical order, from there up to the mill, viz. *Adiutor laborantium*, &c. Now when he put the first handful into the mill, it was then he began upon the first capitulum, and the grinding of the bag (of oats) and the composition of the hymn were completed together; and extemporaneously it was made *sic*.

In the five hundred and sixty-fifth year after Christ's Nativity Colum Cille went to Hi, *ut Beda dicit,* "*Anno dominicæ incarnationis dlxu. quo tempore gubernaculum Romani imperii post Iustinianum Iustinus minor accepit, uenit de Hibernia presbyter et abbas habitu et uita monachi insignis nomine Columba Brittaniam praedicaturus uerbum dei prouinciis septentrionalium Pictorum.*"[1] *Brudi autem filius Melchon regebat Pictos tunc, et ipse immolauit Columbae Hi, ubi Columba cum esset annorum lxxui. sepultus est, post uero xxxiiii. ex quo ipse Brittaniam praedicaturus adiit.*

' Well, this hymn was taken eastward to Gregory as a return for the gifts that had been sent by him, viz. the cross, whose name was the Great Gem, and the Hymns of the Week. But the bearers changed three capitula in it to test Gregory, viz. "*Hic sublatus*," and "*Orbem*," and "*Uagatur*." When however they began upon the reading aloud of the hymn to Gregory, God's angels came and remained standing, until that capitulum was reached. Gregory (too) stood up in

B]   So when Colum Cille put the first feed into the mouth of the mill, he then began upon the *Altus*, and the composition of the hymn and the grinding of the corn were completed together, nor was it as the fruit of meditation but *per gratiam Dei*.

In tempore of Aedan mac Gabrain, King of Scotland, and of Aed mac Ainmerech, King of Ireland, and Falcus was King of Romans at that time. *Causa, quia uoluit Deum laudare, i.e.* to seek forgiveness for the three battles he had caused in Ireland, viz. the battle of Coleraine in Dal-araide, between him and Comgall of Bangor, while contending for a church, Ross Torathair; and the battle of Belach Feda, at the weir of Clonard; and the battle of Cuil Dremne in Connaught, and it was against Diarmait mac Cerbaill that both these were fought.

Ductus est ad Gregorium et furati sunt ministri tria capitula de se, i.e. '*Hic sublatus*' *et* '*Orbem infra*' *et* '*Christo de cælis,*' *et tria capitula pro eis inseruerunt; et ministris cantantibus hymnum Gregorio, Gregorius autem surrexit donec audiret aliena capitula tria, et iterum sedit donec propria. Surrexit iterum et dixit*

---

[1] Bede H. E. lib. 4.

TF] their honour up to that. But when that was reached, the angels sat down; Gregory too sat down and the hymn was concluded after that manner. Then Gregory demanded their confessions of them, for he knew that it was they who had made the changes. So they admit that it was they, and got forgiveness for it. Then he says, that there was no fault (to be found) with the hymn, except the scantiness in it of the praise of the Trinity *per se*, though it was praised through its creatures. And that reproof reached Colum Cille, and was the cause of the composition of *In te Christe*.

Alphabetic order there is *hic, more Hebræo*. Out of the Catholic Faith was taken the foundation of this (first) capitulum, viz. belief of Unity with confession of Trinity. Further it was made in rhythm; in which there are two kinds, viz, *artificialis et uulgaris*. *Artificialis ubi fiunt* feet co-timed, co-divided, with equal weight as to arsis and thesis, and that the *subsequens* comes in the place of the *præcedens* in its resolution; but the *uulgaris* is where there is a correspondence of syllables (as well as) quarter-verses and half-verses; and it is this which is *hic*. Now there are six lines in each capitulum, with sixteen syllables in each line; except

B] *illis, "Confitemini quod egistis." Illi confessi erant et dixit illis, "Cantate igitur hymnum secundum ordinem a suo auctore dictum." Et illi cantauerunt et ille post laudauit laudem, sed dixit, "minus quam debuit deus memoruri in eo memoratus est." Præsentes angeli semper fiunt quando cantatur, sicut uidit Gregorius angelos. Multæ sunt gratiæ hymni huius; quisquis eum cantauerit frequenter, nunquam a persecutione inimicorum et demonum eueniet ei quod timet peruenire, et nesciet diabulus mortem eius; et liber erit ab omni morte absque pretiosa*, i.e. 'death on pillow;' *et non erit in inferno post diem iudicii etiamsi mala multa egerit, et habebit diuitias multas et longitudinem sæculi.*

There is alphabetic order in this hymn, *more Hebræorum*. So then the number of letters in the alphabet is the number of capitula in this hymn. The Hebrews, however, do not put their letters on the sides of their capitula, but each letter over its capitulum to the end of the hymn; and this is the reason of it, because the names of their letters have a meaning, and that meaning runs through the capitula. Further, to Hebrews, this is the cause of the sequence in the order *alphabeti sui, viz. xxii litteræ apud Hebræos*, for there are twenty-two books in the Old Testament. To Greeks, however, the reason of their having twenty-four letters, is *decem sensus hominis* and *decem mandata legis* and *quatuor euangelia*. Whereas to Romans the reason for their having twenty-three letters is that there are *decem sensus hominis* also and *decem mandata legis* and *trinitas*.

TF] in the first capitulum, where there are seven lines, for it is God's praise that is therein. Fitting indeed is that inequality compared with the other capitula, in consideration of the inequality of God compared with His creatures; (fitting is the) number six *autem in creaturis quia sex diebus factæ sunt. Oportet titulum et argumentum esse ante unumquodque capitulum.*

Let this then be the ordinance for the recitation *huius hymni*, that *Quis potest Deo* be recited between every two capitula; and it is thence its grace would be upon it, for thus they sang it *prius*. There are in sooth many graces upon this hymn, viz. angels present during its recitation; no demon shall know the path of him who shall recite it every day, and foes shall not put him to shame on the day he shall recite it; and there shall be no strife in the house where its recitation shall be customary; aye, and it protects against every death "save death on pillow"; neither shall there be famine nor nakedness in the place where it shall be oft recited; *et aliæ multæ sunt.*

B] Now this hymn was composed in rhythm, of which there are two species, viz. *artificialis et uulgaris : artificialis est ubi fiunt pedes cum temporibus æquis et æqua diuisione et cum æquo pondere, viz. arsis et thesis, et ubi sit subsequens pro præcedente in iure resolutionis;* whereas the *uulgaris* is that wherein there is correspondence of syllables and of quarter-verses and of half-verses; and it is this latter that is in this hymn.

Sex lineæ uero in unoquoque capitulo excepto primo capitulo, and sixteen syllables in each line, but seven lines *in primo capitulo*. Fitting it is to have six lines in the capitula in which mention is made of the creatures that were brought to completion in six days; but fitting for seven lines to be in the first capitulum for this reason, *quia narrat de Deo, quia Deus impar est creaturis suis, uel septem gradus ecclesiæ significat, uel quia septenarius uniuersitatem significat, uel septem dona Spiritus Sancti significat.*

Be this now the ordinance for the recitation of this hymn, that there be recited *Quis potest* between every two capitula of it; and it is from this that its grace would be on it, for thus it was sung at first, &c.

Preface to the Hymn *In te Christe*.

T] *In te Christe.* Colum Cille composed this hymn; in rhythm he composed it, with sixteen syllables in each line. Another group of persons say that it was not Colum Cille at all that composed it, save from *Christus Redemptor* down to *Christus crucem;* and therefore *multi* say (only) *illam partem. Locus*, Hi ; *tempus*, of Aed mac Ainmerech ; *causa* because the poet had spoken insufficiently of the Trinity in the *Altus*, and this is what Gregory reproved Colum Cille for.

F] *In te Christe.* Colum Cille composed this hymn in a well-known rhythm ; and why he made it was because he had too slightly commemorated *trinitatem* in the preceding eulogy, for Gregory said it would have been the best of eulogies had it not been for that.

Preface to the Hymn *Noli Pater*.

T] *Noli pater.* Colum Cille *fecit hunc hymnum eodem modo ut ' In te Christe.' Locus,* the door of the hermitage of Daire Calcaig; *tempus idem,* of Aed mac Ainmerech; *causa,* Colum Cille *aliquando uenit ad colloquium regis* to Derry, and there was offered to him the place with its appurtenance. At that time Colum Cille refused the place, *quia prohibuit* Mobi in his case *accipere mundum* till he should hear of his death. But thereafter, when Colum Cille came to the door of the place, there met him three persons of the folk of Mobi, having with them Mobi's girdle, *et dixerunt, Mortuus est Mobi; et dixit* Colum Cille :

"Mobi's girdle
was never closed around 'lua' (?)
Not only was it never opened to (allow) satiety,
it was never shut around a lie."

Colum Cille went back to the king, *et dixit regi,* "the offering thou gavest me early this morning, give it me *nunc.*" "It shall be given," said the king. Then the place is burnt with all that was in it. "That is wasteful," said the king, "for if it had not been burnt, there would be no want of garment or food therein till Doom." "But (people) shall be there from henceforth," said he, "(and to) the person who shall be staying therein, there shall be no night of fasting." Now the fire from its size threatened to burn the whole oak-wood, and to protect it this hymn was composed.

Or it was the Day of Judgement that he had in mind, or the fire of John's Feast, and it is sung against every fire and every thunder from that time to this ; and whosoever recites it at lying down and at rising up, it protects him against lightning flash, and it protects the nine persons of his household whom he chooses.

F] Colum Cille made *hunc hymnum,* in a well-known rhythm ; at Daire Calcaig it was made, *ut quidam dicunt.*

Or it is the Day of Judgement that he had in mind. Or the fire of John's Feast. Or it is to preserve the oakwood when a thunderbolt set fire to the place, after it had been given by Aed mac Ainmerech, and the fire sought to consume it, so it was on that account this hymn was composed. And it is sung against every thunder; and whosoever recites it at lying down and at rising up, is freed from all danger by fire or lightning flash, as (also) the nine persons dearest to him of his folk.

Preface to the Prayer of St. John.

T] *Deus meus. Iohannes filius Zebedei hanc epistolam fecit.* In Ephesus it was made, and further, in the time of Domitian. *Hæc est causa*; a great conflict arose between John and Aristodemus, viz. a priest of Diana's temple, and John said to Aristodemus, "Let us go, O Aristodemus, to the temple of Christ which is in the city, and beseech (thou) Diana there that the temple may fall; and after that I shall go with thee to Diana's temple, and I shall pray Christ that it may fall; and if Diana's temple fall at my instance, then Christ is better than Diana, and it is right for thee to worship Christ thereafter." "Let it be done then," said Aristodemus. After that they went to Christ's temple. *Orauit Aristodemus . . tribus horis Dianam, et nec tamen cecidit templum Christi. Exierunt postea ad templum Dianæ, et orauit Iohannes ut caderet, et statim cecidit. Et Aristodemus temptauit occidere Iohannem, sed non ausus est pro multitudine Christianorum.* "Is there anything that would remove doubt from thee yet, Aristodemus?" said John. "There is," said he, " if thou drink a full cup of ale *cum ueneno, et si non eris mortuus statim, credam deo tuo.*" *Et dixit Iohannes,* "*duc hic.*" "*Dabitur,*" said he, "provided that it be given to the captives, whom it is proposed by the king to put to death *nunc, quia non melius est mori ferro quam ueneno.*" *Ut timeret Iohannes, dixit Aristodemus hoc. Et primus porrexit cani uenenum, et statim mortuus est; et post canem porrexit simiæ, et illa similiter mortua est; et postea datus est illis potus, et mortui sunt statim. Et sic dedit Iohanni; et dixit Iohannes tunc "Deus meus pater etc.," et bibit, et non nocuit ei; et haec est causa* of making *huius hymni. Et suscitati sunt qui mortui fuerunt ueneno, et sic credidit Aristodemus et alii multi cum eo. Et si quis cantauerit hunc hymnum in liquorem aut in aliquid quod possit nocere, in sanitatem redit. In fine uniuscuiusque anni eligitur de populo iuuenis sanctus sine macula peccati ut . . . et . . circum.*

F] *Iohannes Apostolus fecit hanc epistolam*, when *Aristodemus sacerdos* put poison for him *in calicem*, before the king, Domitian, that he might be killed by it (as) is narrated in the Contest of John.

Preface to the Epistle of Christ to Abgar.

T] *Beatus es*, &c. Christ Himself wrote with His own hand this letter, as Eusebius in his history narrates; further it was written at Jerusalem, *in tempore Tiberii Caesaris. Causa uero haec est:*
Abgar the Toparch, King of the land of Armenia, of the land north of the river Euphrates, lay in heavy disease *in Edessa ciuitate*. So there was sent from him an epistle to Christ, that He should come to heal him, for he had heard that He was the Son of God, and that He healed many; and so for the praise of the faith of Abgar Christ wrote this letter. Now this letter is extant *in Edessa ciuitate in qua ciuitate nullus haereticus potest uiuere, nullus Iudaeus, nullus idolorum cultor; sed neque barbari aliquando eam inuadere potuerunt ex eo tempore quo Abgarus rex eiusdem ciuitatis accepit epistolam manu saluatoris scriptam. Hanc denique epistolam legit infans baptizatus stans super portam et murum ciuitatis. Si quando gens uenerit contra ciuitatem illam, in eodem die quo lecta fuerit epistola manu saluatoris scripta placantur illi barbari aut fugantur infirmati.*

F] *Beatus es. Iesus Christus fecit hanc epistolam* when there was *rex Edessae ciuitatis qui dolorem pedis habuit*, and a letter was sent from him to Christ, that He should go and converse with him and heal him; and Thaddaeus gave him this letter after Christ's Passion, and (there still remains extant) the letter; and that it should be · · . . . in God . . . orders . . . that no heretic should (be allowed) to be for the space of an hour in that city.

Preface to the Hymn of St. Fiacc.

TF] 'Patrick was born.' Fiacc of Sletty composed this hymn about Patrick. Now this Fiacc was son of Mac Erca, son of Bregan, son of Daire Barrach,—from whom are the Hy-Barrchi,—son of Cathair Mór; and the said Fiacc was further a pupil of Dubthach mac Ui Lugair, who was high poet of Ireland. In the time of Loegaire mac Neill it was composed. It was this Dubthach who rose up before Patrick at Tara, after Loegaire had decreed that none should rise up before him in the house; and he became a friend of Patrick from thenceforth, and was afterwards baptized by Patrick. Well, he went on one occasion to Dubthach's house in Leinster, and Dubthach gave great welcome to Patrick. Said Patrick to Dubthach, "Seek out for me a man of rank, of good family and morals, who has *tantum* one wife and one son." "Why dost thou seek that, *i.e.* a man of that stamp?" said Dubthach. "For him to enter into orders." "Fiacc is the man," said Dubthach, "but he has gone on circuit in Connaught." While they were engaged over these words, just then came Fiacc on visit with him. Said Dubthach, "Here is the person we spoke of." "Though he be so," said Patrick, "possibly *quod diximus* would not be agreeable to him." "Let there be made an attempt at tonsuring me," said Dubthach, "so that Fiacc may see it." So when Fiacc saw it, he asked, "Why is an attempt being made to tonsure Dubthach?" said (he). "That is wasteful," said he, "for there is not in Ireland a poet the like of him." "Thou wouldst be taken in place of him," said Patrick. "The loss of me from Ireland is less than (would be the loss of) Dubthach," said Fiacc. So Patrick cut off Fiacc's beard *tunc*, and there came great grace upon him thereafter, so that he read all the ecclesiastical order in one night, *uel quindecim diebus ut alii ferunt*, and there was conferred upon him bishop's grade, so that it is he who is the chief bishop of Leinster from thenceforth, and his coarb after him. The place of it is Duma Gobla, north-west of Sletty; *tempus*, of Lugaid mac Loegaire, for he was King of Ireland *tunc ;* but the *causa* was, to praise Patrick, and it was composed after his death, *ut ferunt quidam.*

The Hymn of St. Fiacc.

T F] Patrick was born in Nemthur, this is what is narrated in stories ;
A youth of sixteen years, when he was brought under tears.

Sucat his name (it) was said; what his father was, were worth knowing:
Son of Calpurn, son of Otide, grandson of deacon Odisse.

5 He was six years in bondage ; man's food he ate not.
Many were they whom he served, Cothraige (servant) of a fourfold household.

Said Victor to Milchu's bondsman, that he should go over the waves ;
He struck his foot on the stone, its trace remains, it fades not.

(The angel) sent him across all Britain—great God, it was a marvel of a course!
10 So that he left him with Germanus in the south, in the southern part of Letha.

In the isles of the Tyrrhene sea, he fasted in them, one estimates,
He read the Canon with Germanus, this is what writings narrate.

Towards Ireland, God's angels were bringing him back ;
Often was it seen in visions, that he would come again!

15 A help to Ireland was Patrick's coming, which was expected ;
Far away was heard the sound of the call of the children of Fochlad's Wood.

They prayed that the saint would come, that he would walk about among them,
That he would convert from iniquity the tribes of Ireland unto life.

TF] The tribes of Ireland prophesied that to them would come a new Prince of peace;
20 His succession will remain till the day of Judgement, empty would be the land of Tara, silent!

His druids from Loegaire hid not Patrick's coming;
The prophecy was fulfilled of the kingdom of which they spoke.

Patrick was illustrious till he died, powerful was his expulsion of idolatry;
This was what raised his goodness upwards from him beyond dwellings of mankind.

25 Hymns and Apocalypse, the Three Fifties, he used to sing them;
He preached, baptized, prayed; from God's praise he ceased not.

Cold of weather did not keep him from sleeping at night in pools;
In heaven he won his Kingdom,—by day he preached on hills.

In (fountain) Slan, to the north of Benn-Boirche,—neither drought nor flood took it,—
30 He sings one hundred psalms each night to an angels' King whom he served.

He sleeps on a bare stone thereafter, with a damp mantle around him;
His pillow was a pillar-stone; he left not his body in warmth!

He preached the Gospel to everyone, he wrought mighty miracles widely:
He heals lame and lepers; dead-folk, he raised them to life.

35 Patrick preached to the Scots, he suffered great labour widely
That around him they may come to Judgement, everyone whom he brought to life.

Sons of Emer, sons of Herimon, went all with the devil;
The Transgressor flung them into the deep vast pit.

TF] Till the Apostle came to them, he sent . . . of a swift wind,
40 He preached thrice twenty years Christ's Cross to Fenian pagans.

Over Erin's land lay darkness, its tribes worshipped fairies;
They believed not the true Godhead of the true Trinity.

In Armagh there is a kingship: it has long ago forsaken Emania!
Dun Lethglasse is a great church: Tara even though waste is not dear to me!

45 When Patrick was ailing, he longed to go to Armagh:
An angel went to meet him on the road at midday.

He sent him south to Victor: it was he (Victor) that stopped him;
Flamed the bush in which he was; out of the fire he conversed.

He said, "(Leave thy) dignity to Armagh, to Christ give thanks;
50 To heaven thou shalt soon go: thy prayers have been granted thee.

A hymn which thou hast chosen in thy lifetime shall be a lorica of protection for all;
Around thee in the Day of the Judgement men of Ireland will go to Doom."

Tassach stayed after him when he had given communion to him;
He said that Patrick would soon go: Tassach's word was not false.

55 (Patrick) set a boundary against night that no candle might be wasted with him:
Up to the end of a year there was light; that was a long day of peace!

In a battle fought at Beth-horon against Canaan's people by the son of Nun,
The sun stood still towards Gibeon: this is what letters tell us.

TF] Because the sun stood still with Joshua at the death of the wicked,
60 Light, even were it thrice as bright, would be fitting at the death of the saints.

Ireland's clerics went to keep watch over Patrick from every road :
The sound of the singing prostrated them, each one of them fell asleep on the road.

Patrick's soul from his body after labours was severed ;
God's angels on the first night (after his death) for him kept watch unceasingly.

65 When Patrick departed, he visited the other Patrick :
Together they ascended to Jesus, Mary's son.

Patrick, without sign of pride, much good he thought it
To be in the service of Mary's son : it was a sign of dutifulness to which he was born.

Patrick was born.

Ninine's Prayer.

TF] Ninine the poet made this collect; or, it was Fiacc of Sletty.

We commemorate Saint Patrick,
    chief apostle of Ireland ;
Famous is his wonderful name,
    flame that baptized heathens.
5 He fought against druids
    hard of heart ;
He cast down haughty men with the help of our Lord
    of bright heaven ;
He cleansed Ireland's
10   territories, he the Great Birth.

We pray to Patrick, chief apostle,
    who hath saved us to Doom's day
From judgement by the malevolence
    of dark demons.

15 God be with me, with the prayer
    of Patrick, chief apostle !

Preface to the Hymn *Brigit be bithmaith.*

TFL] 'Brigid, ever-good woman.' May be it was Colum Cille that composed this hymn, and in the time of Aed mac Ainmerech he composed it, if it was he that made it. This is the cause of its composition: a great storm came upon Colum Cille when he went over sea, and he got into Breccan's Cauldron, so he besought Brigid that a calm might come to him, and said ' Brigit bé bith-maith.'

Or, it was Broccan the Squinting that composed it, so that it and ' Ni car Brigit ' were composed at the same time.

Or, three persons of Brigid's household made it: they set out for Rome and reached Blasantia, and there met them outside a man of the city, who asked them whether they were in need of hospitality. They replied that they were, so he took them with him to his house; and there met them a scholar who had come *illic* from Rome, who asked them whence they came and what they came for. They replied that it was ' for hospitality.' "That is an error," said he, "for the custom of this man is to murder his guests"; and they made inquiries about that owing to the hint of the scholar. Well, there was given them poison in ale, but they made a eulogy of Brigid to be freed, and sang 'Brigid ever-good woman!' Then they drank off the ale with the poison, and it did them no harm. So the householder came to look at them, to know whether the poison had killed them, and he saw them alive, and saw a good-looking girl among them. After that he came into the house and began to seek the girl, but he found her not; and he asked them, 'why the girl had gone?' and they replied that 'they had not seen her at all.' So fetters were put on them, and they were to be killed on the morrow if they did not tell about the girl. But the same scholar came to them on the morrow to visit them, *et inuenit eos in uinculis, et interrogauit eos quomodo euaserunt et cur ligati sunt. Responderunt ei et narrauerunt ei omnia quae eis contigerunt secundum ordinem, et dixit scholasticus eis, " Cantate ei laudem quam fecistis." Postquam autem illam cantauerunt inter eos sancta Brigita omnibus illis apparuit. Tunc paenituit ille et demisit illos ex uinculis et dedit suam sedem in Blasantia Brigitae, uel Blasantiam totam, ut alii dicunt.*

TFL]   Or, it was Brendan that composed this hymn ; *nauigans mare et quaerens terram repromissionis audiuit bestiam aliam clamantem et adiurantem uoce humana bestiam aliam conuocantem et rogantem Brendinum et ceteros omnes sanctos Hiberniae insulae, excepta Brigita, ne sibi alia bestia noceret ; et nihilominus tamen uim ab alia patientem usque dum rogaret Brigitam, euadentem uero postquam rogaret Brigitam et nihil mali a persequente patientem interrogantem, ut diceret alia quae eam persequeretur, "postquam Brigitam adiurasti, nocere tibi non possum."   Postquam uero Brendinus haec omnia et honorem quem dedit bestia Brigitae prae ceteris, admiratus est et Brigitam laudauit dicens* " Brigid, ever-good woman."

Locus ergo mare ; causa ad laudem Brigitae ; tempus uero, of Diarmait mac Cerbaill, King of Ireland.

Well, after that, Brendan came to Kildare to Brigid, to learn why the beast *in mari* gave honour to Brigid more than to all the other saints. So when Brendan reached Brigid, he begged her to make her confession, in what way the love of God was in her. Said Brigid to Brendan, " O cleric, give thou thy confession *prius*, and I shall give mine thereafter." Said Brendan, " From the day on which I took religion, I went not over seven furrows without my mind (fixed) in God." " It is a good confession," said Brigid. " And now, O nun, give thy confession," said Brendan. " By the Virgin's Son," said she, " from the hour that I set my mind in Him, I never took it out." " By God, O nun," said Brendan, " fitting it is for the beasts to give honour to thee more than to us."

Or else, Ultan of Ardbreccan composed this hymn, and for the praise of Brigid he composed it. For he belonged to the Dal Conchobair, and so also did Brigid's mother, Broicsech, daughter of Dall-bronach. Further (the hymn) itself was composed in the time of the two sons of Aed Slane, for it was they that killed Suibne mac Colman Móir by the side of Ultan. In Ardbreccan, also, it was composed.

The Hymn *Brigit be bithmaith.*

TFLX]   Brigid, ever-good woman,
    flame golden, sparkling,
    may she bear us to the eternal kingdom,
    (she), the sun fiery, radiant!

5 May Brigid free us
    past crowds of demons!
    may she win for us
    battles over every disease!

    May she extirpate in us
10   the vices of our flesh,
    she, the branch with blossoms,
    the mother of Jesus!

    The true-virgin, dear,
    with vast pre-eminence,
15 may we be free, at all times,
    along with my Saint of Leinster-folk!

    One (of the two) pillars of the Kingdom,
    along with Patrick the pre-eminent (as the other pillar);
    the vestment beyond (even) splendid (vestments),
20 the royal Queen!

    May they lie, after old age,
    our bodies, in sackcloth;
    (but) with her grace may she bedew us,
    may she free us, Brigid!
                      Brigid ever.

Brigitæ per laudem Christum precamur
ut nos celeste regnum habere mereamur.   *Amen.*

Preface to St. Broccan's Hymn.

TF] *Locus huius hymni* Slieve Bloom, or Cluain Mór Moedoc; person, Broccan the Squinting; *tempus*, of Lugaid mac Loegaire King of Ireland, and Ailell mac Dunlainge King of Leinster; *causa*, Ultan of Ardbreccan, whose tutor requested of him that he should tell of the miracles of Brigid compendiously in poetic harmony, for it was Ultan who had collected all the miracles of Brigid.

St. Broccan's Hymn.

TF] Victorious Brigid loved not the world;
    she sat the seat of John on a cliff,
    she slept the sleep of a captive,—
    the saint, for the sake of her Son.

5 Not much of evil-speaking was got!
    with lofty faith (in) the Trinity
    Brigid, mother of my high King,
    of the kingdom of heaven best she was born.

She was not absent, she was not malicious,
10 she was not a mighty, quarrelsome, champion (?),
    she was not an adder striking, speckled;
    she sold not the Son of God for gain!

She was not greedy of treasures,
    she gave, without poison, without abatement;
15 she was not hard, penurious,
    she loved not the world's spending.

To guests she was not acrimonious,
    to miserable weaklings she was gentle;
    on a plain she was built (as) a city;
20 may she protect us (in) hosts to the Kingdom.

TF]   She was no plunderer (?) of a mountain-slope ;
        she worked in the midst of a plain,
        a wonderful ladder for pagan-folk
        to climb to the Kingdom of Mary's Son !

25   Wonderful was St. Brigid's congregation,
        wonderful, Plea to which it went ;
        but alone with Christ was maintained
        her frequent mission to the poor !

        Good was the hour that Mac-Caille held
30   a veil over St. Brigid's head ;
        she was clear in all her proceedings ;
        in heaven was heard her prayer ;

        "God, I pray to Him against every battle,
        in whatever way my lips can reach,
35   deeper than seas, vaster than count,
        Three Persons, One Person, a wonder of a story !"

        A challenge to the battle, renowned Kevin !
        through a storm of snow that wind drives,
        in Glendalough was suffered a cross,
40   till peace visited him after labour.

        St. Brigid was not given to sleep,
        nor was she intermittent about God's love ;
        not merely that she did not buy, she did not strive for
        the world's wealth here below, the Saint !

45   That which the King wrought
        of miracles for St. Brigid,
        if they have been wrought for (any other) person,
        in what place hath ear of any living being heard of it ?

        The first dairying on which she was sent
50   with first butter in a cart,
        she took nought from the gift to her guests,
        nor did she lessen her following.

        Her portion of bacon, after that,
        one evening—the victory was high,—
55   not merely was the dog satisfied with it,
        the company was not grieved.

TF] A day of reaping for her,—it was well reaped,
no fault was found there with my pious one ;
it was dry-weather ever in her field,
60 through the world it poured heavy rain.

Bishops visited her,
not slight was the danger to her,
if there had not been,—the King helped,—
milking of the cows thrice.

65 On a day of heavy rain she herded (?)
sheep in the midst of a plain ;
she spread her upper garment afterwards
in-doors across a sunbeam.

The cunning youth asked alms of her,
70 Brigid, for the love of her King :
she gave away seven wethers,
but it did not lessen her flock's number.

It is of my poetic gift if I were to recount
what she did of good :
75 wonderful for her was the bath
that was blest about her,—it became red ale!

She blessed the pregnant nun,
who thereon became whole, without poison, without disease;
greater than others was the marvel, how
80 of the stone she made salt.

I record not, I enumerate not
all that the holy creature did :
she blessed the flat-faced one,
and his two eyes became quite apparent.

85 Some one brought a dumb girl
to Brigid,—the miracle of it was unique,—
whose hand went not out of her hand
till her utterances were clear.

(Another) wonder was bacon that she blessed ;
90 and God's power kept it safely;
(though) it was a full month with the dog,
the dog did not injure it.

TF]   It was a miracle greater than others:
          a morsel she requested of the (kitchen-)folk
  95   did not spoil the colour of her scapular
          (though) it was flung, boiling, into her bosom

        The leper begged a boon of her;
          it was a good boon that befel him:
          she blessed the choicest of the calves,
 100   and the choicest of the cows loved it.

        He directed her chariot afterwards
          northward to Bri Cobthaig Coil,
          the calf being with the leper in the car,
          and the cow (following) behind the calf.

 105   The oxen, (when thieves) visited them,
          would have been pleased that anyone should hear them:
          against them rose up the river,
          at morn they returned home.

        Her horse parted head from head-stall
 110   when they ran down the slope;
          the yoke was not flung out of balance,
          God's Son directed the royal hand.

        A wild boar frequented her herd,
          to the north he hunted the wild pig;
 115   Brigid blessed him with her staff,
          and he took up his stay with her swine.

        Mug-art, a fat pig for her was given
          beyond Mag Fea; it was wonderful how
          wild dogs hunted it for her,
 120   till it was (close to her) in Uachtar Gabra.

        She gave the wild fox
          on behalf of her peasant, the wretched;
          to a wood it escaped
          though the hosts hunted it.

 125   She was open in her proceedings,
          she was One-Mother of the Great King's Son:
          she blessed the fluttering bird
          so that she played with it in her hand.

TF] ' Nine outlaws (whose weapons) she blessed
130   reddened those weapons in a pool of blood ;
       the man whom they had ill-treated
       was wounded, but hurt to him was not found there!

       What she wrought of miracles
          there is no one who could enumerate aright:
135   wonderful how she took away Lugaid's appetite;
          but the champion's strength she did not lessen.

       An oak the multitude lifted not,
          on another occasion,—excellent and famous (deed)!
          her Son brought it to her (on the prayer) of Brigid,
140   to the place where she wished it to be (?).

       The trinket of silver, which should not have been hidden
          for mischief to the champion's hand-maid,
          was flung into the sea the length of a mighty cast,—
          but even it was found, in the inner part of a salmon.

145 Another wonder of hers was the widow
       who refreshed her in Mag Coil,
       for she made fire-wood of the new (weaving)-beam,
       and that for cooking the calf;

       A miracle greater than any other
150   which the saint effected,—
       in the morning the beam was whole,
       with its mother was the missing calf.

       The trinket of silver, which the smith
          broke not,—this was one of her miracles,—
155   Brigid struck it against her hand
          afterwards, so that it broke into three (parts)

       It was flung into a scale at the smith's;
          thereupon was found a wonder:
          it was not discovered that by one scruple
160   any third was greater than another.

       What she wrought of miracles,
          there is no man who can come at them;
          she blessed raiment for Condlaed,
          when he was taken to Letha.

TF] When she,—it was a danger for her,—
her Son before her failed her not (?):
he put raiment in the basket
of Roncend in a chariot of two wheels

The mead-vat that was brought to her;
170   whoever brought it was not unrewarded (?);
for there was found (honey) in a wall of the house:
it had not been found there up to that!

She gave for behoof of her servant
when he stood in need;
175   not merely was no surplus found there,
but not a drop was wanting.

Upon us may Brigid's prayers rest!
and she against danger be our aid!
may they be on the side of her weaklings
180   before going into the presence of the Holy Spirit!

May she aid us with a sword of fire
in the fight against black swarms!
may her holy prayers protect us
past pains, into the kingdom of Heaven!

185 Before going with angels to the battle
let us reach the church with a run!
commemoration of the Lord is better than any poem:
Victorious Brigid loved not the world.
                              Brigid loved not.

I beseech the patronage of St. Brigid
190   with the saints of Kildare;
may they be between me and pain!
may my soul not be lost!

The nun that drove over the Curragh,
may she be a shield against edges of sharpness!
195   I have not found her like, save Mary:
we honour my Brigid.

TF] We honour my Brigid;
　　　　may she be a protection to our company!
　　　　may her patronage assist me!
200　 may we all of us deserve escape!

　　　Praise of Christ, famous (such) speaking!
　　　　adoration of the Son of God, guarantee of victory!
　　　　may it be without denial of God's Kingdom,
　　' whoever recites it, whoever has heard it!

205 Whoever has heard, whoever recites it,
　　　　may the benediction of Brigid rest on him!
　　　　the benediction of Brigid and of God
　　　　rest upon us, together!

　　　There are two nuns in the Kingdom,—
210　 I implore their aid (?) with all my effort,—
　　　　Mary and St. Brigid;
　　　　may we be under the protection of these two

　　　　Sancta Brigita uirgo sacratissima
　　　　in Christo domino fuit fidelissima.   *Amen.*

Preface to St. Sanctan's Hymn.

TF] 'I beseech a wonderful king.' Bishop Sanctan composed this hymn, and it was on his going to Clonard westward to Inis Matoc that he composed it; he was brother to Matoc, both of them being of British race, but Matoc came into Ireland earlier *quam* Bishop Sanctan. *Causa autem haec est*, to free it *ab hostibus*, and that his brother should be allowed (to come) to him *in insulam; Scoticam uero linguam usque ad horam hanc non habuit sed deus ei tam cito eam donauit. Tempus autem dubitatur.*

St. Sanctan's Hymn.

TF] I beseech a wonderful King of angels,
    for it is a name that is mightiest;
    to me (be) God for my rear, God on my left,
    God for my van, God on my right!

5 God for my help,—holy call—
    against each danger, Him I invoke!
    a bridge of life let there be below me,
    benediction of God the Father above me!

    Let the lofty Trinity arouse us,
10   (each one) to whom a good death (?) is not (yet) certain!
    Holy Spirit noble, strength of heaven,
    God the Father, Mary's mighty Son!

    A great King who knows our offences
    Lord over earth, without sin,—
15   to my soul for every black-sin
    let never demons' godlessness (?) visit me!

    God with me, may He take away each toil!
    may Christ draw up my pleadings,
    may apostles come all around me,
20   may the Trinity of witness come to me!

TF] May mercy come to me (on) earth,
from Christ let not (my) songs be hidden!
let not death in its death-wail reach me,
nor sudden death in disease befal me!

25 May no malignant thrust that stupefies and perplexes
reach me without permission of the Son of God!
  ' May Christ save us from every bloody death,
from fire, from raging sea!

From every death-drink, that is unsafe
30 for my body, with many terrors!
may the Lord each hour come to me
against wind, against swift waters!

I shall utter the praises of Mary's Son
who fights for good deeds,
35 (and) God of the elements will reply,
(for) my tongue (is) a lorica for battle.

In beseeching God from the heavens
may my body be incessantly laborious;
that I may not come to horrible hell
40 I beseech the King whom I have besought.
                        I beseech a wonderful King.

Bishop Sanctan . . . a sage
soldier, angel famous pure-white,
may he make free my body on earth,
45 may he make holy my soul towards heaven!

May there be a prayer with thee for me, O Mary!
May heaven's King be merciful to us
against wound, danger and peril!
O Christ, on Thy protection (rest) we!

50 I beseech the King free, everlasting
Only Son of God, to watch over us;
may He protect me against sharp dangers,
He, the Child that was born in Bethlehem.

Preface to St. Patrick's Lorica.

T] Patrick made this hymn; in the time of Loegaire mac Neill, it was made, and the cause of its composition was for the protection of himself and his monks against the deadly enemies that lay in ambush for the clerics. And it is a lorica of faith for the protection of body and soul against demons and men and vices: when any person shall recite it daily with pious meditation on God, demons shall not dare to face him, it shall be a protection to him against all poison and envy, it shall be a guard to him against sudden death, it shall be a lorica for his soul after his decease.

Patrick sang it when the ambuscades were laid for him by Loegaire, in order that he should not go to Tara to sow the Faith, so that on that occasion they were seen before those who were lying in ambush as if they were wild deer having behind them a fawn, viz. Benen; and 'Deer's Cry' is its name.

The Lorica of St. Patrick.

T] I arise to-day:

    vast might, invocation of the Trinity,—
    belief in a Threeness
    confession of Oneness
5   meeting in the Creator (?).

  I arise to-day:

    the might of Christ's birth and His baptism
    the might of His Crucifixion and Burial
    the might of His Resurrection and Ascension
10   the might [of] His Descent to the judgement of Doom.

T]   I arise to-day:

        might of grades of Cherubim
        in obedience of Angels
        [in ministration of Archangels]
        in hope of resurrection for the sake of reward
15   in prayers of Patriarchs
        in prophecies of Prophets
        in preachings of Apostles,
        in faiths of Confessors
        in innocence of holy Virgins
20   .   in deeds of righteous men.

I arise to-day:

        might of Heaven
        brightness of Sun
        whiteness of Snow
25   splendour of Fire
        speed of Light
        swiftness of Wind
        depth of Sea
        stability of Earth
30   firmness of Rock.

I arise to-day:

        Might of God   for my piloting
        Wisdom of God for my guidance
        Eye of God   for my foresight
35   Ear of God   for my hearing
        Word of God   for my utterance
        Hand of God   for my guardianship
        Path of God   for my precedence
        Shield of God   for my protection
40   Host of God   for my salvation
           against snares of demons
           against allurements of vices
           against solicitations of nature
           against every person that wishes me ill
45   far and near
               alone and in a crowd.

T] I invoke therefore all these forces to intervene between me
and every fierce merciless force that may come upon
my body and my soul:

    against incantations of false prophets
50   against black laws of paganism
    against false laws of heresy
    against deceit of idolatry
    against spells of women and smiths and druids
    against all knowledge that is forbidden the human soul.

55 Christ for my guardianship to-day

    against poison, against burning,
    against drowning, against wounding,
that there may come to me a multitude of rewards;
Christ with me, Christ before me,
60 Christ behind me, Christ in me,
Christ under me, Christ over me,
Christ to right of me, Christ to left of me,
Christ in lying down, Christ in sitting, Christ in rising up
Christ in the heart of every person, who may think of me!
65 Christ in the mouth of every one, who may speak to me!
Christ in every eye, which may look on me!
Christ in every ear, which may hear me!

I arise to-day:

    vast might, invocation of the Trinity
70   belief in a Threeness
    confession of Oneness
    meeting in the Creator.

Domini est salus, domini est salus, Christi est salus;
Salus tua, domine, sit semper nobiscum.

The Hymn of Mael-Ísu.

The Holy Spirit around us,
  in us and with us,
  the Holy Spirit to us,
  may it come, O Christ, suddenly!

The Holy Spirit to inhabit
  our body and our soul,
  to protect us speedily
  against peril, against diseases!

Against demons, against sins,
  against hell with many evils,
  O Jesus, may it sanctify us,
  may Thy Spirit free us!

The Spirit.

[Names of the Apostles.]

Simon, Matthias, and Matthew,
Bartholomew, Thomas, Thaddaeus.
Peter, Andrew, Philip, Paul,
John and two Jameses.

Preface to the Amra of St. Columba.

T] The place for the Amra *usque in finem*, *i.e.* the bit of land that is between Fene in Ui Tigernan in Meath up to Dun na n-Airbed in the district of Masraige eastward of Irarus, or of Chechtraige Slecht from Breifne of Connaught; i.e. for Dallan.

[For] Colum Cille son of Feidlimid, son of Fergus, son of Conall,
5 son of Neill, Dallan wrote this. Now this is the third cause for which Colum Cille came, viz. a refusal that Ireland's kings around Aed mac Ainmerech put on Ireland's poets; for it was owing to the multitude of the poets and to their burdensomeness that Ireland's men were not able to find out what to do with them; for the person who was satirised there, if he did not immediately die, there used to grow poisonous ulcers upon him, till he was con-
10 spicuous to everybody, and till there was deformity upon him always; but upon the poet himself grew the ulcers, and he used to die immediately, if it was without fault that he satirised. Now the poets were at Ibar of Cinntracht in the territory of Ulster, for Ulster's king gave them 'coigny' three years, or (may be) one whole year there. And it was then they set themselves to invent stories,
15 but they were wholly unable (to do it) as they used to tell them; but to impose them on the wholly rude race among whom they were, ready-tongued poets concocted the lying fables. Well, a message came from Ireland's poets to Colum Cille, to the effect that it was to them he should come before he went to Druim Cetta, the place where the kings were who refused them. And so they invoked
20 God's name upon the head of Colum Cille and of the Christian faith . . . was brought under his protection to Druim Cetta. There came afterwards Colum Cille as he came from his boat, seven twenties his number (of followers), *ut poeta dixit:*

25
      Forty priests his number,
      twenty bishops lofty power
      at the psalm-singing without dispute,
      fifty deacons, thirty students.

So he took the poets with him to Druim Cetta. Now Dallan mac Forgaill was under ban of expulsion among the poets though
30 he was a doctor of wisdom and of poetry. But Colum Cille made reconciliation of the poets with the men of Ireland and with Aed mac Ainmerech, in precedence of every other case that was brought before the assembly, so that this is what is said even now-a-days, i.e. "Case of a privileged person before every case." Then Colum Cille requested the kings who were there assembled to give the headship of Ireland's poets to Dallan for his wisdom and for his

T] knowledge in poetry (as being) beyond all. And Colum Cille
35 made a black-poem (?) on going to the assembly along with Cormac's
poets . . . . . .
(and Dallan asked), "What reward shall be given me for the
eulogy?" Said Colum Cille, "Heaven shall be given to thee and
to every one else who shall recite it . . . shall not be more
40 numerous than are hornless dun cows in a cow-shed." "What are
tokens that that shall be given?" said the blind poet. "There
shall be given thee thy sight while composing the eulogy, so that
there shall be visible to thee sky and air and earth"; and when it
would be the end of the eulogy . . . .
Colum Cille made the freeing of Scandlan son of Cinnfaela from
his hostageship, and he bowed down to the Gospel . . . . .
and he gave eight score plough-oxen to him . . . and to the soul-
45 friend; and it was the coarbs of Colum Cille that were soul-
friends . . . . Osraige, so that it is in Hi, and there are due
eight score plough-oxen still to the congregation of Hi from the
Osraige . . . between Aed mac Ainmerech and Aedan mac
Gabrain about Dal-riata, and the Dal-riata were allowed to serve
50 him . . . of the sea between Ireland and Scotland and Gall-
Gaels to the King of Scotland on his behalf. He went . . .

AMRA OF ST. COLUMBA.

T] *Locus huius artis* is Druim Cetta, where was the Great Assembly. In the time of Aed mac Ainmerech and Aedan mac Gabrain it was composed. The person was Dallan mac Forgaill of the Masraige of Mag Slecht in Breifne of Connaught. The cause, to attain heaven for himself *et aliis per se*. Now there are three causes for
5 which Colum Cille came from Scotland into Ireland at that time, viz. [i] to set free Scandlan Mor son of Cinnfaela, King of the men of Ossory, for whom he had gone in suretyship; [ii] to secure residence in Ireland for the poets, for they had been expelled owing to their burdensomeness, viz. thirty persons being the full retinue and fifteen the half retinue of the *ollam*-poet : twelve hundred their
10 number, *ut quidam dixit*.

[vv. 50–57]   Once to Mael-choba of the companies
         at Ibar of Cinn-tracht
         twelve hundred poets resorted
         to the north-west of the Yew.
         'Coigny' of three harmonious years
         gave to them Mael-choba the Chief;
         there shall remain to the day of white Doom,
         (descendants) of the shapely race of Deman.

And [iii] to make peace between the men of Ireland and of Scotland about Dal-riata ; so that Colum Cille came afterwards into the court, and some in the court rose up to give welcome to him, and the poets came to sing him their musical strains. So then Colum Cille said to Aed :—

15   Cormac fairly broke battles,—
       new his praises, withered his treasures,
       it is this I have read (to be) the grace of poetry :
       luck where one is praised, woe where one is satirised, Aed

       Fair the juice that is sucked from their free faces ;
20   woe worth the land that absent is satirised !
       ladder famous—fair the course—living men are pleased
       praises live long after treasures (are gone).

Thereafter Colum Cille begged Scandlan('s release) from Aed, who did not grant it to him ; so he said to Aed, that ' he [Scandlan]
25 would take off his shoes about nocturns, wherever he [Colum Cille] might be'; and so it was fulfilled.

T]   It was Colman mac Comgellain of the Dal-riata that gave the judgement, viz., 'their expedition and their hosting with the men of Ireland,' for there is hosting always with possessions of land; but 'their law of tribute and their tax with the men of Scotland.' And it is that same Colman to whom Colum Cille did the kindness, when he was a little child, *et dixit*,

30   O fair conscience, O pure soul!
            here is a kiss for thee, give a kiss to me!
And Colum Cille said that it would be he who should make peace between the men of Ireland and of Scotland.

Dallan afterwards came to converse with Colum Cille, and recited
35 the prologue to him, but Colum Cille did not let him go past that, (and said) that he should finish it at the time of his decease, that 'it was for a dead person it was fitting.'

Then, Colum Cille promised riches and the fruits of the earth to Dallan for this eulogy, but Dallan accepted nothing but heaven for
40 himself and for every one who should recite it, and should understand it, both sense and sound.

"How shall I know of thy death seeing that thou art in pilgrimage and I am in Ireland?"

So Colum Cille gave him three tokens, as to the time when he should complete his eulogy, viz. that it would be a rider of a
45 speckled horse who should announce to him Colum Cille's decease; that the first word he would speak would be the beginning of the eulogy; and that (the use of) his eyes would be granted him while he was composing it.

'At Ath Feni in Meath was this eulogy sung, *ut Mael-Suthain dixit;* but Fer-domnach (his) coarb states that it was at Slige Assail it was sung, from Dun na nAirbed to the Cross at Tig Lommain.

Tres filiae Orci quae uocantur diuersis nominibus in caelo et in terra et in inferno; in caelo quidem Stenna et Euriale et Medusa,
60 *in terra Clotho, Lachesis, Atropos; in inferno Electo, Megaera, Tisiphone.*

Hoc est principium laudationis.

'Anamain' between two 'n's is this, viz.: 'n' at the beginning of the eulogy, and 'n' at the end; i.e. 'ni disceoil' and 'nembuain.' Or, it is 'fork' of it, viz.: a doubly harmonised 'raicne' metre; i.e. two or three word-utterances beginning with one letter, in unbroken sequence, and a word beginning with a different letter following them.

---

65   'Ni disceoil,' i.e. not folly of a story, i.e. it was not a story about a fool that will be made famous.

T] hid not 'ceis' music from Craiptine's harp,
    that brought a death-sleep on hosts;
    it joined harmony between Maen
    and marriageable Moriath of Morca.
70 Labraid was more to her than every prize.

    Sweeter than every song was the harp
    that was played (to) Labraid Loingsech Lorcc;
    though the king was silent and plunged in secrecy,
    Craiptine's (harp) hid not 'ceis.'

    Three years was he without light,
    Colum, in his Black Church;
75 he went to angels out of his captivity
    after seventy-six years.

    'fo' is a name for 'good' and for 'honour';
    'fi' is a name for 'evil' and for 'disobedience';
    'an' is 'true,'—and it is no weak knowledge,—
80 'iath' is 'diadem' and 'iath' is 'land.'

    'mur' means 'multitude' yonder in the law,
    'coph,' 'victory,'—it is a full-right word.—
    'du,' 'place,' 'du' means 'thy right,'
    'cail,' 'protection' and 'cul' 'chariot.'

85 Ethne pre-eminent in her life-time
    the queen of the Carburys
    the mother of Colum,—bright perfection—,
    daughter of Dimma mac Noe.

    Up to the distance of a mile and a half was clear the voice of
90 Colum Cille in saying his offices, *ut dixit poeta*:
    The sound of Colum Cille's voice,
    great its sweetness above every company;
    up to fifteen hundred paces,
    with wonders of courses, is the distance that it was clear.

95 Hi with the multitude of its relics
    of which Colum was dear fosterchild;
    he went out of it at last,
    so that Down is his old sanctuary.

T]   'Aidbse,' i.e. a name for music or for a 'cronan,' which a number
100   of the men of Ireland used to make all together whatever it was
      that called them together. And this is what the men of Ireland
      did before him in the Great Assembly of Druim Cetta, so that
      there came pride of mind to him. An example of 'aidbse,' *ut
      Colman dixit*, i.e. the son of Lenine :
          Blackbirds (compared) with swans, an ounce with masses,
105   forms of peasant-women with forms of queens,
          kings with Domnall, a mere droning sound with an 'aidbse,'
          a rushlight with a candle, (is) a sword with my sword.

      'Ferb' is employed to express three things, viz. 'ferb' means
      'word,' *ut dicitur*, "if it be of the true-wondrous words of the white
110   pure language"; and 'ferb' also means 'blotch,' *ut dicitur*, "blotches
      will rise on his cheeks after partial judgements," i.e. perverse judge-
      ments ; and 'ferb' also means 'cow,' *ut dicitur*, "three white cows,
      Assal drove them away from Mog Nuadat."

      Angelus dixit uel monachus this following :—
          A humble youth, says 'cet,'
115   *deus ei indulget*
          he testifies *no* and *uet*
          in eternal life *surget*.

          Labraid Loingsech, sufficient his number,
          by whom was slain Cobthach in Dinn-rig,
120   with a lance-armed host from over ocean's water ;
          from them Leinster was named.

          Two hundred and twenty hundred Galls
          with broad lances with them yonder ;
          from the lances which were borne there,
125   hence is 'Lagin' (the name) for Leinster.

      'Tuaim tenma' was its name before there was made the Plunder
      of Dinn-rig, in which . . . . . was killed.

  '   openly he used to lie in the sand ;
          in his lair he was much-suffering ;
130   trace of his rib through his garment,
          it was clear when the wind blew it.

      It is for this reason that he doubles the first word, for the intensity
      or the great eagerness of the eulogy, *ut est, Deus, Deus meus*.
          Now this is its name with the Gael, viz., its 'enunciation'-mode ;
      i.e. this is its 'mood of narration' :—

135   I fear, I fear, after long, long
          to be in pain, pain, not peace, peace
          as each, each, till doom, doom
          at each hour, hour, though fatigue, fatigue.

T]   *Brigita dixit*:
140   Good I deem my smallness;
             to earth descends each race,
             though any one were placed somewhat lower,
             the love of Jesus he would merit there.

          The Amra of Colum—every day
145   whoever he be that recites it in its entirety,
             there will be to him the bright kingdom
             which God gave to Dallan.

          An assembly I gathered,—it is great folly,
             in the house over Druim-lias;
150   O my Lord, O King of noble mysteries
             in which there is . . . .

          There is a woman in the country,
             her name is not said:
             ex ea erumpit peditum
155   like stone out of sling.

          It is a physician's medicine-chest without an ale-bag,
             it is asking of marrow without bone,
             it is a strain of music on a harp without a 'ceis,'—
             so is our state in the absence of our noble organ.

160   May thy bed be in swiftness!
             after thy fight, sail of long height,
             may there be brought in a chariot after a horse
             thy wife, O hero, to her fair church!

       Ferchertne the poet *dixit*:
165   Is name of demon shouted to you?
             he who announces pain for his household:
             may God not leave me, East or West,
             in the track of the demon on whom it is shouted.

          'Cul' is a name for a chariot without fault,
170   in which I used to go with Conor;
             and 'neit' was a name for the battle
             which I used to fight along with Cathbath's son.

          Woe with my looking to him!
             increases on wall glance from below;
175   it was sweeter they sang a drone-murmur
             his two bags towards a glance from below.

T]   Not for that do I wake out of my sleep . . . . after pleasant sweet sleep . . . . . word of Lent without any inquiry . . . Rath of Rathmacc, victory of king's son . . .

180 Example of return to the usual sound is this:—
Were I the sweet-voiced smith,
smith of fire would I cleave to,
weapon that would slay calf of half-tonsured man:
I would grind (corn) for Mael-Sechnall.

185 GOd, God—whom I beseech before I come into His presence.

    i.e. I fear God. Or, I pray before I come into His presence.

Chariot through battle.

    i.e. as goes a scythed chariot through battle, may my soul go through demons' battle to heaven!

190 God of heaven, may He not leave me in the track where it is shouted owing to its smoke from its greatness.

    i.e. for making truth clear he says "God of heaven." Or, from his knowledge that He is not a god that is an idol; "may He not leave me crying in the track of demons from the greatness of their smoke."

Great God (be) my protection from a fiery abun-
195 dance of incessant tears.

    i.e. 'Great God for my protection against the abundance of the fire, in the place where tears are shed a long time at seeing it'; i.e. *quia fit* 'mur,' viz. 'abundance'; and as to 'diutercc,' it is a *compositum nomen*, of Latin and Irish, viz. 'diu' is 'a long time,' and 'dercc' means 'eye,' *ut dixit* Grainne, Cormac's daughter:

200   "There is a person
from whom a long glance would have my thanks,
for whom I should give the whole world,
O Son of Mary, though a losing bargain."

T] God righteous, truly near, who hears my twin-wail
205 from (his) heaven-land of clouds.

>i.e. God True-One. Or, God of the righteous; truly near, *quia est deus ubique et prope omnibus inuocantibus eum*. My twin-wail, i.e. my two wailings, viz. wail of my body and wail of my soul, after clouds in heaven's land. Or, wail of Old Testament and wail of New Testament. . . . to serve him
210 by men with every object.

NOt unworthy of song for descendants of Neill.

>i.e. not without tale. Or, not trifling is the tale of Colum Cille's death, to grandchildren of Neill, or to great-grandchildren of Neill.

They sigh not (as) single plains (but all together);
215 great woe, great noise intolerable.

>i.e. not from one plain is it 'alas' or is it 'groaning' *sed totis campis*: the decease of Colum Cilleis a great woe; noise, i.e. great is the trembling and the shaking that hath come into Ireland at the decease of Colum Cille.

At the time when it tells of Colum being without life, without church.

220 >i.e. the story is to us intolerable at the time when it is told us of Colum's decease, of his being no more in the world or in life, of his no longer abiding in a church.
>
>>*Ubi invenitur* 'ris', i.e. 'story'? Not hard; in the Dialogue of the Two Sages, *ut dicitur*, "delight of a king, smooth stories"; or in the Bretha Nemed, *ut dicitur*, "not payment of a company (that tell) stories"; i.e. he possesses
225 >>not the means of delighting a company (for their) stories

How would a fool speak of him?

>i.e. 'coi' is 'way,' in what way, and 'india' is 'will he narrate'; what then is the way in which a fool will tell of him? Or, compared with him every person up to India was unlearned.

T] Even Nera, about God's prophet.

230 'sceo' and 'ceo' and 'nco' are three Gaelic conjunctive particles. And even Nera son of Morand, or son of Fincholl of the fairy-folk, would not be able to tell of him. Or, even he was unlearned in comparison with Colum Cille.

On land of Zion he hath taken his seat.

i.e. on land of the heavenly Zion he sate down; or the prophet of God used to tell of the sitting that shall be in the
235 land of Zion, i.e. on earth.

No (more) is our sage the profit of (our) soul, for (he hath gone) from us to a fair land.

i.e. we have now none to benefit or to enlighten our soul, for our sage hath gone away from us to a fair land.

Or, from *condio*, 'I salt', i.e. the person who used to salt our stench of sins and trangressions with his teaching.

240 He who preserves alive has died.

i.e. the person who used to preserve us alive hath died. Or, the person who knows our life well hath died.

For he hath died to us, who was destined to secure our forgiveness.

i.e. he who was destined (to secure) our pardon, has died. Or, he who was destined for pity on our wretchedness, hath
245 died.

For he hath died to us who was a messenger to our Lord.

i.e. the messenger who used to go from us to our Lord, hath died; for his spirit used to go to heaven every Thursday.

For now we have no more a sage who should avert terrors from us.

250 i.e. for no longer is alive the person who used to bring us knowledge of peace, and who used to stand in opposition so that there should be no fear in us. Or, the sage who used to go from us into the land of . . . .

T] For we have no king, who shall explain word-truth.

> i.e. he who ran from us runs not back to us; he would state to us truth of word or true-word. Or, he does not come to our reproof, i.e. to our amelioration.

For (we have) no teacher who used to teach tribes of Toi.

> i.e. he who wrought the aid of the tribes in teaching them till they were silent. Or, the teacher who sang (to) the tribes who were about Tai, i.e. *nomen proprium* of a stream in Scotland.

260 Whole world,—it was his.

> i.e. woe to the whole world, which he had, for it is in misery. Or else, he had the whole world.

It is a 'cruit'-harp without a 'ceis'-harp, it is a church without an abbot.

> i.e. 'ceis' is a name for a small harp that accompanies a great 'cruit'-harp in its playing. Or a name for a pulling upon which is the cord. Or, it is a name for the small peg. Or, a name for the tackling. Or, for the heavy cord, *quod est melius, ut dixit* the poet.

De ascensione eius in caelum.

HE rose very high, God's time about Colum of company.

270   i.e. he arose to a great height when God's companies came to meet Colum Cille.

Bright shrine attendance.

> i.e. bright is the shrine for which attendants came. Or else, bright were the peace-folk who came to attend on Colum Cille, viz. angels.

275 He kept vigil as long as he lived.

> i.e. twelve hundred genuflexions by him every day except *tantum* on festival days, so that his ribs were visible through his dress.

T] **He was of brief age.**

> i.e. straight, or insignificant or small (his age), viz. seventy-six years, *ut dixit* the poet.

280 **He was of slight food.**

> i.e. of trifling amount was his sufficiency.

He was head of science of every hill.

> i.e. he was chief in science of every language up to its ridge-pole. Or, a firm chief who used to turn every unlawfulness.

285 **He was a hill, in book law-learned.**

> i.e. he used to teach the books of the law up to its ridge-pole. Or, *quia fuit doctor in libris legis*.

Blazed land south; with him district *Occidens*.

> i.e. he blazed in the south land. Or, the south land was his.
> 290 Or, he benefited it, and he benefited the land of the setting (sun). Or, it is his, just as was Inis Boffin on the sea.

Equally his was *Oriens*.

> i.e. he blazed . . . in the East.

From clerics heart-pained.

295 > i.e. for the clergy at Corccan Ochaide; and it is they whom he sent to Gregory. Or, perhaps his heart was silent with respect to clericship towards each.

Good his death.

> i.e. good his death, *quia fit* 'dibad' and 'bath' and 'ba' and 'teme' are used to denote 'death.'

300 **God's angels when he ascended.**

> i.e. angels of the God of heaven came to meet him when he ascended.

AMRA OF ST. COLUMBA.

De martyrio eiusdem in mundo.

T] HE came to Axalu, great crowds, archangels.

i.e. he came to a place where is the angel Axal. Or, he came to a place where *auxilium* is given to each one, i.e. to a multitude of archangels. Or 'axal' means 'conversation'; i.e. he came to the land in which conversation is made, *quia dicunt hiruphin et zaraphin, sanctus sanctus sanctus dominus deus sabaoth dicentes.* Or, 'axalu' is *ucca* (choice) *sola* (alone), and the word is *compositum*, viz. of Latin and Irish, *sic*; i.e. he came to the one place that is an object of choice to all, *i.e. caelum.*

He reached a land in which it is not night that one has seen.

i.e. he came to a land in which night is not seen.

He reached a land for Moses, we deem.

i.e. in which it is our opinion that Moses is.

He reached plains of customs, that songs are not born (there).

i.e. it is not a custom for any tune to be born in them, for there is never any want of that tune out of them.

That sages heard not.

i.e. sages are not able to tell it. Or, no sage listens to another.

King of priests cast out toils.

i.e. the King of the priests flung all diseases from Him in the time of His death, *ut dicitur, Tristis est anima mea usque ad mortem.*

HE suffered; in a short time he gained victory.

i.e. finely he subdued his passions in the short time that he lived.

T] **Terror of him was on the devil.**

> i.e. the devil was a horror to him. Or, he was deemed a horror by the demon, viz. by the gods of perdition.

To whom celebration was a hanging.

> i.e. to whom Colum Cille's celebration was a 'way of stopping,' or was a 'spear of stopping.' Or, a 'hanging' in its own meaning, i.e. so long as there was heard the voice of Colum Cille at celebration, he was not let out till the celebration was finished; and they used to ask news of him thereafter.

From his powerful art.

> i.e. by the power of his clericship he used to effect that.

Robust right he keeps.

> i.e. he knew the great strength of right *quia idem est*, 'robust' *et* 'robustus.' Or, he preserved his uprightness strongly.

Was known (his) grave, known (his) wisdom

> i.e. the place of his burial was known, viz. Hi, or Down, *ut dicunt alii*. Or, it was known up to Rome, and his wisdom was known.

Sageship to him was granted of deity.

> i.e. there was granted to him sageship of the Deity; from the Son of God he got that. Or, he lived in granted Deity of the Son of God.

Sure good in death.

> i.e. it is certain that the death he departed is good. Or, good was the person who died there.

He was skilled in Axal the angel.

> i.e. he was skilful in the conversation of the angel whose name was Axal.

T] He used[1] Basil-judgements.

> i.e. the judgement of pride that he fell into in the Great Assembly of Druim Cetta, so that it was on that account that Baithin brought a testimony from Basil to subdue the pride. Or, he made use of Basil's Judgements of Doom.

350 He forbade works of chorus, in crowds, in choruses.

> i.e. he forbade, with a view to his mind being (fixed) on God, the eulogy that the hosts made on him. Or, he prohibited the deeds of God owing to the apparition of the black hideous multitudes; and what summoned him therefrom was the testimony from Basil, or the words.

355 *De scientia eius in omni parte.*

HE ran a race which he runs.

> i.e. there overtook him the race which he ran.

For hatred, well-doing.

> i.e. he used to do kindly deeds in return for hatred, *quia fit* '*cais*' 'hatred.'

360 Teacher sewed word.

> i.e. he used to sew the word of teaching, viz. the tutor.

He explained glosses clearly.

> i.e. he was swift at interpreting the glosses clearly. Or, he wounded the glosses, &c.

365 He secured correctness of psalms.

> i.e. he corrected the psalms by obelus and asterisk.

He commented on law-books, books *ut* Cassian loved.

> i.e. it is thus that he read books of law, as he used to read books of John Cassian for their easiness. Or, he read, just as John Cassian read, books *Legis*.

---

[1] There are marginal notes in T; 'i.e. he used 'judgements' or 'words' from Basil. Or, Baithin used dooms i.e. judgements or words from Basil, in instructing Colum Cille that he should not assume pride or loftymindedness, owing to the applause of the men of Ireland. . . . on high. Or, it might be Colum Cille that applied Basil's words to himself to instruct himself.'

T] He fought battles *gulae.*

> i.e. he fought the battle of gluttony. Or, 'culai' is what is good in it, i.e. he fought the battles of the three Culs, viz. battle of Cuil Dremne against Connaughtmen, and battle of Cuil Feda against Colman Mor son of Diarmait, and battle of Cuil Rathen against Ulstermen, in the contest for Ross Torathair between Colum and Comgall.

375 Books of Solomon he followed.

> i.e. he followed the books of Solomon. Or, he attained to the books of Solomon. Or, 'sexus' i.e. 'fexsus,' *ut dicitur* 'fenchas' *pro* 'senchas,' *ut dixit* the poet:
>
>> Poets that are in existence read
>> 'fenchas'-law eagerly with Fergus.

380 Storms and sea-voyages he perceived.

> i.e. 'sina' viz. 'sonenna,' fair-weather periods; and 'rima' 'doinenna,' foul-weather periods; and it is from the word *imber* that 'imrim' is derived. 'Raid' i.e. 'ro-raidestar,' he (fore)told them.

He divided a division with figure, among the books of the Law.

> i.e. he set the history of the Law on one side; and its allegorical sense on the other side.

385 He read mysteries very-wise.

> i.e. 'ros-ualt,' a beast that dwells in the ocean; these are its tokens: when it vomits with its face landwards, poverty and want (shall be) in that land to the end of seven years; if it is upwards, poverty and storm in that air; if downwards, loss and mortality on the beasts of the sea. He used afterwards to tell of the mysteries of that animal to people, that they might
390 be on their guard against him. Or, he read runes with great-sages. Or, it was he himself that was a sage.

Amid schools of scripture; and he joined mutual-fitness of moon about course.

> i.e. he understood how the moon runs in front of the sun *nunc, post nunc.*

T] He perceived a race with branching sun.
> i.e. it is for this reason the sun is called 'branching,' because from it there is light to stars and to men's eyes; *uel nouit cursum fluminis Rheni*, a name that is thence applied to every stream.

Rhine course.
400
> i.e. he was skilled in the course of the Rhine .i. *maris*.[1]

He would number the stars of heaven, who could tell of each very noble thing.
> i.e. I think he would tell of the stars of heaven, he who could recount every noble thing that Colum Cille did. Or, Colum Cille would recount a very noble thing about his endeavour, or about stars.

405 Which we from Colum Cille have heard.
> i.e. we have heard from Colum Cille.

De admiratione et caritate eius.

Who was, who will be alive, that would be more wonderful on lands, very learned, northern?
410
> i.e. what is the place in which he was, and what is the place in which he will be alive, who should be more wonderful and more perfect in the northern land than Colum Cille was?

He used to tell till lately.
> i.e. Colum Cille used to narrate up to lately.

Who knew not falsehood.
415
> i.e. I shall not recognize falsehood now, for dead is the man who used to tell us (what it was), viz. Colum Cille. Or, he used to tell us from now to the ninth descendant of the genealogy of each. Or, the (syllable) 'fet' which is there as

---

[1] The marginal note runs:
> *ut dixit* Finn
> A tale with me for you: ox murmurs,
> summer hath gone, winter is snowing,
> Wind is high, cold sun is low,
> well-running sea forbids race.
>
> very red fern, was hidden (its) form;
> the voice of geese has become common;
> cold has seized birds' wing;
> icy time,—(so) is my tale.

T]   *idem et* uet*us testamentum*, and the (syllable) 'no' is no*uum testamentum;* i.e. he used to tell us both of Old Law and afterwards of New Testimony.

420 A course he made more lucky.

    i.e. luckier than every course was the course that Colum Cille ran.

Towards ladders on city, to world he is borne.

    i.e. towards ladders of the heavenly city he pressed; 'to world' i.e. to him its treasure. Or 'co domun' *ad caelum*.

425 On account of God humanity.

    i.e. this is why he did that, for the humanity of the Son of God; i.e. that the suffering of the Son of God should take effect for him.

On seats he is crowned.

    i.e. on stations for him in the kingdom.

430 He gave the desire of his eyes.

    i.e. he sold everything that was an object of desire to his eye here below.

A perfect sage, he believed Christ.

    i.e. the perfect sage believed Christ. Or, 'creis' is from the verb *creo*, he increased afterwards in Christ. Or, Christ put increase upon him.

435 Also not ale, also not gluttony, satiety: he avoided flesh.

    i.e. he avoided ale, he avoided gluttony, he avoided satiety; he avoided flesh; or past his lips.

He lived 'cath.'

    i.e. *catholicus*.

440 He lived 'cast.'

    i.e. *castus*.

T] Loving-full.

> i.e. 'doit' is 'toit'; full of charity was he (towards) all. Or, perfect was Colum Cille in charity.

445 Famous stone at victory.

> i.e. stone of subduing, *quia fit* 'ond,' a stone; Colum Cille was as a stone of subduing of every evil; and also he lived so that he was a stone of victory, *ut fit* a rock on a promontory of land.

He lived a full benefit.

450
> i.e. he lived so that he gave his full benefit to each.

He lived a great benefit of guests.

> i.e. he had plenty of good even though he did it to guests.

He lived noble, he lived 'obid,' he lived over death.

> i.e. great was his nobleness, and though he was noble, he was humble; and this is why he practised humility, in that he
455 knew death (was) over him. Or, he was mighty over death.

He was gentle, he was a physician, with the heart of every sage.

> i.e. he was *lenis*. Or he was compassionate.
> i.e. he was full of blessings. Or, he was a binder. Or, he was a physician, a healer of all.

Our diadem, Axal of conversation, it was abstemiousness of which he died.

460
> i.e. the diadem that we had in conversation of the angel whose name was Axal; it was of the slightness of his drink that he died, for he consumed neither ale nor food in the year he died save on Saturday and on Sunday.

Was sweet, was unique his art of clericship.

> i.e. everybody deemed his voice a sweet one; and every-
465 body was satisfied with the unique art of clericship which he had. Or, clericship was (only) one of his arts, for he was a poet, a prophet and a sage.

T] To (ordinary) persons he was inscrutable.

> i.e. he was incomprehensible to everybody (on the score) of his talent.

He was a protection to naked persons, he was a shelter to poor persons.

470
> i.e. in clothing and feeding them.

It was afresh he suffered every weight of storm.

> i.e. every heavy storm that he suffered Colum Cille took it as a new one. Or, heavier than every blast to us was this new blast, said the blind man.

From Colum discipline of territories.

475
> i.e. by Colum they used to instruct the territories.

Great dignity we think 'manna.'

> i.e. 'miad' reverence. 'Mar' abundance. 'Manna' the manna. This is what the children [of Israel] said of it: 'man-hu' .i. *quid hoc nisi cibus caelestis*; we expect afterwards,
480 i.e. great reverence will be given to him, of the heavenly food.

Christ will enrol him in His service among righteous.

> i.e. then there shall be given him the reward of his service; amongst the righteous, viz. angels and archangels.

Through his long (period) during which he served.

485
> i.e. he was long in reaching that service.

Wise a sage who reached four men's path.

> i.e. wise is the sage who followed the track of the four, viz. the four evangelists; or he himself reached it *quia apud Finnianum euangelium legit*.

490 Till he went with song.

> i.e. it is thus he went, with song to heaven, i.e. the song of the household of heaven and earth, or of the Old and of the New Testament.

T] To heaven-land after his cross.

> i.e. to the land of heaven he went after cross and passion.

495 Hundred churches' guardian of waves; under completeness of offering.

> i.e. guardian of waves is he, over seas of a hundred churches; and this is a definite (number put) for an indefinite, *ut est*, Hi and Derry. Or, guardian of waves under perfection of offering (up to) that number.

Great-deed, not idol-(worship): he brought together no perverse company.

500
> i.e. great is the amount that he effected of good, and not idol-worship; he nourished no place in which was a perverse company.

. . . .

> i.e. he used to bring them to psalm-singing. Or, he used to milk them, i.e. he used to pacify.

Not long not cold any heresy.

505
> i.e. he sent not from him (as messenger) any one who would inflict evils, and he did not himself practise any heresy; viz. he did not enforce heresy on anybody; or, he did not himself adopt heresy.

He did not . . . . . anything that was not a king's right.

> i.e. he did not regard as distinguished anything, but as according to God's law.

That he may not die world-death.

510
> i.e. that there should not be a fixing to him of death for ever. Or, death in the world.

Alive his name; alive his 'un-stitched.'

> i.e. his soul in the next world.

T] Owing to (a multitude) which he caused (to be) under the law of saints.

> i.e. for the multitude that he drove under saints' law, therefore is his name alive in this world, and his soul in the next.

Wasting attacked his side.

> i.e. he betrayed the fatness of his side, for the form of his rib was visible through his clothes on the sea-shore.

Desires of his body, he checked them.

> i.e. he destroyed the desire of his body.

He checks quarrelsomeness.

> i.e. he destroyed stinginess, *ut poeta dixit:*—
> Do you deem it good
> when truth is spoken to you?
> he enjoins love; treasures approach;
> he takes not quarrel with one whom he loves.

Is not the child the son of Ua Chinn?

> i.e. whose is the child? Not hard, the son in truth of Ua Chinn, viz. Colum Cille. Or, there was not of the son of Ua Chinn either stinginess or quarrelsomeness.

Sin which takes away from jealousy; sin which takes away from envy.

> i.e. he practised no whit of jealousy, he did not commit sin. Or, he did nothing of attack or of envy, nought which would take away sin; *quia fit 'demo,'* viz. I take away.

Good in your judgement the grave (that was) his.

> i.e. it is good for you; you deem good his grave.

Against every toil (from) successions of weather.

> i.e. against every disease of successions of weather, i.e. each season used to exert its quarter(ly) influence).

Through an idolatrous district, he meditated (on its) guilt.

> i.e. on going through a district in which there is idolatry, he meditated on its guilt.

T.] For credulous chariots.

540 i.e. for this reason he passed this judgement upon them, for the credulous chariot of his body. Or, for the clericship he sent away from him his chariots.

Long fight; he sought truth; he fought against body.

 i.e. perpetual warfare; 'soich fir' i.e. he pursued the truth; 'fiched' i.e. he used to make aggression on his body while here below.

545 That a king's son may not come upon two things of God.

 i.e. the son of the king shall not go upon two things of God.

Into a dread voice, into a dread verse.

 i.e. Into the dread voice, viz. *It maledicti*; there shall be no other verse to him but *Uenite benedicti patris*.

550 He was buried before age, before infirmity.

 i.e. he was buried before age came to him; and he was weak i.e. for he had completed seventy-six years.

For hell, in Scotland (was) fear.

 i.e. for fear of hell he went into Scotland.

555 Aed celebrated all mighty-men, a lasting poem of battle on a heavenly champion.

 i.e. Aed mac Ainmerech gave seven 'cumals' to get his name inserted into this eulogy of Colum Cille; and Aed charged the blind (poet) that this poem to the champion viz. Colum Cille, should be more lasting than any (other) 560 poem.

Not undear.

 i.e. to me, but it is dear.

seu insignificant.

 i.e. and not trifling; or 'ni handil'.—he did not 'frame' and he did not stitch together a thing that would be insigni-
565 ficant.

T] Not a champion at all new towards a pacification of
Conall.
> i.e. not a champion at all new is this man towards the
> confirming of a peace with Conall. Or, towards pacification
> of body, i.e. at peace-(making) between body and soul.

Blessing subdued rough tongues, that were at Toi,—
a king's will!
570
> i.e. he subdued the mouths of the rude persons who were
> with the high king (of) Toi, though what they would have
> liked was to utter evil things, but it was blessing that they
> really uttered, *ut fuit Balaam*.

From men by journeyings, with God he stayed.
> i.e. from men he was taken away and with God he abode.

For 'adbud' for splendour, he distributed bright
575 hospitality from his city . . .
> i.e. for his patience and for his fasting the descendant of
> Conall gave pure hospitality in his city. Or, for his pomp
> and for his patience he gave hospitality, &c.; for he did not
> do that *ut faciunt hypocritæ*.

In disease, fair sage and master of household.
580
> i.e. 'udbud,' *nomen doloris .i. proprium*, viz. toil, or 'ingiu
> sechi.' Afterwards the sage was kindly, so that that disease
> should not consume him nor seize him; and also he was a
> *magister* to his household, on that same matter. Or, 'ingiu
> sechi' i.e. now and again his skin encompassed him owing to
> the abundance of his capacities. Or, 'adbud' i.e. in stilling
585
> ambition, in solving questions of the Canon. Or, it is 'dibdud,'
> i.e. destroying falsehoods. Or, it is the name of a booth for
> reading in; or, *proprium loci* in Cenel Conaill.

With an angel he conversed; he spoke in Greek
grammar.
> i.e. he made conversation with an angel, and he learnt
> grammar like Greeks. Or, he conversed grammatically and in
> Greek.

590 Free beyond territory; that I tell.
> i.e. a freeman whom seven districts followed; here it is a
> definite (number) for an indefinite. Or, extern territories

T]   were pursued. 'That I relate;' i.e. it is thus that I make its narration.

The son of Feidlimid fought the north; *fin(em) nouit.*

595   i e. the son of Feidlimid for whom twenty districts used to fight; definite number here also for indefinite; for whom the land to the North fought. *Finem nouit;* i.e. his own death, or *finem mundi.*

There went not to the world; lasting was his recollection of the cross.

        i.e. not well he came into the world (owing to) the shortness of his life; he was however everlasting in the recollection of
600   the cross on his body. Or, there came none hither to the world, who was more constant in his recollection of the cross of the Son of God.

. . . . he said prayers, with deed he verified.

        i.e. that which he wove with prayers of intention to do, he carried out with deed.

He sprang therefrom an illustrious birth, descendant of Art . . . Neill with might.

605   i.e. he was born, a noble birth too, of Art; a descendant of Neill with might, i.e. he was mighty. Or, 'nis Neill conert' is: not towards the powers of Neill he lent his aid, but towards the powers of the Holy Spirit.

He did not commit an injury for which one dies.

        i.e. he did not commit any injury, for which his death would
610   be fitting, if this were a cause for that in general.

Cond's profession broke grief; going 'druib'; greatness his goodness.

        i.e. there was breaking and grief in the city of Conn from the 'do druib' that was on Colum Cille when he went yonder. 'Greatness of his goodness,' i.e. great size is the goodness that
615   was on him from the 'dodruib' that was upon him. Or, there was sighing and sorrow in the profession of Conn.

T] Son, name of cross.

 i.e. a son who gave his name to a cross; or a son with whom the name of Christ's cross was held in remembrance.

620 Up to this his age; *ecce aër*; *certo* 'indias.'

 i.e. up to this his age, i.e. I am sure of his age. *Ecce aer*, i.e. plain to me is the air, for there were allowed to him his eyes whilst he was engaged in praising. *Certo* 'indias' i.e. great were his deeds of skill, as I relate.

Al-liath'; a melodious lion in snow, a new meeting.

625 i.e. 'al-liath,' stands for 'al-lith,' stands for 'lith a aille,' i.e. 'festival of his praise.' As roars a melodious lion in snow at a new meeting, for when the lion utters his roar, there come under him all animals, so that he puts a cast of his tail around them, so that they die in that place, except rat and fox. The hunter comes to him thereafter, and he puts a cast around him so that he dies. *Sic* Colum Cille: the person round
630 whom he puts a cast of his teaching, could not get across it away from him, save unjust persons; the cast of the teaching of God's Son about him. Or, it is 'all-iath' i.e. 'into the land of the rock'; for the lion goes into the land of the cave whilst the frost lasts, so that he utters his roar after coming out into the new rock-cave.

635 Till death how shall I tell.

 i.e. till my death I shall not narrate tales of Colum Cille.

A journey in the body to the upper air; his choice he made joy summer-peace.

 i.e. the journey that he went in the body to the upper air,
640 as went Paul[1]; and that was his own choice; he carried out his choice to the good in which there is peace and joy. Or, he caused that there should be given him his choice with summer-peace, with the peace of summer, for in that season he died. Or, he brought about peace for his congregation by the journey that he made to the upper air.

The famous one, wisdom; it is certain for him.

645 i.e. a sage with good fame opened to them; certain to him, i.e. it is certain that he did that.

[1] 2 Cor. xii. 2.

T] To him not the groan of one house; to him not the groan of one string.

> i.e. 'ong' means 'visitation'; or string (of) timpan harp; or string (is) road. Not visitation of one house thereafter: or not visitation of one string or of one road, to us is the bewailing of Colum Cille. Where is 'ong' found? Not hard: in the Fotha Breth, *ut dicitur*.
> 'ongaib, coscaib carat'
> i.e. with groans, chastisements of friends.
> i.e. for fear of their chastisements, of their visitation with a view to the chastisement of him by his friends. Or, 'ong' is 'ongan,' it was not an 'ongan' of one house to him, but an 'ongan' of many houses. Or, it was not an 'ongan' of one road.

650

Heavy people, word under wave.

655
> i.e. heavy is his bewailing with the tribes; and this story is a word 'under wave.'

For it was due from him: the lamp of the king which was extinguished, was relit.

> i.e. the lamp of the king, of God; it was due to us (to make) this eulogy on him. 'do·r·adbad' i.e. 'ro·dibad' is 'was extinguished, in this world,' was relit, yonder, *in regno caelorum*.

660 Eulogy is this, of the king who made me king, who will redeem us to Zion.

> i.e. eulogy; 'wonderful is the saying,' or 'is the grace'; or 'not-smooth'; or 'wonderful is the course that is under it above.' The 'am' that is in it is the same as 'death' *quia post mortem pretium laudis datum est caeco*. Or, the 'am' is the same as 'nem,' 'heaven,' so that 'am-rath' means 'nem-rath' really, for heaven was given him as the payment for his eulogy. 'Of the king who made me king,' i.e. it was Colum Cille that gave the bardship to me. 'Zion' i.e. perhaps, 'save us unto Mount Zion' or 'to the heavenly city.'

665

May he carry me past torments.

670
> i.e. may·be take me past the demons of the air *ad requiem sanctorum*. Or, past 'riaga' i.e. past the daughters of Orcus.

T] May it be smooth abode-darkness from me

> i.e. may it be easy for me to go past the black abodes, *ubi sunt demones*. Or, 'mendum' i.e. lie, and 'menna' means lies: may he expel from me the black lies.

675 May the descendant of the body of Cathair with nobility see me without stain.

> i.e. may he look on me without stain, a descendant of Cairpre Nia-fer of Leinster; for Ethne daughter of Dimma mac Noe was his (Colum Cille's) mother, of the Carburys of Leinster; and he (Cairpre) was a descendant of Cathair Mor, son of Feidlimid the All-wise.

680 Great re-declension; great of the poem, of heaven, heaven-sun.

> i.e. great is the re-forming I have put on the above words; great is the 'nath' the poets used to make in the beginning for sun and moon; and not greater is the darkening they used to put on them, as I have put. Or, though great they deemed the excellency of sun and moon, not greater do we deem it
> 685 than the excellency of the death of Colum Cille . nid am huan . . . i.e. *quia caecatus sum iterum*.

Prayer of St. Adamnan.

Adamnan made this prayer.

T] Colum Cille, to God he enjoined me (the time) at which I should go, that I should not go earlier.

    i.e. Colum Cille wrought my ordering to God, when I should go; 'that I should not go earlier'; i.e. that it should not be early I should go.

Luck greatly mine, my destiny.

5   i.e. after great luck I shall go; that is my destiny.

Crowds to angel-place.

    i.e. the direction which I say is to the place where there are crowds of angels.

Name of the illustrious descendant of Neill; not small the protection of Zion to archangels of God.

10   i.e. the name of the illustrious descendant of Neill; not small protection i.e. not small is the protection to God of the archangels, *quia idem est 'Hel' et 'deus.'*

In strongholds of God the Father amid the groups of the twenty-four bright elders righteous, who celebrate in song the kingdom of the mystic king resplendent.

15   i.e. 'in strongholds,' viz. in the abodes of God the Father amid the assemblies, the gatherings of the twenty-four bright elders, viz. the twelve patriarchs and the twelve apostles; who sing, *dicentes ter, Sanctus sanctus sanctus dominus deus sabaoth;* of the mystic king i.e. of the resplendent King with whom are mysteries.

T] A cry never came nor shall come.

20   i.e. not only there never came but there never will come a cry of dissension into that quarter.

Right, my powerful Christ; impurity of Colum Cille.

    i.e. there never came impurity into uprightness wheresoever is my powerful Christ. Or, it is *colo* i.e. 'I worship' in uprightness where God is and Colum Cille.

Pedigree of St. Mobi.

T]   Mobi the Flatfaced, son of Beoan, son of Bresal, son of Ailgel, son of Idnae, son of Athrae, son of Lugnae Trín-og, son of Bregdolb, son of Artchorp, son of Cairpre, son of Cormac, son of . . . . .

The Hymn of St. Philip.

T]   Philip apostle, apostle holy;
at a fair, Philip told
(of) the immortal birds, slender,
that dwelt in Inis Eidheand.

5   In the East of Africa they abide;
it is a pleasant labour they perform;
there never came into the world
any colour that was not on their wings.

Their plumage remains on them
10   from the lawful beginning of the world,
without deficiency of one bird of them,
without increase to them in their numbers.

Seven fair rivers in all their length
are in the plains where they dwell;
15   it is this that feeds them for ever,
and they sing songs with fair-custom.

They allotted as share the middle of the night,
being on horses for ever,
to the drone of the angels as they speed
20   in the air overhead.

The first birds sing pleasantly,
—it is not unfitting their being very melodious—
all the wondrous courses
that God wrought before the world.

25   A crowd of them sing after rising
at the time of nocturns,
what God will do, excellent matter,
from earth's beginning till Doom.

The birds whose wishes are good sing
30   in the twilight with its swift-moving locks,
what God will do of wonders beyond
in the Day of the Judgement of the Racings.

Of one and forty on a hundred
and one thousand, 'tis no lie!
was the number to them,—was the grace;
that is its truth in each flock of birds.

If men should hear (these) faultless birds,
this fair equally-balanced concert,
they would all die—great the deed!
on listening to the harmony.

Intercession of Great Mary
after the cutting-off of the Canon
that we may get to dwell yonder quickly
in the land where Philip was.

MISCELLANEA.

(*a*) Find the Poet; his son was Conchobar Abrat-ruad king of Ireland; his son was Mog-Corb *qui cecidit* at the destruction of Bruiden Da Choca; his son was Cu-Corb *qui cecidit* by the hand of Feradach Find Fechtnach.

(*b*) ... not well we went to him, said Cuchulaind ... we ... the Ulstermen; let some one say to Conchobar, why he should come ... it was not that ......

(*c*) ... it is there with poor men ..... upon him, when the five persons went to him under the ..... ; he girt himself with a smooth .... it was sewed of deer-skin, they put a narrow ...... garment over it on the outside.

(*d*) 'mortlaid' i.e. *quando plurimi pereunt de uno morbo; mortali* i.e. 'mort-luad' i.e. swift *mors*, and no wonder; and it is a compound expression of Latin and Gaelic, *sic est* in Welsh, *ut dicitur* 'croebechain' i.e. 'a crai,' is from the word 'cara,' and 'bechain' denotes 'small.'

(*e*) Aed wrote it, and on a little leaf found ..... between two .... quires ..... besides.

The Release of Scandlan Mor.

T] On one occasion Colum Cille went with Aedan mac Gabrain to
the Great Assembly of Druim Cetta, to Aed mac Ainmerech, where
were the men of Ireland, both lay and cleric, for the space of one
year and three months; to ask respite for the men of Scotland they
5 came, and it was not granted them. "There shall be respite till
doom," said Colum Cille, "without attacks eastward from Ireland;"
for there were many causes of quarrel between them and Aed mac
Ainmerech, viz. the chasing of the Dal-riata over-sea, and the chasing
of the sages and the Dal-Osraide after the fall of their hostage, Scandlan. Now when Colum Cille chanced to come to the door of the
fort outside to interview Aed, he heard the outcry of Scandlan owing
10 to the greatness of the suffering in which he lay; viz. twelve fetters on
him, and flesh burning-hot was given to him with only a drop of
water on the finger tip to drink thereafter. Well, Colum Cille
came to talk with Scandlan, and Scandlan said to him, "For
Christ's sake, go back and beg me of Aed, for I am falling to ruin in
15 my indebtedness." Thereupon the cleric went to Aed, but he did not
grant it him. So Colum Cille said, "He shall be free before morning."
"Cumine, you crane-cleric there!" said the queen, with her pretty
face, as she was washing. "'Tis yourself that will be a crane," said
Colum Cille, "(standing) over this ford outside till Doom, and one
of thy wings broken, as is half the tail," and it is so, *sicut uidimus*;
20 "and Scandlan shall come to me before morning," said Colum Cille.
And after that, Colum Cille went across Ciannachta and over Ui
mac Carthaind and over Loch Foyle, and in Corthe Snama and to
Ard mac n-Odrain in Inishowen. And there came a great earthquake
into the camp thereafter with lightning and thunder (in) the evening,
25 and Scandlan was carried off by the power of God past the pickets, and
was whirled away then with a bright cloud before him to Corthe
Snama to . . . . . When he saw the boat coming towards him to
the land, "Who is in the boat?" said Scandlan. "It is Cumine that
is here, son of Feradach, son of Muiredach, son of Eogan. A
debtor is he then to Colum Cille . . . of thy body-side." "A
30 ferrying across to me and a guide," said Scandlan, "and I shall make
thy peace with Colum Cille." He returns thence to Ard mac n-
Odrain, for there dwelt the cleric. Scandlan arises and took one of
his shoes from him. "Who is that?" said Colum Cille. "Scanlan,"
said he. "Thy news?" said Colum Cille. "A drink!" said Scandlan. The cup comes into Colum Cille's hand, and it is given (to
35 Scandlan, who) drinks of it. "Thy news?" said Colum Cille.
"Another drink," said Scandlan. "Go out, Baithin," said Colum

T] Cille, "and bring him another full drink." This also is given him and he drinks. "Thy news?" said Colum Cille. "A drink!" says Scandlan. There is brought him the third full cup, and he drinks. "Thy news?" says Colum Cille. Well, after that, Scandlan narrated to
40 him his adventures till he reached the ferry, and that he did not get his ferrying across from Cumine, till (he promised he) would make his peace with Colum Cille. So peace was then made, and Colum Cille said, "Though great evil is to both Conall and Eogan, the over-plus shall not be with Eogan, except a head and a half, and one cow of Conall's against him in the Day of Judgement."

Three boons accrued to Colum Cille from this expedition viz., (i) the peace of Dal-riata, i.e. their fighting and their hosting to the
45 men of Ireland, and their tax and their tribute to the men of Scotland; (ii) the allowing the poets to remain in Ireland; and (iii) the deliverance of Scandlan.

And after he had made Cumine's peace with Colum Cille the latter said, "Bow down to my will, O Scandlan!" *ut dixit* at giving his gospel to Colum Cille about Scandlan. Then Colum Cille made
50 prosperous the ways that lay before him, and said to him after that to take with him his staff to protect him, and lucky would be the treasure, and bade him bring it thereafter to Laisren mac Feradaich to Ross Grencha. And neither gold nor silver wrought it, for the greatness of the miracle, *ut dixit*. "Take my staff with thee in thy hand," &c.

Dundelga, good the gold place.

The Death of St. Columba.

T]   A rider chanced upon the blind man, and the blind man said to him, " Whence (comest thou ?) " " (from the) side on which is my rear," said the rider. " Thy news? " said the blind man. " The person to whom there is . . . ," said the rider (the descendant) of Ua Neill, " viz. Colum Cille is dead." This then is what the rider did, on the south of . . . . at that time the poets were at Ibar of Cinntracht in the territory of Ulster; for the king of Ulster gave all of them guest-rights there for a year, so that it was there they made the concoction of their own tales of themselves, and these did not happen as they were narrated, but it was to impose them on the stupid race, viz. the Ulstermen, amongst whom they were, that the eloquent poets concocted these lying fables . . . . .
I am Aed.

The Five Divisions of Munster.

T] Five Munsters in Great Munster,
    they are not unknown to the learned;
    I know (the names) of them
    . . . . the stony fertile land.

5   (The first is Thomond)
    from Cuchulaind's Leap
    to Slige Dala of the Horses
    that was on its side.

    The portion of Thomond northward
10 I will name . . . . to you,
    from Slieve Aughty to pleasant Slieve Phelim
    . . . . to virgin Ireland.

    From two other islands a place,
    Ormond to the island of O'Bric
15 . . . to fair Cnawhill
    there is the usual division, pure wise.

    From Cnawhill to full Luachair,
    Mid-Munster will last permanently;
    from Slieve Phelim with beauty
20 to Slieve Cain of the steps.

    Desmond from Slieve Cain
    to the ocean beside the waves.
    West Munster from Luachair a bit west;
    up to Glenn Dian there is a throng.

25 . . . . of whom they are,
    O Tasaig, art . . simple
    betook himself over the vast sea,
    he left it after dividing them into five.

IN PRAISE OF HYMNODY.

F] A holy pope, exalted and excellent, there was in Rome, whose name was Pope Clement. From him Jerome asked a description of the Psalms and Hymnody; and he took to beseeching the Creator aright, that night up till morning, when an angel of God came to him from heaven, with the description of Hymnody. And this is what he told him, "Whoever should recite the hymnody, would be making a song of praise dear to God, for it wipes out all sins, and cleanses the powers of the body and subdues involuntarily the lusts of the flesh; it lessens melancholy, and (banishes) all madness; it breaks down anger, it expels hell's angels, and gets rid of the devils; it dispels the darkness of the understanding, and increases holiness; it preserves the health, and completes good works, and it lights up a spiritual fire in the heart, i.e. the love of God (in place of) the love of man, and it (promotes) peace between the body and the soul

As Jerome said in the seventh chapter of the Medicine of the Soul, "*O homo* . . . there is not anything that is useful to thee in thy mortal state more than praising God, for, if thou praise God, He heals thy soul and thy body together. In truth, O man, inasmuch as this is thy healing, give honour to the Psalms and to the Hymn book", as saith Jerome, that none can . . . more fitly . . . virtues and the description of the psalms . . . . in showing often . . . prayers. *haec Hieronymus ut* . . . .

THE THREE KINGS.

F]   Three Kings came to the house of God,
     three faces like the bright moon,
     from the Eastern learned world,
     heavy . . . smooth, of slow streams.

5   Three came for the lovely child
     to white flowered Bethel;
     three, to whom was granted all knowledge;
     three prophets of the vision.

     Judgement of the great and glorious Lord
10   appeared to the . . . three;
     in the vision to every crowd,
     the Form of the King in the star.

     A lofty star; it was beautiful
     . . the wealthy world
15   he sees; it was a definite help
     during the night of the firmament,

     The three lucky Kings
     followed it full readily;
     the star went before them
20   as an arch of blessing and might.

     It stopped not till it came to the house
     before the three right eagerly,
     The star, brilliant, round, soft,
     over every star swift walking.

25   It is he . . . there
     . . . . unsmooth
     . . . . . was on gallows
     the king of the fourfold world.

F]
30

They bent their white knees,
they gave their three gifts;
He with whom all knowledge remains
is a soul to every single triad.   Three.

35

They recognised His dear face;
Mary the Mother of the Creator,
the holy Virgin, she is our sister
and is akin to every single triad.

40

On the smooth guidance (?) of the star
reaching the king of the world's coming
the three, sweet-sounding, soft, found
wonderful knowledge of the . . ,

Preface to *Benedicite*.

F] *Tres pueri in jornace ignis ardentis hoc canticum fecerunt. In campo uero Sennaar factus est et in Campo Diram speciusiter.*
It was made in the time of Nebuchadnezzar, and they made it to save themselves against fire. For they did not worship the golden image that Nebuchadnezzar had made, and so they were cast *in fornacem. Deus tamen illos cantando hoc canticum de fornace liberauit.* Ananias, Azarias, Misael are their names in Hebrew; Shadrach, Meshach and Abednego, are their names in Chaldee.

Preface to *Christe qui lux es*.

F] Ambrose, sage and bishop, made *hunc hymnum* to praise the Saviour, and in the night it is due to be sung. It was made in rhythm; seven capitula in it, with two lines in each, and sixteen syllables in each line.

Preface to *Quicunque Uult*.

F] The synod of Nicaea made this Catholic Faith; three bishops of them alone made it, viz. Eusebius and Dionysius *et nomen tertii nescimus*. But it is said that it was the whole synod that made it because they gave it celebrity. Now it was made *in Nicæa urbe*, and that town is in Bithynia, which is a country in Asia Minor. Further, it was made in order to expel the heresy of Arius who held that the Father is greater than the Son, and that the Son is greater than the Holy Spirit. So the synod was assembled, viz. three hundred and eighteen bishops with Constantine to Nicæa; but they could not vanquish him owing to his eloquence, till God vanquished him. *Exiens enim de coitu ut purgaret uentrem suum ei contigit ut omnia uiscera cum stercore foras exirent, ut Iudae atque Agitofel contigit.*

NOTES.

THE IRISH PREFACES.

The Prefaces which are found to nearly all the pieces in the *Liber Hymnorum*, in its original form, are a noteworthy feature of the book. They are evidently of a later date than the pieces to which they are prefixed, and were probably composed by scribes who were desirous to place on record the legendary beliefs current in their day as to the composition of the hymns. In the earliest of our manuscript authorities, the *Antiphonary of Bangor* (A), there are no prefaces; and we might therefore suppose that the practice of compiling them did not arise until after the close of the seventh century at earliest. On the other hand the same recension of several of our Prefaces is found in more than one of our MSS. There are only minute variations between the Prefaces in T and F to the pieces numbered 3, 6, 9, 12, 14, 19, 20, 22, and 23; and the same is true of the Prefaces in FB to No. 10, in TFB to No. 11, and in TFL to No. 21. This shows that these prefaces assumed their present form prior to the transcription of any of these manuscripts, that is, before the eleventh century. On the whole we shall not be far wrong if we conclude that the prefaces in T represent the stories current in the tenth century as to the authors of the various hymns.

They are all composed on the same plan, in a rude mixture of Irish and Latin,—and set forth the time, place, author, and occasion of the composition of the pieces which they precede. More than one legend is often recorded, from which it would appear that the scribes did not consider themselves possessed of any certain knowledge on these historical points; and in some instances the subject matter is trivial enough, although in others the information they offer cannot be lightly set aside.

Dr. Todd has remarked[1] that the care taken to record the name of the author of each piece is in accordance with the 23rd Canon of the Second Council of Tours (A.D. 567), which runs thus: "*Licet hymnos Ambrosianos habeamus in canone, tamen quoniam reliquorum sunt aliqui, qui digni sunt forma cantari, uolumus libenter amplecti eos præterea, quorum auctorum nomina fuerint in limine prænotata: quoniam quæ fide constiterint dicendi ratione non obstant.*"[2]

In our translations of these Prefaces we have taken care to reprint (in italics) the Latin words and phrases, only turning the Irish passages into English. The scribes possibly had some Latin original to work on, from which they borrowed here and there *verbatim*; it seems desirable, in any case, to reproduce as closely as possible the curious blending of two languages which appears in these *Præfationes*. In our notes the translations of the Irish glosses are in all cases printed in italics.

[1] *Liber Hymnorum*, p. 56.   [2] Concil. Labb. et Cossart. v. 863.

Preface to the Hymn of St. Sechnall.

It has been said in our *Introduction* (vol. i. p. xi) that the Preface to the hymn *Audite omnes* is wanting in the Trinity College manuscript (T), owing to the loss of a page; but it probably did not differ substantially from that in F. We do not propose to enter into all the obscure details of the legends about St. Patrick and St. Sechnall reported in the two extant Prefaces (F and B). Many of them are also found in the *Tripartite Life of St. Patrick*,[1] an eleventh century compilation, as well as in other places. It seems to us that the F preface is older, as it is shorter, than the story as given in the *Tripartite Life*, and that this again is older than the B preface, which is very diffuse.

A few points in the Prefaces call for special comment.

F. l. 1. The statement that Secundinus was called Sechnall by the Gaels, coupled with the fact that no Gaelic name is given for his father Restitutus, suggests that Restitutus was the first of his family who migrated to Ireland. Who 'the Lombards of Letha' were is not certain, but Letha is here probably equivalent to Armorica in Brittany (see p. 179 *infra*).

F. l. 2. *Darerca*.] According to the Four Masters, Sechnall, Bishop of Armagh, son of St. Patrick's sister Darerca, died Nov. 27 A.D. 447 in the seventy-first year of his age. In the Felire of Oengus (Nov. 27; pp. lxxxiii, clxxiii) and elsewhere his mother's name is given as Liamain, who was another of Patrick's sisters. It is possible that these pedigrees are not to be relied on[2]; but nevertheless there does not seem to be any compelling reason for rejecting the tradition that Sechnall, the reputed kinsman of Patrick, and his successor in the See of Armagh, composed this hymn, and that therefore it may be counted as of the fifth century. The miracles that are so abundantly ascribed to Patrick in the later documents, *e.g.* in the vernacular Hymn of St. Fiacc, are conspicuously absent from this; and it is throughout marked by that simplicity and sobriety of tone which characterise the work of a contemporary. It is noticeable that the saint is spoken of throughout in the present tense, except in one or two stanzas when it is said that he shall *hereafter* receive the reward of his labour, thus suggesting that he was alive when the hymn was written. (See lines 20, 25, 91.) It may therefore take rank with the *Confession* and the *Letter to the subjects of Coroticus* as a document of the first importance for the life of St. Patrick. It will be observed that it makes no mention of his Roman mission.

F. l. 4. *Domnach Sechnaill*.]—That is *Dominica Secundini*, or the Church of St. Sechnall, now Dunshaughlin in the co. Meath.

F. l. 8. *nisi quod minime praedicaret caritatem*.]—The reason assigned by Patrick, according to the *Tripartite Life*,[3] for not dwelling on the duty of almsgiving, explains this more clearly:

---

[1] Ed. Whitley Stokes, pp. 243-249. This is the edition of the *Tripartite Life* to which our references are made throughout.
[2] See Olden, *Proceedings R.I.A.* (1894) p. 415.   [3] p. 245.

"If I preached it, I should not leave a yoke of two chariot horses for any one of the saints in this island, present or future; but unto me would be given all that is mine and theirs."

††B. ll. 16, 17. *Conalle Muirthemne* was so called from Conall Cernach of the Red Branch; it corresponded to the modern Co. Louth. *Dal Araide* was in the East of Ulster, extending from Newry in Co. Down to Slemish in Co. Antrim.

F. l. 13. *secundum ordinem alphabeti.*]—That is, *more Hebraeorum*, as the B preface explains. The instances of the alphabetical Psalms and of the Lamentations will at once occur to the reader. The Celtic hymn writers were much inclined to this device: no less than five pieces in the *Liber Hymnorum*, viz. Nos. 1, 2, 14, 25, and 28 are alphabetical, and there are other instances in the *Antiphonary of Bangor*. Two fragmentary alphabetical hymns attributed to St. Hilary of Poitiers are found in an eleventh century MS. of Hilary *De Mysteriis*.[1] A hymn of this sort (in nearly the same metre, see p. xiii above), on the Day of Judgement, "Apparebit repentina dies magna domini," is given by Trench in his *Sacred Latin Poetry* (p. 290); another is printed by Dümmler (in *Mon. Germ. Hist.* i. 79) beginning "Ad perennis uitae fontem et amoena pascua." And Bede has one in his *Eccl. Hist.* (iv. 18). See also the examples cited by Mr. Warren (*Antiphonary of Bangor*, ii. 51, 52.)

F. l. 16. *three places in which there is found 'in' sine sensu, causa rhythmi.*]—These instances of redundant 'in' are probably at ll. 12, 32, 36, the last of which is noted as superfluous by the glossator in B.

F. l. 29. *Everyone who shall recite it at lying down and rising up shall go to heaven.*]—Dr. Lawlor thinks (*Book of Mulling*, p. 157) that this points to a daily use of the hymn in the monastic offices; it does not seem to us that there is sufficient evidence for this. That special indulgences were attached to its recitation was, however, an old belief. In the seventh century part of the *Book of Armagh* (a composite book written in the year 807 by one Ferdomnach[2]), the second of the four petitions granted to Patrick by the angel Victor was "ut quicumque ymnum qui de te compossitus est, in die exitus de corpore cantauerit, tu iudicabis poenitentiam eius de suis peccatis."[3] Again in the same book (fol. 16) there is another passage referring to the use of the hymn which is sufficiently important to be cited in full. "Patricius sanctus episcopus honorem quaternum omnibus monasteriis et aeclessiis per totam Hiberniam debet habere, id est,

    i. Solempnitate dormitationis eius honorari in medio ueris per tres dies et tres noctes omni bono cibo praeter carnem, quasi Patricius uenisset in uita in hostium.

    ii. Offertorium eius proprium in eodem die immolari.

    iii. Ymnum eius per totum tempus cantare.

    iv. Canticum eius scotticum semper canere."[4]

---

[1] See *S. Hilarii Tractatus de mysteriis et Hymni*, &c. ed. Gamurrini (Romae, 1887).
[2] See Graves in *Proc. R. I. A.* lii. p. 316.
[3] See *Tripartite Life*, p. 296. This is alluded to also in the *Book of Lismore*, p. 166. ed. Stokes.
[4] See *Tripartite Life*, p. 333.

Opposite iii. is written in the margin "ymnus Colmán alo," with evident reference to the story given in the B preface and also in the *Tripartite Life* (p. 247) that St. Colmán Ela recited the hymn *Audite omnes* in his refectory thrice. The *canticum scotticum* is probably the Lorica of St. Patrick (our No. 24).

For another reminiscence of the hymn *Audite omnes* in the *Book of Armagh*, see p. 101 infra. It is probable that the words placed in Patrick's mouth in the *Book of Fenagh* (p. 273, ed. Kelly) also allude to it, viz: "Heaven to him who my lay shall have."

F. l. 32. *Its grace shall be on the last three capitula.*]—This indulgence is mentioned not only in the F and B prefaces, but twice in the *Tripartite Life* (pp. 117 and 247), the words in the former of these two passages being: "Every one who shall sing it from *Christus illum* to the end [co dead] . . . his soul shall not go to hell." In the life of St. Canice, as quoted by Colgan (*Trias*, p. 210) there is a story of a man who was saved from demons by reciting the last three stanzas in this way: "nam uir ille tria capitula de hymno S. Patricii ante mortem cantauit . . . et per hoc liberatus est de manibus nostris.'" Dr. Lawlor, in the valuable essay already mentioned (vol. i. p. xxii) on the office sketched at the end of the *Book of Mulling*, has pointed out that instead of the whole hymn of St. Sechnall, the last three stanzas alone are there directed to be sung, "Christus illum conrici dead" being the very phrase employed. And he has further observed that this usage is also adopted in the same office in the case of the hymn *Celebra Iuda* (our No. 3). Another obvious instance of the same practice is supplied by the hymn *Christus in nostra* (our No. 2), which in the *Liber Hymnorum* is represented only by the last three stanzas. Indeed in this case these are the only verses of the hymn that are extant; and it is described simply as $X\overline{ps}$ *in nostra* in the office noted in the Basel Psalter (P) of which some account has been given in our Introduction (vol. i. p. xxvii).[1]

F. l. 34. Eochaid Ua Flannucain was a famous Irish poet who died about the year 1003.

For St. Patrick's four names see below p. 177.

B. l. 71. *sons of life*] i.e. holy men; the same phrase is used in the Preface to the hymn of St. Hilary (see vol. i. p. 35, and vol. ii. p. 18). A few lines further down in this Preface Sechnall speaks of Patrick as a 'son of life,' i e. 'a righteous man.' *Mac bdis* 'a son of death' in like manner means 'a wicked man.' See Kelly's *Book of Fenagh*, p. 309.

B. l. 78. The hymn *Sancti uenite*.] This is the well-known hymn preserved in the *Antiphonary of Bangor* (fol. 10v°), and familiar in its English version by Dr. Neale, "Draw nigh and take the body of the Lord" (Hymns A. and M. 313). Its author is unknown,[3] and it does

---

[1] Compare *Tripartite Life*, p. 247.
[2] See the Preface to the hymn *In te Christe* (Vol. i. p. 84), where it is said that some persons only recited part of that hymn. The reason in this case, however, is peculiar to the *In te Christe*.
[3] The statement in the *Dictionary of Christian Antiquities* (vol. i. p. 806), that the hymn *Sancti uenite* is attributed by Daniel to Eugenius of Toledo is wrong. Daniel knew nothing about the hymn save that he found it in Muratori's edition of the *Bangor Antiphonary*.

not seem to be extant elsewhere; but it is a distinctively Celtic hymn. It is possible that the gloss in B on *v.* 52 of the hymn *Audite omnes* (p. 10), " ut dicitur Christus, hostia et sacerdos " may refer to a phrase in it; but this is quite uncertain.[1] Another English version is that of D. F. MacCarthy printed in Gaffney's *Ancient Irish Church.*

B. l. 120. *The Cruach,* i.e. the mountain now called Croagh Patrick, in Co. Mayo.

Hymn of St. Sechnall.

This famous and ancient hymn in praise of St. Patrick has been printed many times.

(*a*) Colgan printed it in his *Trias Thaumaturga* (1647), p. 211 from F, with tolerable accuracy. He contented himself with giving only the substance of the preface in a Latin translation.

(*b*) Ware printed it at p. 146 of his *Opuscula S. Patricii* (1656) from two MSS. one of which seems to have been a copy of F, if not F itself (see his words, vol. i. p. xiv); the readings of the other do not agree with any MS. known to us. He says of it: " Est et aliud huius hymni exemplar e quo licet manu recentiori exarato uariantes aliquas lectiones ad marginem apponere uisum fuit " (*l.c.* p. 150). According to his printed text, a collation of his principal MS. with T would give: 10 *Petrum* ; 12 *porta*; 18 *usura* ; 23 om. *et* and *dominum* for dei; 31 *sua* for *iusta*; 34 *ridentur* for *uidentur* (the reading of his second MS.); 54 *qui* and *quisquilia*; 55 *flumine* for *fulmine* (the reading of his second MS.) ; 66 *nuptiali*; 67 *haurit* ; 70 *deitatem* ; 75 *putreant* and *escaque* ; 76 *celesti sallientur* ; 81 *elegit* ; 84 *stabuli obsoluit* ; 89 *ac* ; 92 *sanctis* ; *om.* 1–6 at end. And his secondary MS. had in addition to the above: 12 *et inferni portae aduersus eum non preualebunt*; 76 *satiatur*; 84 *zabuli absoluit*. This MS. seems to be quoted by Ussher in his *Religion of the Ancient Irish* ; at any rate the readings of verses 12 and 81 agree with his citations.[2]

(*c*) Muratori printed the hymn from A in his *Anecdota Ambrosiana* (1713) vol. iv. p. 136; this edition has now been superseded by Warren's *Antiphonary of Bangor.*

(*d*) Todd printed it from T and B in his edition of the *Liber Hymnorum* (1855), with notes and dissertations.

Secondary editions are numerous and need not be here mentioned; but it may be noted that the Irish Preface to the hymn in F was first printed in full in Whitley Stokes' *Tripartite Life of St. Patrick* (1887), pp. 242–6.

We have not been able to discover any independent MS. authority for the piece other than that of the four manuscripts TFAB. There is

---

[1] *E.g.*, in Ps. Aug. *Serm.* clv. we have: " Hoc enim hostia et sacerdos. The phrase occurs in Irish (is sacart ocus is edmairt) in a Homily on the Sacraments in the *Leabhar Breac*, translated by E. Hogan in *Todd lectures*, R.I.A., vol. vi. p. 22.
[2] See Ussher's *Works* (ed. Elrington), vol. iv. p. 317ª.

an eighteenth century paper MS. in the Royal Irish Academy collection (ₙ.¹³.), but it is a mere transcript from Colgan, and of no value. Dr. Reeves stated, indeed, in his article on the *Antiphonary of Bangor*,¹ that there was a copy of the hymn in the "Consuetudinary of St. Patrick's Cathedral," a manuscript then in the possession of Dr. Todd and now in the Cambridge University Library (Add. 710). But this was a mistake, as the hymn is absent from that manuscript, as it is from all the service books of the Anglo-Irish, as distinct from the Celtic, Church which have come under our notice.

An English translation by Bishop Graves with references to the scriptural allusions in the hymn, was published in the *Catholic Layman* ii. No. 54 (Decr. 1853); this has been reproduced by Mr. Olden in his *Epistles and Hymn of St. Patrick*. Another English version is given in O'Laverty's *Diocese of Down and Connor*, vol. i. p. 120.

2 *Patricii*] i.e. *patris ciuium* T i.e. *qui sedet ad latus regis, uel pater ciuium ; Patricius the name of a grade amongst Romans, qui Patricium regit B.*

The explanation *pater ciuium*, as Dr. Wh. Stokes points out,² is probably suggested by the passage from Isidore (Etym. ix. 3): "Patricii inde uocati sunt, pro eo quod sicut patres filiis, ita prouideant reipublicae." Both this and the alternative *qui sedet ad latus regis* are found in Cormac's *Glossary* (p. 35).

3 *simulatur*] *similio* i.e. *I compare B.*
6 *clara*] i.e. *wonderful B.*
inter] i.e. *before men B.*

8 *magnificant*] There is an obvious reference to Mt. v. 16; and it is noteworthy that the text familiar to the writer must have had "*magnificent* patrem uestrum qui in caelis est," the Hieronymian text being *glorificent*. *Magnificent* is read by two Vulgate manuscripts, F and R (in Bp. Wordsworth's notation), which retain traces of Old Latin influence ; it is also the reading of the Old Latin texts cited in critical editions as *ab*. It is natural enough, if we adopt the view that our hymn is a fifth century composition, that its Scriptural allusions should indicate the use of a prae-Hieronymian version of the Bible. In any case, however, the Latin version of the New Testament current in Ireland all through the Middle Ages, though in the main Vulgate, retains traces of Old Latin "mixture"; and we shall find many instances of this phenomenon in the texts cited in the *Liber Hymnorum*.

10] *Petrus*. The manuscript evidence compels us to read *Petrus*, not *Petrum*, which seems more natural. The Latinity of this stanza is peculiar, and the meaning is not quite clear. Dr. Todd takes *cuius* in l. 11 to refer to *ecclesia*, and *aduersus* as equivalent to *aduersitates;* but this does not commend itself to us. The writers of the Preface probably had in their minds l. 12 as one of the three passages where there is a redundant 'in' (see p. 4); but *in* is required by the metre. Taking *aduersus* adverbially, we may translate : "Like Peter on whom the church is built ; and his apostleship he received from God, and against

¹ *Ulster Journal of Archaeology*, 1853. ² *Trip. Life*, p. 370.

his [Church] the gates of hell do not prevail." The B glossator seems to take *ut Petrus* with *fide immobilis*, in this way.

The gloss in B, "Petrus agnoscens", agrees as do many like glosses in the text, with the explanation furnished in Jerome's *De nominibus Hebraicis*. St. Jerome was widely read in Ireland; his works were consulted, for instance, by Oengus the Culdee, and he is quoted frequently and with respect in Irish books and by Irish writers. Columbanus in his letter to Gregory the Great goes so far as to say that the man who contradicts the authority of Jerome will be looked on as a heretic, and rejected with scorn by the Churches of the West. His Irish name was *Cirine*.

The interpretation of Mt. xvi. 18 suggested in the gloss is the usual interpretation with Irish writers.[1] A remarkable paraphrase of the verse occurs in a vernacular Tract on the Liturgy in the *Leabhar Breac*[2]: "that is, upon the firmness of the faith of the first martyrs who were laid in the foundation of the building and of the last martyrs up to Elijah and Enoch."

13 *barbaras nationes ut piscaret, &c.*] This verse was evidently familiar to Muirchu Maccu Mactheni, the seventh century author of the notes in the *Book of Armagh* (fol. 2): "dicens ei adesse tempus ut ueniret et aeuangelico rete nationes feras et barbaras ad quas docendas misserat illum deus ut piscaret." The metaphor ultimately rests, of course, on Mt. iv. 19. In St. Patrick's *Confessio* this last verse is quoted, with the comment: "Unde autem ualde oportebat retia nostra tendere, ita ut multitudo copiosa et turba Deo caperetur," &c.

19 *nauigi*] *i.e. of this voyage of the Church B. The sea is the present life, the ship is the Church, the pilot is a teacher who brings it to a harbour of life, the harbour of life is uita perpetua B=9.*

22 *praebet*] *i.e. preaching and teaching B.*

24 *dictis*] *i.e. by preaching B.*

28 *ducatum*] *i.e. a uerbo duco duxi—dux, ducis,—and thence it makes duco, ducas,—ducatus its passive participle: ducatus further is a noun substantive in form of a participle, of the fourth declension, and it is that which is here B.*

The word is used in the sense of 'guidance,' 'safe conduct.'

31 *stigmata*] *i.e. the relics, &c. B.*

32 *sustentans*] *i.e. he supports T.*

in cruce] *i.e. on the Cross of the Passion B.*

33 *impiger*] *i.e. active B.*

34 *uidentur*] *i.e. in fellowship with Christ B.*

36 The gloss in B notes that the 'in' is superfluous here; but the metre requires it, for *cuius* is a disyllable.

36 *manna*] *i.e. on increase T.*

37 *ob*] *i.e. for B.*

38 The B gloss notes that *que* is redundant here. It is worth observing

---

[1] See Olden, *Church of Ireland*, p. 83.
[2] See *Irish Eccl. Record*, vol. ii. p. 170, or McCarthy, *The Stowe Missal* (Trans. R.I.A. xxvii. vii. 259).

that the enclitic *que* is very commonly used in this hymn and in the *Altus Prosator*, but rarely in the other pieces.

41, 42 The *Etymologion* of S. Isidore of Seville, from which the glosses here are taken, was one of the ordinary text books of the middle ages. Isidore, the "doctor egregius Hispaniae" was perhaps the most learned ecclesiastic of the seventh century, and enjoyed a wide reputation in the schools of Europe. He is counted by Dante as one of the first set of twelve 'blessed saints' in the Tenth Canto of the *Paradiso*.

lumen] The gloss seems to suggest that Patrick shone with a light not his own (*lumen*), but derived from Christ, who is the true *lux mundi*.

42 Observe that the gloss recognises the reading *toto*, now only found in A, as the form adopted *secundum ueteres*.

46 *adimplet*] i.e. *that person; ut de Gregorio dictum est, "Implebat actu quicquid sermone docebat," sic Patricio contigit B.*

The verse quoted is from the epitaph on the tomb of St. Gregory. See Bede's *Eccl. Hist.* ii. 1.

48 *mundoque*] i.e. *in the pure heart B.* The reading of A, *praecedit*, 'excels' is probably the right one.

49 *audenter*] i.e. *boldly B.*

52 *hostia et sacerdos.* See note p. 99 above.

54 *mensam*] i.e. *by measure T.* That is, the glossator understands *mensam* as if it were *mensuram*. But *mensam* is probably used for the Lord's Table. Reading *qui* at the beginning of the line, we may translate: "He despises all the glory of the world for the sake of the divine law, and in comparison with His Table he counts all things as chaff."

ciscilia] . . . *ciscilia sunt purgamenta frumenti, i.e. chaff* T in the left margin. In the right margin of T we have the obscure gloss: "*ciscilium i.e.* broth *or* brothscoa *i.e. the* . . . *which the sea* [*drives*] *to the land.* Or cis cannán, *i.e.* . . . *of Cormac Ua Cuinn. Cannan nomen eius, and it is of this that it was formed, vis. of the* cil-cais *which was on the belly of the animal that was killed there. Or ciscilium, i.e. eyelid, i.e. cilium is the fringe of the eyelid: cis-cilium the hair that sticks on it* [*and brings it*] *down, et quod uerius est. But whichever of these it be, it is all the same to Patrick in comparatione diuinae legis.*"

Ambrosius dicit supercilium .i. super abundantia ; cilon uerbum Graecum quod interpretatur abundantia is the gloss in B. We cannot find the passage in Ambrose to which the glossator refers. *Cilon* is apparently meant for χιλιῶν, *a thousand*.

55 *ingruenti*] i.e. *from the resounding or very heavy thunderbolt B.*

59 *pascere*] i.e. *he used to satisfy B.*

60 The reading *tradit* of A is certainly right, as agreeing better with the metre, and also with the usage of the author, who consistently uses the present tense of the deeds of Patrick.

63 *annonam*] i.e. *provision, i.e. ab hora nona dicta T.*

65 The glossator in B has misunderstood the allusion in this stanza, which is evidently to the parable of the Marriage Feast in Mt. xxii.

67 *uinum*] The glossator in B again seems to mistake the meaning. The 'uinum' is plainly the wine of the eucharist, as the *spirituale poculum* of the next line is the Chalice.

The phraseology is interesting as pointing to Communion in both kinds as the practice of the early Celtic Church. Ussher in his *Religion of the Ancient Irish* (p. 279) is at pains to defend this from objectors by an appeal to the Fathers, and he has collected a host of references bearing on the point. The general question, however, need not now be argued. Bellarmine (*de Euch.* iv, 4) admits that the giving of the cup to the laity was the primitive custom, and the Council of Trent (*Sess.* 21, ch. 2), laid down practically the same doctrine. It was not indeed until the Council of Constance in 1415 that communion in one kind was declared to be the law of the Latin Church. However a few references illustrating the usage of Celtic Christendom may be adduced. There is a postcommon in the Corpus Missal (fol. 57v°) and in the Rosslyn Missal (fol. 4v°) with the opening words : " Refecti cibo potuque celesti, &c., Deus, ut ab hostium defendas formidine quos redemisti pretioso sanguine tui Filii Domini nostri." Again in the vernacular Homilies in the *Leabhar Breac* we have frequent reference to the giving of the cup to the laity, e.g. "those who are most faithful among the people, after receiving the Body and Blood of Christ, &c."[1] and also "that the partaking thereof might not be deemed terror-causing by the faithful, and lest infidels should charge them with partaking of the blood and flesh of a man."[2] Dr. Wh. Stokes has collected a number of instances from the *Book of Lismore*,[3] and Mr. Warren has given many others.[4] It may be observed, however, that the hymn *Sancti uenite*, the language of which is often cited in this connexion, is not altogether relevant ; for according to its title it was to be sung " quando communicarent *sacerdotes*," and so it gives no evidence as to the communion of the laity, although it shows that the practice of the celebrant alone communicating in both kinds was not customary.

68 *propinnansque*] *i.e. that which he used to distribute T.*

The reference in the B gloss is to the grammatical works of Eutychius (saec. vi); there is a fragment of his work in Irish handwriting with Irish glosses in the Paris MS. Bibl. Nat. Lat. 11411.

72 *Israel*] *Israel at one time is disyllabic et 'uir pugnans cum deo' interpretatur ; at another time it is trisyllabic and means "uir uidens deum" B.*

The latter interpretation comes from Jerome[5] and, as Dr. Todd points out, rests on the erroneous derivation of Israel from איש ראה אל. It is found also among the Irish notes on the Pauline Epistles known as the *Würzburg Glosses*, which have been edited by Dr. Wh. Stokes for the Philological Society. Thus on the words *et super Israhel dei* in Gal. vi. 16 the gloss is *i. sanctos uidentes deum, &c.*

[1] Atkinson, *Passions and Homilies*, p. 456, cf. also p. 498.
[2] Hogan, *Todd Lectures*, vi. p. 19. See on the same subject McCarthy, *Stowe Missal*, p. 258.
[3] p. cvii.
[4] *Liturgy and Ritual of the Celtic Church*, p. 134. Compare also Dowden's *Celtic Church of Scotland*, p. 239.
[5] From the *De interpr. nominum*; and the same explanation is found in Jerome's translation of Didymus *de Spiritu Sancto*, p. 151.

73 *fidelis*] i.e. *faithful* B.
74 *condita*] i.e. *salted, a uerbo condio, condis, of the fourth conjugation* TB.
75 *putrent*] i.e. *a uerbo putro, of the first conjugation* B.
essæque] i.e. *chewed* T i.e. *essus a uerbo 'edo' et 'edor' its passive ; essum et essus its passive participle, and distinction of gender in it, i.e. essus essa essum* B.
76 The allusion seems to be to Mc. ix. 49 and Col. iv. 6.
80 *arat*] i.e. *he ploughs* T.
81 *uicarius*] i.e. *steward or tax-collector or 'coarb,' for this is what Jerome says in Epistola de gradibus Romanorum ; that the 'uicarius' is a man who is next to a 'comes' over the city, though he does not come in comitatu cum rege ; 'uicarius' of God is he* T.
i.e. '*coarb*,' *quia Hieronymus dicit in Epistola de gradibus Romanorum, that the 'uicarius' is the man who is next to the 'comes' over the city while the 'comes' goes* (?) *to the king. The 'rex' is God, the 'comes' is Christ, the 'uicarius' is Patrick. 'Uicus' is* fich *i.e. place, so that 'uicus' makes 'uicarius'* B.
We have not been able to identify the passage from Jerome here cited by the scholiasts. It is possible that the letter referred to is the spurious *Epistola de septem ordinibus ecclesiae* (Migne P.L., xxx. 148); but it does not seem to mention the titles *uicarius* and *comes*.
84 The spelling *zabulus* for *diabolus* is not uncommon, and many instances might be given from Irish manuscripts. The interchange of *s* and *st*, of which we have an instance here in F which reads *stabuli*, is worth observing. We have it again in the hymn *Celebra Iuda* at l. 31, where our MSS. read *euangelizæ* for *euangelistæ* and at l. 35 *Zefani* for *Stephani*, and in the Preface to the *Benedictus* (vol. i. p. 57) where we have *Stacharias* for *Zacharias* and *Elistabeth* for *Elizabeth*.
obsoluit] The gloss in B *comdenmach* is perhaps for *cain-denmach*, 'beneficent.'
86 *tractat*] i.e. *he sets in motion psalms and hymns and apocalypse, to build up God's people* B.
Todd read the last words of this gloss as *popuil trine* or 'the people of the Trinity'; but we think that the true reading is simply *popuil de*.
The line is almost identical with l. 25 of Fiacc's hymn; and although, the glossator at that place explains the "hymns" differently, it is tolerably certain that the canticles must be meant. So the notes in the *Book of Armagh* by Muirchu Maccu Machteni have[1]: "omnes psalmos et apocalipsin Iohannis et *omnia kantica spiritalia scripturarum* cotidie decantans."[2]
Mr. Macgregor (*Early Scottish Worship*, p. 25) suggests that by "the Apocalypse" is here meant the *Ter Sanctus*, and the suggestion seems reasonable. See l. 133 of the *Altus* of St. Columba and l. 25 of Fiacc's hymn in praise of St. Patrick.

---

[1] At fol. 7.
[2] See also the *Leabhar Breac Homily on St. Patrick*, in *Trip. Life*, p. 485.

87 *quam*] viz. *a great thing, who believes legem sacri nominis quod est Trinitas TB.*

88, 89 There is a precision of doctrinal statement here, which indicates at least that the Christological controversies of the fourth and fifth centuries left their mark on the language of Celtic Christendom.

89 *praecinctus*] i.e. *girt round B.*

90 *sine intermissione*] *Augustinus dicit, Si quis in unaquaque hora certa tempora orandi obseruat, sine intermissione orat*; i.e. *celebration of each canonical hour T.*

A similar interpretation of St. Paul's precept is found in the Irish writer Sedulius (*in Ep. ad Romanos* ed. Migne col. 16). "Aut ergo dicendum est eum semper orare et non deficere, qui canonicis orationibus quotidie iuxta ritum ecclesiasticae traditionis, psalmodiis precibusque consuetis, Dominum laudare et rogare non desistit. Et hoc est quod Psalmista dicebat, *Benedicam Dominum in omni tempore, semper laus eius in ore meo* (Ps. xxxiii. 2)."

This is rejected, however, by the writer of the Würzburg Glosses, already referred to. He notes (ed. Stokes, p. 315) "What may be the prayer without ceasing? Not hard. Dicunt alii that it is celebration of the canonical hour quod non est uerum &c." It is also rejected in the Benedictine Rule,[1] which observes : " nobis uero non expedit caeteris horis ab oratione uacare."

92 *cum apostolis regnabit sanctus super Israel.* The gloss in B gives the legend which grew out of this verse in later years, viz. *regnabit Patricius super Scotos in die iudicii.* We also find it in Fiacc's hymn v. 52. "Around thee in the day of the Judgement, the men of Ireland will go to Doom." In Muirchu Maccu Mactheni's notes in the Book of Armagh, the *quarta petitio* which the Angel granted to Patrick is "ut Hibernenses omnes in die iudicii a te iudicentur."[2] The legend indeed became very widespread, and reappears in many places; e.g. in the Second Vision of Adamnan[3] at § 6 we have: "It is Patrick who will be their judge and their advocate on Doomsday." So in the *Secreta* in the Corpus and Rosslyn Missals[4] we find an allusion to the same belief: " Hostias tibi quas in honore sancti Patricii offerimus deuotus accipias, ut nos a timore iudicii liberemur."

93 *Audite omnes*, the opening words of the hymn, are added at the close according to the regular Irish practice of which many examples will meet us as we proceed. Mone (*Hymni Latini medii aeui* iii. 242) remarks that this custom is sometimes adopted by German hymn writers. It was probably invented for the purpose of clearly marking the point at which one piece ended and another began, not always obvious of itself in manuscripts written closely and continuously with a view to the economising of parchment. Mone adds that there seems to have been a special tendency among Irish hymn writers to begin their hymns with the word 'Audite.'

The *apparatus criticus* shows that the three antiphons appended to

---

[1] Migne, P.L. clii. 621.
[2] *Revue Celtique*, vol. xii. 420.
[3] See *Trip. Life*, pp. 296, 477.
[4] See Warren, *Celtic Liturgy*, &c., p. 271.

the hymn vary in our manuscripts. The first antiphon in TB is Ps. cxi. 7. The second calls for no comment. The third, which is not found in AB, has reference to the story told by St. Patrick himself in his *Confessio*,[1] of a vision he had in the night when in Britain and of voices which seemed to say to him " Rogamus te, sancte puer, ut uenias et adhuc ambules inter nos." The story is told, with embellishments, by all his biographers ; a strange and extravagant form of it is given in the notes to Fiacc's hymn at l. 16. See *infra* p. 180.[2]

It will be observed that the regular practice of the *Liber Hymnorum* is that antiphons, written by the scribes in pointed handwriting of a different character from that employed for the text, are appended to each of the Latin hymns, and also to some of the vernacular pieces.

vol. i. p. 13.] We have not been able to identify with any known document the half illegible notes written in the margins of fol. 2 of the Trinity College MS. It will be seen that the majority of these notes, which occur on every page up to fol. 22, do not seem to have any bearing on the text; they are memoranda entered in the margins either by the original scribes, or—as seems more probable—by some early owner of the book. For the most part they are extracted from well-known authors, such as Augustine, Gregory the Great, Isidore of Seville, or Hraban Maur. When no reference is given in the text, it may be assumed that we have not been able to identify the piece.

THE HYMN *CHRISTUS IN NOSTRA*.

This is possibly a fragment of an alphabetical hymn, of which all save the last three stanzas has been lost, these last three being preserved owing to the belief (see p. 98 *supra*) that the recitation of these was equal in efficacy to the recitation of the whole. It is evident that the lines beginning *Audite uirginis laudes*, despite the statement of the compiler of the preface, are from a different composition, inasmuch as the metre is quite dissimilar; indeed Ware[3] distinguishes expressly the hymn *Christus in nostra* from the hymn *Audite uirginis laudes*.

We have noted already (vol. i, p. xxvii) the mention of the hymn *Christus in nostra* in the early office sketched on one of the leaves of the Basel Psalter (P). See above p. xxx.

This hymn was printed from F by Colgan (*Trias*, p. 542), who pointed out that it was found at the end of St. Ultan's Life of St. Brigid. He mentions several manuscripts of this Life to which he had access, among them (1) at the monastery of St. Magnus at Ratisbon, in Irish handwriting ; this, he notes, though it gave the hymn, had no antiphon at the end ; (2) a manuscript belonging to the monastery of St. Autbert at Cambray ; (3) one belonging to a monastery in the co. Longford. We have failed to trace any of these ; and in addition to T and F can only produce one other manuscript (V) as authority for our text, a

---

[1] See *Trip. Life*, p. 364.
[2] Compare the legend in the *Book of Lismore*, p. 155, 6.
[3] *Writers*, &c., I. p. 13.

manuscript which though now at the Vatican was originally at Heidelberg.

Of the three persons named in the Preface as possible authors of the piece, a word or two only can be said here.

Ninnid, when a young scholar, so say the later lives of Brigid,[1] came under the favourable notice of the saint, who predicted that she herself, on the day of her death, should receive the viaticum at his hands. On hearing this the youth enclosed his right hand in a locked case, lest it should ever be defiled by the touch of any unclean thing; and so he was known as Ninnid 'Purehand.'

Fiacc of Sletty we shall meet with again as the reputed author of a famous hymn (our No. 19). He died before Brigid.

Ultan of Ardbreccan in the co. Meath, the author whose claims Colgan favours, is also named as the composer of the Irish hymn No. 21 in praise of St. Brigid. All that it seems possible to say with confidence is that the statement in the Preface, that he was one of St. Brigid's biographers, rests on early tradition. He is reputed to have died A.D. 656, and his name lingers in Irish topography, in the form "Cahir Ultan." There is a Latin poem in praise of him, beginning *Fama citat*, &c., printed in Dümmler, *Poet. lat. medii aeui*, i. p. 589.

The words *tria rithim noscarda* in l. 5 of the F Preface are rendered by Colgan *ad imitationem rithmi Noscarii*; but *oscarda* means 'renowned' or 'well-known.' See *Silva Gad.* 124, 21; M.R. 216, 18; *Oss. Soc.* iv. 152.

8 *similem*] i.e. *for Brigid is the Mary of the Gaels* T. This curious statement is frequently met with in panegyrics of St. Brigid. The mediæval Irish were fond of tracing parallels between their own saints and those of the N.T. and the early Christian centuries; but in no case is this parallelism pushed to such extravagant lengths as in the case of St. Brigid. Thus (see p. 39 above) in hymn No. 21, l. 12, she is addressed as "Mother of Jesus"; and again at the beginning of hymn No. 22 (p. 40), she is invoked as "Brigid, mother of my high King."

Dr. Todd[2] quotes a remarkable office of St. Brigid, printed as late as 1622, in which a modified form of the legend, that she had a strong personal resemblance to the BVM, is reproduced. This legend is given by several of the mediæval authorities.[3]

It will be observed that the two strongest expressions in the text of the piece, viz., in l. 8 *Mariæ sanctæ similem* and in l. 15 *Christi matrem se spopondit* are erased in the Vatican manuscript.

13 *laudes*] *uel iura, that is the right reading, in order that it should correspond to 'merita' below* T.

sancta] i.e. *Brigid* T.

14 *perfectionem*] *this should be the proper [order] in the line, viz. perfectionem promisit quam uiriliter implebit* T.

15 *dictis*] *this also should be 'dictis atque factis fecit'* T.

---

[1] Colgan, *Trias*, p. 359.
[2] *Liber Hymnorum*, p. 68.
[3] See *Book of Lismore*, pp. 186, 120.

This is the reading of F.

16 This line is no true part of the verse; it is probably an explanatory gloss on *sancta* of the following line which has crept into the text. Lines 13-16 do not, in short, constitute a stanza at all. The T glossator was evidently conscious that there are metrical impossibilities in the lines as they stand.

Preface to the Hymn of St. Cummain the Tall.

We do not know of any manuscripts which contain this hymn, save T and F. It is alluded to (see vol. i. p. xxv) in the office sketched in the Second Vision of Adamnan and the Book of Mulling; which proves that it was well-known before the ninth century at least. It has been printed with its preface by Todd (*Liber Hymnorum*, p. 72), and also by Malone in his *Church History of Ireland* (vol. ii. p. 273), and in Moran's *Irish Church* (p. 87).

St. Cummain the Tall,¹ to whom the authorship is ascribed in the Preface, was born, according to the chronologies, in 590 and died in 661 or 662. He is commemorated on Nov. 12, in the Martyrologies of Gorman and of Donegal; in the latter book being described as "the blessed preacher of the word of God," and being compared for his way of life to Gregory the Great. He was bishop of Clonfert, and the name survives in local tradition, Kilcummin or the Church of Cummain being the name of a townland in the parish of Tirawley, co. Mayo. The author of a letter to Seghine, fifth Abbot of Iona, on the Paschal question (see Migne P.L. lxxxvii. 969) is a different person.

The shocking story recorded in the Preface as to the manner of his birth is not without parallel in the *Vitae Sanctorum;* and it is far from improbable, as Todd remarks, that a child so born should be dedicated from his infancy to a religious life.² For the genealogies of the various persons mentioned in the Preface we must refer the curious reader to Dr. Todd's learned notes.

l. 5. *Ita's Cell*] now Killeedy in the co. Limerick. The reputed date of St. Ita's death is 569; there is nothing in the narrative which implies that she was alive in Cummain's lifetime.

l. 11. *Ita's coarb*] The 'coarb' (*comarba*) of a monastery was its hereditary head; each religious house was like a spiritual clan, the abbot being the heir of the original founder. He might be either a bishop or a presbyter, according to circumstances; in the Columban houses he was always a presbyter, in memory of the fact that St. Columba himself never became a bishop. But a monastery often had attached to it a resident bishop, for the purpose of conferring orders and consecrating churches, &c.

l. 12. *sinum abbatissae*] *sinum* is a *churn*, or wooden drinking-vessel.

l. 15. *Notice not*] *na rathaig*. According to Todd the repetition

---

¹ So called to distinguish him from St. Cummain the Fair, seventh Abbot of Iona. See Olden, *Church of Ireland*, p. 125.

of these words is necessary for the metre. But this is not accurate, and there is no good reason for such repetition here.

l. 20. *Eoganacht of Loch Lein*] So the *Martyrology of Gorman* at Nov. 12. Loch Lein is the principal Lake of Killarney. *Eoganacht* was the tribe name of the descendants of Eogan Mor, king of Munster in the second century.

l. 35. *upon thee, O Fiachna, &c.*] These words are a gloss, although the copyist of the Preface does not seem to have understood them so. The omission in T of the initial F in Fiachna, as, a little lower down, of the initial letter of Flann, is very common with Irish scribes.

l. 47. *soul friend*] *anmchara*, the ordinary Irish word for a confessor, or spiritual director.

l. 48. *Columcille*] St. Columba died in 597, so that the chronology seems confused. It is possible, however, that when Columcille is mentioned, it is his *coarb* or successor that is meant, who inherited his privileges and was regarded as speaking in his name.

l. 47. *eastward*] *i.e.* to Iona, the seat of St. Columba's famous monastery. In the quatrain ascribed to Columba, there is a play on the word *cummain*, which means 'communion.'

l. 61. *Domnall refuses it, &c.*] These verses, Todd says, "seem to allude to the ancient custom of putting on the raiment of the saint who acted as your penitentiary, in token of submission and humiliation. This, it seems, Domnall refused to do." (*l.c.* p. 83.) But, in truth, the lines are not grammatically explicable; *na gab* ought to mean 'do not take.' Perhaps ll. 57-64 are an interpolation; at any rate the story is more intelligible in their absence.

l. 72. *Daire Calcaig*] *i.e.* 'the oak wood of Calgagh' = roboretum Calgachi (Adamnan *Vita Columbae* i. 2, where see Fowler's note.) This was the old name of Derry, and was superseded by the name *Daire Coluimcille* in the tenth or eleventh century.

The Hymn of St. Cummain the Tall.

1 The opening words of this hymn are, as the Preface observes, borrowed from Nahum i. 15. The glossator in T who says *necessitas metri put here Iuda instead of Iudea* was, seemingly, ignorant of this reference. F has no glosses on this hymn.

2 The repetition of *alleluia* after each stanza (it is apparently only through inadvertence that it is omitted after the first stanza in T) is a device which is found in two hymns in the *Bangor Antiphonary*; the first, "Precamur patrem," being, like that now under consideration, a hymn in praise of the Apostles, the other a hymn for Feasts of Martyrs beginning "Sacratissimi martyres."

3 *clauiculari*] *unde deriuatur hoc nomen? Not hard: from the word 'clauis'; from it (is made) clauicula; 'ris' (is added) to it, so that it makes clauicularis; from this 's' (is dropped) and 'us' (appended) to it, so that it makes of it 'clauicularius,' and its presence here is fitting, quod dixit Christus, &c.*

3 *Petri*] The order in which the Apostles are mentioned follows that of St. Matth. x, the place of Judas Iscariot being supplied by St. Paul, whose name is put immediately after that of St. Peter. This is the regular Gregorian order; it is also found on the Ardagh Chalice. The names which follow Simon Zelotes, viz. Matthias, Mark, Luke, Patrick, Stephen, also (with the exception of Patrick) follow in this order the names of the Apostles in the invocation in the Royal MS. 2. A. xx in the British Museum, printed by Mr. Warren in the Appendix to his *Antiphonary of Bangor*.[1] The list given in Harl. MS. 7653 should also be compared with that in this hymn. For the number of names commemorated see note on l. 37.

6 *alleluia*] *at the end of each (verse is Alleluia, which) interpretatur, &c.* We have not been able to trace the Latin words of this marginal note to any author.

8 *aduocamina*] *i.e. the invocations or the assistances.*

10 *scammate*] *i.e. in the battlefield, or in the combat.* The word is used by Tertullian *ad Mart.* 3.

11 ff. The glossator's interpretations of the Apostles' names, derived for the most part from Jerome, are also given, though with much confusion, in the invocation in the MS. Reg. 2. A. xx already mentioned.

12 *accumbebat*] *in Cannan Galilea.* The glossator seems to allude to the tradition that St. John was the bridegroom at the marriage of Cana of Galilee. It is not certain that this is implied in the words of the hymn itself.

13 *oris*] *i.e. os lampadis interpretatur i.e. for his knowledge and for the excellence of his utterance.*

Pilippi] *i.e. of deacon Philip that, and Cummain enumerates him inter apostolos; qui in Hierapolis ciuitate sepultus est; &c.*

The glossator here confounds Philip the Apostle with Philip the Evangelist, as does also Eusebius in his *Eccl. Hist.* iii. 31. By Eusebius as in the gloss on *prole*, only three daughters of Philip are mentioned, although four are spoken of in Acts xxi. 9. There is an Irish "Passion of the Apostle Philip" in the *Leabhar Breac*,[2] which tells of his stoning and crucifixion at Hierapolis.

15 *impendamus*] *i.e. let us give preces.*

16 *nati*] *i.e. it is the Son of God in truth who stays the waters in the clouds; according to the (mystical) sense the waters are the teachings, and the clouds are the teachers. Niul* cannot be right, for *it e* absolutely demands the nom. pl.; and we have translated accordingly.

19 *fiscali*] *i.e. the treasure chest* (?), *quia fiscus inuenitur; i.e. . . . . fiscalis uel fiscalis cista, ... a chest, viz. he collected taxes for the King of the world.*

We have printed in vol. i. the read ng (*no*) *feda*(*d*) *cista*, 'he used to bear a chest,' given by Stokes in emendation of Todd's *no feda cista* 'a wooden chest'; but we are not satisfied with it. Further the word *main* is not fully legible.

---

[1] Vol. ii. p. 91.   [2] See Atkinson, *Passions and Homilies*, p. 356.

By "the king of the world" the Roman Emperor is, of course, meant.

21 *Iacobi cominus*] *i.e. a mark of definition on him (as compared) with the first James*. Another explanation of *cominus* is suggested in the next gloss, viz., *Christo*. The construction is obscure; probably we should understand *prece* before *alterius* and translate: "let us ask the prayer of James to be near to us aided by the prayer of the other James."

22 *subnixi*] *i.e. later he came to Christ quam prædictus, and they were clubbed in Jerusalem*.

It is not clear whether we should read *sund* (Todd) or *suind* (Stokes). Possibly *o sund* should be read for the pl. *tuarcain o sund* is common enough; and *ra·gab·sat i n-a chend di* means 'they struck him on the head with it' (*Hom-Pass.* 3299).

23 The gloss on *Tathei* confuses (*cf.* Jerome *in Matth.* x. 4) the Thaddaeus of the Abgar legend, whom Eusebius (H. E. i, 13) describes as 'one of the Seventy' with Thaddaeus the apostle; a blunder which we shall meet with again in a gloss on the letter of Christ to Abgar. See, on the whole subject, p. 173 *infra*, and the references there given.

tellura] *i.e. over the corners of the earth, for that indeed is the way in which he writes, et sic scribitur recte per tellura i.e. rura*. *Talmannaib* is from the adj. *talmanda* 'terrestrial' (*Hom-Pass.* 5857, 5878, 5895); and *uillib* means 'angles, corners,' as in *Hom-Pass.* 3728. Cf. Apoc. vii. 1. 'super quatuor *angulos terrae*.'

24 *epistola*] The words 'Beatus es' in the gloss are the opening words of the reputed letter of our Saviour to Abgar, King of Edessa. which is found in our collection (No. 18); see the notes upon it below. The legend that its bearer was one 'Ananias cursor' is as old as Eusebius (H.E. i. 13), to the Latin translation of whose history by Rufinus there is no doubt a reference at the end of the gloss: "ut historia ecclesiastica narrat."

25 *suapte*] *in sua regione uel sua ciuitate, and a syllable is extra here, viz. -pte*. This gloss, like that on *Abgoro* in the preceding line, has been curiously misread by former editors.

27 *Madianus* that is Matthias; his name often appears thus in the Irish texts.

28 *locemur*] *i.e. let us be assembled*.

31 *euangelizæ* i.e. euangelistæ. For this interchange of *z* and *st*, see above p. 104.

37 *bina septim*] *i.e. fourteen, viz. the twelve apostles with Paul and Stephen, quamuis non est apostolus. It may not have been Cummain who put Mark and Luke here. Or, if it be he that put them, it is 'octo ualida' that is right in the line*.

The end of the gloss shows that the F variant, *octo* for *septem*, was current in the time of the glossator, and that there was some doubt as to which was the true reading. It is plain that the difference between .uii. and .uiii. is very slight, and that a confusion might easily arise. There is difficulty whichever we adopt, for seventeen names are mentioned in all. Todd suggests that *septem* is the true reading, and that the 'twice seven' are the fourteen *Apostles*, viz. the Twelve, St. Paul and St. Patrick.

It seems to us, however, that *octo* is certainly the reading of the original text. Without Patrick there are 16 names invoked, and an inspection of the hymn will disclose the fact that there is nothing specifically Celtic about the subject matter, save the invocation of St. Patrick. Further ll. 33, 34 break the sequence of construction; *Marci annuntiantis, Lucae sequentis, Stephani rogantis*, are all dependent on *suffragia* of l. 37. It is therefore certain that the stanza which brings Patrick in is an after-thought, or a supplement introduced when the hymn became popular in Ireland.

The glossator, as usual, is only guessing.

40 *propugnacula*] *i.e. as if it were through ramparts or battlements.*

It will be remembered that the antiphon "exaudi nos" which follows this hymn in the manuscripts, is prescribed for recitation after it in the directory for a monastic service in the Book of Mulling, of which we have given an account in our Introduction (vol. i, p. xxii).

The note in the upper margin of fol. 4 is, for the most part, as will be seen from the references given at foot of page 21 (vol. i), a catena of passages from Latin authors dealing with the primacy of Peter. Hraban Maur (786-856), who is cited here and in other marginal notes in the *Liber Hymnorum*, seems to have been well known in Ireland, as indeed he was all over Europe. In the library at St. Gall there are several MSS. of his works. The "four points of observance at celebrating Easter," given in the Passion of Christ in the *Leabhar Breac*,[1] seem to be derived from Hraban. See Migne P. L., cviii. col. 641.

THE HYMN OF ST. MUGINT.

The Preface need not detain us long, although the full discussion of all the genealogical problems which it suggests would extend over many pages. We must refer our readers to the investigation of these obscure points printed by Dr. Todd.[2]

It is plain at the outset that whatever may be the historical worth of the legend given in the Preface, it has little to say to the hymn. The writer of the Preface, as would appear from the alternative explanations which he gives of the authorship, had not even a consistent tradition to guide him. It is likely that the authorship of St. Mugint was neither better nor worse authenticated than the authorship of Ambrose or of David.

St. Mugint himself is a saint of whom little is known. There is a Welsh St. Meugan who may be the same person; or again Todd may be right in identifying him with one Nennio or Moinenn or Mancend, whose name appears under various forms. At any rate he is described as a tutor of St. Finnian of Moville in the co. Down, which would fix

---

[1] Atkinson, *Passions and Homilies*, p. 387.   [2] *Liber Hymnorum*, p. 97 ff.

the date of the story in the Preface at the beginning of the sixth century. Futerna, the scene of the transaction, is almost certainly Whitherne in Galloway, where there was a large monastic establishment, the celebrated *Candida Casa*, founded by St. Ninian.[1] Rioc, whom legend counts a daughter of Darerca, Patrick's sister (see p. 96 above) is celebrated in the Martyrology of Gorman on August 1.

In the life of St. Frigidianus of Lucca,[2] who is often identified with St. Finnian of Moville, there is a somewhat similar story told of Mugint. No mention is made of Drusticc or Rioc or Talmach; but it is said that Mugint becoming jealous of Finnian's popularity as a teacher, laid a snare for him, which ended in his receiving himself the wound intended for his pupil. And so he said *Parce domine, parce populo tuo, et ne des hæreditatem tuam in opprobrium*. This story is evidently to be traced back to the same source as our Preface.

This hymn, or more properly prayer, seems from internal evidence to have been put together on the occasion of some plague or other visitation of evil by which some monastery or city was afflicted. There is nothing in it which in any way bears out the legend connecting its composition with St. Mugint given in the Preface; nor is there any trace of distinctively Celtic belief. The piece, however, does not seem to exist in this form in any other MSS. save the two copies of the Irish *Liber Hymnorum* from which we have printed it. But the various clauses down to l. 20 are found scattered up and down in a Rogation Litany "ex MS. ordinario insignis ecclesiae Lugdunensis" printed by Martene.[3] The first clause *Parce domine*, &c., occurs frequently in liturgical books, *e.g.* in the Sarum Breviary (preceded by the Antiphon *Ne reminiscaris*), in the Breviary of Aberdeen (after the seven Penitential Psalms), and in the Corpus Missal (p. 211). The second clause *Deprecamur te*, &c. is mentioned by Bede (H.E. i. 26) as having been sung by Augustine and his companions as they entered Canterbury.

Line 20. The true reading is, of course, *uniuersa terra* with F, not *uniuersa tua* with the principal manuscript (T).

Lines 1-3 of the antiphon at the end *Parce domine peccantibus*, &c. occur in almost the same words in a *Deprecatio Sancti Martini pro populo* found on fol. 18 of the Stowe Missal.

PREFACE TO THE HYMN *SEN DÉ*.

Before discussing the structure of the hymn, a few notes explanatory of the Irish Preface must be given.

The pestilence which is said to have been the occasion of the composition of this *lorica* was the terrible "Yellow Plague," which ravaged Europe in the sixth and seventh centuries. The Four Masters put it down to the year 664,[4] and name among the victims, Fechin abbot of

---
[1] Colgan, *A.A. SS.* Mar. 18.   [2] See Olden, *Proc. R.I.A.* (1895), p. 566.
[3] *De ant. eccl. rit.* iii. 527-531 (ed. 1737). Mr. H. A. Wilson has suggested to us that the relation of the piece to these Gallican Rogation Litanies may be a key to the ascription of it to St. Ambrose as author.
[4] See also for an account of it, *Bede*, H.E. iii. 27, and Adamnan, *Vita Columbae*, II. xlvi. (with Reeves' note). Compare Plummer's *Bede*, vol. ii. p. 196, O'Curry's *MS. Materials*, p. 631, and Olden's *Church of Ireland*, p. 68.

Fore, Aileran 'of the wisdom,' Manchan of Liath, and Dermot and Blaithmac, the two sons of Aed Slane, all of whom are mentioned in our Preface. There were, however, several outbreaks of it in Ireland, the most deadly being in the years 543, 550, 664 and 1094; and the country was hardly free from it at any time during the seventh century.

Of St. Colman mac Ui Cluasaig, to whom the authorship of the *lorica* is ascribed, we know nothing save that the Four Masters speak of him as the tutor of St. Cummain the Tall, and record his death along with that of his pupil in 661. There is here an obvious difficulty as to the date; but it might well be that the *lorica* was composed at the beginning of the Plague, before 661, but that its use did not become common until the Plague, which reached its severest point in 664, became very deadly. Indeed the writer of the Preface observes that some held that only two quatrains were written by St. Colman, and that his disciples added the rest. It may be observed that Colman is by far the commonest name in the Irish hagiologies, being chosen by no less than 226 saints according to the tables in the Book of Leinster.

The sin for which the Plague was sent upon the Irish people is described as in our Preface, but more fully, in the Life of St. Gerald of Mayo[1]. With the growth of population, the arable land began to be insufficient for the needs of the country, and so an assembly of clergy and laity was summoned in 657 by Dermot and Blaithmac, kings of Ireland, to take counsel. It was decided, as the Preface tells, that the amount of land held by any one person should be restricted; and, further, the "seniors" directed that prayers should be offered for a pestilence, "to reduce the number of the lower class, that the rest might live in comfort"! St. Fechin of Fore, on being consulted, approved of this extraordinary petition. And so the prayer was answered from heaven, but the vengeance of the Almighty caused the force of the plague to be felt by the nobles and clergy, of whom multitudes, including the kings and Fechin of Fore, were carried off.

It appears from the end of the Preface that an island was a favourite place of refuge during these visitations, as the pestilence did not travel across the sea. As St. Colman is said to have taught in the school of Cork, it is possible that the island spoken of may be that of Inis-Cleire, where a well-known monastery was situated.

The idea that the distance of "nine waves" from the mainland had a special virtue is found elsewhere in Irish literature. For instance, according to the Brehon Laws, a borrowed article carried over "nine waves" by the borrower was forfeit to him. (See *Senchus Mor* iii. 423.) And in the tale of the invasion of Ireland by the sons of Milesius we read that the compact between them and the natives was that the strangers were to go "nine waves" from the shore, and then try to land. If they succeeded in baffling the magical arts of the Druids for

---

[1] See Life of St. Gerald in the *Dict. of National Biography.*

that distance, the country was to be theirs. (Keating, *Hist. of Ireland*, p. 199, ed. O'Mahony.)

THE HYMN SEN DÉ

A critical examination of this poem will show that, whatever truth there may be in the account of its composition given in the Preface, it is not the whole truth. An important article by M. Gaidoz on this hymn appeared in vol. v of the *Revue Celtique* (p. 94), in which it was pointed out that it falls into three natural divisions.

1. The first division (verses 1-38) is plainly the original poem, and it ends, as is the practice of Irish hymnologists, with the words *Sén Dé do·n·fe for·don·te* with which it began. This part of the piece consists of a number of invocations of saints, chiefly Old Testament personages; and from the fragments of Latin phrases which occur here and there at the end of lines, it is natural to suspect that it may be based on a Latin original. This suspicion becomes almost a certainty when we find many of the same saints described in the same way, invoked in the familiar *Commendatio animae quando infirmus est in extremis*, of the Breviary. A few lines of this may be transcribed.

"Libera, domine, animam eius, sicut liberasti Enoch et Eliam de communi morte mundi . . . Noe de diluuio . . . Abraham de Ur Chaldaeorum Iob de passionibus eius . . . Isaac de hostia et de manu patris sui Abrahae . . . Lot de Sodomis et de flamma ignis . . . Moysen de manu Pharaonis regis Ægyptiorum . . . . Danielem de lacu leonum . . . tres pueros de camino ignis ardentis et de manu regis iniqui . . Susannam de falso crimine . . . David de manu regis Saul et de manu Goliae . . . Petrum et Paulum de carceribus . . . Theclam uirginem et martyrem tuam de atrocissimis tormentis . . .

sic liberare digneris animam huius serui tui et tecum facias in bonis congaudere caelestibus."

An Irish Litany presenting striking resemblances to this first division of our hymn is also found at the end of the Felire of Oengus, from which we quote some stanzas:[1]

"Deliver me, O Jesu, O Lord of fair assemblies, as Thou deliveredst Elijah, with Enoch, from the world.

Deliver me, O Jesu, from every ill on earth, as Thou deliveredst Noah, son of Lamech, from the flood.

Deliver me, O Jesu, O King of pure brightness, as Thou deliveredst Abraham from the hand of the Chaldeans.

Deliver me, O Jesu, O King mysterious, gracious, as Thou deliveredst Lot from the sin of the cities.

Deliver me, O Jesu, O King high, wonderful, as Thou deliveredst Jonah from the belly *ceti magni*.

Deliver me, O Jesu, in Thy many-graced kingdom, as Thou deliveredst Isaac from his father's hands.

[1] Wh. Stokes, *Calendar of Oengus*, p. cciii.

Deliver me, O Jesu, when Thou shalt come with Thy saints, as Thou deliveredst Thecla from the beast's maw.

Deliver me, O Jesu, for Thy Mother's intercession, as Thou deliveredst Jacob from his brother's hands.

Deliver me, O Jesu, from every evil that is not . . . as Thou deliveredst John from the serpent's venom.

Deliver me, O Jesu, from hell with its misery, as Thou deliveredst David from the valour of Goliath's sword.

Deliver me, O Jesu, who hast freed all—as Thou deliveredst Susanna with sovranty after the lie concerning her.

Deliver me, O Jesu, because of Thy conflict's intercession, as Thou deliveredst Nineveh in the time of the plague.

Deliver me, O Jesu, I desire that Thou wilt acknowledge me, as Thou deliveredst the people of Israel *de monte Gilboae*.

Deliver me, O Jesu, O Lord who art divinest, as Thou deliveredst Daniel out of the lions' den.

Deliver me, O Jesu, O King famous, gentle, as Thou deliveredst Moses *de manu Pharaonis*.

Deliver me, O Jesu, who hast wrought great marvels, as Thou deliveredst the Three Children *de camino ignis*.

Deliver me, O Jesu, O King of every clan, as Thou deliveredst Tobit from the misery of blindness.

Deliver me, O Jesu, for sake of Thy martyrdom's intercession, as Thou deliveredst Paul and Peter before kings from the vengeance of the prison.

Deliver me, O Jesu, from the anguish of every disease, as Thou deliveredst Job from the devil's tribulations.

Deliver me, O Jesu, O Christ let there not be neglect, as Thou deliveredst David from Saul, from his spoiling.

Deliver me, O Jesu, for Thy Mother's intercession, as Thou deliveredst Joseph from the hands of his brethren.

Deliver me, O Jesu, O King *benedicte*, as Thou deliveredst Israel with holiness from the slavery of Egypt.

Deliver me, O Jesu, for with Thee is my covenant, as Thou deliveredst Peter from the waves of the sea, &c."

There can be little doubt that this Litany and the first section of the hymn *Sén Dé*, both of which are "farced" in the same way with Latin phrases, are based on the Latin text of some prayer like the *Commendatio Animae*. The *Commendatio* is itself ancient; and as M. le Blant has pointed out,[1] its phraseology is remarkably illustrated by the figures carved on early Christian sepulchral monuments,[2] favourite subjects being, The passage of the Red Sea, Noah, The Sacrifice of Isaac, The Ascension of Elijah, Job, David and Goliath, The Deliverance of St. Peter, Daniel in the lions' den, The Three Hebrew Children, Jonah and the whale, and Susannah and the elders.

M. Gaidoz cites a prayer of St. Martin[3] which brings together some

---

[1] *Revue Archéologique*, Oct. and Nov. 1879.
[2] Cf. Anderson, *Scotland in Early Christian Times*. II. 130 ff.
[3] *Migne*, P.L. ci. 604.

of the same topics: "Deus gloriae, Deus qui unus et uerus Deus, qui solus et iustus es, Deus in quo omnia, sub quo omnia, per quem omnia facta sunt, exaudi me orantem sicut exaudisti tres pueros de camino ignis ardentis; exaudi me orantem sicut exaudisti Ionam de uentre ceti; exaudi me orantem sicut exaudisti Susannam et liberasti eam de manu iniquorum testium; exaudi me orantem sicut exaudisti Petrum in mari et Paulum in uinculis, Parce animae meae, &c."[1]

We entirely acquiesce in the conclusion reached by M. Gaidoz viz. "On voit par ces exemples que l'hymne de Colman n'est qu'une paraphrase irlandaise d'une ancienne prière commune à toute l'Église, et que les mots latins dont il est farci appartiennent sans doute à l'original latin qui a servi de modèle au poète irlandais." See also p. xxxix above.

It is only necessary to add that in the subject matter of this first division of our hymn there is nothing distinctively Celtic.

II. The next division of the poem (lines 39–47) is an appendix to the first division of the nature of an antiphon, whether by the original hand or not is hardly now to be determined. Its close is also marked by the words *Sén Dé*. It will be observed that ll. 41–43 are in a different metre from the others, and it may be that, as Gaidoz suggests, the whole of the second section of the poem is itself made up of three groups of verses (viz. 39, 40; 41–43; 44, 45), added at different times. See note on l. 43 and above p. xxxv ff.

III. Yet another set of verses is added (ll. 47–54) which invoke the benediction of St. Patrick, St. Brigid, St. Columba, the three patron Saints of Ireland, along with that of St. Adamnan. The last named saint was not born until 624 (d. 704), and did not rise to eminence until after the reputed date of St. Colman mac Ui Cluasaig's death. The glossator in T shows himself conscious that this last section of the hymn is a later addition, for he observes on l. 46 *Huc usque cecinit Colman*. And the F glossator adds a note which ascribes the authorship of ll. 47–50 to one Dermot, and ll. 51–end to Mugron, the coarb of Columba, who died in 980. See note on l. 47.

Of this hymn we know of no manuscripts save T and F. It was first printed by Todd[2] from T, and afterwards with notes in the *Irish Eccl. Record*, vol. iv. p. 402. A French translation of the hymn and its preface were printed by M. Gaidoz in the article from which we have already quoted. The glosses and marginal notes from F have not been printed before.

1 *do'n'fé*] i.e. *may He bring us with Him T*:
may He take us with Him, in whichever direction we go F
for'don'te] i.e. *upon us from Him, i.e. may it come upon us TF.*
ro'n'feladar] i.e. *may He guard us F*; + *may He put His veil over us for our shelter TF.*

2 *oessam*] i.e. *under His protection TF.*
innocht] The end of the F gloss is illegible; the words *and . . . used to . . . upon it* are all that can be read.
cia] i.e. *in whatever direction we go T*: i.e. *whatever direction F.*

---

[1] Compare the language of the second *Oratio* printed in the Appendix to Hartel's *Cyprian* III., 147.
[2] *Liber Hymnorum*, p. 121.

cain] *i.e. beautiful T.*
temadar] *i.e. may He receive us for our shelter, i.e. may He make our shelter T.*
 i.e. may He protect us against . . . . i.e. who protects F.
 3 *foss*] *i.e. whether stationariness TF.*
 utmaille] *or on journey TF.*
 4 *ruire*] *i.e. great king TF.*
 adessam] *i.e. we beseech TF.*
 5 *itge*] *i.e. we pray TF^m*.
 6 *dian-galar*] *i.e. against the swift disease TF; i.e. against the Yellow Plague T.* The end of the F gloss is illegible.
 fogair] *i e. which threatens, i.e. may make threatening T.* The F gloss is illegible.
 8 *immuntisat*] *i.e. may they come about us T.*
 adamna] *i.e. famine, quia per Adam uenit dolor TF^{me};* an astonishing piece of philology, connecting the Irish word for *famine* with the Hebrew *Adam*. But in reality, nothing is known of the alleged word *adamna* =*hunger*, and we cannot follow the glossator with any confidence. Perhaps we should analyse *adamna* into *a damna*, and translate ". . . against pestilence, lest any cause [of pestilence] visit us." Cf. *damna dogra do't chairdib*, "it is a cause of anguish to thy friends" (MR. 294, 8). Cf. also SM. III. 94, 5.
 9 "The father of the twelve" is, of course, Jacob; although Dr. Wh. Stokes and M. Gaidoz both interpret it of Isaac.
 anuqs . . .] *very noble, i.e. man TF.* The end of the word is illegible in T, but F has plainly *anóser*, which does not seem to fit the glossators' explanation; it means 'their younger [brother],' *a n-óser*.
 11 *snaidsium*] *i.e. may he protect us (here F) TF.*
 12 *Iesu*] *i.e. son of Nun TF^m*.
 13 "Job with the tribulations," goes back to *Iob de passionibus eius* of the *Commendatio Animae*.
 14 *fiadat*] *i.e. 'fiada' i.e. 'fo dia' i.e. good God TF,* an etymological gloss attempting the analysis of the ancient word *fiada*.
 15 *adsluinnen*] *i.e. we appeal to our friendship with him in hac laude T.*
 16 *rop*] *i.e. may He come to our help TF.*
 17 *Maire*] *.i. stilla uel stella maris interpretatur TF.* Of these two interpretations *stilla maris,* from מר a 'drop,' and ים 'the sea,' is probably the original from which *stella maris* was derived, in the first instance no doubt by false orthography on the part of some transcriber. The mistake has however prevailed; the hymn *Aue maris stella* is a sufficiently familiar instance.
 17 *Ioseph*] *i.e. fosterfather of Jesus TF.*
The name of Joseph does not appear in Western Martyrologies until the ninth century; and the insertion of it in the Litany for the *Commendation* of the departing soul was not actually authorised until 1726, by Benedict XIII. Its occurrence here at least indicates for the piece in its present form a date not earlier than 850.
 do·n·ringrat] *i.e. may they summon us for our salvation T: i.e. may they summon us; or, may they name us F.*

18 *do'n·forslaice*] i.e. *may he release us* TF.

The notes on the name of Ignatius in T and F are much defaced; enough remains to show that they recorded the story of his martyrdom. The note in T seems to have been substantially the same as a note at Dec. 20 in a copy of the Felire of Oengus now in the Franciscan Library, Dublin, written by one Ruaidhri O'Liunin, viz. "Episcopus sed post Petrum episcopatum tenuit, sed sub Traiano imperatore passus est Ignatius et leonibus datus est et aliis bestiis."[1] No doubt it comes from some martyrology.

19 *dithrubach*] i.e. *pro deo* also F.

22 *anachl*] i.e. *the king who protected* TF.

luchtlach] i.e. *his people of lake; or, his black people; i.e. Noe cum suis tribus filiis et quatuor uxores eorum* T. The gloss is hardly intelligible; it seems to employ an alternative meaning of *loch*, viz. *lake* or *black*, as an etym. explanation of *luchtlach*, 'crew' (?). Perhaps *luchtlach* is not the right word, for as the line stands it cannot be construed. Something like 'the King who saved Noah from *destruction*' is what we should expect. The gloss in F is illegible for the most part; but it was probably the same as in T.

23 *rex Salem*] The note in the margin of F is almost illegible; what is left yields *it is the opinion of the Hebrews that he was* (*sine*) *genealogia* (*sicut*) *angelus*.

Salem] . . . *it is however the opinion of the Hebrews that this is the same as Jerusalem; and further it is the opinion* (*of others that it was on the banks*) *of the river Jordan, and in it dwelt Melchizedek* F^ms.

References for the Jewish tradition, alluded to in the passage from Jerome cited in the T gloss, that Melchizedek was identical with Shem, are given in Baring Gould's *Legends of O.T. Characters* (vol. i. p. 139, and vol. ii. p. 1.)

incerto de semine] Compare Hebr. vii. 3.

25 *Soter*] i.e. σωτήρ. The occasional introduction of some familiar Greek word is a well-known practice of Irish writers. The glossator in T apparently thought that it was a Hebrew word!

soeras] i.e. *He freed* TF.

Loth] i.e. *declinans interpretatur, i.e. Lot, son of Haran, son of Terah, frater Sarra* TF.

27 *Ur*] The legend given in the passage from Jerome cited in the margin of T was very popular in the East.[2] It is incorporated into the Koran (xxi. 52–75); and Abraham's escape from the furnace of Nimrod was celebrated in the Syrian Church on Jan. 25. There is a trace of it even in the Vulgate; in Neh. [2 Esdr.] ix. 7 we read *Tu ipse domine deus qui elegisti Abram et eduxisti eum de* igne *Chaldaeorum*. The legend is probably based on the fact that אור = 'light' or 'fire.'

Galdai] *the Chaldees i.e. Caldei dicti quasi Casdi, i.e. from Cased son of Nahor son of Terah &c.* F^ms. See Gen. xxii. 22. The etymology is, perhaps, possible.

snaidsi·um] *may He protect us* F.

[1] See Wh. Stokes, *Felire of Oengus*, p. clxxxiii.
[2] Several forms of it are given in Baring Gould's *Legends of O.T. Characters*, vol i. p. 181 ff.

28 *suers·um*] *may He free us TF.*
limpa] *that is, ablatiuus TF.* Possibly *othoin* is equivalent to *o thoind*, 'from the wave.'
Gaba] *i.e. in the peril in which they were sine aqua, quando uenit ex Egypto T.* This gloss takes the word *gaba* as equivalent to *gabud* = 'peril', and refers to the episode recorded in Num. xx. 2 ff.
The note in F gives various explanations: *i.e. in the peril in which they were in the wilderness super aqua, when the people came out of Egypt. Or, perhaps Gaba was the name of the place in which they were then sine aqua. Or, when Samuel son of Elkanah was in the leadership of the people, this is said: Philistines came to them on a hosting, so that the children of Israel came into the places Gibeah and Mizpah, et unde hic i nGabai: and the children of Israel fasted there, and Samuel put water illustrationis over them, et unde dicitur lympha, and Samuel with the children of Israel gained the victory over the Philistines.*
The first and second of these explanations refer to Num. xx. 2. The third refers to 1 Sam. vii. 1-11, 'Gabaa' being the reading of the Vulgate in the first verse. The actual phrase *aqua lustrationis*, occurs Num. viii. 7; but the pouring out of water for purification is recorded 1 Sam. vii. 6.

29 *ruri*] *i.e. great king T.*
anacht] *i.e. He protected T.*
31 *fluithem*] *i.e. a ruler in truth TF.*
locharnaig] *i.e. resplendent TF.*
ar·don·roigse] *i.e. may He be merciful TF.*
33 *foedes*] *i.e. præteriti temporis. Herod Tetrarch, son of Herod, son of Antipater, son of Herod of Ascalon; by him was killed John Baptist and Christ was crucified, and Peter was flung into prison, and it is that is called to mind here F*".
tarslaic] *i.e. He let out F.*
35 *findat*] *i.e. to our good God T; 'fia' = God, and 'dia' from the word* "deus" *F.*
ro·n·tolomar] *i.e. may we please TF.*
38 *snaidsium*] *may He protect us F.*
tomtach] *i.e. threatening TF.*
39 *a Fiada*] *i.e. O good God! TF.*
ro·erthar] *i.e. may there be given TF.*
40 *maccan*] *i.e. angeli F*", *Or, little children who die immediately in sanctitate post baptismum TF*".

With the first interpretation may be compared the promise given to Sechnall by Patrick (see p. 6 above), that a house whose building was begun with the recitation of the hymn *Audite omnes* should have 'about it a watch, consisting of Patrick with Ireland's saints.' The idea of guardian saints and angels is, indeed, common enough. The alternative interpretation possibly contains an allusion to St. Matth. xviii. 10.

43 The marginal note here is unfortunately not completely legible either in T or in F; but the meaning is substantially as follows: *This is a half quatrain, and its other half quatrain is not extant; and as to the other half quatrain, the man to whom it befel to make it, died of the*

plague: i.e. *if it was by a half quatrain to each man that they made it, in the previous lines. But if it was Colman by himself that made this hymn, it was for this reason that he left this half quatrain without the other half quatrain, viz.* 'because my household left the hymn incomplete, I will leave it incomplete.' It would seem that the annotator did not observe that the metre of ll. 41-3 is different from that of the verses which precede and follow, and that, in fact, these lines form no part of the hymn. See p. 114. above.

hil-lethu] i.e. *in breadth T;*
    i.e. *with them, ut quidam dixit :*
      My father and my mother
      while they were in life,
      benediction on the space that took them (?) ;
      was small my . . . with them F^{us}.
This quatrain in the margin of F is much defaced.

43 The aspiration contained in this verse is much like those with which several of the vernacular homilies end'; 'without age' is equivalent to perpetual youth. E.g., in the *Leabhar na hUidre* it is said of the saints that they "will abide continually in the life eternal, without age, without decay."

44 *reraig*] i.e. *great-kings, or time-kings TF;* + i.e. *long life their life F;* + *qui fuerunt ante diluuium F.* In fact the antediluvian saints are meant.

fegad] i.e. *lofty is the sight angelorum et apostolorum TF.*

47 *bendachi*] *Diarmait son of German, coarb of Patrick,*[2] *it is he that added these four verses ; the names of Patrick and Brigid tantum fuerunt ; and Mugron, coarb of Colum Cille made this hymn below, viz. the last two verses* F^{us}. This shows that the glossator of F, equally with the glossator of T, was conscious that ll. 47-54 were a later addition to the hymn. He asserts that ll. 46-50 were added by Diarmait, ll. 51, 52, by Mugron ; but the use of both *rann* and *immun* is perplexing.

Mugron, the thirtieth successor of St. Columba, was abbot of Hy from 964 to 980. The Four Masters describe him as "scribe and bishop, skilled in the three verses." Some verses ascribed to him are found at fol. 42 of the MS. we call Θ.[3]

érlam] i.e. *a ready champion, quite ready to perform wonders and miracles TF.*

Patraic] i.e. *on the patron who is Patrick TF.*

48 *indi*] i.e. *in it T.*

51 *Colum*] i.e. '*dove*' *dictus est from his simplicity T.*

Cille] The notes here in T and F are too much defaced to be read in their entirety, but they were evidently the same in substance as a note found in the *Leabhar Breac* copy of the Felire of Oengus at June 9, viz. : "Colum pro simplicitate eius dictus est. Cille i.e. ar thiachtain co-menicc on cill in ro·leg a salmu hi comdail na lenab comocus. ba head adbertis sen etarru, in tanic ar Colum bec-ni on chill .i. o Thelaig Dub-glaissi hi Tir Lugdach i Cinel Conaill. Crimthan tra

---

[1] See Atkinson, *Passions and Homilies, passim.*
[2] Cf. Stokes, *Trip. Life,* p. xx.
[3] Hp. of Armagh, 848.
[4] Ed. Stokes, p. xcix.

ainm bunaid Coluim Cille:" or (adopting our glossator's version for one clause): "Colum 'dove' he was called for his simplicity. Cille 'of the church,' because of his coming often from the church wherein he read his psalms to a priest of the church. And this is what they used to say amongst them, 'Has our little Colum come from the church?' i.e. from Tulach Dubglaisse in Tir Lugdach in Cenel Conaill. Now Crimthan was Colum Cille's original name." Tulach Dubglaisse, or Temple Douglas near Kilmacrenan, was, as Todd observes, the name of the church in which St. Columba was baptized. Crimthan means 'fox.'

Alban] *i.e. east of the sea* T.

52 *Adamnain i.e. Adamnan son of Loran son of Linne ; Ronnat his mother's name F^{na}*. This is the famous Adamnan, the ninth abbot of Iona (624–704), who was the author of the *Vita S. Columbae*. His father, Ronan, the son of Tinne (there is some confusion about the initial letters in F), belonged to the same royal race as Columba. For further account of Ronan and Ronnat, see Reeves' *Adamnan*, p. xli. Adamnan's day is Sept. 23.

cain] *the four chief Laws of Ireland, viz. Law of Patrick, and of Dari, and of Adamnan, and of Sunday. As to the Law of Patrick, (it forbad) to slay clerics ; the Law of Dari, to steal cattle ; the Law of Adamnan to slay (women) ; the Law of Sunday, to go on a journey* F^{nis}. Substantially the same note is found in the Felire of Oengus (*Leabhar Breac* copy) at March 17th.[1]

The Law of Adamnan was the renewal of a measure passed at the Assembly of Druim Cetta by Columba's influence which prohibited women from taking part in the fierce conflicts which the various clans waged with each other. This important social reform was brought about by Adamnan in the course of a visitation by him of Ireland in the year 697, and was solemnly sanctioned by a convention which met at Tara. See Reeves' *Adamnan*, pp. 1, 179. It is not to be confounded with the so-called *Canones Adamnani*, which were in reference to ecclesiastical matters. They have been printed by Martene and others.

52 *clanna*] *i.e. on the women ; or, super gentes* F.

53 This line is impossible to construe, though the meaning is clear. The terms *foessam* and *comairche* are of frequent occurrence in the Irish Tales and in the Laws, and have a technical sense ; *comairche* was the protection afforded by a chief to a man when in his company, *foessam*, the protection extended to one at a distance.

In the margin of F there are some scribblings in a hand of the 16th century, *e.g.* "Amen dico uobis, omnis homo mendax"; " Pater noster qui es in celis," &c.

The quotation in the margin of fol. 5*b* from St. Gregory the Great is also found in one of the Irish-Latin Homilies in the *Leabhar Breac*.[2] Gregory, as a writer, was so popular in Ireland, that he was called Bél-óir, "the golden-mouthed."

The marginal note on the upper margin of fol. 6 of T has been cut away by the binder of the MS.

[1] Ed. Stokes, p. lxiv. [2] Atkinson, *Passions and Homilies*, p. 444.

Preface to the Hymn of St. Cuchuimne.

Of Cuchuimne, to whom the authorship of the hymn is ascribed in the Prefaces in T and F, we know but little. According to the *Annals of Ulster* he died in the year 746; and he is commemorated on Oct. 7 in the *Martyrology of Gorman*. The name means " hound of memory "; it is perhaps not unnecessary to observe that *hound* was a title of respect among the Irish.[1]

An ingenious identification of Cuchuimne with Cummean, to whom the Irish penitential literature of the middle ages is so much indebted, was suggested jointly by Dr. Wh. Stokes and Mr. Henry Bradshaw in the year 1885. At the end of one of the Paris MSS. of the Irish collection of canons known as the Hibernensis, Mr. Bradshaw read the rubric: *Hucusque nuben & cucuiminiæ & du rinis.* It seems not impossible that *Cuchuimne abbas ex Darinis* may be concealed under the last words of this; and it is curious that the entry in the Annals of the Four Masters preceding that which relates to Cuchuimne records the obit of an abbot of Darinis, an island near Youghal upon which there was a monastic establishment. This identification, however, though not improbable in itself, must not be considered as established. It has been usual, though in like manner without sufficient proof, to equate Cummean the author of the *Penitentiale* to St. Cummain the Fair, the seventh abbot of Iona, large portions of whose life of St. Columba were incorporated by Adamnan into his more elaborate work.

King Loingsech, in whose time the hymn is said to have been written, reigned (according to O'Flaherty's Chronology) from 695 to 704.

The legend in the Preface would seem to indicate that the first half of Cuchuimne's life having been devoted to the study of literature, the second half was spent in profligacy. The obscure verses which tell of this are also found in the margin of the Dublin copy of the Annals of Ulster at the year 746, where they are attributed, not to Adamnan, but to the Nurse of Cuchuimne. They are quoted, probably from the Annals of Ulster, by the Four Masters, and are also found in the margin of the Book of Fenagh (fol. 8).

Several points call for comment in these verses. Todd observes that in such a record of the weakness of Cuchuimne there is great internal evidence of truth. *Co druimne*, 'to the ridge' plainly means 'half-way'; [compare the *Amra* ll. 283, 286], but the phrase is a curious one. The play upon words, *ro·leg* 'he read' in l. 10 and *ro·leic* 'he left' in l. 12 will be observed.

Again, it is impossible to determine the exact meaning in l. 12 of the word *chaillecha*, which means either 'nuns' or 'old women.' Neither term is in keeping with the plain drift of the lines, as referred to in l. 5; so that probably O'Donovan's translation 'hags' is the least offensive.

In l. 18 it is not at all easy to say what *araid cúi* means: *cúi* rhymes

---

[1] See Reeves' *Adamnan*, p. 82.

with *súi*; and so possibly *súi* mod. *saoi* demands here *cúi* mod. *caoi* = 'way, road.' *Raid* might = 'path,' as given doubtfully in the translation. But *raid* might also be for *raith* 'grace,' which would suggest a different interpretation.

The last two lines of the Preface in T plainly do not belong to the Preface at all; they are a gloss on *Mariæ* in l. 2 which has been displaced. This fact is, however, of some significance; for it shows that the glosses (or at least some of them) were copied from an older exemplar by the scribe of T, who here mistook the bearing of one of them. F has here no glosses, and the words in question are absent from the F Preface. See p. 118 above, and vol. i. p. 32.

The Hymn of St. Cuchuimne.

For this hymn we have the textual evidence of five manuscripts TFP KR (see *Introd.* to vol. i. p. xix). It has been printed by Daniel in his *Thesaurs* (iv. 86) from P, and by Mone (ii. 383) from PKR, as well as by Todd from T and P with the aid of Mone's edition. It was also published from P by Bp. Forbes in his Preface to the Arbuthnot Missal, and by Moran in his *Essays on the Irish Church* (p. 225); a translation into English is given in the *Irish Eccl. Record* (i. 204). Our collation of P was made for this edition by Dr. Wickham Legg, and of K and R by Dr. A. Holder. It is possible (see vol. i. p. xxvii) that it forms in P an item of a monastic office, there sketched; but this cannot be regarded as certain.

The metre is characteristically Irish, as explained above (p. xvi).

3 This line points to the practice of antiphonal singing.

4 *uicariam* seems to be used here in the sense of *alternate*; but *uicarius* is found in its usual meaning at l. 81 of the hymn of St. Sechnall.

7 Todd has incorrectly given the various readings of this verse in the several MSS. which he used.

19 *tonicam*] *arrangement of a very long tunic;* and *textam*] *i.e. without a seam in it at all* are the glosses in T.

The legend that the seamless robe was "a purple tunic that Mary made" is also found in the vernacular account of the Passion in the *Leabhar Breac*[1] based on some form of the apocryphal Gospel of Nicodemus.

21 Compare Rom. xiii. 14.

23 *puerperae*] *i.e. puerum pariens in aetate pueri, id est in decimo uel in undecimo.* This apparently contains an allusion to the accounts of the age of the Blessed Virgin contained in the apocryphal Gospels of the Infancy.

24 *pirae*] *i.e. of the horrible* . . . . If we are to read *inna briad*, then probably the Latin *pyra* was expressed in early Irish by some (now unknown) fem. word like *bré*, gen. *briad*.

---

[1] Atkinson, *Passions and Homilies*, p. 367.

The jingling lines at the end of the hymn are not found, as the *apparatus criticus* shows, in either of the Karlsruhe manuscripts. For the collect which follows them in P see vol. i. p. xxvii.

Preface to the Hymn of St. Hilary.

These legends about Hilary are not found elsewhere. We know nothing from other sources which would teach us that he was ever at Monte Gargano in Apulia, nor is the point of the story in the first paragraph in the Preface by any means clear.

The alternative account of the origin of the hymn given in the second paragraph names *Mons Iouis*, now Mount St. Bernard, as the place of its composition. Todd notes that the famous Hospice was founded there at the close of the tenth century, its site having been previously occupied by a miracle-working image of Jupiter. By the philosophers may be meant the attendant priests. The destruction of this relic of paganism must have made a great stir, and the knowledge of it may have caused so well-known a spot to be fixed on for the scene of the story. However that may be, the T scholiast gives the date of Hilary of Poitiers with tolerable accuracy when he says that he wrote in the reign of Valentinian and Valens; as Hilary died in the year 368, the F scholiast goes hopelessly astray about the date.

The city *Susanna* or *Sanna* (for the texts vary) may perhaps be Soissons (as Todd suggests) or Sens. But there is no record of any such journey as that here described in the lives of St. Hilary of Poitiers; and it seems not improbable that the legend of the Prefaces is due to a confusion of him with St. Hilary of Arles (401–449), who made a famous journey on foot across the Alps in midwinter to seek an audience of Pope Leo the Great.

l. 15. *Hilarius orauit pro monacho suo*] In Irish writers the *monachus* of a bishop often means his attendant or chaplain, as we would say now.

The third paragraph in the T Preface, *i.e.* the last paragraph in F, is taken substantially, as our reference shows, from the *De arte metrica* of Bede, a very popular text book in the middle ages.

l. 26. *in psalterio graeco ymnos testmon, hoc est memor fuit nostri*] The reference is to Ps. cxiii. 20 μνησθείς ἡμῶν = *memor fuit nostri* in the Latin Psalters; the scribe had evidently but an imperfect knowledge of Greek.

l. 29. *The Decades*] The commentary of Augustine on the Psalter (the *Enarrationes*) was anciently divided into fifteen Decades, which gave the title *Decades* to the work. It is so called in the *Würzburg Glosses*,[1] as well as in other non-Celtic books.

The Hymn of St. Hilary.

We have given in our text and *apparatus criticus* the readings of six manuscripts which contain this hymn, of which four are now used for the first time, viz. FCGH.

[1] Ed. Stokes, p. 347.

Printed editions of it are numerous. George Cassander published in 1616 the *editio princeps* in his *Hymni Ecclesiastici* (p. 186) from a manuscript which he says contained the Rule of St. Benedict and some other hymns. We have failed to trace this manuscript.

It was published by Muratori in the fourth volume of his *Anecdota Ambrosiana* in 1713 from A, the text of which has lately been made accessible in a more accurate form by Mr. Warren. Todd, in 1869, printed it from T, and registered the variants of Cassander's text and of A in his notes. Secondary editions, such as those of Daniel and Thomasius, need not be described here.

Cassander notes that the hymn is *incerto auctore*; but there is a good deal of evidence for ascribing it to St. Hilary of Poitiers. H and the Prefaces of T and F explicitly name him as the author, and A entitles it *Ymnum sancti Hilari de Christo*. In this last reference Hilary of Poitiers rather than Hilary of Arles is probably meant, although in the Irish Prefaces, as has been said, there seems to be some confusion between these two saints. Hilary of Poitiers was early known as a hymn writer. Jerome speaks of a *Liber Hymnorum* by him,[1] and the Fourth Council of Toledo (A.D. 633) mentions hymns in Church use " quos beati doctores Hilarius et Ambrosius ediderunt." Isidore of Seville (d. 636) in a passage of which a sentence is quoted at the end of the T Preface, says that Hilary was the first Christian author of hymns. Several hymns ascribed to him are extant. One for morning and one for evening use are appended to a letter to his daughter Abra, which is however of doubtful authenticity; and in a manuscript recently discovered at Arezzo, are found three hymns which bear his name.[2]

There is then no difficulty in the way of accepting any good evidence which ascribes a given hymn to St. Hilary. And, as we have seen, four of our manuscripts, one as old as the seventh century, concur in assigning the *Hymnum dicat* to his pen. Another MS. of the eighth century at St. Gall (No. 567 in the Library Catalogue) has at p. 133 at the end of a *Vita S. Hilarii* the words: "Incipit ymnus eiusdem omni tempore, Ymnum dicat turba fratrum, ymnum cantum personnet."[3] Again Hincmar of Rheims in the middle of the ninth century explicitly names Hilary as the author, and quotes two lines (28 and 60). " Et Hilarius in hymno ' et refert fragmenta coenae ter quaternis corbibus,' " are his words. And again : " Et in hymno euangelico pulcherrime a se composito dicit [sc. Hilarius] 'Spiritum dei perfectum Trinitatis uinculum.' "[4] Against all this is to be set the fact that Bede does not name Hilary as the author, when he is describing the metre of the hymn ; but the argument from silence is always a precarious one. The testimony of the *Antiphonary of Bangor* shows at least that the Hilarian authorship was held before Bede wrote, whether he knew of it or not. On the whole, therefore, we are inclined to accept the Hilarian authorship ; although Dr. Julian did not consider the evidence before him

---

[1] *De Script. eccl.* in Hilar.
[2] See Gamurrini, *S. Hilarii Tractatus de Mysteriis et Hymni* (Roma, 1887).
[3] Dr. Ad. Fäh has kindly supplied this information in answer to a letter of inquiry.
[4] *De una et non trina dietate* (Migne, P. L. cxxv. 566, 486).

sufficient to decide in its favour.[1] See the words quoted from Hilary in our note on l. 2.

The last words of the title in C seem to refer to the piece which follows the *Hymnum dicat* in that manuscript, and to have no bearing on the question of its authorship.

Hilary was well-known and respected in the British Islands in the middle ages. In the year 358 he dedicated his book *de Synodis* " Provinciarum Britannicarum episcopis." He is the patron saint of Drumblade in Aberdeenshire ; and there is a " St. Hillary's kirk " in the parish of Fettar and North Yell in Shetland. In Ireland, too, he was known.[2] No work of his is, however, quoted in the margins of our principal manuscript, which contain so many extracts from other famous Latin writers.

Some further references in Celtic ecclesiastical literature to the hymn now under discussion may be given here. We have already (vol. i. p. xxii) quoted the scheme of a monastic or occasional office found in the *Book of Mulling* and in the *Second Vision of Adamnan*, in which *Hymnum dicat* is prescribed for recitation. It seems, indeed, to have been counted of peculiar efficacy. In the tract *De Arreis* printed from Rawl. B. 512 by Prof. Kuno Meyer,[3] the *arreum* or commutation for " a week of hard penance on water and bread is, seven *Biait*, in honest cross vigil, and a Credo and Paternoster and *Hymnum dicat* with every *Biait*." Again in the Story of the Three Clerics as found in the Book of Leinster (p. 283), and also in the Book of Lismore,[4] the *opus dei* undertaken by the third cleric is to sing " a hundred and fifty *Hymnum dicats* every day, with celebrating my hours and my mass." And this was declared by the angel to be the best choice of all, and to him who chose it was promised " long life and the kingdom of heaven."

In the *Book of Cerne* this hymn is one of two pieces which follow a collection of fourteen prayers and hymns expressly stated to be for morning use. With this would agree stanza xxiv of the metrical Rule of St. Ailbe of Emly, viz. :

> The *Hymnum dicat* should be sung
> At striking the bell for canonical hours ;
> All wash their hands carefully,
> The brethren assume their habit.[5]

And to this use in the early morning there may perhaps be a reference in l. 70 " Ante lucem nuntiemus Christum regem saeculo." See also ll. 65-68. It seems probable however (see p. xii. above) that the last four stanzas of the piece are a later addition ; and therefore their witness must be received with caution. The custom spoken of in the T Preface, though based on an obscure legend, seems different : *sic nobis conuenit canere post prandium* says the Scholiast. Whether he refers to a regular monastic custom or only to a special usage that might be supposed to have a peculiar indulgence attached to it, can hardly

---

[1] *Dict. of Hymnology*, p. 642.
[2] See *Felire of Oengus*, p. xxxiv. and *Martyrology of Gorman* at Jan. 13.
[3] *Revue Celtique*, xv. 485ff. Prof. Meyer believes it to be of the eighth century. See vol i. p. xx.
[4] Ed. Stokes, pp. viii. ix.
[5] *Irish Eccl. Record*, vol. viii. p. 183.

now be determined with certainty.[1] The note in the St. Gall MS. No. 567, to which reference has been made above, seems to direct the recitation of the hymn *omni tempore*, that is (apparently) in a daily, and not only an occasional, office.

Internal evidence, at all events, supports the tradition that the hymn was intended for monastic, rather than for private, recitation. The "turba fratrum" of the first verse (see also l. 65) can only mean the members of a monastic society, and the words of praise are in the plural number all through. It is interesting to find that among the *reliquiae* of the great monastery at St. Gall (No. 381, p. 155), there is a hymn which seems to be modelled on this which is before us, thus testifying to the wide popularity of the *Hymnus S. Hilarii in laudem Christi*. It begins:

Iam fidelis turba fratrum uoce dulci [con]sonet
Hymnum dicat et serena partiatur dragmata, &c.[2]

2 *concinentes*] i.e. a uerbo *concino*, i.e. *while we sing together*.

laudes . . debitas is Cassander's reading, and is given as an alternative in the gloss. With this line may be compared Hilary's words in his Prologue to the Psalms[3]: " . . . in quo debitas Deo laudes universitas spirituum praedicabit." Compare the words of the antiphon after the *Te Deum* (vol. i. p. 61). In the passage of Bede's *de Arte Metrica* incorporated in the Preface, the second line as quoted reads *laudes . . . debitas*.

5 *angularis tu lapis*] Compare 1 Pet. ii. 6.

6 Cassander reads *uel* with ACGH ; but the gloss rightly explains the *el* of TF as אֵל i.e. *deus*. Compare the Prayer of St. Adamnan l. 11 (p. 81).

7 Cassander prints *prophetis*, and in l. 9 omits *et* with ACH.

8 *ante saecla tu fuisti* is the text demanded by the metre. See above.

11 Cassander prints *Gabriele*.

12 *aluus* is, of course, the true reading. Cassander has it with all the MSS. except T. The interchange of *b* and *u* is common.

14 *primi*] i.e. *the chiefs ; uel primi ex gentibus hi fuerunt, quia prius ante eos adorauerunt eum pastores ante xiii . . . iuxta turrim Gadder. Molcho eorum senior qui aurum deo regi obtulit ; secundus, Caspar iuuenis qui thus deo obtulit ; tertius, Patifarsat qui myrrham homini obtulit ; unde quidam dixit :*—

Melchar, the giver of the gold,
Caspar gave the abundant frankincense,
Patifarsat gave the good myrrh,
so that he gave them to the royal Lord, &c.

For the Tower Gadder as the scene of the vision of the angels by the shepherds see below, p. 135.

The magi appear under different names, but those by which they are best known are Melchior, Jaspar and Balthasar, of which the forms given in the marginal note are those usually found in Irish books. See

[1] See for a discussion of this, Lawlor, *Book of Mulling*, p. 139.
[2] Migne, P. L. lxxxvii. col. 46. [3] Migne, P. L. ix. 239.

e.g. a homily on p. 199 of the *Leabhar Breac*.[1] In a legendary account of the Adoration of the Magi found on p. 137 of the same voluminous manuscript,[2] they are called Melchisar, Hiespar and Balcisar. In the MS. Harl. 1802 of the British Museum collection written in 1139 by one Mael Brigte ua Mael Uanaig, usually called "The Gospels of Mael Brigid," from its chief contents, there is an Irish poem on the Magi and a note at one place which may be here transcribed: "Haec sunt nomina eorum in Ebreo, Arelius, Arenus, Damascus. i. humilis, fidelis, misericors. In Graeco autem, Malgalath, Galgalad, Sanicis uel Sincerna; nuntius, devotus, gotia interpretantur. Secundum Ug. [sc. Hugh of St. Victor] nomina eorum apud Caldeos, Melcho, Caspar, Patifarsat."[3]

For the mystical significance of their offerings see a Homily in the *Leabhar Breac* printed by Atkinson.[4] The lines from Juvencus quoted by the glossator give the usual mediæval interpretation; they are quoted *e.g.* by St. Jerome (*Comm. in Matth.* II) in a passage read in the Breviary as a lection at nocturns for the Octave of the Epiphany.

15 *offerentes*] *i.e. to shorten it, he did not put 'mirram'; or, it does not fit therein, in uersu; uel, quia postea dicetur.* These are all attempted explanations of the omission of any explicit mention of *myrrh* in l. 15.

Cassander has *thus* in l. 15, and *Herodi* in l. 16.

16 Apparently the construction of the lines requires *inuidens* to be taken as 'a thing *envious* (or distasteful),' to the power of Herod.

17 *paruos*] *query, what is the number of the children that suffered here by Herod? Not hard; MMCXL, ut Gregorius manifestat in Sacramentario.*

What seems to be the same belief as to the number of the Innocents is alluded to in a legend in the *Leabhar Breac* (p. 140). "Two thousand two hundred were slain by them between the city and the plains . . . One hundred and forty children, that is what were slain of them in Bethlehem."[5] Some verses quoted in the *Felire of Oengus* (ed. Stokes, p. clxxxiv) give the number as 2140, with variants 2240 and 2120. An Armeno-Gregorian Calendar (quoted by Neale, *Eastern Church*, Introd. p. 179), gives the number as 14,000; this and the Irish legend probably come from the same source.

18 The allusions in the next two or three lines and in the gloss are all based on the legends in the Apocryphal Gospels, in particular the Gospel of the Pseudo-Matthew, which was known in Ireland and is expressly quoted in the account of the Adoration of the Magi in the *Leabhar Breac*, to which reference has already been made.[6] That the sojourn of the Holy Family in Egypt lasted for four years, that the idols fell down in the presence of the Christ (a story ultimately derived from Isa. xix. 1), that the name of the governor of the city was Affrodosius, all these were early and widely spread legends known *e.g.* to Athanasius and to Cyril of Jerusalem. The Miracles of the Infancy, alluded to in l. 21, are also narrated in the *Evangelium Pseudo-Matthaei*.

[1] Atkinson, *Passions*, p. 237.
[2] Stokes, *Rev. Celtique*, viii. p. 346 ff.
[3] Hogan, *Todd Lectures*, vi. p. 81.
[4] Hogan, *Todd Lectures*, R.I.A vi. 60.
[5] l.c. p. 476.
[6] Hogan, *Todd Lectures*, vi. 73.

18 Cassander prints *occidendus*.
19 *refertur*] i.e. *is brought*. Cassander prints *Herodem*.
20 *adultus*] i.e. *when He grew up*.
21 *quae latent*] i.e. *the things that were not known*. Cf. Jn. xxi. 25.
quae leguntur] i.e. *the things that were known*.
23 Cassander reads *fecit*.
24 This is one of the lines quoted by Bede in the passage from the *De arte metrica* embodied in the Prefaces, the other being l. 9.
The mystical interpretation of the miracles of raising the dead given in the gloss was common in the middle ages.
25 *idris*] i.e. *on the water-pots*. Cf. Jn. iii. 1.
25 Attention should be paid to the small letters placed over and under the words in this and the next line. They are evidently intended to mark the order for purposes of translation by those who were not good Latinists. Several instances of marks of this kind are found throughout the *Liber Hymnorum*. The stanza is, however, probably spurious. See above, p xi.
26 Cassander reads *maerore lentis propina to*.
propinnando] i.e. . . . *was distributed at that hour*. The MS. is so much blurred, that the text is quite uncertain.
poculo] i.e. *fit poculum* . . . *vessel*. The variant *populo* is curiously well attested, but it can hardly be right.
27 *pane*] *It used to be binus et quinus secundum ueteres; nunc autem bini et quini ut Priscianus dicit*. This is a grammatical note in the margin of T. Priscian was well known in Ireland; there is a glossed copy of his works at Leyden written by one Dubthach in 838, and others at St. Gall and Karlsruhe also written by Irish monks.
28 *coruibus*] *curuus*, '*bent*'; *uel coruus* '*raven*'; *uel corbibus quod est hic*.
In the third explanation the glossator has hit on the truth.
Cassander gives this line thus: *et refectis fragmenta coenae ter quaternis corbibus*. *Fefert*, which T has, is of course a blunder of the scribe for *refert*.
29 *discumbente*] i.e. *service by which the whole company was served at table; unde* '*discus*' *deriuatur i.e.* '*dish*.'
We read *amus*, which occurs in the phrase *amus mesi*, 'servant of table', i.e. 'butler', in *Senchus Mor*, ii. 24, 18; Stokes reads *anius* = splendour. Todd's *ani o* is certainly wrong.
30 The marginal note in T calls attention to the fact that *duodecim* must be read as a trisyllable.
31 Cassander reads *queis*. The form *quis* for *quibus* does not occur again in these hymns.
32 The marginal note is quaint:—*misi ab Anna i.e. by Caiphas in truth He was sent, quia ille sacerdos fuit illius anni; sed causa metri dicit* '*ab Anna*'; *et in libris historiarum refertur quod quatuor fuissent principes inter Annam et Caipham, sed filia Annae coniunx fuit Caiphae*. See gloss on l. 47. The succession of high priests was probably as follows: Annas, Ishmael son of Phabi, Eleazar son of Annas, Simeon son of Kanith, and Joseph Caiaphas. It is possible, as Todd suggests,

that the *Libri Historiarum* quoted is the abridgement of Josephus ascribed to Hegesippus and translated by Rufinus; but the manuscript seems to us to read .iiii. not .uii. as Todd states.

33 *tenetur*] i.e. *He is seised.*

34 Cassander has *grassatur*, but puts *grauatur* in his margin. The active form *grassare* 'to attack' is used here and in l. 38 of the *Altus Prosator*, these being the only places where the word occurs in these hymns.

35 *obiecta*] i.e. *the charges that were laid against Christ.* Cassander prints *crimen.*

36 *Cesaris*] *For an insult to him was nomen regis upon anyone else than upon him alone . . . regem esse dicebat.*

37 Cassander has *negandum* and in 38 *grauatur.*

38 *sputa*] i.e. *the spittle.*

flagra] i.e. *the scourges.*

39 Todd notes that an interpretation of the four points of the cross similar to that written in the left margin of T is given by Augustine.[1] Among the Irish glosses at Turin on a fragmentary Commentary on St. Mark's Gospel, we have in like manner: " Ipsa species crucis quid est nisi forma quadrati mondi."[2] The note in the right margin of T is: *Quatuor ligna fuerunt in cruce Christi; cedar its foot, and cypress its tongue, and pine the wedge that was driven through it, and birch the board on which was written the title.* Stokes quotes[3] a similar observation in Irish verse from the MS. H. 3.18 in Trinity College, Dublin.

42 We should apparently read *uinculo.*

Cassander has the following variants: 43 *scissa pendent;* 45 *adfuit . . . myrra;* 47 *præcipit;* 48 *quæ spoponderat.*

50 *uellus*] *uellus sericum i.e. the woollen fleece; that was a good kind of raiment.* Sunt apud Ethiopiam et Indos quidam in arboribus uermes qui bombyces appellantur, qui araneæ more tenuissima fila nent, et unde sericum uestimentum efficitur. The latter part of the note is, in substance, found in Isidore (*l.c.*).

Cassander has: 51 *demouet . . . surgit . . . integer;* 52 *Iudaea mendax . . . uideret;* 54 *moestas . . . tristeis;* 58 *intrat.*

56 *nuntiant* is probably the true reading. See p. xii above.

58 *intrat* is undoubtedly the true reading, but the construction seems confused. The sense is "He enters, the doors being shut, [to them] doubting that He had returned," *ambigentes* being a nom. abs.

59 *dat*] i.e. *He sent the grace of the Holy Spirit on them on the day of Little Easter, quamuis plenius dedit in Pentecostem.* 'Little Easter', i.e. Low Sunday; cf. Jn. xx. 22.

60 *uinculum*] i.e. *that it should not be supposed that it was (a group) of two things or of four things, but of three semper, eo quod patrem et filium coniungit; uel uinculum, quod homines ad deum coniungit.*

Cassander has 61 *precipit . . . baptizare;* 63 *mystica;* 65 *concinimus.*

66 *docemur*] *it is a construction of active for passive that is hic, ut Priscianus dicit.*

---

[1] *Sermo de Symbolo* (Migne, P. L. xl. 698).   [2] Stokes' *Goidelica*, p. 13.
[3] *Goidelica*, p. 66. See also in Bede (Migne, P.L. xciv. 555).

67 The note in margin of T has . . *gallus i.e. cock* . . .

68 *precantes*. The active *preco* is an unusual form ; *precor* occurs twice in our hymns (vol. i. p. 19, l. 7, and p. 197, l. 5).

Cassander has: 68 *cantemus ;* 69 *concinimus uniter ;* 71 *ante lucem nunciemus Christum regem domini ;* and gives the *Gloria* &c., without any antiphons.

The first antiphon at the end of the hymn, *Te decet hymnus* &c. (Ps. lxiv. 2) is found, as Mr. Warren has pointed out,[1] in a fragment of an Irish *officium defunctorum* bound up in the St. Gall MS. 1395. It is perhaps worth adding that in a curious legend about a visit of St. Columba to heaven found in the Book of Lecan, the 'service of heaven' in which the heavenly choir were engaged began with " *Te decet hymnus* and *Benedic anima mea* and *Laudate pueri dominum.*"[2]

The gloss on *Sion* in this antiphon is probably a mistake for *et non in ethrialibus*. See line 114 of the hymn *Altus prosator* (vol. i. p. 79), where this latter word occurs.

The second antiphon, though not following the hymn in the *Antiphonary of Bangor*, is found on another page (fol. 26r°) in that manuscript, where it is headed " post euangelium."

The third antiphon does not occur in any of our manuscripts save T. Dr. Lawlor thought that he had found it prescribed for recitation after the *Hymnum dicat* in the directory for a monastic office in the Book of Mulling, of which a full account has been given in our Introduction (vol. i. p. xxii) ; but we have given reason for believing that he has misinterpreted the few letters that are legible.

Preface to the Hymn of St. Colman Mac Murchon.

A Colman Mac Murchon's obit is recorded by the Four Masters at the year 731, and it is possible that this may be the person to whom the scholiast ascribes the authorship of this hymn. He was Abbot of Moville, but is not said to have been a bishop. It would seem from the Preface that he and his brothers went on missionary pilgrimages abroad, but afterwards returned to Ireland.

The *Ictian Sea* of the Preface is the British Channel ; it is said to have taken its name from the *Portus Iccius* of Caesar, near Boulogne. " Rodan's Island " we cannot identify. Todd suggests that the isle of St. Rovi, off the coast of Brittany, may be intended ; St. Rodincus or Rovin was an Irishman, the founder of the Abbey of Beaulieu, who died Sept. 17, 680. The ' Tyrrhene Sea ' of the F Preface is mentioned in the *Tripartite Life* as having been the scene of some of St. Patrick's wanderings.[3] See also Fiacc's hymn l. 11. The scholiast of T is wrong in the statement that there are 16 syllables in each line, as there are only

---

[1] *Liturgy and Ritual*, &c., p. 180.
[2] See Reeves' *Adamnan*, p. 205. Mr. Macgregor (*Early Scottish Worship*, p. 13) observes that these are also the vesper psalms in the office described in the Voyage of St. Brendan.
[3] Stokes, *Tripartite Life*, p. 26.

the usual 15. In line 7, which would seem to be an exception, *et* is an interpolation in T and is not found in the other manuscripts.

The T scholiast seems to say at the end of the Preface that "the rhythm is on *i*"; but this is so incorrect a statement of the metrical laws which are observed in the hymn, that we hesitate to translate the Preface thus. The rhythm all through consists in the vowel-harmony of the last three syllables.

THE HYMN OF ST. COLMAN MAC MURCHON.

This hymn in praise of St. Michael was first printed by Mone in his *Hymni Latini medii aeui* (vol. i. p. 450) from the Karlsruhe MS. which we have called R, collated afresh for us through the kindness of Dr. A. Holder. This manuscript prefixes the word *unitas*, and thus begins the hymn *Unitas in trinitate*, which neither gives good sense nor suits the metre. It was probably this disguise of the hymn in Mone's collection which led Todd to overlook it and to claim for his edition (from T) that it was an *editio princeps*. An English metrical version of merit by D. F. MacCarthy is printed in O'Laverty's *Diocese of Down and Connor*, vol. ii. p. 18. See on the metre, p. xv above.

The hymn, as has been observed in our Introduction (vol. i. p. xxv), is prescribed for recitation in the office sketched out in the Second Vision of Adamnan, where it is called (as in K) "Michael's hymn," and (probably) in the Book of Mulling. It is, we think, undoubtedly an Irish composition, as Mone, who knew of no manuscripts of it by Irish scribes, adjudged it to be from its linguistic peculiarities.

St. Michael was very popular in Ireland. In the Second Vision of Adamnan we read in section 19: "the three hostages that were taken on behalf of the Lord for warding off every disease from the Irish—are Peter the Apostle, and Mary the Virgin, and Michael the Archangel."[1] There are a large number of fragmentary Irish poems in praise of St. Michael in the manuscript collection of the Royal Irish Academy. There were churches dedicated to him in many localities; the place-name *Temple-Michael* still exists in 6 or 7 counties. Mr. Willis Bund (*Celtic Church in Wales*, p. 330) accounts for the popularity of St. Michael in Wales by the prevalence among the Celts of belief in evil spirits, against which Michael protected the faithful.

1 The Latin gloss on *in omine* plainly has reference to some legend in connexion with the story in the Preface.

omine] *omen* i.e. *augury*: *abominor* i.e. *I separate from the augury for its abomination.*

3 *doctore*] i.e. *God.* Cf. *deus doctor docibilis* in l. 13 of the hymn *In te Christe.*

5 *inergiae* is for *energiae*, used of demoniac possession.

6 For *pes superbiae*, cf. Ps. xxxv. 12.

7 Compare Dan. x. 13: "Ecce Michael unus de principibus primis uenit in adiutorium meum."

9 *truces*] i.e. *horrid.*

[1] Stokes, in *Revue Celt.* xii. 429.

17 For the gloss on Raphael cf. Tobit vi. 6, 7, & xii. 15.

Over *mittat* in the fourth line of the antiphon or supplementary prayer at the end, there is in T a small *i*, indicating a variant *mittit*.

In connexion with L 7 and with this supplementary verse, it will be remembered that it was the task of Michael to weigh the souls in a balance at the Last Judgement,[1] and therefore in the hour of death there were recommended prayers asking his aid e.g. "O Michael, militiae caelestis signifer, in adiutorium nostrum ueni, princeps et propugnator."

It may be observed that the extract from the *Sermons* which go under the name of St. Augustine, in the margin of fol. 8b. of T, is a passage which is read in the Roman Breviary.

Preface to the Hymn of St. Oengus Mac Tipraite.

A visitation of the Columban monasteries in Ireland by Adamnan (see above p. 122) was made in 692, and again in 697; it is probably the latter of these that the scholiast has in his mind. Of Oengus mac Tipraite, we know nothing but this story, save that the Annals of Ulster record his death in 745. Cluain Fota is now called Clonfad, and is in the county of Westmeath. Uisnech "is in the parish of Conry in the diocese of Meath, a little south of which in the parish of Ardmurcher, is *Suidhe Adamnain* (now Syonan), 'sessio Adamnani,' which was probably the spot where the visitation or synod alluded to in the text was held."[2]

The Hymn of St. Oengus Mac Tipraite.

Of this hymn we have no other manuscripts save T and F. St. Martin of Tours was held in great esteem in Ireland, and the legend that St. Patrick was his nephew doubtless grew out of the desire to associate the great Apostle of Ireland with the great saint of Gaul. His life by Sulpicius Severus forms part of the Book of Armagh, and there is an Irish homily on his career in the *Leabhar Breac*.[3] He is one of the three non-biblical saints who have an octave in the *Martyrology of Gorman*.[4] In Ireland, churches were not as a rule called after departed saints, but after living founders, so that the number of churches dedicated to St. Martin is small in comparison with the large number that bear his name in England.[5] His name, however, lingers in many localities, in *Ballymartin* near Belfast; *Templemartin*, (a) near Bandon, (b) near Kilkenny; and in *Desertmartin* in the Diocese of Derry. There are five townlands of the name of *Kilmartin*; and there was an old church of St. Martin in the barony of Forth in the co.

---

[1] See Atkinson, *Passions and Homilies*, p. 453, for an account from the *Leabhar Breac* of the privileges of St. Michael.
[2] Todd, *Liber Hymnorum*, p. 174.
[3] Printed by Stokes, *Rev. Celt.* li. 381.
[4] Ed. Stokes, p. xlvi.
[5] For the connexion of St. Martin with the British Isles see Plummer's *Bede*, ii. 43.

Wexford, in the 13th century.[1] There was also a church in Dublin with this dedication in the 12th century; and before the Reformation one of the 14 altars in St. Nicholas' Church, Galway, bore his name.[2] It is possible that in some instances these place-names may preserve the memory of another Martin, who was a disciple of St. Patrick, but in the majority of cases it is probable that St. Martin of Tours is alluded to.

Mention is made in Adamnan's *Life of Columba* (iii. 12) of a *deprecatio, in qua sancti Martini commemoratur nomen*, which was used in the Liturgy at Iona.[3]

In l. 15 of the Preface, the compound word *gnuis-airmitiu* (cf. *Hom.-Pass.* 4293) should be observed. It is based on *gnuis-airitiu*, an imitation of the word προσωποληψία = *acceptio personarum*.

The antiphon at the close of the hymn or prayer of St. Oengus Mac Tipraite is taken from the life of Martin by Sulpicius Severus, and is given in the Breviary as the antiphon *in primo nocturno* for the vigils of St. Martin's Day. The allusions in the hymn itself are all to well known incidents in the life of the saint.

The marginal note on *dira* in l. 10 is much defaced. All that can be read is : *dialiton there is here i.e. Sechmall* . . . *murchon* . . .

The indulgence mentioned at the end of the Preface: "that it would be a protection against every disease, and heaven for reciting it on lying down and rising up," would seem to point to the use of the hymn as a sort of *lorica* or charm. If used in monastic offices, it would be at the night or early morning hours.

Gloria in Excelsis.

The 'tower Eder' מִגְדַּל עֵדֶר is mentioned twice in the Hebrew Bible; in Gen. xxxv. 16 where the LXX has ὁ πύργος Γάδερ, and in Micah iv. 8, where it has πύργος ποιμνίου; the Vulgate in both cases being *turris gregis*. The place meant in the former passage was near Bethlehem, and St. Jerome[4] identifies it with the scene of the angelic vision to the shepherds; but the *turris gregis nebulosa filiae Sion* of Micah was near Jerusalem. Bede (*in Lc.* ii. 8) is able to explain the *latter* passage as prophetic of the scenes at the Nativity by a slight change of reading (*uenient* for *ueniet*); and it is to some such explanation as this that we owe the statement of the Irish scholiasts that the tower was "a mile east of Jerusalem." It is worth adding that the writer of the Irish Homily on the Nativity in the *Leabhar Breac* follows the more correct geography and speaks of the tower being a thousand paces east of Bethlehem.[5]

The reading *Gabder* of the T Preface is a corruption of *gadder* (which, it will be remembered, is the name given to the tower by the glossator on l. 14 of the *Hymnus S. Hilarii*); and this is a transliteration of the LXX Γάδερ, the representative of the Hebrew עֵדֶר.

---
[1] *The Watchman*, Oct. 15, 1881.   [2] Hardiman's *History of Galway*, p. 246.
[3] See Warren's *Celtic Liturgy*, p. 107.
[4] *Epitaph. Paulae, Epist. cviii ad Eustochium.*
[5] Hogan, *Todd Lectures*, vi. p. 53. So too Jerome in his *Monasticon*.

The authorship of Ambrose suggested in the Preface has nothing to recommend it, and is a mere guess. The Latin version of the *Gloria in excelsis* is ascribed to Hilary with similar improbability in the treatise *De diuinis officiis* which goes under the name of Alcuin, and Hilary is given as the author in the Vatican MS. 5729.

The statement in the B Preface about the number of *capitula* &c. is incorrect. In the B or ordinary version of the hymn it is true that there are seven clauses, but they are not in rhythm, nor are there "seven lines in each *capitulum* and seven syllables in each line." It is possible that the last sentence of the B Preface is a piece of irrelevant information added by the glossator, who had in his mind an Ambrosian hymn of the type of *Veni Redemptor gentium*.

Mr. Warren has printed in his edition of the *Antiphonary of Bangor*[1] the various Irish texts of the *Gloria in excelsis*, and also the Greek text from the *Codex Alexandrinus*, thus bringing out the remarkable affinity between them. We have also given in our *apparatus criticus* the variants from FABS. Of the B text it is right to say that it has little to justify its reproduction save that it is found in an Irish manuscript. It must be borne in mind that the *Leabhar Breac* is a composite book, made up of an enormous collection of pieces of different dates; and whereas the B Preface, which is found at fol. 49 as a marginal note on the Felire of Oengus, is distinctively Celtic, the text of the hymn (at fol. 136) occurs in a late Irish homily, which was probably not put together in its present form until a time when the Anglo-Norman domination had sensibly modified the characteristic features of Celtic worship. The *Gloria in excelsis* is also found in the MS. we have called J, but the text (like that of B) is not characteristic, and has none of the additional clauses which are so interesting in our other MSS.

Not only does the Latin version of the *Gloria in excelsis* in Irish MSS. agree in many particulars with the Greek text; but, as has been pointed out by Dr. Gibson[2] and by Mr. Warren, its use in the Celtic Church seems to have been similar to that of the East. In the Codex Alexandrinus the hymn is entitled ὕμνος ἑωθινός, and to the present day it is sung at night and in the early morning in the Greek Church. So in the *Antiphonary of Bangor*, the title is *ad uesperum et ad matutinam*,[3] and the B Preface notes "at night it is due to be sung." One of the supplementary clauses in F is *ut hanc noctem sine peccato nos transire possimus*. In l. 22 of the piece in T and F (though not in A), we have "nocte ista sine peccato nos custodire," which points in the same direction. Nevertheless it ought to be observed that the T glossator did not understand these words as indicating the hour at which the hymn was sung; he glosses them *huius sæculi*. And again at l. 27 he is careful to explain *in die et nocte* as equivalent to *in prosperis* and *in tenebris sæculi huius*. It would thus appear probable that the old use of singing the hymn at the night offices had fallen into desuetude at the time when the glosses were added; for the glossator goes out of his way to give a mystical interpretation to words which are sufficiently plain in themselves.

---

[1] Vol. ii. p. 76 ff.   [2] *Church Quarterly Review*, Oct. 1885.
[3] In the MS. Galba A. xviii. it is headed: *Hymnus in die dominica ad matutinas*.

In l. 9 the words *et omnes dicimus amen* may have come from a marginal rubric which found its way into the text at an early date. Another illustration is afforded by the last words of Ps. cvi. "Let all the people say, Amen," which is probably in like manner a rubrical direction that has got into the text of the Hebrew Psalter. But Mr. Warren makes the interesting observation that a similar clause is also inserted in the Armenian office for Vespers in the text of the hymn φῶς ἱλαρὸν ἁγίας δόξης. And Mr. Macgregor has suggested that *et omnes dicimus, Amen* is an importation of the phrase "And say we, Amen," which is found in parts of the Jewish Morning Service.[1]

It will be observed that neither in the text of B, which (as we have said) is not distinctively Celtic, nor in that of S, where the *Gloria in excelsis* is found in its place in the Eucharistic service, are there any supplementary anthems like those found in T, F, and A. The variation in these is a phenomenon which presents itself again in connexion with the texts of the *Te Deum*; and it will be seen that some of those with which we are familiar in the *Te Deum* are found in these Irish manuscripts as *addenda* to the *Gloria in excelsis*. For instance *Dignare domine nocte ista [die isto] sine peccato nos custodire* (ll. 21, 22) is in the ordinary texts of the *Te Deum*; it was among the *Preces* used at Prime and was there followed by Pss. cxxii. 3, and cxxxii. 22. Dr. Gibson, in the article to which we have already referred, suggests that these antiphons, which were originally attached to the *Gloria in excelsis*, became linked with the *Te Deum* when this began to take the place of the older hymn in the daily offices of the Church.[2]

MAGNIFICAT AND BENEDICTUS.

Neither the Irish Prefaces to the *Magnificat* and *Benedictus* nor the glosses seem to call for any special remark. The majority of the glosses in T to both of these canticles are taken, as the references we have added show, from Bede's Commentary on St. Luke. They constituted the stock in trade of most commentators of the period, and are found e.g. also in Hraban Maur's *Commentaria in Cantica quae ad laudes dicuntur*. Whether or not they were original with Bede is another question into which we do not here inquire. Bede is often explicitly quoted by Irish writers; the index to our first volume shows how well he was known to our scholiasts.

The text of these Canticles, especially of the *Benedictus*, is interesting in connexion with the question as to the version of the Latin New Testament current in the Celtic Church, which was—speaking generally —Vulgate with considerable traces of the 'European' Old Latin out of which it grew. 'Ab aeuo' in l. 6 is, for instance, quite characteristic. See Wordsworth and White's Vulgate N. T. *in loc.*

The marginal note on fol. 10 of T is made up, for the most part, of extracts from the *Pastoral Rule* of Gregory the Great. This was

[1] Warren, *Liturgy of the Ante Nicene Church*, p. 245.
[2] See *Neue Kirchl. Zeitschr.* 1896, pp. 119 foll. for a discussion by Zahn of these supplementary verses.

one of the most popular books in the middle ages.[1] In the time of Charlemagne there were laws obliging the clergy to read it. It is one of the books which Bede urged Archbishop Egbert to study; and there was a Saxon paraphrase of it attributed to Alfred the Great. In Ireland it was as well known as it was on the Continent. Columbanus in his letter to Gregory (*Ep.* i.) tells him that he had read it with delight. The first extract from it in this note is also embodied in the Irish collection of Canons known as the *Hibernensis* (xxi. 7).

TE DEUM.

This is not the place in which to write a treatise on the authorship and structure of the *Te Deum*; and we therefore confine ourselves to a few explanatory notes. The tradition of the T Preface that it was composed by Augustine and Ambrose is the best known of all the traditions as to its origin, as it has found its way into the Breviary.[2] The title "hymnus quem S. Ambrosius et S. Augustinus inuicem condiderunt" is found in two St. Gall MSS. (23 and 27); and the story is at least older than the middle of the ninth century, for it is alluded to by Hincmar:[3] "ut a maioribus nostris audiuimus tempore baptismatis sancti Augustini hunc hymnum beatus Ambrosius fecit, et idem Augustinus cum eo confecit." This, however, is unhistorical, and the authorship of Ambrose may be ruled out of court.

The tradition of the F Preface is peculiarly interesting,[4] and it is probable that it is based on the real fact. Ten or eleven MSS. of the *Te Deum* give the name of the author as Nicetas or Nicetius. It used to be supposed that Nicetius, bishop of Treves (527–566), was meant; but this is impossible, for a letter of St. Cyprian, bishop of Toulon, which was written before 542, quotes from the hymn and describes it as one "quem omnis ecclesia toto orbe receptum canit."[5] But Dom Morin,[6] and, quite recently, Zahn[7] have identified this 'Nicetius' with Niceta who was bishop of Remesiana in Dacia (392–414), a friend and correspondent of Paulinus of Nola. This person is described by Gennadius (*Catal. uir. illustr.* c. 22) as *Remesianae ciuitatis episcopus*. The MSS. of Gennadius have variants *Romatianae, Romaniciae, Romanae,* &c.; and it is in this last corruption that we find the origin of our scholiast's story that the hymn was made in Rome, and that Niceta, its author, was a *coarb* or successor of St. Peter. Niceta, the bishop of Remesiana, did indeed visit Rome, when he was on his way to visit Paulinus; but it is most likely that the legend with which we are concerned arose from the confusion in the MSS. between *Remesianae* and the more familiar *Romanae*. And it is but a step from 'Romanae ciuitatis episcopus' to

---

[1] See for many references Plummer's *Bede*, ii. 70.
[2] See Batiffol, *Hist. du Breviaire romain*, p. 98.
[3] Migne, P.L. cxxv. 290.
[4] See Introduction to vol. i. p. xiv, for a quotation of this F Preface by Ussher. Ussher also states that Nicetius was named as the author of the *Te Deum* in a Psalter in the Cotton Library (*Works*, vii. 300). This has not been identified, but Rev. A. E. Burn suggests that it may be B.M. Harl. 863 (saec. x–xi), which entitles the *Te Deum* Ymnus sci Nicetii Aepiscopi.
[5] *Monum. Germ. Epist.* iii. 436.   [6] *Revue Benedictine*, Fevr. 1894.
[7] *Neue Kirchl. Zeitschr.* 1896, pp. 106–123.

'coarb of St. Peter.' It appears, then, that the legend of the F Preface furnishes additional strength to the arguments of Morin and Zahn : for here we have distinct witness to the early identification of Nicetius, the author of the *Te Deum*, with Niceta, the bishop of Remesiana.

Bishop John Wordsworth, of Salisbury, in his article on the *Te Deum* in the *Dict. of Christian Hymnology* (p. 1120) has given a collation of the MSS. TFA, and Mr. Warren has added the collation of D in the appendix to his *Antiphonary of Bangor* (vol. ii. p. 93). It has been necessary in accordance with the plan of our edition to give these variants in our *apparatus criticus*, but they have been taken direct from the MSS. The *Te Deum* is found in C, but we have not registered its readings inasmuch as the text is of the ordinary type, and does not show any of the characteristics of the Irish texts.

We do not enter here into the usage as to the recitation of the *Te Deum*. The title in the ninth century St. Gall MS. No. 20 is comparable with that in A : "Ymnus dominicalis pro nocturnis, hoc est ante lectionem euangelii."

1 The verse (Ps. cxii. 1) with which the *Te Deum* opens in the Irish texts is worthy of note. It is prescribed as the antiphon to the Greek evening hymn in the Apostolical Constitutions (Book vii. c. 47). In the account already cited (p. 132) of the "service of heaven" from the Book of Lecan, *Laudate pueri dominum*, which doubtless represents the *Te Deum*, is fabled to have been sung. Morin (l.c.) deems it not improbable that Niceta began the *Te Deum* with these words.

9, 10 Compare the citation of this in the *Amra* (vol. i. p. 171, l. 306) : "quia dicunt hiruphin et zaraphin, sanctus sanctus sanctus dominus deus Sabaoth dicentes," which perhaps witnesses to the insertion of *dicentes* (as in TF) in l. 10 in the *Te Deum* as known to the commentator. The line is also quoted in Adamnan's prayer (vol. i. p. 184, l. 16).

12 The insertion of *uniuersa* is characteristic of the Irish texts. At fol. 22b of S it is inserted in the *Ter Sanctus* in like manner : *pleni sunt caeli et uniuersa terra gloria tua*.

23 This is the reading which had most currency in the British Isles, and very possibly is the original form. But Dom Morin (l.c.) has produced evidence to show the prevalence in Southern Gaul of the now common reading *Tu ad liberandum suscepturus hominem* in the sixth century.

31 The *Te Deum* in its earliest form very probably ended here at the word *munerari* (which, it should be observed, and not *numerari* is the reading of *all* manuscripts). D stops short at this point ; and this is an indication of the extreme antiquity of the text found in that MS. The agreements of D with TFA are remarkable, but it is rather to be considered as giving an ancient form of the *Te Deum*, than as supplying the specially Irish recension.

37, 38 This versicle (Ps. xxxii. 22) is prescribed twice for recitation in S (fol. 33) during the Fraction.

This antiphon, which follows the hymn in T and F, is placed at the end of the volume in A. In that MS. the *Te Deum* is on fol. 10 ; but the antiphon is given at fol. 35 r°. where it is headed *Post Laudate pueri dominum in dominicorum die.* It is given again in a slightly different form on fol. 35 v°. and another fragment of it is on fol. 36. It is not unlike the antiphon prescribed " super *Quicunque* " at Prime on Sundays in the Sarum Office, or at Lauds on Trinity Sunday after *Magnificat* in the modern Roman Breviary: " Te Deum patrem ingenitum, filium unigenitum, te spiritum sanctum paraclitum, sanctum et indiuiduam Trinitatem toto corde et ore confitemur, laudamus atque benedicimus ; tibi glòria in sæcula."

We have not been able to identify the note found in the margin of fol. 10b of T. Passages very like it occur in St. Augustine's sermons (see Migne, P. L. v. 783, vi. 783, xi. 798); but we have not found the exact words.

The passage on fol. 11 beginning " Orationibus mundamur, lectionibus instruimur " occurs, as our reference indicates, not only in Isidore but in the Collection of Canons known as the *Hibernensis.* These opening words are quoted in the Benedictine rule (Migne, P. L. ciii. 621).

PREFACE TO THE HYMN *ALTUS PROSATOR.*

The B Preface tells us that one tradition as to the place of composition of this famous hymn was that it was composed at Duibh Regles, St. Columba's ' Black Church ' at Derry. But the TF Preface, although speaking of the saint's meditation for seven years ' in nigra cellula,' says distinctly that " the place of the hymn " was the Island of Hi (now called Iona through a misreading of the *Ioua insula* of manuscripts).

The indications of date given in the Prefaces are fairly consistent. According to the chronologies Aedan mac Gabrain was king of Scotland from 574 to 606, and Aed mac Ainmerech was king of Ireland from 572 to 599 ; while the Emperor Maurice reigned from 582 to 602 and was succeeded by Phocas. Columba was born in 521 and died on June 9 597, and Gregory the Great, with whom one of the legends here recorded connects him, died in 590.

Columba might well be described as " de nobile genere Scotorum," inasmuch as he belonged to the clan O'Donnell and was great-great-grandson of Neill of the Nine Hostages.

The most plausible of the traditions given in the Prefaces as to the origin of the hymn describes it as a penitential exercise composed by the saint, who was troubled by the memory of three battles in which he had played an active part. The first of these, the battle of Cuil Dremne (now Cooladrummon near Sligo), is recorded to have been fought in 561, the Neill clan under Columba himself gaining a decisive victory over Diarmait, king of Ireland. It was after this battle that he went to Iona, exiling himself from his country, according to one legend, by the advice of St. Molaise of Inismurray, as a penance for the blood which he had caused to be shed. The other battles were that of Coleraine in 579, which arose out of some dispute as to a church between

St. Columba and St. Comgall of Bangor; and that of Cuil Feda near Clonard in 587.[1]

The other story describes the hymn as an extemporaneous utterance, miraculously composed during the grinding of a sack of oats.[2] The hymn *Adiutor laborantium* which he is said to have composed on the way to the mill does not seem to be extant; it is just possible that there may be here an allusion to the hymn *In te Christe* (vol. i. p. 84), the third line of which is *Deus in adiutorium intende laborantium.*

The mention of the stone, variously called Blathnat or Moel-blatha, on which "there is made division in the refectory," and of which it is further said that "luck was left on all food that is put thereon," is interesting. It is probable that the allusion is to the practice of cutting up the *eulogiae* or *pain bénit* at a table in the refectory, which we know to have obtained at Iona and also at St. Kenneth's monastery at Aghaboe in the diocese of Ossory.[3] Dr. Skene considered that he had identified this very stone among the ruins at Iona.[4]

It will be observed that the statement of the TF scholiast as to the donation of Iona to Columba confirms that of Bede, in the assertion that Bruide mac Maelcon, king of the Picts, *immolauit Columbo Hi; i.e. obtulit in perpetuum Columbae Ionam.*[5] Tighernach, and also the Annals of Ulster, represent the island as given by Conall, the king of British Dalriata. Reeves sums up the history thus: "Columba probably found Hy unoccupied and unclaimed, Conall kindly promised not to disturb him, and when the Picts were converted, Brudeus, the supreme lord, of course gave to the infant institution all the right and title which the weight of his sanction could confer."

The legend goes on to the effect that the hymn was sent to Gregory as a return for gifts sent by him viz. a Cross and a Hymnary. The Cross was reputed to be preserved at Tory Island in 1532, as O'Donnell tells in his *Life of Columba.* Of the Hymnary we know nothing; Todd suggests that it may have been a copy of the *Liber Antiphonarius* of Gregory. The messengers sent to Gregory tested him by substituting spurious stanzas for the H, O, and U[6] stanzas of the hymn[7]; but Gregory miraculously discovered their deceit. Gregory's criticism that there was more praise of the creature than of the Creator in the hymn set Columba on the composition of the piece *In te Christe.* See below p. 169.

The TF scholiast observes that the opening stanza is based on the *Quicunque Vult;* see p. 155 *infra.*

The remarks on the rhythm made in the Preface do not call for much comment. A 'verse' includes two lines, according to our way of

---

[1] See Reeves' *Adamnan,* p. 253.
[2] That Columba "often used to carry his portion of corn on his back to the mill, and grind it," is mentioned in the old Irish Life (*Lismore,* p. 180) as a proof of his humility. Cf. also *Lismore,* p. 269, where the same thing is told of St. Ciaran.
[3] See Warren's *Celtic Liturgy,* p. 140, and Fowler's *Adamnan,* p. 82. Compare Dowden's *Celtic Church in Scotland,* p. 168.
[4] *Celtic Scotland,* ii. 100.
[5] See for this use of *immolare* in Celtic Latin, and for a general discussion of the whole matter Reeves' *Adamnan,* p. 435. There is also a note in Plummer's *Bede,* ii. 131.
[6] or X, according to the B Preface.
[7] In ll. 38, 42, of the TF Preface, confusion has been introduced into previous editions by a misreading of the text.

printing the hymn; and the rules laid down are (1) that each quarter verse shall have 8 syllables and (2) that the quarter verse and the half verse shall rhyme, *e.g. uetustus, ingenitus*, &c. See above p. xxvi.

The direction given for the recitation of the hymn is interesting, viz. that 'Quis potest Deo,' which perhaps includes only the first two lines of the supplementary antiphons (vol. i. p. 81), was to be sung at the close of each stanza. These lines are found in all our MSS. of the *Altus*. The second antiphon (ll. 4-9) seems to be quite distinct.

The 'graces' of the hymn which are enumerated seem to show that it was recited as a kind of *lorica*, in time of danger or of sickness. It was said to ward off all death save 'death on the pillow' *i.e.* from natural causes, or, as the B scholiast puts, *mors pretiosa*, which Todd explains by a reference to Ps. cxv. 15 "pretiosa in conspectu domini mors sanctorum eius." The verse found at foot of fol. 237 of B (vol. i. p. 83 and below p. 169), prescribes its sevenfold recitation; and a curious legend printed by O'Curry[1] tells of a boy seized with mortal sickness around whom " the *Altus* was sung seven times," though without effect.

THE HYMN *ALTUS PROSATOR*.

The manuscripts of the *Altus* known to us are seven in number, and they fall into two groups.

T, our principal manuscript, is deficient from l. 80 to l. 127, as a leaf has been lost; for the intervening stanzas, we have taken as our standard the Franciscan copy (F). T is glossed throughout.

F is complete for this hymn; the glosses are few in number and are unimportant; they are written in a hand of the sixteenth century.

B only contains stanzas A-H inclusive; it is copiously glossed, and in many cases the glosses resemble those of T.

TFB all have titles, several lines in length, at the head of each stanza, giving the substance of the argument in the verses which follow; and, as we have seen, they have vernacular Prefaces introducing the hymn, all embodying the same traditions, those in T and F being almost verbally identical. This group of three MSS. we call the "Irish" group.

Our four remaining manuscripts, MEIΠ (for a description of which see vol. i. pp. xvii ff), have neither Preface, titles to the stanzas, nor (with a few exceptions) glosses; and the types of text which they present are markedly similar. There is nothing specifically Irish about these MSS. They all contain the *Altus* among works ascribed to St. Prosper of Aquitaine (403-465), and in three cases at least the hymn follows directly on the *De uita contemplatiua*. This work is well known not to be a genuine work of Prosper's, and is usually attributed to Julianus Pomerius, a Mauretanian priest, who lived *circa* 500.[2] To go a little more into detail as to these manuscripts, which we call the "Prosper group":—

[1] *MS. materials*, p. 78. See also Todd, *Liber Hymnorum*, p. 250.
[2] See Migne, P.L. lix. col. 415 ff. for the *De uita contemplatiua*; no mention is made of the hymn in any printed edition of Prosper or of Julianus Pomerius, so far as we know.

On f. 83 of M we have the end of the third book of the *De uita contemplatiua*, thus: "Quando non res pro uerbis sed pro rebus enuntiandis uerba sunt instituta. Explicit liber tertius. Altus prosator, &c." the hymn then following without any verse divisions, and written as if it were prose. At the end, after *ordinibus*, the next line begins "hic insunt sub hoc corpore epigrammata beati Prosperi, &c."

In E the hymn is found in the same place as in M between the *De uita contempl.* and the *epigrammata*, and is written by the same hand that has written the other pieces. In the margin there was an eleventh century note, which has been cut away by the binder so that only a few letters remain. There were four lines of which the ends were: *nus per al—; I dige— ; pul— ; edit.*

There is nothing to say about I, save that it is reported to be a splendidly executed MS. and that the hymn is found in it among works ascribed to St. Prosper. It is followed by a collect of considerable interest, on which we comment below (p. 168).

II is a MS. of the eleventh century, the hymn following immediately the *De uita contempl.* The verses from l. 79 onward are written in a hand of the fourteenth or fifteenth century, the old leaf having probably become illegible through constant use.

Despite the witness of these manuscripts, however, we believe that the Hymn is a distinctively Celtic composition, and is not the work either of St. Prosper of Aquitaine or of Julianus Pomerius. The genuine works of Prosper are quite different in character, both as regards form and matter. The style of that writer has no resemblance to the rude and barbarous, though vigorous, Latin of this hymn; and the speculations as to the creation and the fall of the 'giants' are foreign to his ways of thinking. And, although in the *De uita contemplatiua* (iii. 1) there is a discussion of the fall of the angels, we cannot find any good reason for connecting the hymn with the name of Julianus Pomerius.

The Irish were fond of cosmogonic speculations; the first poem, *e.g.* in the *Saltair na Rann*, is devoted to them. And it is worth observing how akin are the topics treated in the hymn *Altus Prosator* to those discussed in the Book of Enoch, which widely affected mediæval ways of thinking.[1] Chapters lxxii–lxxxii of *Enoch* which deal with Celestial Physics are not unlike the early stanzas of our hymn; the conceptions of 'the devil's satellites,' of the lightning and the winds issuing from their secret chambers, of the beneficent influence of the rain, of the stately and regular orbits of the sun and moon, have close parallels in the *Altus*; while the Vision of Judgement at the end of *Enoch* reminds us of our stanzas RSTZ.

The Latinity of the hymn, as we have said, is barbarous. It presents some resemblances to two other pieces which have Celtic connexions, viz. the *Lorica* of Gildas (our No. 48), and the curious tract entitled *Hisperica famina*,[2] which is written in a kind of assonant rhythm. Zimmer has given an elaborate discussion[3] of the date of these, and has

[1] See Charles, *Book of Enoch*, pp. 38ff.
[2] See Migne, P.L. xc. 1187.
[3] *Nennius uindicatus*, p. 291 ff. See also H. Bradshaw, *Collected Papers*, p. 463 foll.

come to the conclusion that they belong to the first half of the sixth century, and were most probably produced in monasteries in the south-west of Britain, being certainly Celtic though not Irish. Mai, however, who first printed *Hisperica famina*, considered it to be the work of an Irish monk. But, at any rate, Zimmer's arguments as to the date seem convincing, and they corroborate, so far, the tradition that Columba wrote the *Altus*. Among strange words common to these pieces, we have *iduma* for 'hand' which occurs in all three (see below, p. 163). In the *Hisp. fam.* and the *Altus* we have *dodrans* (see below, p. 160), in the sense of 'the flood of the ocean,' and *tithis* for 'the sea'; 'barathrum,' 'ergastulum,' 'crepido,' are other unusual words in both works; and there is common to both a tendency to form substantives ending in -men, such as 'præsagmen,' 'fatimen,' &c.

But for a full discussion of this curious Latinity the reader must be referred to Zimmer's *Nennius uindicatus*, and the special works there quoted[1]; as the author of the *Hisperica famina* says, 'caetera non explico famine stemata, ne doctoreis suscitauero fastidium castris.' It is enough to say that the Latin of the *Altus* is quite what we might expect from a writer of Columba's date and antecedents, and has no resemblance to the style of Prosper, or the author of the *De uita contemplatiua*.

In the next place, when we examine the text of Scripture underlying the phraseology of our hymn, we find that the author did not use the vulgar Latin, but the older text which was current before Jerome's revision came into use. The following instances will, we think, establish this interesting point.

(*a*) l. 1. '*uetustus* dierum.' This is the O.L. of Dan. vii. 9, witnessed to by Augustine and the author of the treatise *ad Nouatianum*, printed with Cyprian's works. The Vulgate has '*antiquus* dierum.'

(*b*) l. 21. 'serpens . . . *sapientior* omnibus bestiis &c.' Gen. iii. 1, is quoted thus by Augustine, Lucifer of Cagliari and Ambrose; the Vulgate has *callidior*.

(*c*) l. 25. 'refugas . . . parasito *præcipites*.' In the Fleury Palimpsest of the Apocalypse, and in the *Liber de promiss et prædict. dei*, c. iii, which contains Old Latin readings, Apoc. xii. 9, is quoted thus: '*et præcipitatus* est in terram &c.,' the Vulgate having *proiectus*. Again *refuga* was the O.L. rendering of ἀποστάτην, as Rönsch (*Itala und Vulgata*, p. 83) has shown by many examples; *e.g.* Lucifer of Cagliari applies it both to the devil and to his angels (*Athan.* i. p. 2, and *de non parc.* 228). In 2 Thess. ii. 3, Codex Clar. has *refuga* for *discessio* of the Vulgate as the equivalent of ἀποστασία.

(*d*) l. 33. 'collaudauerunt angeli factura pro mirabili.' The Vulgate of Iob xxxviii. 7, which is the passage here in view, is 'cum me laudarent simul astra matutina et iubilarent omnes filii dei.' But the O.L. manuscript from Marmoutier (Tours 18) has a text much more like the words of our hymn, viz.: 'quando facta sunt simul sidera, laudauerunt me uoce magna omnes angeli mei.'

[1] See also p. 243, *infra*.

THE HYMN ALTUS PROSATOR.

l. 111. 'poliandria' is taken from the vox of Ezek. xxxix. 11, 15, 16, which has πολυανδριον *where Vg. has multitudo and Amos.*

(e) l. 113. 'undique conglobantibus ad *compagines* ossibus.' The Vulgate of Ezek. xxxvii. 7, is 'accesserunt ossa ad ossa, unumquodque ad *iuncturam* suam'; but Ambrose and the O.L. translator of Irenaeus have 'unumquodque ad suam *compaginem*.'

(f) L 117. The description of the Pleiades as *Uirgiliae* in this stanza reproduces the O.L. of Job ix. 9: 'qui facit *uirgilias* et uesperum, &c.' which is witnessed to by Ambrose, and is found in the margin of the *Codex Gothicus legionensis*.' The Vulgate has 'qui facit Arcturum et Oriona et *Hyadas*.' See, however, p. 166.

(g) l. 125. 'cadent in terra sidera, ut *fructus* de *ficulnea*.' The Vulgate of Apoc. vi. 13, has 'sicut *ficus* emittit *grossos* suos.' Now the *Gigas* text of the O.L. Apocalypse has 'sicut *ficulnea* deicit grossos suos'; and Primasius and the *Liber de promiss. et praedict. dei*, c. xvii. read '*ficus*' and '*fructus*.' Thus both *fructus* and *ficulnea* of the hymn rest on good O.L. authority. In the adaptation of the *Altus* by Hraban Maur, to be presently spoken of, it will be observed that Hraban has replaced *fructus* by the more familiar *grossos*.

The writer of the hymn, then, used a prae-Hieronymian text of both Old and New Testaments. This fact, of itself, would indicate that he was not Prosper of Aquitaine or Julianus Pomerius; and it falls in well with the tradition which names Columba as the author, for the scanty evidence on the subject which is forthcoming teaches us that it was the Old Latin rather than the Vulgate which was current in the Irish Church in the fifth and sixth centuries. This is certainly true of the Scripture quotations in the genuine remains of St. Patrick, which are Old Latin of the so-called "European" type. It is possible that legend has preserved for us the truth as to the introduction of the Vulgate into Ireland. It is said in the Life of St. Finnian of Moville (who died, according to the Annals of Innisfallen, in 576) that he was "the first to bring the Gospel to Ireland," a statement which is repeated in a gloss in the *Leabhar Breac* copy of the Felire of Oengus.[2] This has reference to a highly valued manuscript brought over by Finnian, which is said to have been copied clandestinely by Columba; and the most plausible explanation is that it was a manuscript of Jerome's version, which hitherto had been unknown in Ireland. But, however that may be, it is probable that the Irish Church in the days of Columba used the Old Latin version of Scripture; and it is certain that traces of it lingered for centuries even when the Vulgate text had come into use.

In this connexion attention may be drawn to the 'titles' prefixed to the stanzas of the *Altus* in the 'Irish' group of MSS. These are evidently the additions of some scholiast, though at what date they were composed it is impossible to say. The title of the first stanza which alludes to Columba as 'the *latest* and noblest of Ireland's prophets' perhaps points to a date not very far removed from the times of Columba himself. And the fact, which will be noticed further on, that in some instances alternative titles are suggested, shows that they

[1] Berger, *Notice sur quelques textes latins inédits de l'ancien Testament* (1893), p. 21.
[2] See Olden, *Church of Ireland*, p. 61, and Stokes, *Felire of Oengus*, p. cxliv.

must have been in existence for a considerable period before the date of the earliest of our Irish MSS. of the *Altus*. But whatever their date (and they were most probably put together about the eighth century), they retain conspicuous traces of an Old Latin Version of Holy Scripture.

Against the tradition that Columba wrote the *Altus*, there is only one argument of any importance, and that rests on the fact that allusions to the hymn are extremely scanty in Irish literature. One of these we have mentioned above (p. 142); another is found in an ancient poem entitled *Mesca Coluimcille* found in the Bodleian MS. Laud 615, which professes to record a prophecy delivered by Columba shortly before his death. One stanza runs thus:

'My *Altus* angelic and holy:
'My *Easparta* for Thursday;
My *Amra* with the King of the pure bright moon;
'Here I leave after me.'[1]

But the absence of many references to the hymn, save in the formal *Lives* of the saint, may perhaps be accounted for by the prevalence of the legend given in the Prefaces, which suggested it was not quite orthodox. In any case the argument from silence is a very unsafe one to use, and not sufficient in this case to set aside the evidence of tradition, corroborated as it is by the internal characteristics of the poem, that Columba was the author.

The Prosper MSS. may then be taken as witnessing merely to the knowledge of the *Altus* in the Gallican Church. And in this connexion it is interesting to find that a large part of the hymn is embodied in a long poem by Hraban Maur (786-856), beginning *Aeterne rerum conditor*. This furnishes not only a valuable piece of evidence as to the popularity of the piece, but gives us what amounts to an additional early authority for its text. We have thought it worth while to print here so much of the poem as bears upon the textual criticism of the *Altus*. The omitted lines 24-60 deal with the Trinity, ll. 69-100 with the Fall, ll. 106-220 with the Incarnation and Life of Christ, and ll. 274-295 contain prayers. It will be observed that the following portions of the *Altus* are reproduced, though not always in regular order, and sometimes with slight modifications of reading: ll. 1-31, 38, 60, 75-79, 95, 99, 101-114, 122-135. The stanzas which Hraban has not taken up into his poem have little religious reference, and are concerned with the operations of nature rather than specially Christian themes. We have printed the text given by A. Dümmler in his *Poetae Latini aeui medii*, vol. ii. p. 197 (1884)[2]; the poem will also be found among Hraban's works in Migne, P.L. cxii. 1610.

---

[1] See Reeves' *Adamnan*, p. lxxx.
[2] Dümmler observes that some writers, e.g. W. Grimm (*Gesch. des Reims*, p. 684), have argued that Hraban is the original author of the *Altus*; this is, however, quite impossible. It was Hraban's constant practice to borrow the verses of other writers. See Dümmler, l.c. p. 157 n.

De Fide Catholica rythmo carmen compositum.

Aeterne rerum conditor et clarus mundi formator,
deus in adiutorium intende tu humilium ;
cordeque tibi deuotûm festina in auxilium.
Da mentis fida regmina ac uerbi clara munera
5   da uotis cordis optima et facti dona plurima ;
sensum corde purissimum famen ore pacificum

Ut tuam laudem famine in primis possim dicere,
magnam, miram ac praeclaram, digna uoce iustissimam
meaeque sim miseriae compunctus memor ultimae.
10 Deus salus credentium deus uita uiuentium
deus deorum omnium deus et princeps principum
deus summus amabilis deus inaestimabilis.

Altus prosator uetustus dierum et ingenitus
eras absque origine primordii et crepidine
15 qui es eris in saecula saeculorum infinita
Cui est unigenitus Christus proles carissimus
dicentis de corde uerbum satum ante Luciferum
coaeternus in gloria deitatis perpetua

Cum quo simul et filio in sempiterno saeculo
20 spiritus sanctus aequalis regnat et honorabilis
in eadem substantia deus manens per saecula.
non tres deos nec profero sed unum deum praedico
salua fide in personis tribus gloriosissimum
summum iustum rectissimum super omnes mitissimum.

•   •   •   •   •

40 Bonos creauit angelos ordines et archangelos
principatus et uirtutes thronos dominationes
potestates et cherubin gloriosa et seraphin
uti non esset bonitas otiosa ac maiestas
trinitatis in omnibus largitatis muneribus
45 sed haberet caelestia quibus det priuilegia.

Sed caeli regni apice stationis angelicae
claritate pro fulgoris uenustate speciminis
superbiendo ruerat Lucifer quem plasmauerat
Apostateque angeli eodem lapsu lugubri
50 auctores cenodoxiae peruicacis inuidiae
caeteris remanentibus in suis principatibus.

Draco magnus teterrimus terribilis et antiquus
qui fuit serpens lubricus sapientior omnibus
bestiis et animantibus terrae ferocioribus,
55 tertiam partem siderum traxit secum in baratrum
locorum infernalium diuersorumque carcerum
refugus ueri luminis parasitus praecipitans.

l. 2

```
        Dum pius mundi machinam praeuidens et armoniam
        polum et siccum fecerat atque aquas diuiserat
 60     herbarum format germina uirgultum ac arbuscula
        solem lunam ac sidera ignem ac necessaria
        aues pisces et pecora bestias animalia
        tum demum honorabilem ipse condidit hominem

        Huic praecepit firmiter manere immortaliter
 65     suam sacram imaginem seruare uenerabilem
        sequique iussa domini uicarius cum sit dei
        'esto' dixit humillimus rector mundi et dominus
        nam cuncta tibi tradidi ac dominatu subdidi
        quae sunt modo uiuentia ac terra germinantia

                •           •           •           •           •

100     Grassatis sicque duobus protoplastis parentibus
        post tota ruit propago et absque adminiculo
        auctor peccatum auxerat ad inferna detraxerat
        creuerunt homicidia dum creuit philargyria
        habundabat luxuria, dum anxit gastrimarchia
105     tota nefanda crimina iam possidebat glarea

                •           •           •           •           •

220     Ipso de caelis domino descendente altissimo
        praefulgebit clarissimum signum crucis et uexillum
        plangor super se nimius erit tum cunctis gentibus.
        tectisque luminaribus duobus principalibus
        cadent in terram sidera ut grossus de ficulnea
225     eritque mundi terminum ut fornacis incendium

        Clangor buccinae quaternas sonabit terrae per plagas
        discurrunt coruscantia fulgura et tonitrua
        tunc in montium specubus abscondent se exercitus.
        ergo erit dies ille dies planctus et lacrimae
230     dies irae et uindictae tenebrarum et nebulae
        dies magnae angustiae laboris ac tristitiae

        In quo cessat mulierum amor ac desiderium
        hominumque contentio mundi huius et cupido
        cum caelo terra ardore conflagrant atque lumine.
235     Tuba primi archangeli strepente admirabili
        erumpent munitissima claustra ac poliandria
     ,  surget homo a tellure restauratus a puluere.

        Undique conglobantibus membrorum conpaginibus
        animabus aetralibus eisdem obuiantibus
240     certant sancti cum munere Christo regi occurrere.
        Altithronus glorioso rex sedebit in solio
        angelorum tremebunda circumstabunt et agmina
        cunctis iudex cum propria secundum reddet merita.
```

```
        Stabimus et nos pauidi ante tribunal domini
245     reddemusque de omnibus rationem affectibus
        nostra uidentes posita ante obtutus crimina,
        librosque conscientiae patefactos in facie :
        in singultus erumpemus et fletu diro gememus
        subtracta necessaria operandi materia.

250     Tunc fideles nam caelestem urbis summae Hierusalem
        sustollentur ad patriam introibunt ad gloriam
        ubi fulget uera pacis lux Christus sol mirabilis.
        Ymnorum cantionibus sedulo tinnientibus
        sanctis tripudiantibus angelorum et millibus
255     in paterna claritate se gaudent Christum cernere.

        Sic uiginti felicibus quatuor senioribus
        coronas iam mittentibus agni dei sub pedibus
        laudatur tribus uicibus trinitas, aeternalibus
        bis binis coram stantibus unitis animalibus
260     terra laude sonantibus 'Sanctus sabaoth dominus'
        hac sancti manent gloria a saeculis in saecula.

        Zelus ignis furibundus consumet aduerarios
        nolentes Christum credere deo a patre uenisse
        retro ruunt perpetui in ignis flammas impii.
265     ubi habentur tenebrae uermes et dirae bestiae
        ubi ignis sulphureus ardet flammis edacibus
        ubi rugitus hominum fletus et stridor dentium.

        Ubi gehennae gemitus tonitruus et horridus
        ubi ardor flammaticus sitis famisque maximus
270     ubi tortor durissimus auget poenam cum laribus.
        Sathan atro cum agmine quo tenetur in carere
        religatus in Tartara in aeterna incendia
        Cocytique Charybdibus submergetur in gentibus.
```

*   •   •   •   •

```
295     Nuncque rogo ut iubeas et in me hoc perficias
        quamdiu in ergastulo sum clausus carnis sedulo
        ore corde et opere te canam laudem, kyrie,
        Doxa tibi altithrone rex caelorum sanctissime
        qui me tuo iuuamine consolaturus optime
300     laus et honor cum gloria in saeculorum saecula.
```

The printed editions of the *Altus* are as follows :—

Colgan printed it from F in his *Trias* (1647) p. 473 ; this was the *editio princeps*.

The next edition was that of Todd in 1869, who gave it from T and B, using Colgan's text where these manuscripts are deficient.

In 1871 Reifferscheid printed the hymn from M in his Catalogue of the MSS. of the Ambrosian Library.[1] He was unaware that it had ever been published before, and he knew nothing of its author.

[1] *Sitzungsberichte der Wiener Akad. (Philosoph. Hist. Klasse)*, vol. lxvii. p. 545.

In 1875 A. Boucherie published the text from E in the *Revue des langues romanes* (vol. vii. p. 12). He, too, was in ignorance that it had previously been made accessible.

In 1881 Ch. Cuissard printed the hymn from I in the *Revue Celtique* (vol. v. p. 205). He was aware of the editions of Colgan and Todd, but not of those of Reifferscheid and Boucherie. Boucherie then printed in the *Revue des langues romanes* for 1882 (p. 293) a letter comparing the text of E with I and T.

The next printed edition was that of the Marquess of Bute (1882); but this is popular rather than critical. It is based on Todd's text, and is chiefly valuable for its apposite citations from the Vulgate.

In 1884 Sir J. Gilbert published from F a transcript of the text, which is much more accurate than Colgan's, in the *Facsimiles of National Manuscripts of Ireland*, Part iv. App. xxi.; reproducing in facsimile the first stanza and all the initial letters of the hymn.

In 1885 Dümmler called attention in the *Revue Celtique* (vol. vii. p. 237) to the existence of the Munich MS. which we have called II. The collation of this has been kindly made for us by Dr. L. Traube. For E and I we have used the texts printed (apparently with minute accuracy) by Boucherie and Cuissard.

Several translations of this difficult hymn are in print. The first, a metrical version, was made by Dr. J. Smith in his *Life of St. Columba* (1798), but it is of little value. Todd gives a literal rendering in his *Liber Hymnorum*; Boucherie (*l.c.*) gives a French version; the Marquess of Bute added a prose paraphrase to his edition; and a free metrical rendering by Rev. Anthony Mitchell is printed at the end of Dowden's *Celtic Church of Scotland*. A good version is given by Mr. Macgregor in his *St. Columba* (1897), and a metrical paraphrase by Mr. Stone in his *Lays of Iona*. We have thought it necessary to include a literal translation in this edition, as many passages of the hymn are obscure.

    The High Creator, Ancient of Days, and Unbegotten
was without origin of beginning and without end;
He is and shall be to infinite ages of ages
with Whom is Christ the only begotten and the Holy Spirit,
5 coeternal in the everlasting glory of the Godhead.
We set forth not three gods, but we say there is One GOD,
saving our faith in three most glorious Persons.

    He created good Angels, and Archangels, the orders
of Principalities and Thrones, of Authorities and Powers,
10 that the Goodness and Majesty of the Trinity might not be inactive
in all offices of bounty,
but might have creatures in which
it might richly display heavenly privileges by a word of power.

From the summit of heaven's kingdom, from the brightness of
  angelic station,
15 from the beauty of the splendour of his form,
  through pride Lucifer, whom He had made, had fallen;
  and the apostate angels too by the same sad fall
  of the author of vainglory and stubborn envy,
  the rest remaining in their principalities.

20 The Dragon, great, most foul, terrible, and old,
  which was the slimy serpent, more subtle than all the beasts
  and fiercer living things of earth,
  drew with him the third part of the stars into the abyss
  of the infernal regions and of divers prisons,
25 apostate from the True Light, headlong cast by the parasite.

The Most High, foreseeing the frame and order of the world
  had made the heaven and earth. The sea and waters He
    established;
  likewise the blades of glass, the twigs of shrubs;
  sun, moon, and stars; fire and necessary things;
30 birds, fish, and cattle; beasts and living things:
  and lastly man first-formed to rule with prophecy.

So soon as the stars, the lights of the firmament, were made,
  the angels praised for His wondrous handywork
  the Lord of the vast mass, the Builder of the heavens,
35 with praise giving proclamation, meet and unceasing;
  and in noble concert gave thanks to the Lord,
  of love and choice, not from endowment of nature.

Our first two parents having been assailed and seduced,
  the Devil falls a second time, with his satellites;
40 by the horror of whose faces and the sound of whose flight
  frail men, stricken with fear, should be affrighted,
  being unable with carnal eyes to look upon them;
  who now are bound in bundles with the bonds of their prison-
    houses.

He, removed from the midst, was cast down by the Lord.
45 The space of the air is closely crowded
  with a disordered crew of his rebel satellites; invisible,
  lest men infected by their evil examples and their crimes,
  no screens or walls ever hiding them,
  should openly defile themselves before the eyes of all.

50 The clouds carry the wintry floods from the fountains of the sea—
  the three deeper floods of Ocean—
  to the regions of heaven in azure whirlwinds,
  to bless the crops, the vineyards and the buds;
  driven by the winds issuing from their treasure houses,
55 which drain the corresponding shallows of the sea.

The tottering and despotic and momentary glory
of the kings of this present world is set aside by the will of GOD!
Lo! the giants are recorded to groan beneath the waters
with great torment, to be burned with fire and punishment;
60 and, choked with the swelling whirlpools of Cocytus,
overwhelmed with Scillas, they are dashed to pieces with waves and rocks.

The waters that are bound up in the clouds the Lord ofttime droppeth,
lest they should burst forth all at once, their barriers being broken
from whose fertilising streams as from breasts,
65 gradually flowing through the regions of this earth,
cold and warm at divers seasons,
the never failing rivers ever run.

By the divine powers of the great GOD is suspended
the globe of earth, and thereto is set the circle of the great deep,
70 supported by the strong hand of GOD Almighty;
promontories and rocks sustaining the same,
with columns like to bars on solid foundations,
immoveable like so many strengthened bases.

To no man seemeth it doubtful that hell is in the lowest regions,
75 where are darkness, worms, and dread beasts,
where is fire of brimstone blazing with devouring flames,
where is the crying of men, the weeping and gnashing of teeth,
where is the groaning of Gehenna, terrible and from of old,
where is the horrid, fiery, burning of thirst and hunger.

80 Under the earth, as we read, there are dwellers, we know,
whose knee ofttimes bendeth in prayer to the Lord;
for whom it is impossible to unroll the written book—
sealed with seven seals, according to the warnings of Christ—
which He Himself had opened, after He had risen victorious,
85 fulfilling the prophetic presages of His Advent.

That Paradise was planted by the Lord from the beginning
we read in the noble opening of Genesis;
from its fountain four rivers are flowing,
and in its flowery midst is the Tree of Life,
90 whose leaves for the healing of the nations fall not;
its delights are unspeakable and abounding.

Who hath ascended to Sinai, the appointed mountain of the Lord,
Who hath heard the thunders beyond measure pealing,
Who the clang of the mighty trumpet resound,
95 Who hath seen the lightnings gleaming round about,
Who the flashes and the thunderbolts and the crashing rocks,
Save Moses the judge of Israel's people?

The day of the Lord, the King of Kings most righteous, is at hand:
a day of wrath and vengeance, of darkness and cloud;
100 a day of wondrous mighty thunderings,
a day of trouble also, of grief and sadness,
in which shall cease the love and desire of women
and the strife of men and the lust of this world.

Trembling we shall be standing before the judgement seat of the Lord,
105 and shall give account of all our deeds;
seeing also our crimes set before our eyes,
and the books of conscience open before us,
we shall break forth into most bitter cries and sobs,
the necessary opportunities of action being withdrawn.

110 As the wondrous trumpet of the First Archangel soundeth,
the strongest vaults and sepulchres shall burst open,
thawing the (death) chill of the men of the present world;
the bones from every quarter gathering together to their joints,
the ethereal souls meeting them
115 and again returning to their proper dwellings.

Orion wanders from his culmination the meridian of heaven,
the Pleiades, brightest of constellations, being left behind,
through the bounds of Ocean, of its unknown eastern circuit;
Vesper circling in fixed orbits returns by her ancient paths,
120 rising after two years at eventide;
(these), with figurative meanings, (are) regarded as types.

When Christ, the most High Lord, descendeth from heaven,
before Him shall shine the most brilliant sign and standard of the Cross;
and the two chief luminaries being darkened,
125 the stars shall fall to the earth, as the fruit from a figtree,
and the surface of the world shall be like a fiery furnace.
Then shall the hosts hide themselves in the caves of the mountains.

By chanting of hymns continually ringing out,
by thousands of angels rejoicing in holy dances,
130 and by the four living creatures full of eyes,
with the four and twenty happy elders,
casting down their crowns beneath the feet of the Lamb of God,
the Trinity is praised with eternal threefold repetition.

The raging fury of fire shall consume the adversaries,
135 unwilling to believe that Christ came from God the Father;
but we shall forthwith fly up to meet Him,
and so shall we be with Him in divers orders of dignities
according to the everlasting merits of our rewards,
to abide in glory, for ever and ever.

   Who can please God in the last time,
   when the glorious ordinances of truth are changed?
   Who but the despisers of this present world?

A.

[THE HOLY TRINITY.]

The title is *De unitate et trinitate trium personarum*; the argument is the text upon which the capitulum is founded, *ut in Daniele uel in Esaia legitur*, '*uetustus dierum sedebat super sedem suam.*' *Uetustus dierum aeternus temporum erat. Uetustus dierum deus dicitur, pro multitudine dierum ante quos deus erat, uel quia fuit ante omnia tempora.* It is indeed a prophet's text that he gives, *quia ipse propheta fuit*, and he took it from Daniel in particular, because it is he who was later and nobler [than the other prophets]; so too Colum Cille was latest and noblest of Ireland's prophets. *T*:

"*De unitate et trinitate deitatis trium personarum* is the title; but the argument is *ut dicitur in Daniele*, '*ecce uidebam sedes positas, et uetustus dierum sedebat super sedem suam.*' Now, *altus* and *almus* are used to denote 'nobility,' *et ideo ponitur hic*, because it denotes 'height' and 'depth,' *ut Cicero dicit* '*altum mare*' *et* '*altum caelum*,' whereas *almus* denotes '*nobility*' *tantum*." *B*.

As to the reference to Cicero, we may note *De off.* i. 151, and *De nat. deorum*, ii. 104.

prositor] i.e. *genitor* i.e. *the great sower T*.

Seminator uitis; sertor agri; sator horti; sero, seui, satum; seminor, idem; sator; prosero, ui, situm; with the ending -*or*, *so that it makes prositor* B^{uo}.

The word is only known in the feminine to the lexicons; the Isidorian Glossaries have '*prosatrix, genetrix*.'

uetustus] i.e. *aeternus* i.e. *senior of the times* i.e. *elder and chief of our tempora T.* For the reading here adopted of Dan. vii. 9, see above p. 144.

2 *absque origine*] i.e. *without matter, or without origin T.*

primordii] must be pronounced as a trisyllable. See p. xxviii above.

crepidine] i.e. *without end, for crepido is found in the signification of* '*boundary*' *or* '*foundation*', *ut in lege dicitur, sacerdos decurrere faciet sanguinem ad crepidinem altaris, id est, ad fundamentum B.* Other instances of '*crepido*' being used in the sense of '*end*' or '*boundary*' will be found at Exod. ii. 5, Judges vii. 23.

4 We have had the gloss on *Christus* before (vol. i. p. 12); it comes from Isid. *Etym.* xvii. 2.

5 *perpetua* is necessary for the rhyme, and so we have translated; *perpetuae* is either a mere blunder of the scribe of T, or else an orthographical peculiarity. The substitution of *ae* for *a* in Irish MSS. is not uncommon.

6 We have not been able to identify the reference to Jerome in the T gloss; but the comparison given there is common enough. See e.g. [Aug.] *Serm. ad fratres in eremo* (Migne, P.L. xl. 1321), and Ambrose (Migne, P. L. xvi. 737).

7 *salua*] i.e. *the Catholic Faith* . . . . *and under its protection T.*

This gloss is in part illegible, but it is sufficiently plain that it refers to the parallelism between this first stanza and the *Quicunque Vult*, which has been already pointed out in the Preface, and is indeed obvious.

This first stanza, unlike all the others, has seven lines. It is just possible that l. 7 may not have been in the hymn as originally written, but added in the interests of orthodoxy. It was, however, known to Hraban Maur, and is reproduced by him as l. 23 of his hymn *Aeterne rerum conditor*.

B.

[The Creation of the Angels.]

The title is: *De formatione nouem graduum; tribus prætermissis non per ignorantiam, sed pro angustia capituli prætermisit*. The argument is '*Fiat lux et facta est lux*' TFB.

8 *angelos*] *For this reason he omitted to place Cherubin and Seraphin along with the others, because they are further from human beings in respect of knowledge and abode. The nine grades are these, viz. angeli, archangeli, uirtutes, potestates, principatus, dominationes, throni, cherubim et seraphim T^{nc}*.

This is the usual list of the nine orders of heavenly beings, derived ultimately from the Celestial Hierarchy of Dionysius the Areopagite, and based on such passages as Eph. i. 21 and Col. i. 16. It was familiar to Irish writers,[1] as it was to all Western Christendom in the middle ages.

The Latin gloss on *angelos* comes from the treatise *De ecclesiasticis dogmatibus* of Gennadius of Marseilles, which was often ascribed (as here by the glossator) to Isidore.

10 *otiosa*] *i.e. sine operatione i.e. inactive or idle in not bestowing treasures T*.

So also B. The phrase *ut non esset bonitas dei otiosa* occurs in the treatise *De eccles. dogmatibus* (c. x) just mentioned. Compare also Hrab. Maur. *de Uniuerso* iv. 10.

11 *largitatis*] *i.e. for God was bountiful towards His creatures B*.

12 *priuilegia*] *i.e. the privileges and the honours viz. every grade above another; i.e. quasi priuata lex T*:
i.e. *great honour or preeminence of angel over the rest of the creatures B*. The reading *preuigilia* of T is a mere blunder of the scribe.

13 *magnopere*] *i.e. with the great deed; or, mightily, i.e. greatly T*:
i.e. mightily B.

possibili] *i.e. by the powerful utterance, i.e. by the powerful praise that angels put upon Him dicentes, Sanctus, sanctus, sanctus, dominus T*.

That *possibilis* shall be taken, as the glossator takes it, in the sense of 'powerful' seems demanded by the context. But the glossator has not understood that *fatimine* refers to the Divine Voice of Power, not to the praises of the angelic host.

fatimine] *i.e. from the word 'fateor' B*. The F glossator evidently did not understand the word.

---
[1] See Atkinson, *Passions*, p. 452, and Stokes' *Book of Lismore*, p. cv.

C.

[THE FALL OF THE ANGELS.]

The title is, De transmigratione nouem graduum principis. The argument is taken from the Apocalypse, Vidi stellam de caelo cecidisse in terram; et in Esaia, Quomodo cecidisti Lucifer qui mane oriebaris TFB.

For *principis* the B scholiast has *angelorum, uel de peccato Adae*. With the reading *principis*, the allusion is, no doubt, to those passages of Scripture where Satan is called *princeps* e.g. Jn. xii. 31, Eph. ii. 2, &c. The alternative title *de peccato Adae* found in B, though certainly wrong, is interesting as indicating that at the time of the production of that manuscript the titles to the several stanzas of the *Altus* were not stereotyped. Two alternative titles to the Q stanza are found, in like manner, in the Franciscan manuscript (F).

speciminis] *i.e. of the form T:*
i.e. of the shape or of the form B.
16 Compare 1 Tim. iii. 6.
17 *apostataeque*] *i.e. ruerant i.e. the off-starting angels T,* &c.
eodem] *i.e. by the same fall T.*
lugubri] *i.e. lamentable, viz. by themselves et aliis, quia demones suum lapsum lugent T;*
i.e. lugubri i.e. flebili viz. about great grief to themselves and to all other of created beings, for the transgression angelorum deceived them B.

The additional glosses on this word in T^ms and in B are due to a confusion of *lugubri* with *lubricus* of l. 21. That in T^ms is: *uel lugubrium lignum est super quod etiam aues stare non possunt for its slipperiness; (a name) which from this was applied to everything slippery.* This is given over again in B^ms on *lubricus* in l. 21, which see. This confusion, like the alternative titles to which we have called attention above, shows that the original source of the glosses in T and B must be sought at a date considerably prior to the production of these manuscripts.

18 *cenodoxiae*] *i.e. inanis gloriae uel superbiae; uel, of the common glory, nam ' cenon' Graece commune Latine dicitur, i.e. common; ' doxia,' uero gloria T:*
i.e. ' ceno,' uanae, ' doxia' Graece gloria interpretatur, viz. ' of the long entry' a diabolo contra hominem B.

In the B gloss *in dermait sir* of the MS. should probably be *ind formait sir* = peruicacis inuidiae.

19 Compare Jude 6, 'angelos uero qui non seruauerunt suum principatum,' &c.

D.

[THE FALL OF THE ANGELS.]

The end of the title seems to witness to a various reading *siderum* for *stellarum* in Apoc. xii. 4, but we do not know of any authority for this.

There are, it will be observed, in this stanza, and occasionally afterwards, a few Latin glosses in M which Dr. Ratti holds to be of the twelfth century. They have been omitted by Reifferscheid.

20 Compare Apoc. xii. 9, 'draco ille magnus, serpens antiquus.'

21 *serpens*] *i.e. in the tempting of Adam B.*

lubricus] *i.e. slippery T:*

lubricus a lubro quod est nomen leuissimi cui oblenita scinipes adhaerere non possunt summitatem ; omnis leuis de quo quis labitur lubricus ; dicitur of that tree on the top of which birds live; and of their dung is made silk T^ss.

i.e. lubricus, eo quod ibi labitur, lubrum, viz. a tree in Oriente, on which flies do not stick because of its slipperiness sed cadent, and from it the name is given to everything slippery ; and birds are in its top, and it is from their dung that silk is made B^os.

sapientior] *i.e. he is cleverer T:*

The end of the B gloss is: *uel sapientia* 'more foolish,' *ut dicit, sapientia huius mundi;* cf. Gen. iii. 1, 'serpens erat callidior cunctis animantibus terrae,' and p. 144, above.

22 *feracioribus*] The reading of T is to be discarded for *ferocioribus* of the other MSS. and of Hraban.

23 *tertiam*] *there are three modes of explaining it, one third in aere and one third maris . . . et terrae and one third in barathro, viz. in inferno T^os:*

in barathrum] *i.e. in infernum TF:*

i.e. into a place of gore T:

i.e. in puteum i.e. quasi uoratrum i.e. uorago ut Circirius dicit, Barathrum i.e. hiatus terrae viz. putereus in profundo maris et terrae. Barathrum i.e. a place in which old people are put, and they are not drawn out of it till death ; and from it the name is applied to every other horrible thing B.

We have not been able to identify 'Circirius,' if indeed that be the name in the manuscript. And the gloss 'dico' in M we do not understand.

25 *refugas*] *i.e. deserters B.*

This seems to be the best reading; but *refugax* may be right. Hraban has *refugus . . . praecipitans*. See above p. 144. *Refuga* always means *apostate* in the Old Latin versions of Scripture. Cf. *ut refuga legum et exsecrabilis* 2 Macc. v. 8, the only place where it is preserved in the Vulgate.

parasito] *i.e. by the juggler, i.e. by himself, who is a juggler T:*

i.e. parasita, juggler, or liar, or stinking pit B. Parasitus is used by Martial (ix. 29) in the sense of 'actor,' 'player,' &c.

It is tempting to read *paradiso* and to translate 'headlong thrust from paradise,' but the testimony of the MSS. for *parasito* which is confirmed by Hraban, is too strong.

praecipites] *i.e. headlong flung ; i.e. (into) hell T: i.e. flung down a diabolo B.*

The gloss has *rind-(t)raigthechu*, where *rind*, 'point,' corresponds to Lat. *prae*, and *traigthechu* is an adj. (from *traig*, 'foot') corresponding to *-pites* of *praecipites*, whose true analysis the glossator did not understand.

The Old Latin text (*h*) of Apoc. xii. 9, has "et praecipitatus est in terram," which gives us the clue to the use of the word *praecipites* here.

E.

[The Creation of the Earth and of Man.]

26 *machinam*] i.e. *the mass*; or, *the trap B.* The word *chuithech* is frequently used in *Senchus Mor* for 'trap,' 'pitfall'; cf. I. 272,2: III. 260,2; 456, 17.

armoniam] i.e. *the mutual fitness that there is between created things TB : ut dicit Boethius i.e. man and man (?), &c. B.*

28 *uirgultorum*] i.e. *of the wood, or of the* . . . . *B.* Todd translates *inna ruba*, ' of the forest.'

arbuscula] i.e. *the shrubs B.*

Compare S. Gall. 65, a. 7, for *fualascach*.

31 *demum*] i.e. *at last B.*

protoplastum] i.e. *first-formed B.*

praesagmine] i.e *by host-leadership T :*

Praesagmine i.e. by prophecy, i.e. Christi T⁻⁸; or, by host-leadership T⁻⁸ B :

i.e. *leadership agminis hominum. Praesagmen enim a presule et agmen componitur. Agmen dei 'host-leadership,' so that it was for Adam, ut Cic. dicit, Deus cuncta creauit, Adam uero ea cum nominibus nominauit T⁻⁸.*

The gloss in B^{ms} is only verbally different.

The first explanation of *praesagmen* as 'prophecy' is undoubtedly right (see *praesagmina* in l. 85), and the allusion is to the idea that Adam named all the beasts in the spirit of prophecy.

F.

[The Praises of the Heavenly Host.]

The title refers to the ancient opinion that the stars created on the fourth day were angels; see *e.g.* Greg. *Moral.* xxviii. 14.

The quotation from the Book of Job is introduced as from the 'Wisdom of Solomon' in the Irish group of MSS., and is taken from a praeHieronymian version of the Latin Bible. See above, p. 144.

32 *etheris*] i.e. *of the æther TB.*

33 *pro mirabili*] i.e. *on account of the very great workmanship B.* Cf. Bar. iii. 35 "[stellae] uocatae sunt et dixerunt Adsumus; et luxerunt ei cum iucunditate, qui fecit illas."

34 *opificem*] i.e. *deed-doer* i.e. *opus et faciens TB.*

35 *praeconio*] i.e. *from the praiseful resounding word (?) viz. Sanctus sanctus sanctus dominus deus Sabaoth B.* The word *óndurdonail* is unknown to us; it is possible that *dordan* may be involved in it.

concentu] i.e. *from the excellent united (om. B) song TB.*

37 *naturae*] i.e. *not in their (om. T) nature was planted God's praise;*

sed in uoluntate et potestate sua, sicut ostendit ante ubi dicit '*amore et arbitrio*' *TB*:

T adds: *ut dicunt, for they would be able facere malum if they had not the love of God.* The glossator apparently takes 'amore et arbitrio' to refer to *God's* love and will.

The quotation from Augustine added in B we have not succeeded in identifying.

G.

[THE FALL OF MAN.]

39 The gloss on *secundo* explains that Satan's first fall was from heaven to earth, the second from earth to hell. This is worked out more fully in the curious marginal gloss in T (which has been overlooked by previous editors), viz. :—

ruit] i.e. *diabolus fell first de caelo through his first crime ; secundo de aere through his second crime. Or,* '*ruit*' *pro* '*irruit*' *hic causa rhythmi ponitur quasi diceret, he threatened an attack on God tantum, secundo on Adam. Aliter: ruit, i.e. he fell at first through tempting God ; he fell secundo through tempting Adam. Causa secundae perditionis diaboli is told ; the name* '*fall*' *is given hic to the pain that was inflicted on the devil for the temptation primorum duorum parentum, after the pain that was inflicted on him prius for tempting God T^{us}*.

zabulus] i.e. *a Greek word,* '*de-consiliarius*' *interpretatur ; uel infirmus after* . . . . *Or, perhaps, from the word* '*diabulus*' *was made* '*zabulus*' *through z out of d by cutting B*.

That is, the glossator first equates *diabolus* to $\zeta a + \beta o v \lambda o s = de\text{-}consiliarius$. The second explanation is that it is = 'infirmus *iar gennaith*,' where the last word (plainly written in the MS.) is unintelligible ; perhaps it is meant for a proper name, *secundum Gennadium* (?).

41 *consternarentur*] i.e. *they would be terrified T: that they might not terrify, quia inuisibiles sunt demones B*.

42 *non ualentes*] i.e. *that they might not show B*.

fascibus] i.e. *in their bundles and in their bandages like bundles, as if every bandage of them were bound in its special place like bundles T^{us}B*.

Thus the allusion in l. 43 is to the words of St. Matth. xiii. 30. 'Alligate ea fasciculos ad comburendum,' where *fasciculis* is the reading of at least one MS. of the Irish family (see Wordsworth *in loc.*).

ergastolorum] i.e. *of the torture-prisons ; or, of the work-prisons ; ergastulum enim opus ex* . . . *longum interpretatur T*.

In the *Book of Enoch* we have a similar idea ; "the fallen angels, whose spirits continue to tempt man, are bound fast under the hills of the earth"; and the stars are "bound until the time when their guilt should be consummated" (x. 12, xv. 11, xviii. 16).

H.

[THE SECOND FALL OF THE ANGELS.]

44 *e medio* is sufficiently explained by the glosses in TB. The similar gloss in M shows that the reading *remedio* of that MS. is a mere blunder of the scribe.

deiectus] *i.e. he was cast down* T.

45 It is possible that *cuius* should be taken with *aeris*, rather than, as we have done, with *satilitum*. If so the allusion would be to Eph. ii. 2 "princeps potestatis aeris huius."

constipatur] *i.e. is condensed*; or, *is filled* B.

satilitum] *i.e. of the officers* TB.

46 *globo*] *i.e. by a circle*; or, *by a company* B.

perduellium] *conduellium i.e. of the two-battled ones viz. inter se inuicem semper*; or, *battle contra deum et homines, i.e. quasi duobus bellis bellatorum. Aliter perduellium i.e. enmity quia fit perduellis inimicus* T.

The B gloss is not substantially different, but it gives a reference to Cicero which we have not been able to verify.

The gloss in the margin of E, which is only partially legible, we take from Boucherie's article on the hymn.

exemplaribus] *i.e. from the examples demonum* B.

imbuti] *i.e. instructed* B.

We take *fortchi* as for *forcthi*, 'learned' or 'instructed'; or perhaps it is (*f*)*oircthi* = 'damaged.'

49 *oculis*] We can make nothing of the illegible gloss on this word.

I.

[THE CLOUDS AND THE SEA.]

50 *inuehunt*] *i.e. they raise or carry* T.

pontias] *i.e. the seas* T: see p.

brumalias] *i.e bruma a breui motu solis in eo*; *it is for this reason* . . . . *rather than* . . . . *on account of the quantity of water*; *bruma edax uel edacitas interpretatur* T.

With this last etymology cf. Isid. *Etym.* v. 35.

51 *tribus*] *i.e.* . . . . *the three dodrants mentioned hic are the three dodrants of retardation, i.e. the three full* . . . *of the equinox*; . . . *and the sun also*; *it is a dodrant of an hour with respect to retardation and half an uncia, ut Baeda dicit*: *but he left out the half-uncia causa rhythmi*; *or it is following Philip that caused him to leave it out. Profundiores autem are they, because they fill more the river mouths and the lands, and the clouds bring water to them the more* . . . *on each depth maris. And 'mare' i.e. on every arm of the sea they come over upon the land. Quique paludes i.e.* . . . . *sea, so that they fling them at the time of their ebb* (?) *Quique i.e. thesauri, that is, the winds that bring* . . . *the pools* $T^{...}$.

This obscure and half obliterated gloss seems based on a misunderstanding. *Dodrans* in l. 51 means, as often, 'the flood of the ocean.'

But the glossator has gone back to the original meaning 'three-quarters of an hour.' It is thus used by Pliny (*Nat. Hist.* ii. 14 *De lunae motu*), and thence by Bede, of the moon's retardation, the period of which is described as a 'dodrans' *plus* a 'semi-uncia,' *i.e.* 45 minutes *plus* 2½ minutes. And the glossator remarks that the odd 2½ minutes or 'semi-uncia' was omitted by the poet *causa rhythmi*. The 'Philip' whom Bede followed was a disciple of Jerome who died in 455. He wrote a Commentary on Job which Bede largely used; and, as the glossator notes, Philip omits mention of the *semi-uncia* when speaking of the moon's retardation.

The idea of *three* dodrants is probably due to a further confusion, arising from a reminiscence of the fact that a *dodrans* was equivalent to *three*-quarters of an hour.

It is hardly worth while to expend more space on an analysis of this curious theory of the tides. It is, however, interesting in connexion with the statements of the *Amra* (ll. 390–400) that Columba was skilled in astronomical science, and in 'the course of the sea.'

52 *climatibus*] *i.e. from heights* T.
The construction of this stanza is very obscure; we have taken l. 51 as parenthetical, and *maris* in l. 52 with *fontibus* in l. 50. This is awkward; but we cannot make sense of the words in any other way.

ceruleis] *i.e. from the dark blue waves, or the dark blue blasts* T. Previous editors have equated *athchaib* to *achthaib*, 'fields' from *achad*; but *turbines* could not be 'fields.' For *athach* 'blast,' cf. FM. 1121, 1146, '*athach* gaoithe móire.'

53 *profuturas*] *i.e. the things that will benefit* T.

55 The explanation of *quique* by *uenti* or *flamina* in the T gloss seems to be the only possible way of making sense. E by reading *quaeque* supports this view.

The writer of the hymn seems to have thought, with some mentioned by Isidore, that the tides are caused by the winds.

reciprocas] The gloss on this is quite illegible.

K.

[THE PUNISHMENT OF SINNERS.]

56 The reference to the 'giants' is explained by the scholiast in the *Titulus* by Job xxvi. 5; but the marginal note in M brings out that it is the giants who perished at the flood that are in the mind of the poet. So in Wisd. xiv. 6 we have: "ab initio cum perirent, superbi gigantes." The 'giants' were held in the early cosmogonies to be the descendants of the fallen angels; so that we have here another reminiscence of speculations like those found in the Book of Enoch.

58 The gloss in the margin of T (by a later hand) is only partly legible; it evidently alludes to the giants under *Mount Etna*.

59 The gloss *in scriptura* in T shows that *comprobantur* is to be taken in the meaning of 'recorded,' 'attested,' which it might very well have.

aduri] *i.e. that they be burnt* T.

60] *i.e. morasses of hell T.* The four rivers of Tartarus are also mentioned, though not named, in the Second Vision of Adamnan and in other Irish compositions. Mone observes in reference to another poem (*Hymni medii aeui* i. 409) that the mention of these 'heathen names' in a hymn may be taken as pointing to an early date; for in the later middle ages they would not have been understood by the people.

Carubdibus] *i.e. from the whirlpools . . . . . for the greatness of the tempest of the whirlpool it is likened to whirlpools of Cocytus and . . . . leading to hell T.*

Carubdibus turgentibus i.e. from the rocks that are heaped or rough or glowing with heat; or, from the whirlpools that are raging T^{no}.

strangulati] *i.e. retenti i.e. held de scillis i.e. this is a story that is recorded here. . . . Scilla filia Porci &c. T^{ng}.*

61 *fluctibus*] *i.e. from the Scillan waves, i.e. from the waves of the whirlpool whose name is Scilla, et in Sicilia est, and for the greatness of its storm besides T.*

scrupibus seems to point to a form *scrupis*, meaning 'rock'; but *scrupus* is the only known form. There may be a confusion with *rupis*, 'rock,' or *scrobis*, 'dyke.'

L.

[THE RAIN AND THE RIVERS.]

62 *crebrat*] *i.e. filters T.*
cribrare is to drop as through a sieve. Compare 2 Reg. xxii. 12 "cribrans aquas de nubibus caelorum."

63 *simul*] *i.e. when the barriers are burst; or, when the barriers are manifested; i.e. ruptis ligationibus quibus quodam modo nubibus aqua T.* *Fritecoirse* no doubt means 'barriers,' but its analysis is obscure. It seems = *frith-tecor*, as the equivalent of *ob-iex*. *Tecur*, with the idea of 'keeping back' is well known (MR 216, 12 and 162, 15); but if this be the word, then the final *se* must be the demonstrative particle which seems here uncalled for. Again the analysis of *anata n-* is uncertain; for even on the basis of the dictum "forma simplex *an* temporali magis significatione...poscit sequentem notam relatiuam" (Zeuss² 709), we should hardly get *anatambristi* and *anatafaillsigthe*.

65 *pedetemtim*] *i.e. paulatim; i.e. foot-goings T.* This is an etymological gloss on *pede-temptim*.

telli] The gloss corroborates the reading, and notes that *tellus* is sometimes counted a noun of the second declension.

per tractus] *i.e. through circuits T.*

istius] *good here, from the word . . . . in rod or cast . . . . est quicquid . . T^{ng}.* It is a pity that the note is illegible, for an explanation of *istius*, which has little meaning here, would have been welcome. *sithbe* means 'chief,' 'leader' as well as 'rod.' See O'Dav. 116.

67 *influunt*] *i.e. they flow forth T.*

M.

[THE FOUNDATIONS OF THE EARTH.]

The version of Job xxvi. 7, 8, quoted in this and the preceding title is nearer to the O. L. text already cited (p. 144), than to the Vulgate. The words 'molis mundi uirtute dei continetur' are probably a reminiscence of Isa. xl. 12, 'Quis appendit tribus digitis molem terrae.'

68 *appenditur*] *suspended T.*

dialibus] *i.e. diuinis, . . . diuinus secundum ueteres ; or may be . . . . would be right here T.*

The word *dialis* is frequent in Adamnan's *Vita Columbae*.

69 *circulus*] *i.e. the great abyss in which was implanted the law of a circle T*

70 The true reading must be *suffultus*, but there is no MS. authority for it.

iduma] The gloss explains that this is a Hebrew word for 'hand' *i.e.* connected with יד. In the curious piece known as the *Hisperica Famina* (see p. 143) the word occurs and is again accompanied by the gloss; *i.e. manu.*[1] So also the B copy of the Lorica of Gildas (vol. i. p. 208) glosses *idumas* in l. 36 by *manus*.

The dots underneath *iduma* and *ualida* in T show that these words are to be taken together.

72 *promontoriis*] *i.e. from promontories T.* The gl. however, seems to be *o arusaib*, whereas 'promontories' would require *o rosaib*.

solis is, of course, a mere blunder of the scribe of T for *solidis*.

N.

[HELL.]

The punctuation of Lc. xvi. 22 adopted in the title 'Et sepultus est in inferno' follows the true Vulgate text. Wordsworth *in loc.* should be consulted for a discussion of the point.

75 Compare Ecclus. x. 13, "cum enim morietur homo, hereditabit serpentes et bestias et uermes."

After line 79 a page is lost in T. Consequently we have adopted F as our standard from l. 80 to l. 127.

O.

[THE WORSHIP OF THE UNDER WORLD.]

In the title the words of Phil. ii. 9, 10, on which ll. 80, 81 are based, are quoted as 'in Apocalipsi,' through a confusion between *Apocalypsis* and *Apostolus*, which is not infrequent; *e.g.* it is found again in the titles to the T and Z stanzas.

81 *precario* seems to be used adverbially, 'in prayer.'

82 *reuoluere* is probably a reminiscence of an Old Latin text of Apoc. v. 3, where the Vulgate has *aperire*.

[1] Migne, P.L., xc. 1187.

83 Colgan could not read the latter part of this line in F; and it was emended by Todd into "septem licet praemonitis." This, however, was only a guess.

85 For *praesagmina* see note on l. 31 above.

P.

[THE GARDEN OF EDEN.]

The quotation of Apoc. ii. 7 and xxii. 2 in the title preserves Old Latin readings, *manducare* for *edere* (Vulg.), and *curationem* (Primasius has *curatione*) for *sanitatem* (Vulg.). *Quinto* in the former quotation is a mere blunder of the scribe for *uitae*.

86 *a prohemio*. The Vulgate of Gen. ii. 8 is "plantauerat autem dominus deus paradisum uoluptatis *a principio*"; it is possible that here an Old Latin rendering is preserved.

89 *et tua* of F is probably a mere blunder for *etiam* of the other MSS.

91 With *inenarrabiles* compare 1 Cor. ii. 9, and with *deliciae*, Ezech. xxviii. 13.

Q.

[THE THUNDERS OF SINAI.]

We have already (p. 156) called attention to the alternative title registered for this stanza. The verse Apoc. xvi. 18, is introduced by the words *in chanoin* i.e. 'the text.' See title to cap. A.

92 *condictum*] This is a not uncommon word in ecclesiastical Latin, *e.g.* in Adamnan and in Bede. Cf. Gen. xviii. 14 "iuxta condictum reuertar ad te."

94-96. Compare Exod. xix. 16 "ecce coeperunt audiri tonitrua, ac micare fulgura, et nubes densissima operire montem, clangorque buccinae uehementius perstrepebat." The *lampades* are mentioned in Exod. xx. 18.

For *iacula* as applied to the lightning flashes, compare the account of the theophany in Ps. xvii. 15: "Et misit sagittas suas, et dissipauit eos; fulgura multiplicauit et conturbauit eos."

R.

[THE DAY OF JUDGEMENT.]

The splendid treatment of this theme by Thomas of Celano (*flor.* 1225) in the hymn *Dies Irae* is too familiar to need further mention.

99 *dies* . . *uindictae:* Compare Isa. xxxiv. 8 "dies ultionis domini."

104 Compare 1 Jn. ii. 17.

S.

[THE DAY OF JUDGEMENT.]

107 Compare Dan. vii. 10; Apoc. xx. 12. The interpretation of the 'books' of the latter passage as 'libri conscientiae' is also found in the

Liber de promiss. et praedict. dei iv, to which reference has already been made : ' Libri aperti, conscientiae singulorum' are the words.

109. The sense is : "for the night cometh when no man can work."

T.

[THE GENERAL RESURRECTION.]

For the quotation in the title of 1 Thess. iv. 6 as in "Apocalipsi" see above on the title to the O stanza. Cf. Apoc. viii. 7ff.

110 With this stanza the stately verses of the *Dies Irae* may be compared :

> Tuba mirum spargens sonum
> per sepulchra regionum
> coget omnes ante thronum
>
> Mors stupebit et natura
> quum resurget creatura
> iudicanti responsura.

111 In our translation we have taken *claustra ac poliandria* as the nominative to *erumpent*.

Boucherie emends *frigola* of his MS. into *friuola* and translates "voleront en éclats les clôtures les plus solides et les enceintes des cimetières, objets d'un vain luxe pour les hommes de la génération présente." Although we are not certain that we have translated the lines correctly, this must be wrong. Hraban seems to have felt the difficulty for he replaces l. 111 by one of his own : "surget homo a tellure restauratus a puluere."

The whole stanza recalls the Vision of Ezekiel (xxxviii. 7-12) ; see p. 145 above.

114 The metre demands *ethralibus* with EI ; *obuiantibus*, the reading of the Prosper MSS. and of Hraban, is better than *obeuntibus*.

V.

[TYPES OF CHRIST.]

The title of this stanza is given incorrectly by Colgan, thus : "De tribus syderibus thronos septem significantibus &c."; and his mistake has been reproduced by Todd and the Marquess of Bute. But there is no doubt about the true reading of the MS. which we have printed. The three stars meant are, probably, the three conspicuous stars in Orion. In the tract *De signis caeli* printed among Bede's works,[1] we have : "Orion obliquus quidem Tauro habet in capite stellas splendidas tres." And a little further down in the same work we read : "Hae autem stellae Pleiades et uirgiliae necnon et subuculae dicuntur"; the designation *uergiliae* for the Pleiades, of which *Uirgilio* in l. 117 is a corruption, was quite usual. Isidore (De nat. rerum 26 *de*

---

[1] Migne, P.L. xc. 947.

nom. astr.) gives them the same name, and it is also found in the Old Latin version of Job ix. 9 as we have noted above (p. 145). The words "astrorum splendidissimo" in l. 117 are possibly in like manner a reminiscence of the Old Latin, the Vulgate having "micantes stellas."

The 'tria sidera' of the title may, however, be Orion, Lucifer, and Vesper; this would fall in well with Philip's Commentary on Job xxxiii. 32, as given by Bede, which makes both Lucifer and Vesper types of Christ, the former of His Divine, the latter of His human nature.

In any case, the meaning seems to be somewhat as follows. In the preceding stanzas the Day of Judgement and the general Resurrection have been treated; we now go on to consider the second Advent of Christ, which is described in detail in the X stanza. And the idea here is that His coming is certain and will be at the appointed time, although He be now removed from the sight of men. Even so is Orion invisible through half of his diurnal course; and Venus in the course of her motion through the heavens returns surely to the same place after a period of nearly two years.[1] That is to say, we understand the first half of the stanza to refer to the diurnal movement of Orion, which, as a matter of fact, sets a little before the Pleiades (and did so in Columba's day and country); and in the second half there is reference to the less obvious annual movement of the heavenly bodies, Venus being selected as a well-known and conspicuous example.

Line 121 points out that the preceding lines are meant to illustrate a spiritual truth, viz. the certainty of the Second Advent, though it be long delayed.

118 The word *tithis* for the Ocean is frequent in Latin of this period. Compare Reeves' *Adamnan* p. 184 n.

120 In illustration of the old word *uesperugo* (and indeed of the whole stanza) we may quote Plautus *Amphitruo* ii. 118: "Nam neque se septentriones quoquam in caelo commouent, neque se luna quoquam mutat atque uti exortast semel, nec Iugulae neque Uesperugo neque Uergiliae occidunt, ita statim stant signa." The word also occurs in a text-book much read in Ireland in the middle ages, the tract *De nupt. Phil. et Merc.* (cap. *de stella Veneris*) of Marcianus Capella: "Nunc faciens ortum, ut in Luciferum, nunc post occasum solis effulgens, uesper, uel uesperugo nominatur." This book was generally condemned by the Westerns on account of the 'pagan' ideas which it set forth; but it was popular among the Celts. See *Dict. Christian Antiquities*, pp. 1851, 1858.

X.

[THE SECOND COMING OF CHRIST.]

123 It was a common opinion that the 'sign of the Son of Man' would be a luminous cross in the heavens. See *e.g.* Chrysostom and

---

[1] The synodic time of Venus is 584 days, which is roughly described by our author as "biennium." This seems to be borrowed from Philip on Job xxxviii. 32, as copied by Bede: "hunc igitur Luciferum appariturum terris *post biennium* autumnat in oriente nasci." For this and some other observations on this stanza we are indebted to Rev. M. H. Close.

Jerome on Mt. xxiv. 30, and Cyril Hieros. *Cat.* xv. 22. The idea, indeed, is as old as the *Didache* (xvi. 6): καὶ τότε φανήσεται τὰ σημεῖα τῆς ἀληθείας· πρῶτον σημεῖον ἐκπετάσεως ἐν οὐρανῷ, εἶτα σημεῖον φωνῆς σάλπιγγος, καὶ τὸ τρίτον ἀνάστασις νεκρῶν. The third line of the *Dies Irae*, according to the later Gallican version, is "crucis expandens uexilla." And the hymn *Vexilla regis* is followed in the Roman Breviary, on Sept. 14, by the versicle and response: "Hoc signum crucis erit in caelo: cum dominus ad iudicandum uenerit."

125 A paraphrase of Apoc. vi. 13. See above p. 145.
126 Cf. 2 Pet. iii. 10.

Y.

[THE WORSHIP OF HEAVEN.]

Here we resume again the text of T.

128 *tinnientibus*] *i.e. when they sing the songs* T.

129 The word *tripudium* 'a dance,' occurs once in the Vulgate, viz. at Esther viii. 16.

uernantibus] *i.e. they were frequent* T.

The word properly means 'to be spring-like,' but is used in Ovid (*Tr.* 3, 12, 8) of the singing of birds.

131 The interpretations of the glossator are all common; the last one is found in Jerome's *Prologus galeatus*.

133 *tribus uicibus*, i.e. of course, the *Ter Sanctus* of Apoc. iv. 8.

Z.

[THE DESTRUCTION OF THE UNGODLY AND THE REWARDS OF THE RIGHTEOUS.]

134 *Zelus ignis furibundus.* This phrase may possibly point to a version of Hebr. x. 27 different from that of Jerome, which is quoted in the title.

135 This line would seem to point to a period and locality where the Divinity of our Lord had been questioned: this would hardly be Gaul in the seventh or eighth century, but it might very well be Scotland or Ireland in the sixth, where Christian preachers had frequently to address themselves to their pagan fellow-countrymen. And this falls in with the authorship of Columba.

137 Cf. 1 Cor. xv. 41, 42.

139 The reading of T, *gloria* for *secula* at the end of the line is a mere blunder of the scribe.

The second antiphon may have been added, as Todd suggests, in consequence of the tradition about Gregory's censure of the hymn for containing too scanty praise of the Trinity. See above p. 25.

The last line may contain an allusion to Mc. xii. 35.

The words of the antiphon *Quis placet deo* seem intended to point the same moral as that suggested by the seer in the Book of Enoch. In the last days, the order in their courses of the heavenly bodies will be disturbed; the world will be convulsed; the 'ordinances of truth,' the undeviating laws of nature, will be 'changed.' In such a time of physical upheaval and confusion, only those who have set their heart on heavenly things will be safe.

The collect *Deum patrem ingenitum* is only found in the " Irish " group of manuscripts.

After the words *ueritatis ordinibus*, i.e. at the end of the second line of the antiphon *Quis placet deo*, the following collect is found in I:

" Adesto domine officio seruitutis nostrae, ut quia tu dignatus es lauare pedes discipulorum tuorum opera manuum tuarum ne despicias, quae nobis retinenda mandasti, sed sicut his abluuntur exteriora inquinamenta corporum, ita per te omnium nostrorum interiora lauentur peccata. Per dominum nostrum, &c."

This collect is well known as prescribed for the ceremony of *pedilauium* on Maundy Thursday. It is found e.g. in the Leofric Missal (ed. Warren, p. 226), where it is called *oratio post mandatum*, and in the Missal of Robert of Jumièges (p. 275), and in the Book of Evesham (p. 84). Again in the Book of Lismore[1] it is told of St. Brigid that on a certain Maundy Thursday the saint washed the feet of four sick persons "who were biding in the church." Older documentary evidence for the same practice in the Celtic Church is afforded by the prose Rule of the Culdees in the *Leabhar Breac* (B). The passage will be found at p. 206 of Dr. Reeves' memoir on the Culdees[2] (it should be observed that Dr. O'Donovan's rendering there given is not free from inaccuracies): "The selanns are not made on Maundy Thursday, but skimmed milk, or a goblet of beer, and if there happen to be any honeycombs, for this is usual on solemnities and high festivals without vigils or debt for it. Whey and bread, and dinner is taken after nones. Now at the *pedilauium* the *Biait* is to be sung, while the *pedilauium* is going on. The preaching of the *pedilauium* afterwards." *Biait* here obviously stands for the Beatitudes, beginning *Beati pauperes spiritu* &c. (see vol. i. p. xxv).[3]

These instances sufficiently illustrate the prevalence of the practice of *pedilauium* in the Celtic Church; but we know of no evidence which directly connects with it the recitation of the *Altus*. It is possible that the antiphon *Quis placet deo* may have been used at that service, which would account for the juxtaposition in I of the collect *Adesto domine*.

T fol. 12 marg.] This note, copied at vol. i. p. 82, occurs in a homily in the *Leabhar Breac*, transcribed in Atkinson's *Passions and Homilies*, p. 445.

F fol. 3 marg.] This note, copied at vol. i. p. 83, is in a late Irish hand. Its translation is: "Benediction from O'Domnal mac Dabog son of Mael-tuile with this book; and it is Colum Cille who sent them themselves for cure, from the battle of Cuil Dremne. And from Maeltuile son of Mael-fith .. are the race of Mac Mael-tuile, *i.e.* of the descendants of Neill of the Nine Hostages. *Finit*." See above p. 140.

---
[1] p. 191, ed. Stokes. Cf. also p. 176.
[2] *Trans. R.I.A.*, vol. xxiv (1864).
[3] For the baptismal *pedilauium*, see Warren, *Celtic Liturgy*, &c. p. 217. See also *Irish Eccl. Record*, vol. vi. p. 645.

B fol. 237a marg.] This note gives a direction for the recitation of the hymn:

> "Recite to seven times the *Altus*
> which gives no 'law' to hard demon;
> there is no disease in the world,
> nor shower that it will not drive back."

B fol. 238b marg.] The connexion of this note with the hymn is not very plain; possibly it has reference to the fall of Satan through pride, sung of in stanzas C H &c.:

> "There is a triad
> that is not allowed to the poor of the living God:
> thanklessness with his life, whatever it be,
> grumbling, and pride."

'The poor of the living God' suggests St. Matth. v. 1; Dr. Lawlor observes that this may perhaps indicate a connexion of this metrical note with the *Altus* through the *pedilauium* (see p. 168 supra).

With the form of the verse we may compare another marginal note in B (fol. 71): "Three things there are through which God's pleasure is attained, viz.: chastity in youth, austerity in middle life, sadness in old age."

On fol. 6 of F there are written in the margins in a sixteenth century hand a few lines of a metrical martyrology for February and March, together with one or two other Latin scraps. They are hard to read, and do not seem worth reproducing here.

THE HYMN *IN TE CHRISTE*.

The Irish Prefaces need no comment; they refer to the tradition found in the Prefaces to the *Altus* (see above, p. 25), that Columba composed the hymn *In te Christe* in consequence of the criticism made by Gregory upon the scanty praise of the Creator in the former hymn. As was observed above (p. 141) the hymn entitled *Aaiutor laborantium* in the T Preface to the *Altus* may possibly be the one now before us.

We know of no copies of the *In te Christe* save those contained in the two manuscripts (T and F) of the *Liber Hymnorum*. It was first printed by Colgan (*Trias*, p. 475) from F. A metrical translation by Rev. A. Mitchell appeared in the *Scottish Standard Bearer* for June, 1897. Mr. Macgregor has printed another in his *St. Columba*.

The hymn naturally falls into two parts, the verse 'Christus Redemptor' (l. 17) beginning the second division. And the statement of the T scholiast that some held that Columba only composed the five lines 17–21 is very interesting. The fact is that the hymn is made up of a large number of liturgical phrases, many of which appear elsewhere; and there is nothing in either matter or Latinity in the least like the poem *Altus prosator* in the case of which we have found good reason for accepting the Columban authorship.

Thus Mone has printed[1] a hymn on the Day of Judgement from a thirteenth century Reichenau MS. in which we have the stanza:

" Deus uita uiuentium, spes morientium
salusque omnium in te sperantium,
miserere omnium ex hac luce migrantium."

Again lines 10–12 of the poem of Hraban Maur, printed above (p. 147), in which so much of the *Altus* is embodied, reproduce several phrases in the *In te Christe:*

" Deus salus credentium, deus uita uiuentium
deus deorum omnium deus et princeps principum
deus summus amabilis deus inaestimabilis."

This is plainly a case of borrowing on the part of Hraban Maur.
A hymn of St. Anselm[2] begins in like manner with the words:

" Deus pater credentium, salus in te sperantium."

And in a long prayer in the Basel Psalter (see vol. i. p. xxvii) we have:
" Tu es liberator credentium. Tu es spes laborantium . . . Tu es creator omnium . . . Tu es princeps omnium uirtutum. Tu es amator uirginum. Tu es fons sapientium. Tu es fides credentium &c."[3]

How far back phrases of this sort go it would be hard to tell. In the Sarum *Ordo ad faciendum catechumenum* there is a collect which opens with the similar words: " Deus immortale praesidium omnium postulantium, liberatio supplicum, pax rogantium, uita credentium, resurrectio mortuorum."[4] It is, therefore, difficult to speak with confidence as to the origin of a piece which is made up for the most part of familiar and obvious expressions of devotion. Tradition, no doubt, must be reckoned with; but there is little, if anything, that can be described as Celtic in the language of the hymn. The *uirtutes* spoken of in l. 6 are perhaps the *powers* believed by the pagan Celts to be resident in the forces of nature. The *Deus in adiutorium* of which l. 3 is a paraphrase was a favourite ejaculatory prayer with the Irish. And Todd has pointed out[5] that the use of the pluperfect for the perfect, which occurs in lines 22–25 is a peculiarity that is also found in the writings of Adamnan; perhaps, too, the expression 'lorica militum' in l. 19 betrays Celtic ways of thinking. Again, the structure of the piece is comparable with that of the *Lorica Patricii* (No. 24): see especially ll. 32–40 and 59–67 of that remarkable invocation. But such indications afford an insecure basis for theory.

The antiphon at the end shows that it was the custom to sing this hymn at the services of the Canonical Hours, the gloss upon which is interesting:

decim] *Ten canonical hours Colum Cille used to celebrate, ut ferunt; and it is from the history of John Cassian that he got that.*

[1] *Hymni medii aeui*, i. 407.   [2] *Ibid.* iii. 1.
[3] Warren, *Celtic Liturgy*, p. 185; printed also by Forbes in his Preface to the Arbuthnott Missal.
[4] Cf. also Muratori, *Lit. Rom. uet.* ii. 155.
[5] *Liber Hymnorum*, p. 255; see Reeves' *Adamnan*, p. lxi.

In the commentary on the *Amra* (l. 367) it is said of Columba that he was a student of the writings of Cassian. But although this may well be believed, there is no notice of the observance of *ten* Canonical Hours in Cassian's *Institutes ;* our reference is to a passage in which he speaks of the use of services at seven fixed hours and refers to Ps. cxviii. 164. Mr. Macgregor (*Early Scottish Worship*, p. 12) thinks that "the discrepancy may be reconciled by adding Compline and counting the two parts of Matins and Vespers as respectively two distinct offices."

Preface to the Hymn *Noli Pater*.

We have here the story of the founding of the Church of Derry by Columba. It may be read elsewhere *e.g.* in O'Donnell's Life of Columba (see vol. i. p. xix), or in the *Leabhar Breac* (fol. 32a), or in the Book of Lismore (ed. Stokes, cf. 174 ; cf. also p. 305), but our Prefaces furnish the oldest extant authorities for the legend Aed mac Ainmerech, according to the Irish Annals, died in 598 or 599 ; but it appears that the grant of territory to Columba must have been made in his name when he was quite a lad, as the foundation of Derry is set down at the year 545. Of Mobi the Flat-faced, who was the instructor of Columba at the monastery of Glasnevin, we shall hear again, as his genealogy is registered in the T copy of the *Liber Hymnorum*. The obscure quatrain about Mobi's girdle is found in the Book of Lismore (ed. Stokes, p. 26), and it is quoted in the Martyrology of Donegal at Octr. 12.

The Hymn *Noli Pater*.

The tradition that connects the hymn with St. Columba is pretty constant, and the style of the piece is not altogether dissimilar to that of his more famous *Altus*. The abrupt way in which one subject after another is introduced will be observed, and the harshness of the Latin is also remarkable. We have found it in two MSS. (O and Q) of O'Donnell's Life of Columba, from the latter of which a portion of it was printed by Colgan, who also printed the F text (*Trias*, pp. 397, 476). An English translation is given by Mr. Macgregor in his *St. Columba*.

There are two Irish glosses in T of which we give the translation at this point :

2 *uridine*] *i.e. by Fire ; or by Yellow Plague*.

5 *exultent*] *i.e. they rejoice ;* the right reading is probably *exaltent*.

uagi also seems to be wrong ; *uaga* would give good sense, and we have *uaga fulmina* in Ovid, *Met.* i. 596.

The story that the hymn was miraculously composed by Columba to check the progress of a fire may be dismissed without comment ; and there is nothing to commend the scholiast's second theory that it was written in view of the Day of Judgement. But his third explanation that it was 'the Fire of St. John's Feast' that the writer had in his mind is very interesting, and has some evidence in its favour. A glance at the hymn shows that it is likely to have been composed with reference to some feast of St. John the Baptist, as he is introduced in a seemingly unnecessary way in a prayer for deliverance from disaster.[1] What feast was this?

Todd found here an allusion to the widespread custom of kindling fires on Midsummer Eve, a custom which has prevailed in many countries from distant ages, and is probably derived from prae-Christian folk-lore. In the first place it will be observed that there is no mention of the *Eve* of St. John (though Stokes so translates),[2] but of his *Feast*; and there is no tradition of fire on St. John's Day (June 24). In the next place, although in modern Ireland these Midsummer fires are not unknown, it is curious that there is an Irish tradition that they are of *Danish* origin[3]; there is no evidence that this custom prevailed during the period of Celtic Christianity. We must look out then for some other explanation of the scholiast's phrase. We find our explanation in the legendary belief (described at p. xxiv. vol. i.) in a dreadful visitation of fire and plague which was to come upon Ireland on the Feast of the Decollation of St. John the Baptist (Aug. 29) in a certain year. It was this which the writer of the *Noli pater* had in view. And so we find the glossator on *uridine* (l. 2) explaining this word: 'by Fire; or, by Yellow Plague.' Thus we have a remarkable confirmation of Dr. Lawlor's most ingenious identification[4] of the rubric in the Book of Mulling: 'Benedictus usque ad Ioh . . ' with lines 6-11 of the hymn before us. The *Noli pater* is one of the pieces prescribed for recitation in the penitential office that was used with special reference to the dreaded pestilence; though no doubt it was used on other occasions too, and the note at the end of the Preface shows that it served as a *lorica* to be said night and morning.

THE PRAYER OF ST. JOHN.

The legend of St. John and the poisoned cup has had wide circulation, and is familiar from the artistic representations of the Apostle, in which he appears holding in his hand a chalice from which a serpent is emerging. It probably grew out of such passages as St. Matth. xx. 23 and [St. Mark] xvi. 18; and is quoted by many writers, *e.g.* by Isidore (*De ortu et obitu patrum* c. 72).

The fully developed form of the legend which we have in the T Preface is found in the *Passio S. Johannis* which goes under the name of Mellitus, and in the *Historia Apostolorum* of one Abdias, the date of which is about 540. These books have a common source, so that the

---

[1] It has, however, been pointed out above (p. xxv) that ll. 1-6 (which form an invocation and a prayer) are metrically distinct from the lines which follow, in which St. John the Baptist is lauded. The rubric in the Mulling office to which attention is drawn in the text has explicit reference only to the latter portion of the piece; but the glossator's note on l. 2 seems to connect the early portion as well with the prediction of the Yellow Plague on the 'Feast of St. John.'
[2] *Goidelica*, p. 104.
[3] O'Curry makes this statement in his index to the R I.A. MSS. (B. Cat. 449).
[4] See vol. i. p. xxiii.

story goes back earlier, but we need not pursue its intricate history here.[1] It is printed in Fabricius' *Cod. Apocr. N.T.* iii. 604.

It would appear that the prayer\ *Deus meus* was used as a *lorica* or charm. In the *Book of Cerne* (C), where it follows another more familiar prayer attributed to St. John, beginning *Aperi mihi pulsanti ianuam uitae* &c., a few words from the *Passio S. Iohannis* of Pseudo-Mellitus introduce it; but in the Book of Nunnaminster (N) it is simply headed 'Contra uenenum,' and is followed by the Lorica of Gildas (our No. 48). But the source from which it is taken in N is evidently the same as that of C, as the words which follow 'Et cum hoc dixisset &c.' (see vol. i. p. 91) are from the *Passio*. Its use as a charm in Ireland is indicated by what seems to be an invocation of the four evangelists at the end in the manuscripts TF; an ancient custom which has lingered down to our own day in the form : " Matthew, Mark, Luke and John ; Bless the bed that I lie on." See p. 244, below.

In the Senchus Mor (*Ancient Laws of Ireland*, i. 2), there is a couplet of magical words said to have been used by Patrick as a charm against poison. " And whoever pronounces these words over poison or liquor shall receive no injury from it. Or, it was the *In nomine dei patris* he then composed and pronounced over the liquor."

The piece is not distinctively Celtic ; but it has been shown above (vol. i. p. xxvii) that it seems to have been well known in the Celtic Church, inasmuch as it forms part of an ancient monastic office found in the Basel Psalter. In the Epilogue to the Felire of Oengus (l. 477) we have an allusion to St. John's deliverance from the poisoned cup, which has been incidentally quoted above (p. 116). The end of the T Preface is unhappily illegible, and we have not ventured upon any conjecture as to it.

1 The gloss on *Deus* indicates that it is to be taken with the *extinge* in l. 9.

2 *cui*] i.e. *it is to thee.*

4 The etymological gloss on *uipera*, as well as the subsequent gloss on *regulus*, is taken from Isidore (*l.c.*)

5 *quieta*] i.e. *inactive*, i.e. *sea-monster*.

The gloss seems to confuse κῆτος with *quietus !* We had the word *antach* before in a gloss on *otiosa* at l. 10 of the *Altus*. The *rubeta* here mentioned is a kind of toad which lives in bushes.

6 *regulus* = βασιλίσκος, a common word in the Vulgate for a serpent.

spalagius = φαλάγγιον, a kind of venomous fly.

The Letter of Christ to Abgar.

The famous "Letter of Christ to Abgar, the King of Edessa," has been the subject of much learned discussion, which we do not here reproduce. Many references will be found in Lipsius' articles in the *Dictionary of Christian Biography* on *Abgar* and *Thaddaeus*. Lipsius

[1] See Zahn, *Acta Iohannis*, cxiv, 137.

traces the original form of the legend to a date as early as 200 A.D., but the earliest text of this curious apocryphal correspondence is found in Eusebius (H.E. i. 13), who says that he saw the 'original' Syriac documents at Edessa. Our version follows very closely the Latin translation of Eusebius by Rufinus; but the T preface introduces the legend of the privileges which the city of Edessa enjoyed in consequence of the favour shown it by Christ, which seems to be a later addition to the story.[1]

We are here concerned not with the literary but with the liturgical history of the piece, and especially with the acquaintance with it which appears in the remains of the early Irish and British Churches.

In our *Introduction* (vol. i. p. xxvii) we pointed out that this *Epistola* is prescribed as a lection in the monastic office found in the Basel Psalter (P); and it would seem that its presence in the *Liber Hymnorum* is to be accounted for in like manner. The prayer *Domine deus* &c., by which it is followed in both T and F suggests that here too it is a lection for use in a monastic service. That it was well known in Ireland appears from the fact that there is an Irish translation of it, preceded by a legend as to its origin similar to that of our scholiasts, in the *Leabhar Breac* (fol. 146). In this last mentioned passage there is no mention of the privileges of the city of Edessa. And it will be remembered that the hymn *Celebra Iuda* alludes to it in the lines (23, 24):

"Tathei tota famosa per tellura
Abgoro misi Iesu cum epistola,"

upon which the glossator has remarked that the real bearer of the letter was not Thaddeus but 'Ananias cursor,' as Eusebius records.

The piece is also preserved, as our *apparatus criticus* shows, in the interesting manuscript which we call J (see vol. i. p. xviii). Here the words which follow the letter, and the prayer which is added at the end, show that it was used as a kind of charm. 'Si quis hanc epistolam secum habuerit securus ambulet in pace' are words which do not point to the reading of the letter in the public worship of the Church, but to a superstition connected with the possession of its text. This superstition was by no means confined to the Middle Ages.

An author of the year 1726[2] makes the following curious statement in the course of a critical discussion of the letter to Abgar: "The common people in England have it in their houses in many places fixed in a frame with our Saviour's picture before it; and they generally with much honesty and devotion regard it as the Word of God, and the genuine Epistle of Christ." And in the year 1895 the present writer was shown a roughly printed sheet, containing the letter to Abgar in English and one or two other apocryphal pieces, which he was informed has a wide circulation at the present day among certain classes of the Eurasians in our Indian Empire as a sovereign preservative against fever, when worn about the person.

---

[1] It is, however, found in the *Peregrinatio Silviae*, a piece written at the end of the fourth century, and is also (probably) alluded to by Ephraem Syrus; although Eusebius says nothing about it.
[2] J. Jones, *New method of settling the authority of the N.T.*, ii. 3.

The gloss on *discipulis* in l. 8, *i.e. apostolis*, seems to confuse the Thaddeus of the legend, who is said in Eusebius' account to have been 'one of the Seventy,' with Thaddaeus the Apostle (see above, p. 111).

It may be observed that the extract from St. Augustine at the top of fol. 15 (see vol. i. p. 95) is read in the Roman Breviary among the lections for the Octave of All Saints. The connexion with the text is, as usual, difficult to trace; it is *possible* that the word 'custodis' with which it opens may have some reference to the prayer, "Custodi nos in bonis . . . " with which the epistle is closed, but we cannot say that we have any evidence by which to support this conjecture.

The Hymn of St. Fiacc.

This important piece was first printed (from F) by Colgan in his *Trias* (p. 1), with Latin translation and notes. Passing by many reprints of Colgan's text, the next edition of critical value was that of Dr. Whitley Stokes in *Goidelica* (1866), which was based on T. The second edition of *Goidelica*, to which our references are made throughout, appeared in 1872. In 1874 a complete photographic reproduction of the piece from T was given in Gilbert's *National manuscripts of Ireland*, Part i (Plates xxxii–xxxv). And finally Dr. Stokes printed the text of F afresh in 1887, adding for the first time the *marginalia* which are so numerous in that manuscript, and giving an English translation of the whole.[1]

Other editions of value are those of Windisch,[2] and Zimmer;[3] and articles in the *Revue Celtique* (vol. vi) by Stokes and Thurneysen are important. Dr. Todd's edition of the *Liber Hymnorum* was interrupted by his death before the text of Fiacc's hymn was ready for press.[4]

We know of no manuscripts of the hymn worth collating save T and F. There is a paper copy (saec. xix) in Egerton 154, and there are at least two others in the Library of the Royal Irish Academy $\left(\frac{23}{E.\ 16}\ \text{and}\ \frac{23}{L.\ 16}\right)$; but they are of no independent value. Translations are numerous, but the only one, besides those of Stokes and Colgan, to which reference need here be made is the metrical rendering of Sir Samuel Ferguson.[5]

A few words must be said as to the date and reputed author of the hymn. The Irish Preface states that it was written by Fiacc, Bishop of Sletty, who was a contemporary of St. Patrick. This Fiacc is mentioned in the Martyrologies of Oengus and Donegal at Oct. 12, and his pedigree is traced in the Preface from Cathair Mór, who was King

---

[1] *Trip. Life*, pp. 402-426.
[2] *Irische Texte*, p. 10. In this edition illustrative passages from the *Vita* by Jocelin and from other sources, as well as copious linguistic notes, are given.
[3] *Keltische Studien*, ii. 160 ff.
[4] The hymn is also printed in O'Conor's *Rer. Hibern. Script.* i. lxxxviii., in the *Irish Ecclesiastical Record* for 1868 (vol. iv. p. 269), and in Haddan and Stubbs' *Councils*, vol. ii. pt. ii. as well as in many other books.
[5] *Trans. R.I.A.* (1885) vol. xxvii. p. 105.

of Ireland, according to the recognised authorities, in 174. But it is certain that the number of descents recorded in the Preface is quite too small to bring Fiacc down to the time of Patrick; and we may dismiss the pedigree as untrustworthy. It is tolerably plain, when we proceed to examine the hymn, that it is not the work of a contemporary of Patrick. The references in its first line to existing 'histories' of the saint, and in l. 12 to 'writings' about him suggest a date subsequent to his time. Again in ll. 20, 44 the desolation of Tara is mentioned; but this brings the date down to a period later than 561.[1] At the time of its composition St. Sechnall's hymn was known as a *lorica* (ll. 51, 52), and the words "Around thee in the Day of Judgement the men of Ireland will go to judgement" are apparently a development of some such statement as that in l. 92 of the hymn of St. Sechnall. See above p. 105. And, further, the seat of the Primacy seems already to have been a matter of dispute when the piece *Genair Patraic* was composed. For all these reasons, coupled with the fabulous and extravagant character of the *Acta Patricii* which it records, in marked contrast with the sobriety of St. Sechnall's hymn, it is necessary to bring down its date to a period long subsequent to the days of St. Patrick.

It is possible that the date can be more exactly determined. There is a considerable resemblance between the latter half of the hymn and some of the notes written by Muirchu Maccu Mactheni in the seventh century and preserved in the Book of Armagh. Muirchu states that he wrote these notes "dictante Aiduo Slebtiensis ciuitatis episcopo," and so it seems that the source of this information was the see of Sletty, where Fiacc had been bishop. Dr. Loofs[2] has argued from these facts that the hymn is based in part on Muirchu's notes. In any case it is probable that it is not earlier than the eighth century, a date which is corroborated by linguistic considerations. But see above p. xl.ff.

1 *Nemthur*] *i.e. that is a city which is among Britons of the North, viz. Ail Clúade TF*⁻*ᵒ*.

Ail Clúade is another name for Dumbarton on the Firth of Clyde, which has been generally held to be Patrick's birthplace. The matter is fully discussed in Todd's *St. Patrick*, p. 354 ff. An ingenious account of the hitherto unexplained *Nemthur* has been offered lately by Mr. E. B. Nicholson.[3] In St. Patrick's confession, as given in the Book of Armagh, Patrick's home is said to have been "uico Bannauem Taberniae." Here Mr. Nicholson finds a corruption of *Bannauenta Britanniae*; and he points out that *Bannauenta* was the lofty Borough Hill near Daventry, thirteen miles from Northampton. In other words Patrick lived in his youth at Daventry. Again in Muirchu's Life of St. Patrick[4] we read that Patrick was *Brito natione, in Brittanis natus*, and that his father or grandfather was [de] "uico Bannauem thabur indecha ut procul a mari nostro quem uicum constanter indubitanterque comperimus esse *uentre*." The Brussels MS. is here corrupt, but it

---

[1] See Petrie, *History and Antiquities of Tara Hill* (*Trans. R.I.A.*, xviii.), p. 125.
[2] *Antiquae Britonum Scotorumque ecclesiae*, p. 42 ff, and Stokes, *Trip. Life*, p. cxii.
[3] *Academy*, May 11, 1895. See *Eng. Hist. Review*, Oct. 1895.
[4] Stokes, *Trip. Life*, p. 494.

certainly seems to identify the mysterious *Bannauem* with some place called *Ventre*. And this place-name, curiously enough, has got into the life by Probus under the form *Neutriae* or *Nentriae*, which is something like the *Nemthur* of our hymn.[1] If this interpretation of *Nemthur* be accurate, Fiacc's hymn is a witness to Daventry as St. Patrick's birthplace. We are not, however, inclined to accept Mr. Nicholson's conjecture.

2 *dobreth*] i.e. *was given* T.F.
deraib] i.e. *under captivity, viz. under the sorrow of captivity* T.
3 *succat*] i.e. *it is British, and 'deus belli' in Latin* T.
i.e. *it is British, 'deus belli'; uel 'fortis belli' in Latin; for 'su' in the British is 'fortis' and 'cat' is bellum* F^{us}.

Succat son of Calpurn. This is the genealogy of Patrick: son of Calpurn, son of Potid, son of Odisse, son of Gorniad, son of Mercud, son of Ota, son of Muric, son of Oric, son of Leo, son of Maxim, son of Hencret, son of Ferin, son of Brittus, a quo sunt Brittani nominati. Multa Patricius habuit nomina ad similitudinem Romanorum nobilium, i.e. Succat first, suum nomen of baptism, a parentibus suis; Cothraige, his name in his captivity in Ireland; Magonius, i.e. 'magis agens' quam ceteri monachi, his name when studying with Germanus; Patricius, his name when in orders, and it was Celestinus, coarb of Peter, that conferred it on him F^{us}.

This pedigree of St. Patrick is found, with slight variations, in the Leabhar Breac Homily,[2] in another passage in the Leabhar Breac, and in the Book of Leinster.[3]

The earliest mention of the four names of Patrick is found in Tirechan's collections in the Book of Armagh[4]: "sanctus Magonus qui est clarus, Succetus qui est . . . , Patricius . . . , Cothirthiacus quia seruiuit quatuor domibus magorum." They are also given in the Leabhar Breac Homily,[5] in another passage in the Leabhar Breac,[6] and in the lives of Patrick generally.

itubrad] i.e. *this is what was said a peritis* T.
fissi] i.e. *it were right to know it* T.F.

5 *se bliadna*] i.e. *he was in his captivity (six years) after the fashion of the Little Jubilee Hebraeorum*.[7] *The cause of his captivity was this. Patrick and his father Calpurn, his mother Conchess, daughter of Ocmus, et quinque sorores eius, viz. Lupait and Tigris and Liamain and Darerca et nomen quintae Cinnenum, [et] frater eius, viz. deacon Sannan, all went from the Britons of Ail-Cliade over the Ictian Sea southwards on a journey to the Britons of Armorica, that is to the Britons of Letha; for relatives of theirs were there at that time; and besides, the children's mother Conchess was of the Franks and a near relative of Martin. It was the time when seven sons of Sechtmaide, king of Britain, were in exile from Britain. Now they made a great foray among the Britons of Armorica, ubi Patricius cum familia fuit, and they killed Calpurn*

---

[1] *Irish Eccl. Record*, viii. (3rd series), p. 229.
[2] The lists are transcribed in Stokes' *Lismore*, p. 293.
[3] *Trip. Life*, p. 302.
[4] Stokes, *Lismore*, p. 294. See p. 7 above.
[5] *Trip. Life*, p. 433.
[6] *Ibid.* p. 441.
[7] Deut. xv. 12.

there and carried off Patrick and Lupait to Ireland with them: Lupait they sold in Conalle Muirthemne, and Patrick in the northern part of Dal-Araide F^me.

maissi] i.e. *good food and clothing T.*
ni·s·toimled] i.e. *he did not consume it TF.*
6 *Cothraige*] i.e. *the name Cothraige clave to him; i.e. 'cethair aige,' because he served four tribes T:*

cethair aige was probably intended to mean 'four chiefs'; for *aige* is constantly used in the Brehon Laws, *aige fine*, 'head of the tribe,' 'chieftain.' The F gloss has '*cethair aige*' i.e. .... *quatuor domibus seruitium*; this seems to correspond to the explanation of Cothirthiacus (*cethar-thige*) in the Book of Armagh (p. 177 *supra*). Quite possibly *Cothraige* is an older name, connected with *catu*, 'battle'; but this is only conjecture.

7 *asbert*] i e. *he said T:*
said Victor to the slave, i.e. said Victor—the angel communis Scotticae gentis—quia Michael angelus Hebraeorum gentis, ita Victor Scottorum; ideo curauit eos per Patricium F^eu.
gniad] i.e. *to the serf, to a servant, or to a slave TF.*
Mil] i.e. *a soldier T:*
Milcon] *genetiuus est hic; Michul son of Ua Buain, king of the north district of Dal-Araide F^no.* See p. 3.
tessed] i.e. *that he should go TF.*
tonna] i.e. *over sea; eastward to study T.*
forruib a chois] 'he set his foot,' i.e. *in the shape of a bird, angel Victor used to come to Patrick when he was herding the swine of Milchu son of Ua Buain in Arcal, that is the nomen uallis magnae in the north of Dal-Araide by Slemish;¹ and in Scirit especially he was wont to come to him. That is an ecclesia hodie in ualle illa, and there remains the trace of his feet still on the stone. And Victor said to him, "It is time for thee to go over sea to learn, for it is to thee that God has assigned the duty of being teacher to the inhabitants of this island in after time." "I will not go," said Patrick, ac si diceret .. et stetit . . . nec perueniret ad Germanum . . . domino meo. "Go," said the angel, "and ask him." So Patrick went and asked him, but he got not consent, unless he should give him a mass of gold the weight of his own head. Said Patrick to him, "By my debroth, God is able for that, if it be His will;" (that was a genus iuramenti with Patrick, ac si diceret "by my God of judgement.") Patrick went back again to his swine in the wilds and narrated to Victor omnia uerba domini sui. The angel said to him, "Follow yonder boar and he will root up a mass of gold out of the ground, and take it with thee to thy master." Et sic factum est. And the angel carried Patrick in one day sixty miles (or a hundred, ut alii dicunt), viz. from Slemish in Dal-Araide to Cell Ciannain . . . on the banks of the Boyne to the north, eastward of Monasterboice. And Ciannan sold him to the shippers who were at Inber Boinne² for two copper cauldrons; these he carried*

---

[1] Reeves identified this with the valley of the Braid in Co. Antrim; Scirit is now the parish of Skerry.
[2] i.e. the mouth of the Boyne, also called *Inber Colptha* (l. 37 below).

away with him (to hang them) against the wall of his house, but his hands clave to them and the hands of his household. Et ille penituit et absolutus est Patricio, duxit et a nautis eum in libertatem ; et baptizatus est Ciannan a Patricio postea F⁼*.*

This story is also found in the Life of Patrick in the Book of Lismore (p. 154); it is inconsistent with the account of Patrick's escape found in the *Confessio*, according to which it was suggested to him by a voice in his sleep.

The oath *dar mo De broth* is mere jargon; *De broth* ought to mean something like 'God's doom-day'; but even then there would be a difficulty, because the genitive *Dé* could not precede its governing noun.

8 *es*] i.e. *his footstep TF*.
bronna] i.e. *it does not fail therein F*.
9 *dofaid*] '*he sent*' i.e. *Victor sent Patrick over mount Elpa T*:
i.e. God or the angel sent or brought. How does he come to say '*over Alpa*'? Not hard. From Britain the angel brought him, so that '*over Alpain*' would be rightly used, viz. over the mount of Elpa, for this Alba *was olim a name for the whole island of Britain, ut Beda dicit in principio suae historiae,* '*Britannia insula est, cui quondam nomen erat Alban,*' *eo quod pars quam illi tenuerunt suo uocabulo nominauerunt et uetus nomen Alban quod inuenerunt mansit F*⁼*.*

The 'mount of Elpa' or Drumalban is the mountain chain dividing Argyleshire from Perthshire; Alba was the ancient name of Scotland.

retha] i.e. *this course TF.*
10 *German*] *Germanus, abbot of the city cui nomen est Altissiodorum ;*' *it is with him that Patrick studied, and Burgundy is the name of the province in which is illa [ciuitas]. Perhaps illa prouincia was in the south of Italy, sed uerius that it is in Gaul.*

Now Germanus came into Britain to drive out of it the heresy of Pelagius, quia creuit multum in se, et sic uenit cum Patricio et aliis multis with him. Now while he was mightily expelling it on this side, he heard that the same heresy was growing up in his own city after his departure. So they went eastward, he and Patrick with him, but they were unable to expel it from their midst. Then Germanus said to Patrick, "What shall we do about them?" Said Patrick, "let us fast upon them," said he, "in the gate of the city for three days and three nights, and if they do not turn, iudicet deus super se." Well then, about nocturns of the third night the earth swallowed up ciuitatem cum suis habitatoribus; and the city stands nunc ubi clerici ieiunauerunt, i.e. Germanus et Patricius cum suis F⁼*.*

Letha] The Latin glosses give the usual explanations. Letha is used by Irish writers as the equivalent of both *Latium* or Italy, and Letavia or Armorica, *i.e.* Brittany. There can be little doubt that the latter is its meaning here. The supposition that we have at this point of the hymn an account of St. Patrick's journeying to Italy arose out of understanding *Elpa* in l. 9 of the *Alps*.

11 *ainis*] i.e. *he remained behind F*.

[1] Auxerre.

12 *legais*] i.e. *Patrick read* F.
lini] i.e. *writings* . . . F.
13] *do·d·fetis*] i.e. *they brought him* T.
15 *fo·ro·chlad*] i.e. *was heard or was expected* F.
16 *ro·clos*] i.e. *throughout Ireland* TF.
macraide] i.e. *Crebriu and Lesru, the two daughters of Glerand mac Ui Enna, dicentes* "*Hibernenses ad te clamant 'ueni sancte Patrici saluos nos facere*'" T:
i.e. *son of* . . . i.e. '*riad*' *his son* F. The word *maccrad* is a collective noun; but this gl. seems to analyse it as if it contained a word *riad*, whose meaning cannot be assigned with any certainty.

Now Patrick had studied with Germanus the canon and the ecclesiastical ordo; and he said to Germanus that oftentimes it befel him in heavenly visions to be invited, and that he heard the voice of the children (from the wood of Fochlad. Therefore Germanus bade him, "Rise and go) ad Celestinum that he may confer orders upon thee, for it is he who should confer them." Uenit ergo Patricius ad eum et nec ei (Celestinus) honorem dedit, because he had sent Palladium ante ad Hiberniam ut doceret eam. Uenit ergo Palladius in Hiberniam, and landed in Ui Garchon in the Fortuatha of Leinster, and therein he founded churches, viz. Tech na Romanach[1] *and Cell Fine*[2] *and* . . . *But no good welcome was given to him illic, so he departed thence to go round Ireland* . . . *to the north, and a great storm overtook him so that he got to the south-east head of* . . . . . *and he founded a church there called Fordun, and Pledi*[2] . . *nomen eius ibi. Now Patrick went ad insulas Tyrrheni maris, after he had been refused ordination a papa Celestino, et tunc inuenit the Staff of Jesus in insula quae dicitur Alanensis* . . . *mount Arnon. So Patrick came iterum ad Germanum, et narrauit ei omnia quae in noctibus uidebat. Misit ergo Germanus Patricium ad Celestinum, et Segetium cum eo, ut perhiberet testimonium propter se: sixty years was fully completed by Patrick tunc. Now after that Celestinus heard Palladium decessisse, et tunc dixit* "*non potest homo quidquam accipere in terra nisi datum ei fuerit desuper.*" *Then Patrick was ordained in conspectu Celestini et Theodosii iunioris, regis mundi. Amatorex, Autissiodorensis episcopus, conferred orders on him—on Patrick—and Celestine lived only one week after Patrick's ordination* . . . *Sixtus uero ei successit, in cuius primo anno uenit Patricius in Hiberniam. He (showed) great (welcome) to Patrick, and gave him a quantity of relics and many books.*

Now when orders were conferred on Patrick, Celestinus heard the voice of the children calling him. The children that are spoken of hic were named Crebriu and Lesru, viz. two daughters of Glerand son of . . . *son of Nene, and to-day they are saints. Patrick baptized them, and they rest in Cell Forcland to the west of the Moy. This is what they said, out of their mother's womb,* "*Hibernenses omnes clamant ad te*"; *and they were often heard singing this throughout all Ireland, uel usque ad Romanos F*ne.

A full discussion of the account given here by the scholiast of the mission of Palladius will be found in Todd's *St. Patrick*, pp. 286, 290.

[1] Now Tigroney in the Co. Wicklow.
[2] This has been identified with Killeen Cormaic near Dunlavin.   [3] i.e. Palladius (?)

The country of the "Fortuatha" or "stranger tribes" of Leinster, where he is said to have landed, was the district round Glendalough in the co. Wicklow. Here, according to the story, he found two or three churches, but produced no lasting impression; and, leaving, he was driven by storm round the north coast of Scotland until he found himself at Fordun in Kincardineshire.

We then have an account of the mission of Patrick by Pope Celestine, about which controversy has run so high. This is not the place to discuss it fully. A good account of the materials will be found in Todd's *St. Patrick*, p. 321 ff.

The "Staff of Jesus" was long counted one of the most precious possessions of the See of Armagh; it was removed in Anglo-Norman times to Christ Church Cathedral at Dublin, where it was destroyed by Archbishop Browne with other relics of antiquity at the Reformation.[1]

Caille Fochlad] *i.e. name of a district which is in Amalgada, in the north-east of Connaught, and it is a church to-day* $F^{=g}$.[2]

17 *imthised*] *i.e. that he might go about F.*

lethu] *i.e. of 'Italy'; or, 'latitudine' terrarum F.*

18 *tintarrad*] *i.e. that he might convert TF.*

chlóen] *i.e. from iniquity, i.e. from worshipping idols F.*

20 *code*] *i.e. to Judgement (Day) T.*

Temrach] *i.e. Tea-mur, viz. an old rampart in which was buried Tea wife of Erimon son of Miled* $F^{=g}$.

tua] *i.e. without glory T.*

21 *druid*] *these are the druids, viz. Lucru and Lucat-Mael, and what they said was this:*

> 'Adze-head will come
> over mad-head sea,
> his cloak hole-head,
> his staff crook-head,
> his table in the west of his house;
> all his household will answer, Amen, Amen' $TF^{=g}$.

These celebrated verses were held to have been the composition of the pagan Druids, and to have been a prophecy of the introduction of Christianity into Ireland. We first meet with a mention of them in the seventh century notes by Muirchu Maccu Mactheni preserved in the Book of Armagh. "Haec autem sunt uersiculi uerba, pro linguae idiomo non iam manifesta:

> 'Adueniet asciciput[3]
> cum suo ligno curuicipite
> et sua domu capite perforato.
> Incantabit nefas a sua mensa
> ex anteriore parte domus suae:
> respondebit ei sua familia tota, fiat, fiat.'"

---

[1] See Todd's *Book of Obits and Martyrology of Christ Church, Dublin*, vi-xx.
[2] Caille Fochlad has been identified with a place near Killala in the Co. Mayo.
[3] 'Asciciput' is a compound of *aaria*, 'adze,' and *caput*; it is the Latin equivalent of *taikend*, which is thus a nickname for a tonsured missionary.

This is a Latin translation of an Irish original now only preserved in a corrupted form in our F gloss, in the Egerton copy of the *Tripartite Life* (p. 34) and in the Leabhar Breac Homily on St. Patrick.[1] "It is clear," writes Todd, "that no pagan Druids ever wrote these verses, and it is evident also that they were written when the orientation of Churches was the rule and the altar always in the eastern end of the building. The allusion to the shaven tonsure, the clerical habit, and the episcopal staff proves beyond question that this stanza cannot be older than the beginning of the seventh century."[2]

These inferences, however, cannot be sustained. If we compare the Latin with our F gloss, we see that lines 1, 4, 6, of F agree with Muirchu (although l. 4 is Muirchu's l. 2); but lines 2, 3, and 5 are different. (*a*) L. 2 is absent, and in its place is found *Incantabit nefas a sua mensa*. This line must have been the work of a pagan; no Christian could thus have described the Christian Eucharist. (*b*) In l. No. 3, Muirchu has *sua domu* for "his cloak" or "cowl" of the Irish text. It is impossible that Muirchu should have thought *domus* to be the Latin for the Irish name of a "cloak," and therefore it is plain that he was working on a different text. (*c*) The words "his table" go with l. 2 in Muirchu, and lines 5 and 6 go together. The sense, in his version, is that while the priest performs his part of the service *a sua mensa*, the choir answer *ex anteriore parte domus suae*. This is hardly definite enough to justify Todd's inference that the altar was at the east end. Indeed the F gloss expressly places it in the west, although the later texts (mentioned above) have altered 'west' to 'east.' The age of the verses is impossible to determine; all we know is that they were prior to Muirchu's time.

ni cheilltis] *i.e. they did not hide* F.
22 *ro·firad*] *i.e. was fulfilled* F.
23 *leir*] *i.e. in piety* T:
　　　　　i.e. was excellent for piety F.
co mbeba] *i.e. up to his death* TF:
　　　　　i.e. till he (departed) from the world F.
sab] *i.e. was strong* TF.
clóeni] *i.e. falsity* F.
24 *a feua*] *i.e. his goodness* TF.
25 The glossator seems to have misunderstood this line. There is no reference to any special hymn, whether the *Te Deum* or the Hymn of St. Sechnall, both of which he mentions; but to Patrick's general habit of singing canticles. See above, p. 104.
26 *pridchad*] *i.e. he performed preaching* F.
baitsed] *i.e. he performed baptizing* F.
arniged] *i.e. he practised prayer and repentance* T:
　　　　　i.e. he practised prayer or cleansing F.
27 *gebed*] *i.e. it did not take from him (the practice of) going in* F.
linnib] *i.e. to the waters* F.
28 *consena*] *i.e. he strove after* TF. *Consena* is here treated as a

---

[1] *Ibid.* p. 448. See *Lismore*, p. 157.　　　[2] *St. Patrick*, p. 411.

preterite, but cf. MR 262, 5, "ni tuit rig . . nach *coisenad* Cellach a coscar, &c.," where it is possibly sec. fut. See also LU 19β4.

fri de] *i.e. in the daytime TF.*
i ndinnib] *i.e. on hills TF.*

29 *slan*] *i.e. nomen fontis of Slan (was given) because every sick person was cured, over whom the water passed, and it is at Saul; repleuerunt Ulstermen illam propter molestiam turbarum exeuntium ad illam T:*
i.e. proprium . . . of a well in se, et ob id Slan dicta est eo quod omnes sani reuertebantur ab ea propter gratiam Patricii. Alii dicunt that it was in Saul or in Dal-Araide; but Ulstermen repleuerunt illam propter molestiam turbarum exeuntium ad illam sicubi fuit F^{us}.

For a full note upon Saul and the fountain there, see Reeves' *Antiquities of Down and Connor*, p. 220.

benna] *i.e. to the north of Benn Boirche*[1]*; i.e. Bairche was a cowherd* [bo-aire] *of Rossa Rig-bude king of Ulster, from whom are named the peaks* [benna], *quia ibi habitabat frequenter cum pecoribus suis F*^{us}.

ni's gaibed] *i.e. Patrick; or, the well F.*

30 *cét*] *i.e. two fifties TF.* That is, two-thirds of the Psalter.
This record of Patrick's devotion and asceticism is borne out by his *Confessio*: "fides augebatur et spiritus agebatur ut in die una usque ad centum orationes, et in nocte prope similiter; ut etiam in siluis et in monte manebam et ante lucem excitabar ad orationem per niuem, per gelu, per pluuiam; et nihil mali sentiebam, neque ulla pigritia erat in me."

31 *foaid*] *i.e. he used to sleep TF.*
iarum] *i.e. after that TF.*
32 *timnai*] *i.e. in warmth, i.e. in heat F.*
33 *pridchad*] *i.e. he practised preaching F.*
lethu] *i.e. in 'Italy,' or in 'latitudine' saeculi F.*
34 *luscu*] *i.e. lame TF.*
truscu] *i.e. with lepers TF.*

35 *Scotaib*] *From Scotta daughter of Pharaoh king of Egypt nominantur. And this is what it arose from, viz. Etarnel son of Góedel Glas son of Fenius Farsa, a man of service, uoluit scire linguas. Uenit a Scythis ad campum Sennaar, ubi sunt diuisae linguae; et ita uenit, i.e. cum septuaginta duobus uiris, et misit eos sub regiones mundi ut discerent linguas, unum ad unam misit et postea uenerunt ad eum cum peritia omnium linguarum. Et habitauit in campo Sennaar et docuit ibi linguas. Et audiuit Pharaoh rex Egypti illum studiosum esse, et uocauit eum ad se ut doceret Egyptios circa linguas et dedit ei filiam suam et honorem maximum, et ab illa Scoti nominati sunt. The Gaels were so called from Góedel Glas, son of Fenius Farsa, father of Nel F*^{us}.

seth] *i.e. toil or disease F.*
36 *tissat*] *i.e. they will go TF.*
cach] *i.e. everyone TF.*

37 *Meicc Emir*] *Six sons of Miled and six sons of Bile, son of Bregon simul uenerunt ad Hiberniam, sed clariores sunt filii Miled quam filii of Bregon. Haec sunt nomina filiorum Miled: Eber, Erimon, Ir, Donn,*

---

[1] The *Benna Boirche* are the Mourne mountains in Co. Down.

Amargen, Colptha. From Eber are the men of Munster, *et ab eo Momonia dicitur*; but from Erimon is the whole of Conn's Half; and Leinster with Ulster are from Ir. Fewer now are the descendants of the other (sons), *et nescio ubi sunt.* But from Donn *nominatur* Tech-Duinn to the west of Ireland; from Colptha, further, is Inber Colptha *ubi the Boyne in mare exit* F^{m4}.

lotar] i.e. they went F.

cisal] i.e. with a rock of trouble, i.e. with the devil who is a rock for his hardness T.

i.e., and for its permanence, with which tribute is exacted from everyone for sin F^{ms}.

38 *fo·s·rolaic*] i.e. the devil flung them down(?), i.e. carried them off with him F^{ms}.

in tarmchosal] i.e. the place . . . . in which are places for wounding with charge against each. Or, the low after-road, for the devil is low on the road. Or the transgressor, i.e. he to whom there is a very low place. Or, the cause of seizing each one to himself, i.e. sins F^{ms}.

isel] i.e. to hell TF.

39 *co·nda·tanic*] i.e. that is the time he was busy seizing them F.

40 *Fene*] i.e. they were so called from Fenius Farsa, *unde apud nos 'Oic Fene' pleni dicuntur ab illo*. Gaels *autem, ut dixi*, from Góedel Glas, son of Nel son of Fenius Farsa, *ut alii dicunt* F^{ms}.

41 *temel*] i.e. there was darkness, viz. of idol worshipping F.

side] i.e. folk of the Sid they worshipped F^{ms}.

That is to say, they worshipped the mysterious inhabitants of the fairy mounds. See Skene, *Celtic Scotland*, ii. 108.

44 *ni·m·dil*] i.e. not dear to me is Tara, though desert TF^{ms}.

Or, he does not forgive me, *ac si diceret* he would not make my sleeping with thee, though it is desert. Or, not from it is there a fault, i.e. not sorrow though Tara is desert. Or, it is not pleasing to me, to Patrick or to God F^{ms}.

Dunlethglasse is the modern Downpatrick.

45 *lobra*] in disease, i.e. at Saul, in order that his resurrection should be at that spot T:

i.e. at Saul was Patrick when disease came to him, so that he came on the road to Armagh, in order that his resurrection should be at that spot F^{ms}.

The F glossator seems to hold the belief that Patrick was buried at Armagh; the T glossator that he was buried at Saul. For a discussion of St. Patrick's burial place, see Olden, *Proc. R.I.A.* (1893), p. 655, and Reeves' *Antiquities of Down and Connor*, p. 224.

46 *ar a chend*] i.e. to meet him, to summon him to go to Victor. He was his soul-friend, and he is the common angel of the Gaels; *sicut est Michaël Iudaeorum, ita Victor Scotorum* F^{ms}. Compare the gloss on l. 7.

47 *dofaith*] i.e. he took him on the road southward when he was going from the east F.

ar·id·ralastar] i.e. he addressed (?) him; *quia misit Victor angelum ad Patricium inuitandum ad se*, that he should not go to Armagh F^{ms}. Compare *Trip. Life*, p. 253.

lassais] i.e. *it flamed* F.
ten] i.e. *out of the fire* TF.
adgladastar] i.e. *he conversed* TF.
49 *orddan*] i.e. *thy voice and thy preeminence to Armagh, as if thou thyself wert present there* T:
i.e. *thy dignity and thy preeminence to Armagh ; thy faith and thy charity to Down* F.
Crist] i.e. *for His divinity* F.
50 *mo's·rega*] i.e. *soon thou wilt go to heaven* T.
ro·ratha] i.e. *there has been given to thee, O Patrick, thy prayer* F=g.
du gude] i.e. *all thou hast asked of God has been given to thee* TF=g.
51 *doroega*] i.e. *thou hast chosen* F. The hymn in question is probably the *Audite omnes* or hymn of St. Sechnall in praise of St. Patrick. But see above p. xliv.
i't biu] i.e. *in thy lifetime* F.
53 *Tassach*] i.e. *Patrick's artificer ; he it is who first put a cover on the Staff of Jesus ; and Raholp to the east of Down is his church* F=g.
This Tassach or Assicus was one of Patrick's three artificers or silversmiths,[1] the others being named Bite and Essu. Tassach is often mentioned in the *Tripartite Life*. The words of l. 54, "Tassach's word was not false," were possibly introduced in allusion to a story that he once, to his lasting shame, had told a lie ; but the phrase is common.[2] His name is thus commemorated in the Felire of Oengus at April 14 :

> " The royal bishop Tassach
> gave, when he came, the Body of Christ,
> the truly strong King,
> at the communion to Patrick."

This story of his having given Patrick his last communion is also in Muirchu's Memoir.[3]
Raholp is near Ballyculter to the north-east of Downpatrick.
54 *mos·n·icfed*] i.e. *to Saul iterum* T :
i.e. *to Saul, when it was said to Tassach, 'cur non pergis cum Patricio'* ? F.
ille ait, ueniat Patricius iterum huc F=g.
55 *les*] i.e. *candles* TF.
occai] i.e. *with Patrick* F.
56 *sith-laithe*] i.e. *the day of peace ; in Mag Soile this was* F.
The 'long day' spoken of in this line comes from Jos. x. 14 : 'non fuit antea nec postea tam *longa dies*.' The verses which follow refer directly to the battle of Beth-horon, where the sun stood still 'contra Gabaonem.' The legend alluded to here is given more intelligibly in the *Tripartite Life* (p. 255 ; see also p. 487), where it is said that 'an angelic radiance abode in Mag Inis till the end of a year after Patrick's death,' even as the sun went back ten degrees on the sun-dial of Ahaz, and as the sun stood still in the days of Joshua. An earlier account 'de uigilis primae noctis iuxta corpus Patricii quas angeli fecerunt' is found in Muirchu's notes in the Book of Armagh.[4]

[1] Brigid also had a bishop, one Condlaed, as her 'principal artist.' Cf. Todd's *St. Patrick*, p. 26.
[2] *Trip. Life*, p. 97.   [3] *Ibid.*, p. 297.   [4] *Ibid.* p. 297.

58 *assoith*] i.e. *he stayed, namely deus* F.
adfeit] i.e. *which tells* T.
littri] i.e. *story of the book of Joshua* TF.
60 *ciasu*] i.e. *though it was ' trebairech,' i.e. though there were therein three times the light, it would not be unjust. Or, though it was ' trebairech,' i.e. though the tribe was chief, i.e. princeps. Or, though his tribes were great* F^{ne}. Evidently the word was unknown.
ba huisse] *were fitter* TF.
eitsecht] i.e. *at death* TF.
61 *Herenn*] *Haec insula quinque uocabula tenet, uiz. Ériu and Banba and Fotla and Fail and Elca ; and this is why each of these names was applied to it. When the sons of Miled came hither from Spain to Ireland, and when they reached Slemish in Ciarraige Luachra,*[1] *they saw the mountain full of birds under shields . . . . so that great fear seized them . . . . a woman coming towards them, and that she was . . . .* F^{ne}.
dollotar] i.e. *they went* F.
62 *cetail*] i.e. *of the music angelorum* F.
fo's'rolaich] i.e. *terrified them* i.e. *put them into a prostrate position* F.
set] i.e. *on the road outside* F.
63 *sethaib*] i.e. *after much suffering* F.
ro'scarad] i.e. *his body* F.
64 *cét-aidche*] i.e. *after his death* F.
ar·id·fetis] i.e. *they played music ; or, they sang (?) cum eo* F.
65 *conhualai*] i.e. *he departed ; or, slept* F.
adella] i.e. *he visits* TF.
n-aile] i e. *Sen Patrick* TF.
66 *malle*] i.e. *this is what Patrick son of Calpurn promised to Sen Patrick, that they should go together to heaven. And what they tell is that Patrick was there from March 19 to August 24, to the end of the first month of autumn, in Rath . . outside . . , and angels with him awaiting Sen Patrick* TF^{ne} :
Dicunt alii that it was in Ross Dela in Mag Locha there used to be relics of Sen Patrick ; sed uerius est in Glastonbury of the Gaels, viz. a city in the south of England F^{ne}.

These lines (65, 66) are thus interpreted by Todd (*St. Patrick*, p. 306) : " In other words, Patrick after his death went in the Calendar to the day next after the festival of the other Patrick ; the other Patrick met him on the day after his own festival, and both ascended together to heaven." The relations between the Patrician and Palladian legends have been reconsidered of late years by Mr. Olden (*Church of Ireland*, p. 405 ff.) ; he holds that the Apostle of Ireland was the Sen Patrick or Patrick senior of the native records, who never left the country, and that in the ninth century by the blending of the acts of Palladius with his, "the St. Patrick of popular belief, the missionary of Celestine," came into existence. These conclusions have, however, by no means met with general acceptance.

[1] This Slemish is not the mountain of that name in Antrim, but is near Tralee in Kerry.

For the legend connecting the name of Patrick with Glastonbury, see Ussher, *Works*, vi. p. 454.   Rossdala is in the co. Westmeath.

67 *airde*] *i.e. without a sign F.*
ro menair] *i.e. he meditated to do F.*
68 *geillius*] *i.e. service, in friendship F.*
sen] *i.e. it was a good blessing F.*

The Prayer of Ninine.

Of Ninine, the reputed author of the following piece, little is known. In a note in the B copy of the Felire of Oengus at July 6, he is mentioned in connexion with the nun Moninna: "Moninne of Slieve Gullion and Sárbile was her name previously. Or Darerca was her name at first. But a certain dumb poet fasted with her, and the first thing he said was *ninnin*. Hence the nun was called Mo-ninde, and the poet himself Nine Ecis." He is mentioned again at Dec. 11.

We know of no MSS. of this hymn save T and F. It seems to us to have merit, and, short as it is, to be equal in poetic feeling to most of the other Irish pieces in the *Liber Hymnorum*. See p. xlix above.

1 *admuinemmair*] *i.e. we go in reliance on him TF.*
7 *dedaig*] *i.e. beautifully hath repressed T.*
9 *fonenaig*] *i.e. hath purified, hath made its purification, its cleansing T.*
10 *iath-maige*] *i.e. land T.*
mor-gein] *i.e. great is the birth; Patrick or great birth (i.e. many of births F); we are praying him, i.e. births of the men of Ireland all TF.*
12 *do'nn'esmart*] *i.e. who will save us, i.e. who will effect our deliverance TF.*
13 *a brithemnacht*] *i.e. from the judgement of Doom TF.*

The Hymn *Brigit Bé Bithmaith.*

This hymn has been printed from T by Stokes in *Goidelica*, and also by Windisch in his *Irische Texte*. We have used four MSS. in our *apparatus*, TFLX. It is also found in the Royal Irish Academy MSS., $\frac{23}{N.\ 3}$ and $\frac{23}{N.\ 4}$ and elsewhere; but these later authorities are not worth collating. On its metre, see above p. xxxiii.

The preface in L (see Stokes, *Lismore*, pp. 52, 198) is substantially the same as that in TF, and was possibly, as Stokes observes, derived from some copy of the *Liber Hymnorum*. We have departed in the case of this MS. from our usual practice in giving a full collation; for there is nothing to be gained by registering minute differences of orthography in a late manuscript like L.

A partial (Latin) translation of the F preface is found in the Trinity College MS. classed E. 3. 28.

There are five different legends as to the author given in the Preface:

(a) Columba is said to have written the hymn as he was sailing in a storm through the wild channel of Corryvreckan between Rathlin and the mainland.[1] The hymn is ascribed to Columba in the title in X; and Colgan (*Trias*, pp. 472, 609) adopts this view.

(b) It is attributed to Broccan the Squinting, who is the reputed author of the next hymn *Ni car Brigit*. See p. 40.

(c) There is a story about its composition by three students of Brigid during an adventure in the city of Placentia.

(d) The claims of St. Brendan the Navigator are mentioned. This was the famous St. Brendan of Clonfert (d. May 16, 577), whose voyage in search of the Fortunate Islands is the subject of a well-known legend. The story given here is found again in one of the F notes on the hymn *Ni car Brigit*. See p. 196 below.

(e) St. Ultan of Ardbreccan, the uncle of St. Brigid, is also given as a possible author; it will be remembered that the hymn *Christus in nostra*, No. 2 in our collection, is also put down to him. We have called it in accordance with usage "Hymnus S. Ultani"; but it can hardly be as early as this title would indicate.

1 *Brigit*] i.e. *power* . . . . *atque her powers* . . . T^{ad}.
    i.e. *flame-arrow* T^{ad} F^{ma}:
    i.e. *flame that the men of Ireland fear* F:
    i.e. *men they terrify* F:
    i.e. *Brigid, or power* . . . . . *exhibited in wonders and miracles* F^{ma}. Similar glosses are found in the margin of the B copy of the *Felire* at Feb. 1.

be] i.e. '*woman*,' *ut dicitur* '*fair woman*' TF.

bithmaith] *ever-good woman is Brigid,* i.e. *woman good through the ages, viz. for ever* F^{ma}.

3 *do·n·fe*] i.e. *may she take us* TF^{ma}.

4 *tind*] i.e. *fiery, or resplendent* T.

taidlech] i.e. *shining* F.

6 *drungu*] i.e. *past companies* T.

7 *ro·roena*] i.e. *may she overthrow* ; i.e. *may she break* F.

8 *tedma*] i.e. *of every vice* F.

9 *do·ro·dba*] i.e. *may she destroy* TF.

10 *colla*] i.e. *vices of our flesh* TF. This gloss indicates merely the order of the words in l. 10. For the extravagance of the language used cf. pp. 107, 190.

11 *blathaib*] i.e. *with virtues* TF.

13 *inmain*] i.e. *dear to us, or to everybody* T.

14 *orddain*] i.e. *with splendid dignity* TF.

adbail] i.e. '*ada*' = *right*, '*bil*' = *safe*; i.e. *it is right that the dignity and the supremacy of St. Brigid should be safe for ever* T: *with vast dignity is Brigid, viz. with dignity which it is fitting should be safe,* i.e. *enduring* F.

---

[1] See Reeves' *Adamnan*, p. 29. The channel was called "Breccan's Cauldron," from the tradition that Breccan, grandson of Neill of the Nine Hostages, was swallowed up in it. The name is now appropriated to the strait between Scarba and Jura.

17 *leth-cholba*] *i.e. as there are two pillars in the world, sic Brigid and Patrick in Ireland T.*
    famous . . *i.e. just as would be a pillar in dividing a house, sic Brigid and Patrick divided out the kingship of Ireland inter se, so that it is she who is head of the women of Ireland, and Patrick who is head of the men F.*
    flatha] *i.e. kingship of Ireland TF.*
18 *Patraic*] *i.e. head of the men of Ireland is Patrick; head of the women of Ireland is Brigid T.*
19 *ligaib*] *i.e. over beautiful ones T:*
    i.e. Brigid i.e. she is a garment that surpasses every beautiful garment F.
21 *sinit*] *i.e. that is a treasure (?) TF:*
    i.e. after old age F.
22 *cilicc*] *i.e. in penitence; quia cilicium nomen uestis which is made out of goat's or camel's hair TF.*
26 The versicle at the end which is found in X, is found in T and F at the close of the next hymn *Ni car Brigit.*

The Hymn of St. Broccan.

St. Broccan, who, according to the Preface, composed this panegyric upon St. Brigid in the monastery of Slieve Bloom or of Clonmore, is said to have died on Sept. 17, 650. The date of Lugaid's death, however, is put down to 507; so that there is nothing of historical value to be got out of this Preface. St. Broccan was a disciple of St. Ultan, and the statements in the Preface are reproduced in the Martyrology of Donegal at Feb. 1 and Sept. 4. See above, p. 107.

The hymn was first published by Colgan (*Trias*, p. 515); and it has since been printed with greater accuracy from T by Stokes in *Goidelica*, and by Windisch in his *Irische Texte*. The collation of F and the glosses therein contained are here given for the first time; some of the legendary *marginalia* in F, but not all, have been printed in Stokes' *Lismore*. The hymn is also contained in the R.I.A. MSS. $\frac{23}{N.4}$ and $\frac{23}{N.15}$; but these are late copies and of no independent value.

This hymn is very difficult; many of its grammatical puzzles have been already discussed in the glossary. The writer alludes in brief and obscure phrases to legends which may have been well known to his contemporaries; but which are far from well known to us. And hence, too, it has come about that the marginal notes that have been added in F are of such portentous length. Windisch has remarked that the order of the incidents in the Life of Brigid by Cogitosus is almost exactly their order in the hymn; and it is hardly possible to doubt that this points to some literary connexion between the prose *Vita* and the rhythmical panegyric. Windisch has printed extracts from Cogitosus as an Appendix to his edition of the *Ni car Brigit*; and they are worth consulting. See, on the whole piece, p. l.ff. above.

1 *car*] *i.e. she did not love TF.*
Brigit] *i.e. flame-arrow TF.*
2 *siasair*] *i.e. she sat TF.*
3 *ailt*] *a maiden; or, in altitudine F.*
5 *mor*] *i.e. it was not easy TF.*
ecnaig] *i.e. to speak evil of her TF.*
The meaning of this line is plainly that Brigid afforded little occasion for speaking ill of her.

6 *hiris*] *i.e. it is she who had the holy faith of the Trinity in her TF.*

7 *rurech*] *i.e. of my high King T.*
The extravagance of this language will be observed; nevertheless it is plain that Brigid is not *identified* in the mind of the writer with the B.V.M., for 'Mary and Brigid' are *both* mentioned in the last line of the hymn. See above, p. 107. Cf. Matth. xii. 50.

8 *cinis*] *i.e. she is the best who was born T.*
9 *ecnairc*] *i.e. she was not a detractor; i.e. she made no detraction of any one TF.*
elc] *i.e. she was not wicked TF;*
> or, *she was not troublesome F.* The meaning of *elc* (*elcnide*) is quite uncertain.

10 *chair*] *i.e. she loved not the battle of the sorrowful (women) T.*
The line is full of difficulties; all that is certain is that the glossator's explanation is wrong. (a) *cair*, after *pu* or *bu*, must be a predicative substantive; it cannot mean 'she loved.' F has *car* 'brittle,' but an attributive adjective is just as impossible here, as a verb. The only alternative seems *caur, cur* 'champion.' (b) *ban-chath* might mean 'white battle,' if the texts read *bán*. But, even if it is intended as a compound of *ban* 'female,' it ought not to mean 'battle of women' as the glossator says; unless it can be proved that prefixed *ban* is used to express the subjective genitive. The nearest analogy is *ban-rdd* given in the *Würzburg Glosses* as explanatory of *uerbosae* (1 Tim. v. 13), where *rdd* is not the collective affix, but the infinitival subst. Thus, as *ban-rdd* is *uerbosus*, *ban-chath* may be *bellicosus*. (c) *brigach* must mean 'mighty,' 'forceful'; it cannot be 'sorrowful' as the gl. has it. But it is to be observed that the words *na mban* are not legible in the gl., and it is just possible that *bronach* there may have a totally different reference, viz., to Brigid's grandfather Dall-bronach, and that we have here an allusion to some incident now unknown.

12 *rir*] *i.e. she sold not TF.*
dibad] *i.e. for perishable (?) treasure TF;* but the gl. is not fully legible. Cf. gl. 43.
13 *seotu*] *i.e. she was not greedy for treasures TF.*
ernais] *i.e. she gave TF.*
neim] *i.e. without rebuke TF.*
15 *calad*] *i.e. she was not stingy TF.*
16 *cair*] *i.e. she loved not the world T.*
The position of the governed genitive in this line is noteworthy.
cathim] *i.e. consumption of the world by herself TF.*

17 *acher*] i.e. *angry or fierce TF:*
   or, '*acer*' = *ac hir*, i.e. *in ira F.*
18 *bai*] i.e. *kind she was T.*
truagu] i.e. *mercy for the wretched sick T.*
19 *maig*] i.e. *Leinster T.*
arutacht] i.e. *she built TF.*
cathir] i.e. *Kildare T.*
20 *dollaid*] i.e. *of God TF.*
ro·n·snade] i.e. *Brigid; or, civitas TF.*
22 *genais*] i.e. *she did bonum T.* An impossible translation.
23 *amra*] i.e. *the city; or Brigid TF.*
24 *ascnam*] i.e. *to visit TF.*
26 *Plea*] i.e. *Placentia* (?), *viz. a city which belongs to Brigid in Italia. Or. Plea is a city which belongs to Brigid on the Ictian Sea; and it is its Rule that the folk of Brigid observe. Et sic factum est id,* i.e. *Brigid sent seven persons from her to Rome to learn the Rule of Peter and Paul, for it was not permitted to herself by God to go. When they got back to Brigid, there did not remain with them one word of the Rule. "The Virgin's son knoweth," said Brigid, "small is your profit, though great your labour." Misit iterum alios septem uiros; similiter contigit eis quam primis et tunc misit alios septem uiros and her blind youth with them, for whatever he heard, he stored up in memory on the spot. Well, when they got as far as the Ictian Sea, a great storm came upon them, so that they let down anchoram; it caught on the dome of the oratory, so that they cast lots inter se about going down, and it was on the blind youth that it fell to go down. Et exiit et absoluit ille anchoram et stetit there, to the end of a year, learning the Rule, until the rest of the party got back to him from the East. And there overtook them a great storm again in the same place, so that they let down anchoram adhuc, till the blind youth came to them from below with the Rule of celebration illius ecclesiae secum ad se; and he brought up along with himself a bell for them; and the bell belonging to the folk of Brigid to-day is that same bell of the blind youth; and the Rule they have is the Rule the blind youth brought with him from Plea F*no*.*

This story, as Stokes observes,[1] is also found in the notes to the Leabhar Breac copy (p. 82) of the *Felire* of Oengus. This copy has for *Muir Icht* = 'the Ictian Sea,' *Inber Mara*, i.e. the Straits of Gibraltar (?). The legend is interesting in its assertion that the Rule of Kildare was not the Roman Rule, but the Rule of the submarine city Plea.

There are two curious Irish stanzas on p. 23 of the Codex Boernerianus (G) of the Pauline Epistles,[2] the first of which seems to have reference to a phrase in this story. It begins 'Téicht do Roim · mór saido · beic torbai · in rí chondaigi hifoss &c.'; i.e. 'To go to Rome is much trouble, little profit. The king whom thou seekest here, unless thou bring him with thee, thou findest not &c.' Scrivener's account[3] of these verses is that they were probably written at Rome by some disappointed pilgrim. But from the similarity of phrases in our

---
[1] *Book of Lismore*, p. 334.
[3] *Introd. to Criticism of N.T.* (4th ed.), i. 180.
[2] Published by Matthaei in 1791.

legend, it is not out of the reach of possibility that the verses have grown out of it.

conhualai] i.e. *it went away; i.e. from her Rule; she was gentle with power* T:

i.e. *with her cry* F.

The latter part of this gloss seems to refer to *cain-bai* of l. 18. The F gl. analyses *conhualai* as = *co-nual !*

27 *gaba*] i.e. *it was alone with Christ she was when in peril* TF:
or, *till she took* [*went ?*] T: *till she died* F.

28 *dana*] i.e. *which is usual towards guests* TF:
or, *frequent was her visit to sufferers* T.

29 *fo*] i.e. *good was that* TF.

fo-huair] i.e. when Brigid wished to have the Order of penitence conferred on her, she went to Cruachan Bri Ele in Offaly,[1] when she heard of Bishop Mel being there, and there were seven nuns along with her; but when they arrived, the bishop was not there to meet her, but had gone northward to the territory of the Ui Neill. So she went on the morrow with Mac Caille as guide, northward over the Bog of Faichnech,[2] and God caused the bog to become a smooth flowering plain. But when they got near to the place where Bishop Mel was staying, Brigid said to Mac Caille, that he should place a veil over her head, that she might not go without a veil over her head to the clerics, and that is probably the veil that is alluded to. Well, after she had entered into the house where Bishop Mel was staying, there blazed up a fiery column out of her head up to the ridge-pole of the church. So Bishop Mel saw that, and asked, "Whose are the nuns?" Mac Caille said to him, "That is the renowned nun from Leinster, even Brigid." "My welcome to her," said Bishop Mel; "it was I that foretold her when she was yet in her mother's womb," said he.

Once on a time Bishop Mel had gone to Dubthach's house; he saw (his) wife in trouble, and asked, "What is the matter with the good woman?" said he. "I have cause enough," said she, "for the bondmaid who is washing your feet is more liked by Dubthach than I am." "That is a natural feeling on thy part," said Bishop Mel, "for thy seed shall serve the seed of the bondmaid."

"What have the nuns come here for?" said the bishop. "To have orders of penitence conferred," said Mac Caille. "I shall grant it," said the bishop. So that after that, orders were read over her, and it was the order of a bishop that it befel Bishop Mel to confer on Brigid, though it was only the order of penitence that she herself wanted; and it was then that Mac Caille held up a veil over Brigid's head, *ut ferunt periti*; and from this the coarb of Brigid has always a right to have bishop's orders and a bishop's honour upon her. While the ordination was being read over her, she held the foot of the altar in her hand, and over that foot seven churches were burnt (in after times), but it was not burnt there. *Dicunt alii*, that the church in which ordination was conferred upon Brigid was in Fir Telech.[3] Or, it is in Ardagh of Bishop Mel, *ut alii dicunt*. Well,

---

[1] This mountain is now Croghan in King's Co. The ruins of the church of Bishop Mac Caille are said to be still visible (Todd, *Obits and Martyrology of Christ Church, Dublin*, p. xcix.)
[2] Now Boughna Bog.   [3] Now Fartullagh in Co. Westmeath.

after that, Bishop Mel preached eight Beatitudes Euangelii to them, eight nuns as they were, after all had gone under orders, and each of them chose her Beatitude. Brigid indeed chose the Beatitude of mercy. On that occasion she said that she would never eat food without (a preaching) to her beforehand; and Natfraich was lector to her always from that time forward, and he was of the men of Turbi F^a.

The story of Brigid's 'ordination' is also found in the Book of Lismore (p. 188), and in the notes to the B copy of the *Felire* at Feb. 1. See also *Quinta Vita*, c. xxxi.

congab] i.e. he raised *T*.

Mac Caille] i.e. he was brother to Bishop Mel, and it was he that blessed the veil over Brigid's head; Mac Caille held the veil over her head, while Mel was blessing the veil *T*.

Both were sons of Darerca, Patrick's sister; hence we read *brathair*.

31 *menn*] i.e. was manifest *TF*.
33 *no·d·guidiu*] i.e. I beseech him *TF*.
34 *mod*] i.e. in every way *T*: in whatever way *F*.
ro·sasad] i.e. they would reach *TF*.
35 *domnu*] i.e. deeper quam mare *TF*.
36 *amru sceóil*] i.e. more wonderful than stories . . . from him . . . . seven years Kevin remained standing in Glendalough, with a board under him merely, and he without sleeping during that time, ut ferunt, in 'cross-vigil,' so that the birds made their nests in his hands, ut ferunt F^a.

Stokes (*Lismore*, p. 344) compares a story told by Giraldus Cambrensis of a blackbird that laid and hatched her eggs in the hand of the same St. Kevin.

37 *cath*] i.e. to the sage *T*:
    i.e. to the sage . . . dictus est 'cadus,' and 'cad' is from that F^a.
    i.e. Kevin, a virgin. Or, his mouth, i.e. his face; or, good was his speech *F*.

The glossator is attempting to justify *cath* in the sense of 'sage,' by equating it with Latin 'catus.'

Coemgen or Kevin is styled 'caith-fer' = 'man of battle' in the Felire of Oengus at June 3; *ob*. 618.

Coemgen] Brigid used to prophesy to Kevin, sage, illustrious, that there would rush upon him a wind through snow and storm, under his lair in Glendalough; for this is what is told, that Kevin remained in a standing position to the end of seven years without sleep, and the joint of his elbows around him on high. Or, it might be 'athrec' (?) tantum. Or, as Kevin remained under his lair without sleep, sic Saint Brigid was not sleepy *T*^a.

cloth] i.e. renowned, viz. illustrious *TF*^a.

Line 37 is impossible to explain; there is nothing to show that Brigid has any relation whatever to the details of this stanza.

38 *luades*] i.e. the wind drove snow through storm; towards the effectuation of a trisyllable is that, for it is in the midst of the two halves

there should be put ante quod non additur in fine F⁻ᵉ. This obscure gl. seems to refer to the position of *snechta* in the line.

da loch] i.e. *of the two lakes F.*
40 *con·idn·arlaid*] i.e. *till it advised* (?) *T*:
i.e. *till it . . . F.*
saith] i.e. *after disease, or after labour T.*
41 *suanach*] *sic sancta Brigida fuit sicut Kevin*, i.e. *sleepy F.*
42 *huarach*] i.e. *it was not for hours there used to be* (and at another time there used *not to be F⁻ᵉ*) *the love of God with her, sed semper habebat TF⁻ᵉ*.

A later hand has added in F: i.e. *not during (certain) hours (merely) was the love of God with her, but always.*
43 *chiuir*] i.e. *she sold not TF.*
cossena] i.e. *she strove not for T.*
dibad] i.e. *wealth T.*
44 *che*] i.e. *of this world here below T*:
 i.e. *on this side F.*
46 *fertaib*] i.e. *head-pillow under the miracles is the following TF.*

In other words, this is the beginning of her miracles; *cennadart* is used of the place of the bed where the sword was hung up in SG 120, 39.

48 *cairm*] i.e. *what place*, i.e. *ubi F.*
50 *fenamain*] i.e. *wain, which her mistress sent to her to the summer herding-place to get butter T*:

Once on a time the angel came to Brigid, and sent her to release her mother who was with the druid, named Mac Midrui. Her mother was a Connaught woman, and her father a Munster man, and she was at that time in Mag Fenamain in (Arad) Cliach.[1] Now when Brigid got as far as that, there was her mother with an eye-disorder in the milking-yard; so she went along with the druid's charioteer to her mother, and took the cooking in her absence, and used to practise great charity with the provisions; and the druid heard of it. The charioteer went home. Said the druid, "How are things going on at the milking-yard?" "I am thankful indeed," said the charioteer, "and the calves are fat, and the guests are thankful." But the practice of charity by Brigid was evil in the eyes of the druid and his wife; so they came with a big basket, to take advantage[2] of Brigid, and to reduce her to slavery hereafter, i, plenty of butter were not found with her. And indeed she had nothing but a churning and a half, so she recited this verse:

> My kitchen
> a kitchen of a fair Lord,
> a kitchen that my King hath blest,
> a kitchen with something in it!

---

[1] Now Kilteely in Co. Limerick.
[2] The word *citim* is used to express "to take unawares, at a disadvantage"; cf. FM III. 1574 tarraid *citim* ngabála ar (place); fuair boeghal gabála; 1600 fuaratar *citiw* ar [men]; 2224 fuair *cit* 7 *clang*; 2226 fuair uain 7 *edarbaegal* ar; 1896 ar nach flagthar *faill*.

Et dixit iterum:

> May Mary's Son, my friend, come
> to bless my kitchen;
> Ruler of the world to its extremity,
> may there be plenty with Him!

Et dixit tertio:

> O my great King,
> who art able for all these things,
> bless, O God—a cry without prohibition—
> with Thy right hand this kitchen!

She divided the churning (into three) *sub numero trinitatis*; but a half-churning she brought out of the kitchen. "It is good," said the druid's wife, "for the filling of a big basket is that." "Fill ye your basket," said Brigid, "and God will put something into it . . . . the druid and his wife." F=⁹.

This story is also found in B, L, and Θ. See the references in Stokes' *Lismore*, p. 320, and Cogitosus, *Vita*, c. 4.

The verses are given in Egerton 161 as a charm, the recitation of which will replenish an empty larder.

51 *rath*] i.e. *for feeding poor people* T.
52 *lenamain*] i.e. *the following which guests put upon her* T.
In other words, the crowd of beggars who were always about her.
54 *hard*] i.e. *was great* T.
coscur] i.e. *the marvel* T.
56 *toscur*] i.e. *the guest*, i.e. *the good company*. Or, *the country-fellow:* or, *the . . . . . or, the deed that Brigid wrought in giving food to the dog* TF=⁹.

Compare Cogitosus c. 6.

57 *lathe*] *one day in the 'Land of the Benediction' in Airiud Boinne beside Clonard, this miracle was performed; or at Domnach Mor beside Kildare, i.e. wetness in every place but dryness in Brigid's field* F=⁹.

This story is in Cogitosus c. 7.

mad-bocht] i.e. *well was it reaped, ut quidam poeta dixit:*

> 'Thy cake . . . .
> if thou give it to guests
> well reaped was it for her pipers (?)'

And another:

> 'He used not to give to a human being
> anything that was well . . . (?)
> of his reaping, the good . . of his cooking.' F=⁹.

58 *chraibdig*] i.e. *with Brigid* TF=⁹.
59 *tair*] i.e. *it was dry weather* T:
    i.e. *it was dry the whole time* F=⁹.
60 *anmich*] i.e. *splendid raining* T:
    i.e. *great wetting* F=⁹.
61 *epscoip*] i.e. *seven bishops came to Brigid out of Ui Briuin Chualand,*[1] *from Bishops' Hill particularly to Kildare. And Brigid*

---

[1] This district was partly in Co. Dublin and partly in Co. Wicklow.

asked of her cook i.e. of Blathnait, if she had food. Illa dixit, Non. And there was great tribulation in Brigid on that account, viz. that she had no food illis. And the angel told Blathnait to take the cows to Loch Lemnachta north of Kildare, and milk them, though they had been twice milked before. Well, the cows were taken, and were milked; and the milk ran over the vessels, and would have overflowed even the vessels of all Leinster if they had been brought to them, et inde stagnum nomen accepit F="1".

See *Book of Lismore*, p. 197. A short form of the story is in Cogitosus c. 8. It is also found in the margin of the B copy of the Felire at Feb. 1.

do'da'ascansat] i.e. they visited TF.

62 *diuir*] i.e. was not little, or, was not insignificant F.

63 *fororaid*] i.e. unless he had helped T:
             i.e. unless he had succoured F.

65 *argairt*] i.e. she herded TF:

Brendan was four years at sea, seeking the Land of Promise. During that time there was a monster following him in the wake of the boat. At one time another monster came up to it to kill it, and the monster supplicated Brendan and all the other saints of Ireland against the other monster, but that did not protect it till it supplicated Brigid. So after that Brendan said that he would not remain any longer at sea, until he knew why this miracle was wrought for Brigid beyond everybody. Brendan came thereafter on a journey towards Brigid, and that was revealed to Brigid. At that time Brigid was herding sheep in the Curragh of the Liffey, so she went to meet Brendan to Domnach Mor to the west of Kildare; so they saluted each other.

At Licc Brendan one day after that, Brigid during the heat flung her wet cloak over the sunbeams and it stetit thereon. Brendan told his gillie to put his cloak on them, but it fell off them twice; the third time Brendan himself flung it angrily, and it remained on them tunc. Brigid enquired of her cook, what quantity of food she had. She replied that she had nothing but one-eighth of barley grain. That was taken to the mill of Rath Cathair west of Kildare, twice, and they refused to grind it there, for Ailell mac Dunlainge king of Leinster chanced to be there at that time, viz. at Rath Cathair. Well, Brigid's servant went the third time, when it was flung into the mill-race along with its sack. So after that Brigid passed the word on Rath Cathair, that there should neither be smoke nor fires nor human beings in it till Doomsday, and so the whole mill disappeared underground. But Brigid's attendant took his sack out of the mill-race, and its other half of meal of malt, and made a feast out of that for Brendan and Brigid and her folk, so that they were thirty days simul consuming that feast; and each of them made his confession to his fellow. Said Brendan first, that from the time he took piety he had never gone over seven furrows without his mind on God. "It is good," said Brigid, "Deo gratias ago." Said Brigid further, that (from the time she had fixed) her mind in God, she had never withdrawn it at all. Brendan admires that, "It would be true,"

---

[1] Reading *ola* for *ola*; perhaps we should read *olc*, 'evil.'

said Brendan, "though [we said that] thou surpassest us in every point." Sic narrauit ei omnia quae in mari a bestiis audiuit, and they did so thereafter F⁼⁹.

With the earlier part of this note the story in the Preface to Ultan's hymn (p. 38 above) may be compared. It seems also to be found in substance in the Irish MS. at Rennes.[1]

lathe] i.e. *on a day* T.
anbige] i.e. *of great wet* TF.
66 *réde*] i.e. *on the plain of the Liffey* TF.
67 *scarais*] i.e. *she spread open* TF.
iarum] i.e. *after that* F.
forbrat] i.e. *her cowl, or any upper garment of any kind whatsoever* F.
68 *deslem*] i.e. *on a ray, i.e. on the sunbeams that rested on her right hand* T.

This story is in Cogitosus c. 9.

69 *macc*] i.e. *the robber who came to Brigid* TF.
in mac amnas] i.e. *at Rath Derthaige in Offaly was wrought this miracle, viz. there came a robber to Brigid four times, and carried off from her on each occasion a wether of the sheep of Dubthach's wife, so that she reproached Brigid. But Brigid replied, "Look over your sheep to see if they are all present." Then they looked, viz. Dubthach and his wife, and found them all complete without any missing* F⁼⁹.

This story is in L and in a slightly different form in Θ as well as in Cogitosus c. 10. See *Book of Lismore*, p. 331.

ro·das·gaid] i.e. *he begged* TF.
70 *rig*] i.e. '*For the sake of the King in whose absence [away from whom] thou art, give some of the sheep to me,*' said he TF.
71 *dobert*] i.e. *she gave* TF.
73 *sous*] i.e. *it is of my art, i.e. of my poetry* F.
atchous] i.e. *if I should relate* TF.
75 *amra*] i.e. *good. In Kildare was wrought this miracle, viz. there was a poor man on whom the king of Leinster had a claim for ale, and he had nothing to make it with, so he came to Brigid. Brigid was just then in a bath when the poor fellow entreated her that she would assist him. So after that Brigid blessed the bath-water in which she lay, and made of it new ale, which was given to the man, and by him to the king* F⁼⁹.

Compare Cogitosus c. 11.

lothrugud] i.e. *in which she herself was* T.
76 *senta*] i.e. *she blest* TF.
laid] i.e. *it was red ale* TF⁼⁹.
77 *senais*] i.e. *she blest* F⁼⁹.
comail] i.e. *pregnant* TF⁼⁹.
78 *galar*] *a nun who was with child came to Brigid, and she healed her* T:

A nun there was in Cluain Moiscna,[2] *and she was with child, and Brigid chanced upon her [when going] to the church; so she came after that to Brigid, and was pure thereafter* F.

This is in Cogitosus c. 12.

---

[1] *Rev. Celt.* xv. 88, 89.   [2] Near Fartullagh, in Co. Westmeath.

79 *mo*] i.e. *the greater was the wonder for another miracle's being wrought* F.

80 *saland*] *In the Curragh of Liffey was wrought this miracle, viz. a man came past Brigid with salt on his back, and Brigid said to him, "What is there on thee?" "Stones," said he. "Be it so," said Brigid, and it was fulfilled just so. Once more*[1] *he comes in this direction, and so came iterum past Brigid, et illa dixit ei, "What is there on thy back?" "Salt," said he. "Be it so," said Brigid; and so it was verified* F=*s*.

This story is in L. See Stokes' *Book of Lismore*, pp. 195, 329. Compare also Cogitosus, *Vita*, c. 13.

81 *ruirmiu*] i.e. *I have not counted* T:
    i.e. *I am not able to number it* F.
airmiu] i.e. *I am not able to number it* TF:
    Or, *I do not enumerate everything she did in miracles* F.

82 *noeb-duil*] i.e. *Brigid* T:
    i.e. *the holy creature* F.

83 *bennachais*] i.e. *she blessed*; i.e. *the flat-faced*; *in Cluain Corcaige in Offaly was wrought this miracle, viz. a leper was brought to Brigid, who bade him take out the clump of rushes that was in his neighbourhood from the place where it was; so he took it out, and there sprang a well of water from that place; so he sprinkled the water over his face and became whole* F=*s*.

This is told briefly in I. and in Cogitosus c. 14. See Stokes' *Book of Lismore*, pp. 197, 330.

85 *ingen amlabar*] i.e. *in Cluain . . . was wrought this miracle. a dumb girl was brought to Brigid, and Brigid took the girl's hand into her hand, and did not let go the girl's hand out of her hand till her speech was plain* F=*s*.

This is fully told by Cogitosus c. 15.

86 *hoen*] i.e. *of Brigid's miracles* T.

89 *tinne*] i.e. *bacon* T.
amra] i.e. *a flitch of bacon was given to her as an offering in Cell Finnend . . . this was wrought: and it was forgotten by her household . . . in Kildare, and it was there up to the end of a month, with a dog guarding it, which not merely did not let other animals defile it, but also did not (itself eat it); . . . . . (and it remained good) as if people had eaten it the same (night?)* F.

This is told by Cogitosus c. 16.

90 *ro·d·glinnestar*] i.e. *guarded it, and preserved the joint* T:
    i.e. *kept it safely* F.

93 *mo*] i.e. *greater was the other miracle in comparison with it* F.

94 *do·tlucestar*] i.e. *she requested* TF.
mir] i.e. *it was in the kettle* T:
    i.e. *a poor fellow begged from Brigid a bit that was in the kettle. And the food therein was not at all cooked yet, so she requested of the (kitchen-)folk (to give a piece) of food (and they) threw the bit towards the man; it fell on Brigid's breast, but it did not spoil her dress* F=*s*.

---

[1] The text seems to be *tic ille quidem*, but there is a difficulty in the transcription of the last word which makes the passage obscure.

This is in Cogitosus c. 17.

95 *maforta*] *i.e. in the singular; viz. her vestment that, from the word 'mafortis' i.e. 'coif-veil' TF*ⁿ*⁹.*
i.e. kerchief, that is over . . . *; in Kil(dare) was wrought this little miracle sic F*ⁿ*⁹.*

96 *brothach*] *i.e. hot TF.*
focres] *i.e. was flung, viz. into Brigid's breast F.*

97 *in clam*] *may-be it was a leper of Patrick's who came to ask for a cow, and he did not take any but the best cow in Brigid's milking yard; (and then he asked for) the calf (that was best), so Brigid blessed the calf that was best in the booley, and the cow loved (that calf as if it had been her own) after that F*ⁿ*⁹.*

This is in Cogitosus c. 18.

ro·gaid] *i.e. he begged F.*
ailgais] *i.e. his prayer F.*
con·id·rualaid] *i.e. so that she gave TF.*

99 *senais*] *i.e. she blest F.*
forglu] *i.e. the choice T.*

100 *carais*] *i.e. it loved the chosen calf of the cows TF.*
101 *reraig*] *.i. she drove, viz. permitted him to drive it to Bri T:*
i.e. Natfraich Brigid's lector . . . . *she used to give, that not* . . . *at any time that the land was not* . . . . *at present, till there should be given her town as far as* . . . *from the time that he begged* . . . *Brigid about letting* . . . *out, and he was let into it after that; he begged of Brigid* . . . *it was given to him; but* . . . *with the calf; he begged (of) Brigid a calf* . . . . *would not take* . . . . *even though over Ireland he should go F*ⁿ*⁹.*

This note is very difficult to read, as the surface of the MS. is much rubbed.

102 *B. C. Coil*] *proprium nomen loci in Bregia T:*
*was king of Breg Cobthach Coil; and as to Natfraich, he was the driver of the car tunc F*ⁿ*⁹.*

105 *in daim*] *i.e. a friend came to Brigid* . . . . *Mor in the Curragh of the Liffey, and a request with him to her, that Brigid would abide with him that night; and then was stolen (her herd of oxen) in her absence. It was brought to the river Liffey, and the river rose up against them, so that the robbers put their clothes on the horns of the oxen as they were going across it. The oxen go away back from them to their home, and they wend their way to Kildare to Brigid, with the robbers' clothes on them F*ⁿ*⁹.*

The story is given in Cogitosus c. 19 thus: "Et quodam interuallo temporis alii nequissimi fures . . . boues ipsius furati sunt. Sed eos eadem reuertentes uia impetus ingentis fluminis inundatione aquarum subito facto conturbauit. Non enim flumen instar muri erectum scelestissimam bouum fraudem B. Brigidae per se transire permisit, sed eos fures demergens et secum trahens boues de eorum manibus liberati loris in cornibus pendentibus ad proprium armentum ad bubulum reuersi sunt."

do·da·ascansat] *i.e. they re-visited TF.*

106 *fo*] i.e. *good* T F.
ro·das·cload] i.e *he would hear them* F.
107 *conuccaib*] i.e. *it rose* T F.
doub] i.e. *the river* T F.
108 *a tech*] i.e. *Kildare* T.
109 *breit*] i.e. *under-cloth (?) that is put under the horse's neck* T F.
scarais] i.e. *at Ri Cuind this was wrought; between Forraig Rath and Cell Culind*[1]; *was Brigid . . . Natfraich in one chariot . . . to them there . . . . Kildare . . . ; Natfraich at that time preached to them the word of God, and he lets slip from him (the reins . . . one of) the two big horses got his head out of the yoke so that it was eating grass . . . . so that Ailell mac Dunlainge, the king of Leinster, saw that, and he was going to Maisten and he gave . . from his neck that he might help . . ; and Brigid said for this act of humility, There shall be to thee the kingdom of Leinster till Doom and to thy progeny after thee* F^m*9*.

The sense will be gathered from the corresponding passage in Cogitosus (c. 20) " cum quadam die ipsa sanctissima Brigida cogente aliqua necessitate utilitatis conuentionem plebis uisitaret in curru sedens binis uehebatur equis. Et cum in suo uehiculo meditatione theorica caelestem agens in terris uitam suum ut solebat dominatorem oraret, de alto procidens loco alter bruto animo equus saliens sub curru et irrefrenatus habenis fortiter se extorquens et de iugo semetipsum absoluens, equo altero solo sub suo remanente iugo, exterritus per campestria cucurrit ; et sic manus diuina iugum pendens sine praecipitio sustentans, et uidente turba ob testimonium uirtutis diuinae secura in suo orans uehiculo, cum uno equo sub curru posito ad plebis conuentionem discursu placabili illaesa peruenit."

Observe that 'He' in l. 101 is Natfraich, Brigid's charioteer.
110 *do·rertatar*] i.e. *they ran* T F.
112 *ro·reraig*] i.e. *he helped* T:
i.e. *they helped, or assisted* F.
– laim] i.e. *hand of the king of Leinster*, T.
113 *tathig*] i.e. *a wild boar that was in a certain wood to the north of Kildare, and he did not allow other pigs near him ; and Brigid blessed with her staff the wood at Ross na Ferta in Kildare to the north of Clocthech, so that after that the boar was at peace with them ; it was he that became leader to them always* F^m*9*.

This is in Cogitosus c. 21.
114 *do·sefhain*] i.e. *he chased* T F^m*9*.
os] i.e. *the wild pig* T F^m*9*.
117 *mug-art*] i.e. '*pig high*,' or '*pig fat*' T F^m*9*.
di] i.e. *to Brigid* T F^m*9*.
A fat pig the king of Fotharta Tire gave—that land is in the South of O'Kinsela—every year to Brigid ; as an offering . . . the king of the Kinsela to Brigid ; and the king of Fotharta further said that he would not give it to him, nor could he give it to Brigid in violation of his protection, but he would let it away outside, and wherever God would send

---
[1] I.e. Old Kilcullen in Co. Kildare.

it . . . *And it went to Mag Fea*[1] *to Uachtar Gabra i.e. to the place where Brigid was F=9.*

This is in Cogitosus c. 22.   The O'Kinsela country was in co. Wexford.
dobreth] i.e. *was taken TF=9.*

118 *amra*] i.e. *it was good TF=9.*
120 *Uachtur-Gabra*] i.e. *a big hill in the plain of Leinster TF.*
121 *asrir*] i.e. *she gave TF.*

sinnach] i.e. [*a man had killed a tame*] *fox of the queen at Maisten in Ui Muredaig, and a movement was made to kill him for it. At that time Brigid chanced to be at Maisten, and she said* . . *the son of the* . . . [*the king said*], *Thou shalt get him under thy protection, provided that it would perform the trick that the other fox used to perform. Brigid afterwards blessed the wood and struck a hand-tree, so that a fox of the same tricks came to her. And Brigid gave it for the sake of the wretch. So the man was let off. The fox went into the wood, and nothing could be done to him, though all the dogs of Leinster were after him F=9.*

There is a shorter form of this story in the Book of Lismore (p. 196). It is also given by Cogitosus c. 23.

123 *conselai*] i.e. *he ran away; or, it stretched T.*
124 *do'sefnatar*] i.e. *though they chased TF.*
125 *menn*] i.e. *was plain TF=9:*
       in Cell Brigte i.e. *in Kildare itself that was done F=9.*
126 *mathair*] .i. *Brigid was unique de matribus Christi T.*
127 *senais*] i.e. *she blessed T.*

en] i.e. *a bird,* i.e. *a silver chain that a certain man brought as an offering to Brigid, and she gives it to the little girls that were along with her; for they were not pleased at nothing being given to them; and there came a certain leper to her, to beg something of her, so she gave him the chain without the knowledge of the girls; and they wept when they learnt it, so she asked them,* " *What equivalent would you ask to be given you for it?* " *In lieu thereof it pleased them,* " *that we should have yon little bird, for it is pretty.*" *Brigid blessed the bird, so that it was tame from one hand to another. What was the land of the bird from that time forth? Not hard* . . . *regionis, in which was found the true gold F=9.*

This explains line 128; the bird was so tame that it could be passed from one hand to another, without its trying to fly away. Cf. p. 43. above, and Cogitosus c. 24.

129 *nonbur*] .i. *of the Ui Loscain were they, ut ferunt F.*
senais] i.e. *Brigid blessed F:*

Nine brothers of Leinster, who wanted to go to . . *in Conn's Half, for it is they who killed him* . . *they came to Brigid to bless their arms* . . . *tunc* . . . *miracles in Kildare. So Brigid blessed their arms for them. After the blessing of their arms, the men went southward, and the man chanced upon them, and they killed him. On the morrow after they had killed him as they thought* . . . . . *they did not get a drop of blood out of him, so that they were thankful for that; and the man escaped per gratiam Brigitae F=9.*

---
[1] Mag Fea is a level plain in the barony of Forth, Co. Carlow.

This is in Cogitosus c. 25.

130 *minna*] *i.e. their arms* T. The reading of F, *amesat*, and its gl. *aggau* [their spears?] are alike unknown.

131 *for da'corsatar*] *i.e. whom they set upon* T.

132 *greta*] *i.e. wounds; or, was wounded* T.

collann] *i.e. for it was not upon a real person they inflicted their wounds but it was upon a pillar-stone* T.

134 *do'rurme*] *i.e. would make its enumeration* TF.

135 *amra*] *i.e. good* F:

ro'gab] *i.e. he took* F.

136 *tren-fer*] *i.e. three strong men there were building the ditch of a man of Alene, where there is a small fort of the king of Leinster. These are their names, Mureth and Fiad and Lugaid. A dinner of a hundred men, each man of them ate. Now Lugaid was entrusted to the Churches for his feeding, but the other two men to the laity. Well, Lugaid begged of Brigid that she would diminish his appetite and would not take away his strength, and Brigid wrought that for him, and she blessed his mouth, so that his appetite was not greater than that of an ordinary man; and after that he went, and lifted up the stone, which the others, a hundred men of them, could not do before, from the ditch on to the top . . . .* F=9.

Compare Cogitosus c. 26.

digaib] *i.e. she diminished his allowance, but none the less was the strength of Lugaid; i.e. Lugaid was a mighty man that lived in Leinster, and he was . . . i.e. food of a hundred he consumed as his food . . .*

. (she took away his voracity) but did not diminish his strength T.

137 *omna*] *i.e. it fell on the road, so that it took . . . . but the (men of) Offaly were unable to raise it. And one time Brigid chanced to be on that road, and the (men of) Offaly implored of her to lift up the oak from the place where it lay; and she lifted it up after that through the might of the Son of God, so that it is still in the same place from that time to this* F=9.

This is in Cogitosus c. 27.

138 *digrais*] *i.e. wise* F.

doth] *i.e. famous the deed* F.

139 *dobert*] *i.e. he gave, viz. Christ* F.

140 *airm*] *i.e. to a place* F.

ro'chloth] *i.e. in which it was . . . in which it was good* F.

both] *i.e. her (it?) to be (there)* F.

141 *set*] *i.e. a pin* T.

chleth] *i.e. not to be hidden* T:

i.e. that it was not right to hide or to conceal F.

142 *fraicc*] *i.e. towards a bondmaid* TF.

Niad] *i.e. Nia, proprium nomen alicuius poetae* T:

i.e. the champion F.

143 *focress*] *i.e. was flung* TF.

ro'it] *i.e. the length of a cast* TF.

144 *iach*] *i.e the salmon* TF:

i.e. a silver pin the king of Leinster gave her as a reward for her complaisance: he took her with him home to . . . he took it from the hand

of the bondmaid . . . . *and he flung it from him into the sea to her detriment* . . . . *the poet asked asked the pin with the bondmaid* . . . *of a salmon the pin was found.*
At that time Brigid chanced to be in the house of . . . . *(prayer) of Brigid towards God that there might be shown her the pin for which* . . *and an angel came,* . . . *and ordered her to cast nets into the water i.e. into the sea, and a salmon would be caught in them, and the pin would be found in the middle; et sic factum est et liberata est ancilla de necessitate illa F*ᵘ⁹.

The story is in Cogitosus c. 28; and is to the effect that a man deposited a silver pin with a woman 'quam dolose retraxit illa ignorante et iecit in mare.' Brigid saved the girl from evil consequences by predicting that the pin would be found in a salmon, which accordingly came to pass. There is a somewhat similar story told in the romance of Froech and Find-abair, printed by O'Beirne Crowe from the *Book of Leinster*.[1]

145 *amra*] i.e. *good TF*.
di] i.e. *for Brigid TF*.
amra di] i.e. *Once Brigid chanced to be at the fort of the king of Breg in Mag Coil in Fingal hodie, and the queen refused her (hospitality). A certain widow woman that dwelt beside the fort outside gave her a welcome, and (killed her calf) for her and set fire to her new weaving-beam under it. On the morrow through the favour of Brigid both calf and beam were quite whole. But now when the king heard of that, viz. that Brigid had come, (he went) to interview her, and that widow woman met him; as soon as the king saw her, he fell in love with her through the favour of Brigid, and took her to wife, and from her is the origin of the* . . . *Carrolls ut ferunt F*ᵘ⁹.
The first part of this story is in Cogitosus c. 29.

146 *ar·do·utacht*] i.e. *feasted (?) her TF.*

149 *arailiu*] i.e. *this miracle was the greater for being wrought there also TF.*

150 *ar·id·ralastar*] i.e. *she effected TF.*
152 *dith*] i.e. *it sucked TF.*
153 *set*] i.e. *the valuable; or, the trinket gift F.*
i.e. *the trinket of silver, viz. three brothers to whom their father left a bar of silver, and the smiths of Ireland were unable to divide it exactly into three parts for them; so Brigid broke it, divided it TF*ᵘ⁹: *with her fist in Kildare T:* . . . . *was the miracle wrought F*ᵘ⁹.
This is in Cogitosus c. 30.
combaig] i.e. *he did not break TF.*

154 *di*] i.e. *it was a great miracle by Brigid.*
155 *ro·sm·bi*] i.e. *she broke it; or she smote T.*
157 *focress*] i.e. *it was put TF.*
ceird] i.e. *with the smith (in the smithy?) TF.*
159 *fuirecht*] i.e. *was not found T.*
162 *fail*] i.e. *was not found T.*
dune] i.e. *persons coming (?) F.*

[1] R.I.A. *Irish MSS. Series*, I., i, 147.

do·da·decha] *i.e. who narrates* T.

163 *senais*] *i.e. she blessed* F.

. . . Brigid blessed Condlaed the Pious (and he) tried twice to go to Rome. Brigid again blessed him, so he tried the third time . . . . Brigid gave her cowl to another man, a leper, once when she was guarding . . . . . to Brigid upon him, *quia non fuit intus cere* . . . . garment to Brigid, and it was brought, and she had only one garment that she could give him, so he enquired of Ron-cend, *i.e. the sub-deacon*, on account of the size of her garment . . . to see if he had not a garment. "There will be," replied he, "provided thou put prayer up to God." Thereafter there was found a garment in a basket that was with Ron-cend in a chariot of two wheels; they were under the chariot. Or, not the name of a person at all was Roncend, but a garment that had a resemblance to the skin of a seal's head; it was found there, and it was afterwards given to Condlaed. Thereafter he, Condlaed, set out on a journey to go to Rome. Brigid said to him, "Though thou set out thou shalt not arrive." So it was fulfilled, for wolves ate him at Scecha F^m.

In a note at May 3 in the Felire of Oengus, the story is briefly told that Roncend, otherwise Condlaed, Bishop of Kildare and Brigid's chief artificer, tried to go to Rome in disobedience to Brigid's orders, but was devoured by wolves on the way. See p. 191 above, and Todd's *St. Patrick*, p. 23; compare Cogitosus c. 31.

dillait] *i.e. garment* TF.

164 *dobreth*] *i.e. he used to go; i.e. a semetipso it was brought* F^m.

Letha] *i.e. to Rome* TF^m.

166 *mac*] *i.e. Christ; preceding her* T.

ni·s·derbrad] *i.e. he defrauded her not* TF^m.

167 *dobert*] *i.e. he gave* TF^m.

criol] *i.e. in a basket of seal's skin was the garment* T.

169 *ol*] *i.e. the vat* F: *i.e. ale which the king of Leinster claimed from the king of Ui Culduib, and it was owed to the latter by a man of his people; and he came to Brigid to ask her to help him, for he had nothing to give as he had given the ale to Brigid; but the king of Ui Culduib did not accept that [excuse] from him, et proinde uenit ad Brigitam, et necessitatem habuit, so that after that there was put water into the vats that were at hand in the neighbourhood of Brigid's house, and Brigid blessed that water, so that it became mead. And the poor man took it home with him then, and there was no mead that was better than it, and there was neither plus uel minus of it than was due de misero* F^m.

This story is in Θ and in a shorter form in L. See Stokes' *Lismore*, p. 331.

di] *i.e. to Brigid* F.

dobreth] *i.e. was given* TF.

170 *ances*] *i.e. it was not deep* TF.

thucai] *to the person who gave the vat to Brigid* T.

171 *frith*] *i.e.* . . . . *after drinking what there was in it, by Brigid and her household* T.

173 *asrir*] *i.e. she gave* T.

a hathaig] *i.e. to a man of her folk TF.*
175 *furecht*] *i.e. was not found TF.*
177 *itge*] *i.e. may they be upon us, her prayers T:*
   i.e. may her prayer be of assistance to us F.
178 *con·don·fair*] *i.e. may she succour us T:*
   i.e. may she effect our help F.
179 *leith*] *i.e. may the weaklings and the wretched be on our side praying for us T.*
181 *do·n·fair*] *i.e. may she effect our assistance T.*
182 *ialla*] *i.e. against demons T.*
ciara] *i.e. black ; i.e. black flocks demoniorum F.*
183 *ro·n·snadat*] *i.e. may they effect our deliverance TF.*
186 *eclais*] On a vellum fragment bound up with T we have an etymological gloss, whose reference is probably to this verse: "*eclais* i.e. *uaid* and *clais*, 'trench of the cave'; or, *clais* 'stripe,' 'that is sewed (*uaig-*) upon each one'; or, *eclais* from *ecclesia*, 'collectio iustorum,' the congregation of the righteous being therein." See vol. i. p. 190.
187 *taithmet*] *i.e. recollection, i.e. correspondence TF:*
   i.e. meeting T.
fiadat] *i.e. of the good God F.*
nath] *i.e. better than any poetry T:*
   is the poetry that is made for God T⁻⁹ :
   than any poem F.
189 *ateoch*] *i.e. I beseech T.*
erlam] *i.e. 'high her hand'; vast her hand [readiness], towards working miracles and marvels TF.*
193 *reided*] *i.e. she drove ; i.e. she proceeded TF.*
Currech] *i.e. 'racing of horses'; a cursu equorum dictus est TF⁻⁹.*
194 *fegi*] *i.e. against (sharpness) of the edges T.*
195 *fuar*] *i.e. I found not T.*
set] *i.e. her like T.*
196 *admunemar*] *i.e. we bless, or we beseech T.*
Brigi] *i.e. my Brigid T.*
conacna] *i.e. may she help TF.*
200 *ternam*] *i.e. may we escape TF.*
201 *clothach*] *i.e. illustrious TF.*
209 *riched*] *i.e. 'rig-iath' or 'king-land,' in the land of the heavenly King TF.*
210 *dichill*] *i.e. violation of her protection (?)* . . . . *F.*

The note in the lower margin of fol. 17 of T is, as Mr. Warren has observed (*Antiphonary of Bangor*, ii. 35), a favourite one with Irish scribes. To the instances of its occurrence which he has collected might be added the following. It occurs in the Preface to the Yellow Book of Lecan ; and in the Stowe MS. C. 3. 2 (R.I.A. Collection). At fol. 1 of Egerton 89 the scribe has written : "In nomine patris et filii et spiritus sancti Amen." *In nomine dei* was a common dedicatory form on inscriptions in Rome and Gaul. See Petrie, *Christian Inscriptions in the Irish language*, ii. 150.

The Hymn of St. Sanctan.

This hymn exists only in the manuscripts T and F, so far as we know. The text of T has been printed by Stokes in *Goidelica*, as well as by Windisch; and the Preface from F has been reproduced by Nigra (*Il manoscritto irlandese di S. Gallo*, p. 21). An English translation of this F Preface is found in the Trinity College MS. classed E. 3. 28.

The date of Sanctan, who according to the Martyrology of Gorman, presided over the church of Killdaleas in Leinster, is quite unknown; and it was unknown in the days of the scholiast who wrote the Preface. "Famous Bishop Sanctan" is named in the *Felire* of Oengus at May 9, as well as by Gorman.

Inis Matoc mentioned in the preface has been identified with an island in the lake of Temple Port, Co. Leitrim, but there is no certain knowledge of the place.

1 *ateoch*] *i.e. I beseech T.*
amra] *i.e. good, or, mirabilis T:*
    i.e. good, or, wonderful, viz. at saving and protecting anyone against dangers F.

2 *tressam*] *i.e. for there is not a nomen fortius quam nomen illius quod liberet hominem T.* Cf. Phil. ii. 9.

3 *lorg*] *i.e. after me TF.*
tuathum] *i.e. northward of me TF.*

The invocations in the *Lorica* of Patrick may be compared with these.

5 *togairm*] *i.e. dei T:*
    i.e. it is a holy invocation of God F.

6 *guasacht*] *i.e. in which I am, in danger T:*
    that I may not be in danger F.

7 *drochet*] *i.e. may each one come to it; or, 'droch-sét' = 'bad road,' for the badness of the road across which it is made; or, 'set diriuch = 'direct road,' for 'droch' is 'diriuch,' T:*
    i.e. 'set diriuch' = 'straight road,' for 'droch' is 'stretched out' in Gaelic F.

8 *issum*] *i.e. under me (my) face viz. countenance F.*

9 *do·n·foscai*] *i.e. may he awake us from the death of sin, or at Doomsday T:*
    i.e. may he effect our awaking at Doomsday; or may he overshadow us, viz. he made that so that it is figurative, so that it is . . . to him, quia ad similitudinem dei facti sumus F"9.

10 *baile*] *i.e. it is to him alone to whom there is not certain the death of piety, for if it were we . . . and death T:*
the Holy Spirit, ac si diceret, the spirit of Heaven, the household of heaven . . . God from His Countenance . . . certain death of piety . . . the Father, i.e. in this fashion, i.e. may the lofty law of God overshadow us; aliter, lofty Trinity may it awake us F"9.

The phrase 'death of piety' seems to mean 'death in a state of grace.'

11 *dn*] *i.e. in miracles and marvels T.*
13 *fine*] *i.e. our deeds ; viz. our sins F.*
14 *fiadu*] *.i. ' good God' TF.*
dillocht] *i.e. unvitiated, i.e. without fault God exists T :*
    i.e. its faultiness is increased abundantly faulty F.
15 *guallocht*] *i.e. against every fault of lying T.*
16 *ni·m·thairle*] *i.e. may they not visit me T.*
dibocht] *i.e. without God with him T.*
poor in respect of God : i.e. without God with me ; or, not poor, without poverty in respect of the world's wealth F.
17 *seth*] *i.e. every sorrow or disease T.*
18 *frisinnle*] *i.e. may he minister T :*
i.e. may Christ effect the settlement of my questions ; i.e. may Christ come towards the suffering F.
20 *testa*] *i.e. may the testifying Trinity (?) come to my assistance ; or ' triple' i.e. three T :*
till the testifying Trinity come to overtake me, to protect me before crime or error befal F.
Perhaps we may compare 1 Jn. v. 3 " tres sunt qui testimonium dant in caelo.".
21 *tolam*] *i.e. ' toi-ellam ' = silence-prepared ; i.e. may it come in silence and in readiness T.*
22 *celar*] *i.e. that is not hidden in songs TF :*
    or, the battle-songs . . . or spear-shaft F :
    i.e. his songs are not hidden TF.
On the word *celar* see the Glossary (which must be referred to for most of the difficulties of this poem).
23 *ni·m·thairle*] *i.e. of death the pang (be it not) to me in slaughter ; i.e. may he not put colour of corpse on me ; or, may he not put stumbling on me F.* There were two readings : F* has *·thasle*, and apparently *taisi li* is intended as a sort of ety. gl.
amor] *i.e. the cry of death is ' uch ach ' ! T :*
of death the cry ; i.e. song of death ; or ' ach ' and ' uch,' for this is the cry of death F.
24 *mortlaid*] *i.e. communis morbus F.*
    i.e. quando plurimi pereunt uno morbo i.e. swift death T :
    i.e. death swift, sudden death F^m *:*
    i.e. unnatural TF.
See note on this word printed at p. 84.
25 *ni·m·thairle*] or, *' ni·m·thuisle' i.e. let him not put stumbling on me T.*
erchor] *i.e. temptatio diabolica F.*
amnas] *i.e. ' am-inas' i.e. bad condition T.*
26 *medras*] *i.e. omen-knowledge TF :*
    i.e. which prognosticates the knowledge T.
bodras] *i.e. troublesome knowledge i.e. which troubles the knowledge ; disponitur i.e. a cast . . . which perturbs beyond the Son [of God] T.*
27 *ainsi·unn*] *i.e. may he protect us F.*

ern-bás] *i.e. against every iron death TF.* This is a common word in the Irish Tales. Cf. LL 132β40; 133α13; 150β35; 194β31, &c.

28 *thein*] *i.e. against death TF.*
threthan] *i.e. against three-wave TF^{ug}:*
    quia ferunt periti nautae that it is the third wave that most frequently sinks naues T^{ug}, F^{ug}.
torbas] *i.e. which humbles death (?) . . . ; dry death (?); or, weariness (?) death TF^{ug}.*

29 *éic-lind*] *.i. against every water of death; which produces death; or against every . . . F:*
    or, against everything which water drowns (?) T:
    against everything that . . . F.
eslinn] *i.e. that is unsafe T.*

30 *ainbthib*] *i.e. which is with storms and with horrors T.*

31 *do·mm·air*] *i.e. may it come to my assistance T.*
thratha] *i.e. either day or night T.*

32 *gǽth*] *i.e. against hurt, of wind TF.* Yet the text seems to refer to 'perils of *waters*'; perhaps *gaeth* in both text and gll. is used in the sense of "a shallow stream into which the tide flows and which is fordable at low water" (MR 288, 5). Cf. the end of the gl. on l. 51 of the *Altus Prosator.*

33 *luathfe*] *i.e. I shall set going T:*
    I shall utter F.
molthu| *i.e. praises TF.*

34 *bages*] *i.e. it contended T:*
    which engages [to do] F.
Both words are, however, used to gloss *glorior*, 'I boast.'
baga] *.i. for deeds F.*
finna] *i.e. good TF.*

35 *friscera*] *i.e. He will reply TF.*

36 *lurech*] *i.e. God TF.*
arbaig] *i.e. which boasts TF.*
mo thenga] *i.e. out of which it may make battle TF.*

37 *digde*] *i.e. at praying God TF.*

38 *sigith*] *i.e. may it be lasting F.*
sethrach] or, *sethach*, 'laborious' *T.*

39 *ris*] *i.e. that I may not go to* TF.

40 *ateoch*] *i.e. I beseech TF.*
ad·ro·etach] *i.e. I besought TF.*

THE LORICA OF ST. PATRICK.

The legendary story of the composition of this famous hymn is given in the *Tripartite Life* (p. 45 ff.). The tale runs that Patrick and King Loegaire met at Tara Hill, when the latter was presiding at a heathen festival, which was to begin with the extinction of all fires throughout the country. But Patrick disregarded this regulation and defiantly lighted his paschal fire on the Hill of Slane in full view of the king and his druids. Then followed a contest between the saint and the druids, in which Patrick triumphed, as Moses of old triumphed over the magicians of Egypt. The king thereupon purposed to kill Patrick by a treacherous assault; but he and his companions escaped, being miraculously transformed into deer. And the hymn or charm which he recited in his flight was the *Lorica S. Patricii*, commonly called, as the Preface informs us, *Faeth Fiada*, or "The Deer's Cry." The end of the story tells of the conversion of the king to the Christian Faith. Save for the mention of the hymn, this legend is, in substance, contained in Muirchu Maccu Machteni's memoir in the Book of Armagh. That Muirchu does not say anything of the hymn is undoubtedly unfavourable to the truth of the legend that it was composed by Patrick.

The title *Faeth Fiada* is perplexing. *Faed* certainly means 'scream' or 'cry,' cf. MR 72, 23, 230, 19. But the MSS. have not *faed*, but *fáeth*, which Colgan prints *feth*; and *feth* means 'peace,' 'calm.' On this hypothesis, the title should mean, "The Deer's Repose." It is possible, however, that a quite different explanation may be the true one. *Feth fia* is found in the *Book of Ballymote*, 345β in a gloss on the word *druid*; it there is equated with *aisdinecht* and seems to mean 'the divination.' O'Donovan, similarly, in his *Supplement* to O'Reilly's *Dictionary*, translates *feth fia* 'magical darkness.' O'Curry observes that *feth fiadha* was a *spell*, peculiar to druids and poets, who by pronouncing certain verses made themselves invisible.[1] And thus our Lorica may have gained its title not from any tradition about St. Patrick and the deer at Tara, but from its use as a charm or incantation to ensure invisibility.

The piece was first printed by Petrie in his essay on the *Antiquities of Tara Hill* (1839), with a translation by O'Donovan. A much better translation was given by Dr. Whitley Stokes in the *Saturday Review* for Sept. 5, 1857; and the same editor has printed the hymn in *Goidelica* from the manuscripts T and Θ, as well as in the Rolls' *Tripartite*. Another valuable edition is that by Windisch in his *Irische Texte*.

The only MSS., save T and Θ, which we know to contain the piece are Egerton 93 and Egerton 190. The latter is quite modern, and of no value; the collation of the former which we have made does not seem worth printing, but we have had it before us while preparing the translation given above. Our register of the variants of Θ has been derived from Dr. Stokes' transcript of that MS. in *Goidelica*.[2]

Metrical translations by J. C. Mangan, J. J. Murphy, and Mrs. C. F. Alexander will be found in Dr. Wright's little volume on *The Writings of Patrick the Apostle of Ireland* (p. 109). Dr. Sigerson has printed in his *Bards of the Gael and Gall* (p. 137), a translation in which the irregular rhythm of the original is imitated.

That the hymn is of early date there can be little doubt. As we have said, it is not mentioned in Muirchu's memoir, but in a passage already cited (p. 97) from Tirechan's collections in the Book of Armagh there occurs the injunction "Canticum eius scotticum semper canere," as one

[1] Atlantis III., 386. [2] See Vol. i p xx.

of the four special honours to be paid to Patrick in all Irish monasteries. And there seems no good reason for hesitating to identify this "Canticum Scotticum" with the piece before us. The language of the hymn is so uncouth in its grammatical forms that it affords no sure basis for argument. But, at least, it is more likely that these grammatical anomalies should be survivals of perversions of some older form of speech than that they should have been deliberately constructed in times subsequent to St. Patrick to give the piece an archaic flavour. Again, internal evidence would suggest that the hymn was written at a time when paganism had still considerable influence. True, the druids lived on in Ireland long after it became a Christian country; and some of the old superstitions have survived to our own time. But nevertheless lines 47–54 appear *prima facie* to have reference to existing and recognised pagan belief.

In his *Essay on Tara Hill*, published in 1839, Petrie stated that some portions of this hymn were then in use among the peasantry, and repeated at bedtime as a protection against evil. We do not know whether this is still true; but it is worth while to observe that the structure of the piece seems to have been followed more or less closely in the composition of later charms of a similar character. For example, in the manuscript belonging to the Royal Irish Academy classed $\frac{23}{E. 16}$ there is at p. 237 a lorica, a portion of which is worth printing here for comparison in the translation kindly made for us by Mr. E. J. Gwynn :—

" God be with me against every sorrow, even the One noble Three,
The Father, the Son, and the Holy Spirit!

. . . . . .

The Trinity be my protection against swarms of plagues,
Against sudden death, against terror, against treacheries of marauders!
May high Jesus keep me against the Red Plague!
Against demons at all times, the Son of God is my shield,
10 Against disease, against hurts, against thunder, against fire.

. . . . .

Against weapons, against terror, against venom of darts,
Against danger, against treachery, against hidden poisons,
Against every form of sickness he pours on the world.
Every (blessing) without pain, every pure prayer,
Every ladder that reaches heaven shall be an aid to me,
Every good saint who suffered on the surface of the earth,
20 Every chaste disciple who was tortured for Christ,
Every meek, every gentle, every candid, every pure person,
Every confessor, every soldier, who happens to live under the sun,
Every venerable patron saint who should reach me for luck,
Every one, gentle or simple, every saint who has suffered the Cross.

. . . . . .

Every righteous modest son under the roof of the glassy heaven,
30 From the sunset in the west to Mount Zion eastward,

May they protect me henceforth against the demons of the mist,
They, the comrades of the King's Son in the lands of the living.

36 May I be under the hand of God against every danger!"

This last lorica naturally falls into three divisions. In lines 1–6 the might of the Trinity is invoked; then from line 7–16 the dangers are enumerated against which protection is desired; and finally the aid of saints and angels is asked in the warfare against evil. The Lorica of Gildas (vol. i. p. 206), in like manner, begins with an invocation of the Trinity, goes on to invoke saints and angels, and then proceeds to a detailed enumeration of the parts of the human body which might be subject to injury.[1] The structure of Patrick's Hymn is more complex than either of these, and it presents features, such as the special invocations of Christ in His Incarnate Life, which they do not contain; but the likeness is obvious. It will be observed that the fine idea of lines 11–20 in Patrick's Hymn has been developed in the later pieces into a formal invocation of saints and heavenly powers. The opening invocation of the Trinity, which is found in all three loricas, is undoubtedly a very ancient Celtic form. It will be remembered that the hymn of St. Colman Mac Murchon (vol. i. p. 44) begins in like fashion: "In Trinitate spes mea fixa, non in omine."

The grammatical peculiarities of the poem, first of which is *niurt* (which is *dat* in l. 2, *acc* in l. 9, and *nom* in l. 32), have been pointed out for the most part in the Glossary.

The opening word *atomriug* has been variously translated; but 'I arise' is the rendering we have finally adopted. It is thus not in any special grammatical connexion with the following lines, all of which have reference to *tocuiriur* (l. 48) 'I invoke,' the one principal verb in the piece. The general meaning of the clauses is "each day, when I arise, I invoke, &c."

l. 8. There is an etymological gloss on *adnocul* 'burial' on the last of the vellum fragments bound up with T. See vol. i. p. 190. It is as follows; "*adnacul* i.e. *ead + nae + 'cul, ed* meaning 'law,' and *nae* 'man,' and *cul* 'observance'; *i.e.* 'observance of the law of man.'"

l. 9. Stokes compares the words of the Milan Gloss (24 a. 18), *cluasa dæ diar n-eitsecht intan mbimmi isnaib fochaidib*, "God's ears to hear us when we are in the sufferings." The likeness is undoubted, but we should hesitate to conclude therefrom that the glossator borrowed from the lorica, although we are disposed, as we have said, to acquiesce in the traditional authorship of St. Patrick.

l. 13. With lines 13–20 may be compared the very similar language of a Latin prayer found in the manuscript Reg. 2. A. xx (J). It is headed *Oratio matutina*, and is as follows:—

> Ambulemus in prosperis huius diei luminis
> In uirtute altissimi dei deorum maximae
> In beneplacito Christi in luce spiritus sancti
> In fide patriarcharum.

[1] See below, p. 244.

```
     5        In gaudio angelorum in uia archangelorum
              In sanctitate sanctorum in operibus manachorum
              In martyrio martyrum in castitate uirginum
              In Dei sapientia
              In multa patientia in doctorum prudentia
    10        In carnis abstinentia in linguae continentia
              In trinitatis laudibus
              In acutis sensibus in bonis actibus
                    SEMPER CONSTITUTI.
              In formis spiritalibus
              In diuinis sermonibus in benedictionibus
    15        In his est iter omnium pro Christo laborantium
              Quod ducit nos post obitum in gaudium sempiternum.¹
```

l. 60. In the Lorica of Mugron, preserved in two manuscripts of the Royal Irish Academy $\left(\frac{23}{G\ 4}\text{ and }\frac{23}{G\ 5}\right)$ we have some invocations which seem to be modelled on ll. 61–65 of the Lorica of Patrick, viz. :

"The Cross of Christ with me in my good luck, in my bad luck;
The Cross of Christ against every strife, abroad or at home;
The Cross of Christ in the East with courage (?), the Cross of Christ
  in the West at sunset;
South, North without any stay, the Cross of Christ without any delay;
The Cross of Christ above towards the clear sky, the Cross of Christ
  below towards earth.
There shall come no evil nor suffering to my body or to my soul,
The Cross of Christ at my sitting, the Cross of Christ at my lying;
The Cross of Christ all my strength, till we reach the King of
  Heaven!"

This Lorica of Mugron,² according to a colophon at the end, was copied by Michael O'Clery from the "Book of Armagh," *i.e.* not the famous manuscript which now goes by that name, but another volume used by the Four Masters in their work.

THE LAMENTATION OF ST. AMBROSE.

This curious piece has not been printed before, and we have not found it elsewhere. It is alphabetical, and not only so, but the lines in each stanza begin for the most part with the same letter, as will be observed on inspection. A somewhat similar piece is ascribed to Isidore (Migne P.L. lxxxiii. 1251); and Mr. Warren has printed (*Antiph. of Bangor* II. 101) an alphabetical set of prayers from the manuscript we have called J, which will bear comparison with it.

The notes written at this point in the margins of T (see vol. i. pp. 142, 3) are interesting. That at the top of fol. 20b we have not

---

[1] The phraseology of the collect in the Stowe Missal (fol. 27), printed in Warren's *Celtic Liturgy*, p. 244, may also be compared with these lines.
[2] The translation given above is due to Mr. E. J Gwynn.

succeeded in identifying. It seems to be a fragment of bad hexameter verse.

The extract at the top of fol. 21 from Augustine is from a passage now prescribed in the Roman Breviary as a lection at the third nocturn in the *Commune Doctorum*.

Then comes the verse Apoc. vii. 12, which is also found in the Breviary more than once; *e.g.*, it is the Capitulum at Nones on All Saints' Day. We do not quite know what to make of the rubric (?) which follows: " Uespere psalmus cotidie cantatur post prandium uel ballenium." The word we read *psalmus* is almost illegible, and we are not sure about it. In any case it is not probable that the so-called *Lamentatio Ambrosii* is the piece referred to; so gloomy a penitential would hardly have been counted suitable " post prandium," as a kind of grace after meat. But as we have remarked before, (vol. i. p. xxix) the presence of this rubric suggests the use of the *Book of Hymns* at daily choir services, and so is interesting as being one of the very few direct pieces of evidence we have got for the fact.[1]

The ethnological and etymological notes at the top of fol. 21b seem to be merely memoranda. The Irish words in the fragment may be translated: *scenopodi i.e. the one-legged men ; i.e. the broadfooted men . . . labrosi ; their lower lip they thrust out beyond their (chin)*.

M. Berger has printed[2] a remarkable penitential piece ascribed to St. Patrick in a tenth-century MS. now at Angers, but which he supposes to have been written at Tours. It presents some points of interest in connexion with the *Lamentatio Ambrosii*, and we reproduce it here.

INCIPIT CONFESSIO SANCTI PATRICII EPISCOPI.

Deus, Deus meus, rex omnipotens, ego humiliter te adoro. Tu es rex regum, dominus dominantium. Tu es arbiter omnis saeculi. Tu es redemptor animarum. Tu es liberator credentium. Tu es spes laborantium. Tu es paraclytus dolentium. Tu es uia errantibus. Tu es magister gentibus. Tu es creator omnium creaturarum. Tu es amator boni omnis. Tu es princeps omnium uirtutum. Tu es gaudium omnium sanctorum tuorum. Tu es uita perpetua. Tu es laetitia in ueritate. Tu es exultatio in aeterna patria. Tu es lux lucis. Tu es fons sanctitatis. Tu es gloria Dei patris in excelso. Tu es saluator mundi. Tu es plenitudo spiritus sancti. Tu sedes ad dexteram Dei patris in throno regnans in saecula.

Ego peto remissionem peccatorum meorum, Deus meus Iesu Christe. Tu es qui neminem uis perire sed omnes uis saluos fieri et ad agnitionem ueritatis uenire. Tu, Deus, ore tuo sancto et casto dixisti: In quacunque die conuersus fuerit peccator, uita uiuet et non morietur. Ego reuertar ad te, Deus, et in omni corde clamabo ad te, Deus meus, et tibi nunc uolo confiteri peccata mea. Multiplicata sunt delicta mea

---

[1] The note on fol. 22 is an extract from a Canon of the *Hibernensis* collection dealing with the duties of *principes*, which apparently means *kings*. It may possibly, however, refer to the duties of an abbot. The general tenor is not unlike that of Sedulius' treatise *De rectoribus Christianis*.

[2] *Revue Celtique*, xv. 155.

super me, quia peccata mea numerum non habent ante oculos tuos, Domine, reus conscientia testis adsisto. Rogare non audeo quod inpetrare non mereor. Tu enim scis, Domine, omnia quae aguntur in nobis, et erubescimus confiteri quod per nos non timemus admittere. Uerbis tibi tantum obsequimur, corde mentimur. Et quod uelle nos [? non] discimus, nostris actibus adprobamus. Parce, Domine, confitentibus, ignosce peccantibus. Miserere tu rogantibus, quia in sacramentis tuis meus sensus infirmus est. Praesta, Domine, ut, qui ex nobis duro corde uerba non suscipis, per te nobis ueniam largiaris, Iesus Christus Dominus noster.

Confitebor tibi, Deus meus, quia ego peccaui in caelo et in terra et coram te et coram angelis tuis et coram facie omnium sanctorum tuorum.

Peccaui per neglegentiam mandatorum tuorum et factorum meorum.
Peccaui per superbiam et per inuidiam.
Peccaui per detractionem et per auaritiam.
Peccaui per luxoriam et per malitiam.
Peccaui per fornicationem et per gulam.
Peccaui per falsum testimonium et per odium hominum.
Peccaui per furtum et per rapinam.
Peccaui per blasphemiam et per desiderium carnis.
Peccaui per ebrietatem et per odiosas fabulas.
Peccaui per contentiones et per rixam.
Peccaui per iuramentum et iracundiam.
Peccaui per laetitiam terrenam et transitoriam.
Peccaui per terrorem et per suauitatem mentis meae.
Peccaui per dolum et per murmurationem.
Peccaui per instabilitatem mentis fidei et per dubietatis impietatem.
Peccaui per inmisericordiam et per spernationem hominum.
Peccaui per praua et per iniqua opera [et] iudicia.
Peccaui per neglegentiam et per obliuionem operum Dei.
Peccaui per uagationem et per discretionem mentis meae.
Peccaui per inpacientiam et per spei inperfectionem.
Peccaui per duritiam et per cecitatem cordis uel mentis.
Peccaui per [in]obseruationem amoris Dei et proximi.
Peccaui per inoboedientiam et per amissionem bonorum constitutorum.
Peccaui per amissionem caelestium desideriorum et per amorem terrenarum rerum.
Peccaui per studia iniquitatis et per dolosa argumenta.
Peccaui per exempla iniqua et per humanitatis obsordes.
Peccaui per accidiam uanam et per stuporem mentis.
Peccaui per fictam humilitatem et amissionem amoris Dei.
Peccaui per maledictionem et per diuinationes.
Peccaui per inperfectionem uotorum meorum et per machinamenta iniqua.
Peccaui per scrutationem maiestatis Dei et caelestis uitae.
Peccaui per pompas corporis et per ambitiones fauorum hominum.
Peccaui per intemperantiam hilaritatis et furoris.

Peccaui per tedia et per desidiam mentis.
Peccaui per consilia iniquitatis et per redditionem mali.
Peccaui per concupiscentiam et perpetrationem libidinis.
Peccaui per consentionem et per conscientiam actuum iniquorum atque uerborum.
Peccaui per dominici diei operationes et per inlecebr[os]as cogitationes.
Peccaui per tristitiam seculi et per amorem pecuniae et per ambitiones honorum.
Peccaui per inquietudinem et per amaritudinem mentis.
Peccaui per inutilem laetitiam et per scurilitatem, per dolorosa uerba et per intemperentia[m] clamoris.
Peccaui per disperationem et per inpuritatem confessionis.
Peccaui per inperfectionem et neglegentiam emendationis.
Peccaui per audatiam et disperationem.
Peccaui per acceptionem munerum iniquorum et per punitiones impietatum.
Peccaui per simulationem et per memetipsi placationem.
Peccaui per silentium rectitudinis et iniquitatis et adulationis.
Peccaui per comessationem et per polluti cibi acceptionem et per suggestiones diaboli et per dilectationem spiritus et per conscientiam carnis.
Peccaui in oculis meis et in auribus meis.
Peccaui in manibus meis et in ore meo et in labiis meis et in omnibus factis meis.
Peccaui in lingua et in gutture.
Peccaui in collo et in pectore.
Peccaui in corde et in cogitationibus.
Peccaui in mente et in operationibus.
Peccaui in manibus et in pedibus.
Peccaui in ossibus et in carne.
Peccaui in medullis et in renibus.
Peccaui in anima mea et in omni corpore meo.

Si nunc erit uindicta tua super me tanta quanta in me ipso fuerunt peccata mea multiplicata, iudicium tuum quomodo sustineo? Sed habes te sacerdotem summum ad quem confiteor omnia peccata mea. Id tibi soli, Deus meus, quia tibi soli peccaui et malum coram te feci. Et quia tu es, Deus, solus sine peccato, obsecro te, Domine Deus meus, per passionem atque per signum salutiferæ crucis tuæ atque per effusionem sanguinis tui, quo tu concedas mihi remissionem omnium peccatorum meorum. Peto te, Domine meus Iesu Christe, quod mihi non reddas secundum meritum meum, sed secundum magnam misericordiam tuam. Iudica me, Domine, secundum iudicium indulgentiae tuae. Ego te peto et adiuro, Deus meus omnipotens, ut tu in me colloces amorem et timorem tuum. Suscita in me paenitentiam peccatorum meorum et fletum pro nomine tuo. Da mihi memoriam mandatorum tuorum et adiuua me, Deus meus, dele iniquitatem meam a conspectu tuo et ne auertas faciem tuam ab oratione mea. Ne proicias me a facie tua. Ne derelinquas me, Deus meus, ne disces-

seris a me, sed confirma me in tua uoluntate. Doce me quid debeam
non agere, quid facere aut loqui, quid tacere. Defende me, Domine
Deus meus, contra iacula diaboli et contra angelum tartari suggerentem
et docentem multa mala. Ne deseras me, Domine Deus meus, neque
derelinquas unum et miserum famulum tuum, sed adiuua me, Deus
meus, et perfice in me doctrinam tuam. Doce me facere uoluntatem
tuam, quia tu es doctor meus, et Deus meus qui regnas in secula seculorum. Amen.

An Abridgement of the Psalter.

The preparatory note to this collection of 365 verses gathered from
the Book of Psalms in regular order, states (*a*) that it was made by
Pope Gregory, and (*b*) that the recitation of these 365 verses is not only
equivalent to a recitation of the whole Psalter, but that it has the
virtue as well, "sacrificii et fidelis animarum commendationis." This
highly convenient arrangement for getting rapidly over one's devotions
recalls the Celtic doctrine explained (p. 98), that the recitation of the
last three verses of a hymn was as efficacious as if the whole hymn were
said.

We have other instances of these collections of versicles from the
Psalter. There is one printed among Bede's works, entitled *Libellus
Precum* (Migne P.L. xciv. 515). A *Psalterium abbreuiatum* attributed
to St. Jerome is frequently met with in service books. And the idea
that the recitation of certain verses had peculiar efficacy occurs in a
curious form in a legend of St. Bernard of Clairvaux. A demon once
mocked him by the assurance that he knew of eight verses, the recitation
of which was equivalent to the recitation of the whole Psalter. The
saint begged to be told what these verses were; and, the demon refusing
the information, he declared that he would henceforth daily recite the
entire Psalter, so that the precious verses might always be included.
The demon then disclosed the situation of the verses; they were
Ps. xii. 4, xxx. 6, xxxviii. 5, lxxxv. 17, cxv. 16, cxli. 5, cxli. 6.[1]

In the *Book of Cerne* (C), eleven folios (from fol. 87b to fol. 98b),
are taken up with an exactly similar collection to that before us. The
versicles selected in C are not always the same as those in T, and the
collection is not quite as long, but the general plan is the same. At
the beginning there is an almost defaced title, of which the last letters
seem to be: " . . . entia forsorum eal ' said eps decerpsit." The
name of Ethelwald appears on fol. 21a, so it is possible that this may
be the name of the bishop who made the C collection. In C the
number of separate *orationes* is not easy to determine; but we counted
over 260 coloured initial letters.

If the number of versicles in T be counted, it will be found that
there are only about 240 instead of 365 as promised in the title; but
on examination it will be seen that there is an obvious gap between
fol. 24b. and fol. 25, for we make a sudden advance from Ps. xlii. 3

[1] Wordsworth's *Ecclesiastical Biography*, II. 66, note.

to Ps. lxix. 6, whereas both before and after the text has been fairly continuous. This indicates that a page, or more probably two pages, has been lost from T at this point. If the MS. were not thus mutilated, we should no doubt find our full number of 365 verses.

The number 365 seems, for whatever reason, to have been a favourite one with Irish writers. Nennius[1] says, *e.g.* that St. Patrick founded in Ireland 365 churches, and consecrated 365 bishops. We may be quite as sceptical as Todd was[2] as to the accuracy of these figures; but the choice of the number 365 is here significant. Again the Irish tract *de Arreis*, on the penitential commutations,[3] begins with the words: " The *arreum* for saving a soul out of hell, viz. : 365 paternosters and 365 genuflexions and 365 blows with a scourge on every day to the end of a year, and fasting every month saves a soul out of hell." And it is by no means unlikely that the old tradition that there were 360 crosses on the island of Iona may have a great deal more truth in it than Reeves was willing to allow.[4]

Both the plan of this collection of verses from the Psalms and their number, are, then, distinctly Celtic. The triple division of the Psalter, usual in Irish books, next claims attention. It will have been observed that several times in the Book of Hymns, the Psalter has been described as "the Three Fifties." This is indeed the regular Celtic designation for the Psalter; and it is worth observing that the phrase first occurs, so far as we know, in the *Prologus in librum Psalmorum* of Hilary of Poictiers, whose relations to Celtic Christianity have been touched on above (p. 127). His words are: " Tribus uero quinquagesimis psalmorum liber continetur: et hoc ex ratione ac numero beatae illius nostrae expectationis exsistit." (Migne P. L. ix. 239). In Irish Psalters these divisions are nearly always clearly marked by large initial letters, sometimes elaborately illuminated; *i.e.* the initials of the Psalms *Beatus uir* (i), *Quid gloriaris* (li) and *Domine exaudi* (ci), are treated with special care. A good instance is the Southampton Psalter (Σ); another is the Psalter of Ricemarch at Trinity College, Dublin. In the collection of versicles in the Book of Cerne (C), of which we have spoken, the triple division is thus indicated by large letters at the points Psalm i. 1–3, and ci. 2. In the collection before us it seems to have been made even more conspicuous. The first point of division occurred on one of the lost folios; but the first and third divisions are preceded by the introductory versicle *Deus in adjutorium*, the initial D being specially large, and the second and third are concluded by the *Pater noster*.

The short office at the end will be observed. The *Credo* and the *Pater noster* are followed by the prayer: " Ascendat oratio nostra usque ad thronum claritatis tuae domine, et ne uacua reuertatur ad nos postulatio nostra. Amen. Amen. Amen. Alleluia." This prayer is found in the Stowe Missal (S) with the rubric *Haec oratio in omni*

---

[1] See Usher, *Works*, iv., 322
[2] *St. Patrick*, p. 28.
[3] It has been printed from the manuscript θ by Kuno Meyer in the *Revue Celtique* xv. 485ff.
[4] See his *Adamnan*, p. 419, for the tradition, which Reeves scouts without serious examination.

missa cantatur. And the long prayer which concludes this portion of the *Liber Hymnorum* seems also to have had Eucharistic associations.

It will be observed that the text of this Abridgement passes continuously on from fol. 25 to fol. 29; this is due to misplacement of the folios by the binder.

At the top of fol. 23b a late hand has written the letters of the alphabet in the margin; but there are no more *marginalia* like those with which the earlier pages are covered. And the handwriting now entirely changes its character, and is of a later date than that of the pieces which we have hitherto considered. The remaining hymns are written in ink of a different colour, and the scribe is less skilful than his predecessors. We shall also see that the vocabulary has changed, and that many words, hitherto unused, occur.

THE HYMN *ALTO ET INEFFABILI*.

In the Life of St. Ciaran of Clonmacnoise (c. 26), as quoted by Colgan, we read: " Unus ex praecipuis Hiberniae est et merito numeratur Apostolis iuxta quod de ipso cecinit eius condiscipulus et coapostolus sanctissimus Columba in hymno quodam quem in eius composuit laudem dicens:

Quantum Christe O apostolum mundo misisti hominem
Lucerna huius insulae lucens lucerna mirabilis, etc."[1]

The first line of this couplet is almost identical with line 8 of the piece *Alto et ineffabili*, which suggests that this may be the hymn in question. It is mentioned again in the manuscript (wrongly) called the *Book of Kilkenny* in Marsh's Library at Dublin, where at fol. 148aa we read: "Et fecit sanctus Columba ympnum sancto Kiarano," a hymn which Ciaran's successor at Clonmacnoise called *clarus et laudabilis*. Columba, the story goes, asked in return for some earth from St. Ciaran's grave, with which he calmed the stormy water on his way back to Iona.[2]

This St. Ciaran, who is to be carefully distinguished from St. Ciaran of Saighir, was the founder of the great monastery of Clonmacnoise, and in its *Annals* the year of his death is given as 547. He is counted one of "the twelve Apostles of Ireland," and in the Martyrology of Donegal (at Septr. 9) he is compared to the Apostle St. John. He was known in his life time as Ciaran mac an t-saor, or "Son of the Carpenter"; and was a friend of St. Kevin, as of St. Columba. His memory still survives in the place called "Temple Kieran," about four miles from Navan. In Cornwall the name of Ciaran (of Saighir) has become corrupted to *Piran*, to whom there were many churches dedicated.

At the end of the *Vita S. Kiarani* contained in the two manuscripts which we call Y and Z, a composite Latin hymn is found which we reproduce here[3]:

---

[1] Compare the same story in the life of St. Ciaran in the *Book of Lismore*, ed. Stokes, p. 263 ff.
[2] See Reeves' *Adamnan*, p. 263.
[3] The piece will be found at fol. 130 of Y, and at fol. 94 of Z. Their texts are almost identical.

Matre Quiarani sedente in curru uolubili
sonitum magus audiuit perdixitque seruulis
uidete quis sit in curru nam sub rege resonat
coniunx inquiunt Beodi sedet hic artificis

5   Magus inquit gratum cunctis ipsa regem pariet
cuius opera fulgebunt ut Phebus in ethere
miles Christi Keranus sancti sedes spiritus
spiritali pietatis uirtute floruerat

Uitulum uacce lactentem iam cani concenserat
10 Keranum inde grauiter mater reprehenderat
uitulum cane uoratum ab ipso exegerat
cuius ossa mox apportans ipsum restarauerat

Mulieris regie caput decaluatum
seue zelo pelicis fuerat nudatum
15 In Querani nomine cum esset signatum
aurea cessarie fulserat ornatum
Cum Queranus studiis sacris teneretur
atque tempus posceret ut operaretur
pro ipso ab angelis tunc mola mouetur
20 textus euangelicus in stagnum ceciderat
Sic uoluto tempore per Querani merita
integrum de gurgite uacca reportauerat

cum puer oraret dominum precibusque uacaret
ignis ab excelsis uenerat arce poli
25 Defunctusque puer conspexit brauia uite
et sancti magnum glorificant dominum
de celis lapsus rutilans accenditur ignis
et peragit proprium protinus officium

Alto et ineffabili apostolorum cetui
30 celestis Ierosolime sublimioris specule
sedenti tribunalibus solis modo micantibus
Queranus sacerdos sanctus insignis Christi nuntius

Inaltatus est manibus angelorum celestibus
consumatis felicibus sanctitatum generibus
35 quem tu Christe apostolum mundo misisti hominem
gloriosum in omnibus nouissimis temporibus.

This hymn is plainly made up from different sources. Ll. 1–12, ll. 13–19, and ll. 20–22, are all distinct from each other and from ll. 23–28, which are in elegiac metre, as well as from ll. 29–36 (the first two stanzas in T) which form, perhaps, the only specifically Celtic fragment in the whole. Mr. H. A. Wilson has suggested that ll. 13–19 may possibly be responds, like some of those in the Aberdeen Breviary. But without entering upon any investigation of the sources of its various parts, this composite piece is sufficiently interesting to justify printing it in its integrity. YZ preserve the true readings *ineffabili, cetui* (l. 1), *speculae* from *specula*, a watchtower (l. 2), and *sedenti* (l. 3).

The vocabulary is remarkable. The words *ineffabilis, coetus, sublimis, specula, micare, sacerdos, inaltare, sanctitas, genus* do not occur elsewhere in the *Liber Hymnorum*.

Dreves (*Analecta hymnici medii aeui* xix. 172) has printed the stanzas found in T; but without reference to the manuscripts YZ.

The legends about St. Ciaran which are obscurely alluded to in this hymn will be found in Irish in the life of the saint in the *Book of Lismore* (p. 265ff), and in Latin in *Acta Sanctorum ex codice Salmanticensi* (p. 155ff).

With l. 3. cf. the observation of Stokes (*Lismore*, p. 356) that 'currus sub rege resonat' was a common proverbial expression, and occurs again in the Vita Sancti Aidui (*Cambro-British Saints*, p. 233). Cf. also Colgan's *Vita tertia* of St. Brigid c. 1.

l. 9. The story in this stanza is in *Lismore*, p. 267.

l. 15. The spelling *Quiaranus*, of which *Queranus* is a further corruption, illustrates the not uncommon interchange in Irish MSS. of C and Q.

l. 17. The story of the manuscript, which was uninjured by water, is in *Lismore*, p. 275.

l. 23. The allusions in this and the following lines are explained by the story in *Lismore*, p. 277.

l. 32. Dreves prints *uirgo* for *insignis*; but the latter is the reading of T.

THE HYMN OF ST. MOLAISE.

This alphabetical hymn was first published in the *Irish Eccl. Record*, v. 224 (1869), and has been also printed in Dreves' *Analecta*, xix. 222, but with some inaccuracies. It was known to Ussher, who doubtless had read it in T. In his *Antiquitates*,[1] he says: "Ad Laisreanum pergo, Hibernice Molaisse dictum . . . quem antiquissimus hymnus iuxta alphabeti ordinem in laudem ipsius compositus Macculasrium nominat:

> Lucerna erat in tota
> Macculasrius Hibernia
> Nadfraich et sanctus filius."

St. Molaise of Devenish, who is to be distinguished from St. Molaise of Leighlin[2] (Apr. 18, 638), and also from St. Molaise of Inismurray (Aug. 12), was the son of one Natfraich; he is celebrated in the Martyrologies on Sept. 12, and the *Annals of Ulster* give 563 as the year of his death. His *Acta* may be conveniently read in *Acta Sanctorum ex codice Salmanticensi*, p. 791; and there is an interesting

---

[1] *Works*, vi., 531.
[2] It is from St. Molaise of Leighlin that the village of Lamlash, in the island of Arran and St. Molio's Cave in Holy Island, derive their names.

Life of him in the R.I.A. manuscript collection $\frac{23}{\text{A. 43}}$. An English translation of his *Life* from the MS. Add. 18205 in the British Museum is printed by Mr. S. H. O'Grady in *Silua Gadelica*.

He was the founder of the monastery at Devenish, an island in Lough Erne, and for many centuries his memory lingered there. A stone coffin, called the Bed of St. Molaise, used to be shown to pilgrims, and was supposed to have healing virtues. For a description of his so-called 'Shrine' see Todd, *Proc.* R.I.A. vii. 331.

It has been suggested with some plausibility that this hymn is derived from an office for the Feast of St. Molaise, of which a fragment is extant as a marginal note in the Martyrology of Donegal at Sept. 12, viz.: "Antiphona communis: Uir dei dum uerbum uitae populo predicaret, uisus est a terra paululum sublimari et in aere pendere et mirati sunt uniuersi. Adesto nobis, quaesumus domine, ut beati Lasreani confessoris tui atque abbatis interuentu ab omni inquinatione mundemur corporis et mentis per Christum dominum nostrum."

The vocabulary of this piece is unlike anything else in the *Liber Hymnorum*, and indicates a later date than the majority of the hymns. The words *abbas, omnino, ecclesiasticus, anthleta, macula, subagrinus* (a curious word, apparently meaning *rustic*), *supplex, submissus, ieiunus, lucerna, peritus, obitus, securus, particeps*, and *prae* (in the last line in the sense of *beyond, as compared with*) do not occur elsewhere in the collection.

The Hymn of Mael-Isu.

This hymn is printed in *Goidelica* by Stokes. A metrical translation is given in Dr. Sigerson's *Bards of the Gael and Gall* (p. 192). Possibly the Mael Isu, named as the author, is Mael Isu, the grandson of Brolchan, who died in 1086, according to the Annals of Tighernach. Other poems by him are found in the Book of Lismore (at fol. 52), in the Yellow Book of Lecan, and in the margin of the B copy of the *Felire* of Oengus at Dec. 31. This last is a curious devotional piece in Latin and Irish, and has been translated in Olden's *Church of Ireland*, p. 426.

It will be observed that the date of Mael Isu of necessity brings down the date of this part of our principal MS. (T) to the end of the eleventh century at the earliest. But we have already remarked (p. 218) that the handwriting of the MS. changes in character at fol. 23b, and that the later pieces have certainly been added at a time long subsequent to the transcription of the more important part of the book. On the metre see p. lviii above.

A writer in the *Irish Ecclesiastical Record* (v. 224) has identified Mael-Isu with Molaise, a hymn in praise of whom immediately precedes the one before us; but there is no ground for this identification. Mael-Isu means "the tonsured servant of Jesus."

The Names of the Apostles.

This quatrain calls for no comment. As usual *Madian* is the form assumed by the name Matthias; and *Partholon* is the equivalent of Bartholomew. It occurs in the *Felire* of Oengus as a note at July 31, where there is special mention of "the twelve apostles who excel every number." See p. 110 above.

The Hymn *Ecce Fulget Clarissima*.

This hymn in praise of St. Patrick is found in T, and also in the manuscript we designate W. at fol. 122. In the latter it forms part of an office for St. Patrick's Day, and is divided into two parts, collects, &c., being inserted between ll. 12 and 13. From these two manuscripts it has been printed, though not very correctly, by Dreves' *Analecta*, xix. 233.

Colgan printed the hymn in his *Trias* (p. 189). He says that he took it from a book entitled "Officium sancti Patricii impressum Parisiis anno MDCXXII." This book we have not seen, but Colgan's text is almost the same as that contained in a volume edited by Thos. Messingham: "Officia SS. Patricii, Columbae, Brigidae, et aliorum quorundam Hiberniae sanctorum ex ueteribus membranis et manuscriptis breuiariis desumpta. Parisiis MDCXX." In this the hymn appears in the office for the translation of the relics of the patron saints of Ireland to Downpatrick, which took place in the year 1186.[1] As the old distich says:

"Hi tres in Duno, tumulo cumulantur in uno,
Brigida, Patricius, atque Columba pius."

The text of the hymn in this book and in Colgan differs considerably from both T and W, and must have been derived from some MS. now lost, or at least unknown to us. For instance Colgan's text exhibits the following variants amongst others: 2 *om* qua; 4 puritatis *pro* dignitatis; 5 felici hic ortus; 7 rectus; 8 duxerat; 13 sacra; 14 dominum *pro* omnium; *om* 15 and 16; 22 dono suae.

It may be remarked of this, as of the last two hymns, that its vocabulary shows it to be of a different period from the hymns in the *Liber Hymnorum* proper. The following words found in it do not occur in the rest of the book: *solemnitas, transcendo, pueritia, prosapia, baptisma, studeo, praescius, clemens, dirigo, fructiferus, idolatra* (apparently for *idololatrâ* in the sense of *idolatrous*), *mergo, aduenio, gentilis, gentilitas, confluo, respuo, colo, liber, remeo, patria, astutia, expello, quapropter, dilectissimus, praesul, psallo, alterno, uitium, perfruor, uisio, paraclitus*.

The hymn has been recently printed from T, with an English translation, by Dr. C. H. H. Wright.[2]

[1] See Reeves, *Eccl. Ant. of Down and Connor*, p. 227.
[2] *The Writings of St. Patrick*, p. 39.

The Hymn *Phoebi diem*.

This hymn has been recently printed by Dreves (*Analecta*, xix. p. 98) from T; we do not know any other text of it, nor have we been able to trace its history. It was probably an office hymn of a late period; the vocabulary is strangely different from any other piece in our collection. No less than 40 words (exclusive of proper names) do not occur elsewhere in the *Liber Hymnorum*, viz.: *orbita* (the orbit), *decus, laurea, ministro, spina, tanquam, lilium, stirps, profero, mortalis, celebs, fugo, blanditia, eger, leuamen, egens, cibarium, hostilis, monstro, aruus, caelicus* (bis, a rare word), *relinquo, oliua, regalis, sumo, ferculum, fulgidus, kalendae, sarcina, solutus, palatium, comptus, flos, lacteus, adhaereo, pudor, speculum* (a mirror), *precamen, substantialiter, personaliter.* Further, the use of *flamen* for the Holy Spirit in l. 17; and the position of *ut* after its verb in l. 16, are noteworthy features. The metre is Celtic, with internal rhythms.

l. 2. *gaudium* must be a scribe's blunder, as *gaudia* is required by the metre.

l. 5. The construction seems to be: 'She avoided yielding to the allurement of the flesh.' Dreves reads *celeras* for *cedere*, but this would destroy the metre.

l. 7. Dreves conjectures that the two last words should be *uicit praelium*; and we are inclined to adopt the conjecture; the MS. reading is untranslateable.

ll. 9, 10. It must be remembered that Brigid is called in the Hymn of St. Ultan *ueri dei regina*. This stanza takes up the language of the Canticles (see esp. iii. 9, *ferculum fecit sibi rex Salomon*), and applies it to Brigid as the Spouse of Christ, with a side reference to the Queen of Sheba and her visit to Solomon. The words *ornant oliuae uasculum* we do not clearly understand.

l. 11. February was *Numae mensis*, and St. Brigid's Day is Feb. 1.

l. 14. The text prefixed to the Irish *Lives* of St. Brigid was: *Hi sunt qui sequuntur Agnum quocumque ierit* (Apoc. xiv. 4).

The Preface to the Amra.

The 'Amra' or 'Eulogy' composed by the poet Dallan mac Forgaill in honour of St. Columba, is not extant in its integrity; and consequently it is impossible that a satisfactory edition of it should be produced. The piece was early remarked as obscure, and commentators in the middle ages spent much ingenuity in the endeavour to explain its strange phrases. The unfortunate fact is that of the *Amra* itself, but little has been preserved, while we have many texts containing prefaces to the poem, and glosses on the more difficult portions. Very few complete lines are now extant; and for the most part the glossators seem to have had little basis, in grammar, in tradition, or in common sense, for the superstructure of so called explanation which they produced. Thus it has come about that the *Amra* as we have it, is only a strange medley of isolated phrases and unintelligent comment, which presents little attractiveness to an editor.[1] But as the plan of these volumes is to present to the reader every piece contained in the two manuscripts of the Irish *Liber Hymnorum*, we have found it necessary to print the *Amra* as it stands in T. Such translation as we could furnish has been supplied, and a few explanatory notes are added; but we have not attempted to collate all the manuscripts. There is no ground for hoping for any reconstruction of the original work from the fragments that remain.

The main texts are the following: (1) Our principal manuscript, T, which we have reproduced *verbatim*. Dr. Whitley Stokes has already printed this in *Goidelica*, but he has altered the order of the verses or sections, so as to bring them into conformity with the more rational order of the L. na hUidhre text, and thus his reprint does not readily convey to the reader an exact picture of his exemplar. (2) The manuscript Rawl. B. 502. We have had a photograph of this in our hands, while writing our translation. (3) The *Leabhar na hUidhre* (LU) in the Library of the Royal Irish Academy. This has been reproduced, with a translation, by Mr. O'Beirne Crowe.[2] (4) The *Yellow Book of Lecan* (YBL), classed H. 2. 16 in the Library of Trinity College, Dublin. This has been published in photographic facsimile by the Royal Irish Academy. (5) The *Leabhar Breac* (B), of which a facsimile from a hand transcript has also been published. This is a fragmentary copy. (6) The *Saltair na Rann* at the Bodleian Library. (7) The vellum manuscript classed Stowe C. 3. 2 (Saec. xv?) in the Royal Irish Academy's Collection, a fine copy with a very full gloss, the longest that we have seen. (8) The manuscript we call X also contains fragments of the poem. There are fragments of the *Amra* in most manuscripts which deal with the works of Columba, *e.g.* in the copy of the Old Irish Life at the Advocates' Library in Edinburgh[3]; but we do not attempt a complete classification.

The legend of the composition of the *Amra* is briefly as follows. In the year 575, Aed, son of Ainmere, King of Ireland, summoned the petty princes, heads of tribes, and principal clergy to a great convention at Druim Cetta, mainly with the purpose of banishing the bardic poets, whose exactions on behalf of themselves and their retinue were becoming intolerable. Aedan mac Gabrain, King of Argyle, was also present with the view of determining the question as to the independence of his kingdom of Dalriata, which had heretofore paid tribute to Aed. And St. Columba revisited Ireland on this occasion with the threefold motive of defending the cause of the bards, of keeping the peace between his native and his adopted country, and of bringing about the release of Scandlan, Prince of

---

[1] Mr. Strachan has given linguistic reasons in the *Rev. Celt.* xvii. (1896) p. 41 ff., for holding the date of the *Amra* in its present form to be much later than that of Dallan mac Forgaill. He assigns the text preserved in T to the early part of the ninth century.
[2] *The Amra Choluim Chilli of Dallan Forgaill* (1871).
[3] Stokes has printed translations of these portions in *Lismore*, pp. 316, 17.

Ossory, who was kept in ward by Aed. His intervention was successful, and in gratitude for his efforts on behalf of the bards, Dallan mac Forgaill, otherwise called Eochaid Righ Eigheas, the principal *ollamh* of Ireland at that time, composed the Eulogy in his honour, which goes by the name of the *Amra Coluim Cille*.

The introductory piece [pp. 53, 54 above] which we call the *Preface*, is followed by the Prologue proper on pp. 55–60, the poem itself not appearing until p. 60. We have numbered the lines so as to facilitate reference between the original and the translation; and it will be observed that (following the practice of the scribes) we have printed what is left of the *Amra* proper in large letters, the explanations of the glossators being in smaller type. The lines of the introductory piece on pp. 53, 54 we have numbered separately. It is evident that many of the explanatory notes of the scribes have, in our copy, been disturbed from their appropriate places.

p. 53. l. 2. *Fene* is glossed in T: *i.e. a hill.*

l. 3. The *Masraige* were a Firbolg tribe, inhabiting the district of *Mag Slecht*, a plain lying round Ballymagauran in Co. Cavan. Dallan mac Forgaill was of their race.

Irarus is now Oris in Westmeath.

Breifne of Connaught practically included the modern counties of Leitrim and Cavan.

l. 5. *Dallan mac Forgaill* is reputed to have also composed the *Amra Sionain*, or eulogy in praise of St. Senan. He is commemorated in the Irish Martyrologies on Jan. 29. His name still survives in *Kildallan* in the diocese of Kilmore, and *Desert Dallan* in Raphoe.

l. 7. For the deadly effect which the satires of the bards were supposed to have, see O'Curry, *Manners and Customs of the Ancient Irish*, ii. p. 217.

l. 13. *Ibar of Cinntracht, i.e.* 'the Yew Tree at the Head of the strand,' is now Newry in the Co. Down.

We have retained the old word *coigny*, which signifies the right of entertainment, billeting, food, &c., claimed by the bards for their retinue. It was reduced, as a result of this convention, to provision for 24 attendants in the case of each *ollam* or principal bard, and 12 in the case of each *anrad* or minor poet.

l. 18. *Druim Cetta*, the scene of the Great Assembly, is identified with the mound called the Mullagh, in Roe Park near Newtownlimavady in the Co. Derry: Adamnan (i. 10) Latinises it *Dorsum Cete*.

ll. 24–27. A similar retinue is mentioned in the old Irish Life (*Lismore*, p. 178) as having accompanied Columba to Iona. Here they are particularly interesting, as they "not only illustrate the ancient frequency of bishops, but confirm what Bede said of the subjection of the bishops of the neighbouring provinces to the Abbot of Hy."[1]

l. 38. The virtue which was attached to the recitation of the eulogy is referred to again in the prologue to the *Amra* ll. 34, 145. We

---

[1] Reeves, *Antiquities of Down and Connor*, p. 132 ff. Compare the verses about the members of the Community of St. Mochta in the *Felire* (ed. Stokes), p. cxxxii.

have already (p. 146) quoted a quatrain which speaks of the *Amra* as well known in connexion with the name of Columba.

The release of Scandlan Mor, son of Cinnfaela (or son of Colman, according to Adamnan)[1] is described more fully in the piece of which a translation is given at p. 85 above. Here it is sufficient to note the record of the tribute paid in return from the men of Ossory (*Osraige*) to the monastery of Iona.

THE AMRA OF ST. COLUMBA.

ll. 50-57. We have already observed that many notes and illustrations of the scribes and commentators upon the *Amra* are found in T out of their context. No doubt in most cases they were marked by the scribes in such a manner that their true bearing would be readily perceived. The proper place of these verses, for instance, is marked with an asterisk which is still plainly visible. They are introduced from some now lost poem to illustrate the number of the retainers of the bards. Their burdensomeness had been often a subject of complaint, and the matter had been brought before several kings in succession, the third of whom was Mael Choba, son of Deman, son of Carell, king of Ulster. He granted them a respite from exile for three years, and these verses were, accordingly, composed in his honour.

ll. 15-22. The relevance of these verses is explained in the Edinburgh *Vita*. The king had refused to retain the poets. "'Say not so,' saith the cleric; 'for the praise which they will make shall be enduring for thee, even as the praise which the poets made for Cormac, descendant of Conn, is enduring for him, and the treasures which were given for it were perishable, but the praise abides after them.' And the cleric composed this little 'rhetoric,' i.e. *Cormac cain, &c.*"[2]

l. 17. The words *grace of poetry* are glossed in T *grace of knowledge*.

l. 23. The story of Scandlan's release is more fully told in the fragment *De liberatione Scandlani*, of which a translation is given at p. 85 above. See the notes *in loc.*

ll. 25-34. *Colman mac Comgellain*. The tale runs that Columba had observed the beautiful spirit of Colman, when a child; that he had thereupon addressed him in the verses ll. 30, 31; and had prophesied that he should be a peacemaker between Ireland and Scotland. And so it happened, for at the Assembly of Druim Cetta, Columba asked him to settle the dispute between the Irish and the Scotch Dalriads. His sentence amounted to this, that the Scotch were to be free from tribute to Aed, King of Ireland, but that they were to join in hostings and in expeditions (save those by sea) when required by the Irish. This practically made Aedan mac Gabrain an independent sovereign, and secured the freedom of the Scotch Dalriata.

---

[1] *Vita Columbae*, i. 11. See Reeves' note on the passage.
[2] Translated in Stokes' *Lismore*, p. 312.

ll. 35-45. This account of the composition of the *Amra* by the blind poet Dallan mac Forgaill explains itself. In the LU text, which preserves the order of the sections much better than T, l. 41 is followed by the verses which appear in our edition as ll. 144-148, an evident displacement.

l. 48. *Mael Suthain*. This is probably Maelsuthain O'Carroll, the author of the *Annals of Innisfallen*, who was anmchara or confessor to Brian Borumha, and whose handwriting is to this day preserved on a page in the Book of Armagh. He died in 1009. *Ferdomnach*, whose name is mentioned in support of a different tradition concerning the place where the *Amra* was first sung in its entirety, was elected coarb or successor of St. Columba in the year 1007, and died the following year. These names fix a limit in one direction as to the date of this Prologue; in its present form it cannot be earlier than the eleventh century.

l. 49. *Slige Assail* was one of the five great roads of Ireland; it divided Meath into two parts.

Tig Lommain was on the shore of Loch Owel in the county of Westmeath. It was here (according to the most popular tradition) that the eulogy was finished, after the tidings of Columba's death had been brought to Dallan by the rider on the "speckled horse." See p. 87 above.

l. 60. This note in explanation of who are meant by the "daughters of Orcus" should be placed after l. 670, where it is found in LU.

l. 62. *Hoc est principium laudationis*. What follows is a commentator's note on the structure of the poem, which began and ended with *n*, viz. '*Ni* disceoil' (l. 211) and 'amhuain' (l. 681).

l. 65. This note on the meaning of *ni-disceoil* should come, as in LU, after l. 213.

l. 66. *Ni chelt ceis, &c.* These nine lines of verse[1] are quoted by the commentator from some old poem on the Plunder of Dinn-rig, to illustrate the usage of the obscure word *ceis* which occurs at l. 262. They should follow after the words "*ut dixit* the poet" (l. 267) as they do in LU, in YBL, and in the Stowe MS. A gloss on *ni chelt* in T has *Ross mac Finn or Ferchertne poet cecinit*. The verses themselves occur three times in the Book of Leinster (pp. 269β, 311β, and 377β). They are concerned with the tale of the charm of Craiptine's harping, which at a feast so bewitched the revellers that the lovers Maen, otherwise called Labraid the Mariner, and Moriath of Morca were able to slip away unobserved. Labraid the Mariner lived, according to the annals, in the sixth century B.C. The famous poet Ferchertne, and Craiptine, the first harper who is named in Irish legend, had charge of him in his boyhood when he was dumb, and it was under their care that the youth Maen recovered his powers of speech. Henceforward he was known as *labraid* (i.e. *he speaks*).

---

[1] Lines 66-68 are printed as prose in vol. I. p. 164; for the passage is only partly legible, and it is possible that only a paraphrase was there given. But we have printed it as poetry in the translation (p. 57 *supra*).

ll. 73-76. This quatrain should follow l. 279, as it does in LU and YBL. The 'Dub-*recles*' or Black Church was the ancient Church of Derry. In the fourteenth century it was called the *Cella Nigra de Deria*.[1] The quatrain is quoted in the Annals of Tighernach, and of the Four Masters, in the latter case under the year 592. But it may be taken as established that St. Columba died June 9, 597, at the age of 76 years. See l. 550 *infra*.

ll. 77-80. This quatrain should follow l. 210, as in LU. It is quoted to illustrate the use of the word *iath*.

ll. 81-84. This quatrain in like manner should follow l. 197, as in LU. It is quoted to illustrate the use of *mur*. These verses are like the jingling rhymes of Latin grammar, which boys are set to learn.

l. 82. *coph* is glossed in T: *or, cu, i.e.* '*dog*.' Possibly the idea of the glossator is that $cu = q = \unicode{x05E7} = coph$.

ll. 85-88. This quatrain giving the maternal descent of St. Columba, should follow l. 679, as in LU and the Stowe MS. See p. 235 *infra*.

ll. 89-94. This note and the quatrain belong to l. 330, where they are found appended in LU. They are quoted in a note in the *Felire of Oengus* (ed. Stokes, p. ci); and occur in a poem headed "Mongan cecinit do Colum Cille" in the MS. we call X. The sweetness and power of Columba's voice are reckoned by Adamnan[2] among his miraculous gifts. See l. 465. St. Brendan of Clonfert was said to have a voice of like power (*Lismore*, p. 250).

ll. 95-99. This quatrain should follow l. 338 (as in LU, YBL, and the Stowe MS.) It alludes, of course, to the translation of Columba's relics to Downpatrick. See p. 222 *supra*.

ll. 100-107. This note should come after l. 354, as in LU. It is explanatory of the word *aidbse* or 'chorus.' The quatrain is ascribed to Colman mac Lenine, the founder of the Church of Cloyne, who died in the year 600. They are also quoted in the *Book of Leinster*, fol. 8, and in Cormac's *Glossary*, s.v. *adann*.

The old word *coilgg-se* in l. 107 is glossed in T: *i.e. a sword*.

The word *aidbse* signifies a kind of low, murmuring chorus at the end of each verse; from its name of *cronan* it seems to have been produced in the throat, like the purring of a cat. *Dord* was used for a humming or droning noise, without melody.[3]

ll. 108-112 supply a linguistic note (displaced as usual) on *ferb*, which occurs in l. 360. Substantially the same explanations of the word are given in Cormac's *Glossary*.

In l. 109, T has a gloss on *bain*, viz. *true*, and in l. 111 has a gloss on *o'sn'acht*, viz., *he drove them*.

l. 112. Mog Nuadat is now Maynooth in the Co. Dublin.

ll. 113-117. This note should follow l. 419 as it does in LU.

ll. 118-127. These lines consist of two quatrains, and a paraphrase of a third, from the Dinnsenchus on 'Laigin' or Leinster, in the Book of Leinster (159a and 377a). They are not found in LU. But as in

---

[1] Reeves, *Adamnan*, p. 277. See also p. 140, *supra*.
[2] *Vita Columbae*, i. 37. See Reeves' note *in loc*.
[3] See O'Curry, *Manners and Customs of the Ancient Irish*, iii. 246, 371 f.

the Stowe MS. they form part of the gloss on l. 263, they seem to be added to explain who was Labraid Loingsech, already mentioned in ll. 70, 72. He defeated and slew Cobthach at the battle of Dinnrig, formerly called 'Tuaim tenma,' in the year A.M. 4658, according to the Four Masters. Dinn-rig is on the Barrow near Leighlin Bridge. The story is that Labraid introduced into Ireland the broad lances called *laighni*, from their use of which the people of the principality of Gaillian received the name of *Lagenians* or Leinstermen.

ll. 128-131 should follow l. 277, as in LU and in the Stowe MS. They are added by the commentator to illustrate Columba's ascetic habits of self-discipline. See *Lismore*, p. 180, and also p. 228, where a similar thing is told of St. Finnian of Clonard.

l. 128 *isin ganium*. The gloss in T is: *Or in the winter*.

ll. 132-8. This is a note explanatory of the repetition "God, God. . ." at the beginning of the *Amra* in l. 186. It follows the note ll. 61-64 in LU. The LU text explains that there are three standard devices in Irish poetry; the *return to the usual sound* (of which we have an example in ll. 181-183), the *enunciation mode* of which it gives an illustration not in T, and *reduplication*, as an example of which it cites ll. 135-8. Such devices are common in modern poetry; cf. e.g. "Pibroch of Donuil Dhu, Pibroch of Donuil, &c."[1]

ll. 139-143. This stanza is not found in LU; but occurs twice in the Stowe MS., first as part of the gloss on l. 297, and again on l. 565. It is introduced, as usual, to illustrate linguistic usage.

ll. 144-147. This quatrain in LU follows the statement at l. 41, about the indulgence attached to the recitation of the *Amra*.

ll. 148-151. This obscure quatrain is apparently added to illustrate the formation of certain words by 'beheading' or cutting off the last letter, *ru ra* instead of *run ran* being the example here. So at least the stanza is introduced in LU after a note on *culu* (l. 187).

ll. 152-155. These verses furnish an unedifying illustration of the use of the word *deilm*, and should follow l. 217, as in LU.

ll. 156-160. This quatrain does not occur in LU, but, in the Stowe MS. and in YBL, it is part of the gloss on ll. 262, 3; it is cited in like manner by the Four Masters *sub ann.* 592 to express the bereavement caused by Columba's death.

ll. 160-163. This quatrain should follow l. 189, as in LU. It is quoted to illustrate the use of the word *neit*, i.e. 'battle.'

ll. 164-168. This is the quatrain from which the quotation is made in l. 193. It is not given in LU, but is found in the Stowe MS.

There were three famous poets of the name of Ferchertne, the earliest of whom was contemporary with Labraid Loingsech (see on l. 66).

ll. 169-173. This quatrain, which is not found in LU, is in illustration of the words *cul* and *neit* in l. 187. It is also given in Cormac's Glossary, *s.v. cul*, where it is ascribed to Cuchulaind.

ll. 173-176. This difficult quatrain, which is not in LU, is in illustration of the word *derc* in l. 199.

---

[1] See Sigerson's *Bards of the Gael and Gall*, p. 47 ff.

ll. 177–179. These words are not intelligible to us.

ll. 180–184. The stanza is not found in LU, but is an illustration of one of the standard methods of expression in Irish verse. See note on ll. 132–8 above.

l. 185. We now come to the *disiecta membra* of Dallan mac Forgaill's eulogy; hitherto we have only been dealing with the work of the commentators. It seems to have been anciently divided into sections, which are marked in the MSS. by large capitals, and in most cases by Latin titles. The explanatory matter printed in small type contains the various (and often absurd) explanations of the scholiasts.

Lines 185–210 contain fragments of the *exordium* of Dallan's poem, which apparently began with an invocation of God.

l. 199. This Grainne was the daughter of Cormac Mac Art; her story is told in the "Pursuit of Diarmait and Grainne," edited by Mr. S. H. O'Grady for the Ossianic Society in 1857.

ll. 211–268 are headed in LU " de moestitia omnium rerum in morte Columbae, uel de exitu Columbae," and in YBL, " De tristitia omnium rerum in morte Columbae." There is no Latin title to this section in the Stowe MS., but it is marked by the usual large initial letter. l. 211 was always counted the *principium laudationis* (see l. 62); the preceding section being only an *exordium*.

l. 211. For Columba's descent from Neill of the Nine Hostages, who was King of Ireland from 379 to 405, see on l. 526.

l. 223. The *Dialogue of the Two Sages* is found in the *Book of Leinster*; an account of it is given in O'Curry's *Manuscript materials*, p. 383. The Two Sages were Ferchertne the royal poet of Emania, and Neidhe, son of Adhna.

The *Bretha Nemed* is one of the many tracts dealing with some of the questions discussed in the Brehon Laws.

l. 230. The words *in faith De*, 'about God's prophet,' go with the next section (In faith De de Sion suidioth) in LU and the Stowe MS.; they seem to be misplaced in T.

In the list of historians and poets given in the Book of Ballymote, quoted by O'Curry,[1] two persons of the name of Nera are mentioned: 1. Nera, druid and lawgiver, son of Morand, a celebrated judge (*fl. cir.* 14 A.D.); and 2. Nera, son of Fincholl, of Sidh Femin, in the Co. Tipperary, of unknown date.

l. 247. This legend is mentioned twice again in the LU copy (under ll. 339, 637); it is given in the Edinburgh copy of the Old Irish Life,[2] and is also preserved in a quatrain in the *Book of Fenagh*.[3]

l. 251. The missing word is perhaps *Hi*; or *heaven* (see l. 310).

l. 256. This is of some importance historically. King Bruide, who died in 584, was succeeded by Gartnaid son of Domlech, who belonged to the Southern Picts and had his royal seat at Abernethy to the south of the Tay. His people had been converted to Christianity in the previous century by Ninian, but they had fallen away. Gartnaid is said

---

[1] O'Curry, *Manners and Customs of the Ancient Irish*, ii. p. 51.
[2] See Stokes' *Lismore*, p. 315.
[3] Ed. Kelly, p. 209.

to have dedicated a new church to St. Brigid at Abernethy, and this revival of Christianity among the Picts is here ascribed to the teaching of Columba. See l. 570, and the legend from the Edinburgh copy of the Old Irish Life quoted in Stokes' *Lismore*, p. 315.

l. 267. See the verses at l. 67, and also at l. 156, in continuation of this theme.

The two kinds of harps in use in Ireland were called the *cruit* and the *timpan* harp respectively; on the distinction see O'Curry, *Manners and Customs*, &c., iii. 236, 252f.

l. 275. *Figill* has not the special meaning in Celtic phraseology, which *vigil* has with us. *Cros-figill*, for instance, is the recognised term for an exercise of devotion (which may be by day or night) in which the hands are extended so as to form a cross.

l. 279. See ll. 73-76 for the verses referred to by the commentator.

ll. 282, 285. The subject of Columba's learning is treated of again in the section entitled *De scientia eius in omni parte* (ll. 356 ff).

l. 291. *Inis Boffin on the sea*, i.e. the island of that name off the coast of Donegal.

l. 295. There is no mention in the LU copy of any visit of Columba to Gregory; but there is a miraculous tale about it in the *Book of Lecan*, quoted in Reeves' *Adamnan*, p. 205. The story apparently grew out of some legend like that in the preface to the *Altus* (p. 24 *supra*).

ll. 303-320. This section is headed in LU and in the Stowe MS. "De regione ad quam peruenit Colum Cille et de pluribus gradibus eius." It is not marked by any title or large initial letter in YBL.

l. 303. The word *Axal* remains a puzzle, despite the desperate efforts of the glossators to explain it. The usual explanation is that *Axal* was the name of Columba's guardian angel, *Demal* being the demon that tempted him; and this agrees with ll. 345, 460, where the angel Axal is again mentioned. It is probable that *Axal* is a corruption of *auxiliarius*.[1] The third book of Adamnan's *Vita* is filled with accounts of the angelic visitations and counsels which Columba was privileged to enjoy.

l. 310. Cf. Apoc. xxi. 25. What followed in the original poem was evidently a description of the heavenly city.

l. 320. Apparently this refers not to Columba but to his Master.

ll. 321-354. This section is headed in LU and in the Stowe MS. "De martyrio eius."

l. 326. *Celebrad* means here, as always in Irish ecclesiastical literature, the service of the choir or recitation of the daily offices, as distinct from *oifrenn*, which is the word of the celebration of the Eucharist. The meaning of the passage is that the recitation of the offices by Columba rendered powerless the assaults of the devil. See ll. 89-94, which come in at this point.

l. 337. See ll. 95-98 and the note there.

l. 347. One explanation of these words is that when he was received at the Assembly of Druim Cetta with the performance of an elaborate piece of music (*aidbse*) and the applause of the multitude, Columba

---

[1] So the *Vita Columbae* in the *Leabhar Breac*, p. 236.

became much elated; whereupon Baithin found it necessary to quote from Basil to abate his pride. The other explanation is that Columba was a student of the works of Basil.

l. 350. Baithin having rebuked Columba, the saint came to himself, and, stopping the music, forbad Dallan to proceed with the eulogy. See l. 35 *supra*.

l. 360. The rest of the gloss on this is found at l. 108.

l. 365. This is an interesting observation, establishing an acquaintance, if not on the part of Columba (which is the tradition), at least on the part of the scholiast, with Jerome's *apparatus criticus*, which is ultimately based on Origen's work. In the Commentary on the Psalter (8th century?) edited by Kuno Meyer[1] from Rawl. B. 512 (our Θ), there are references to the various Greek versions as well as to Jerome's critical labours.

l. 367. It will be noticed that the scholiasts are doubtful whether this implies that Columba read the works of Cassian, or whether it only means that he was a student of Scripture, as Cassian was. But see p. 171 *supra*. The 'Libri legis' probably refer to the N.T. rather than to the O T., the Gospel being counted the 'new law.'[2] Mr. Macgregor[3] interprets this gloss as suggesting that Columba and his community followed the arrangement of scripture lections drawn out by Cassian.

l. 372. The three battles with which the name of Columba was associated have already been mentioned (p. 140 *supra*).

l. 380. Columba's skill in the interpretation of weather signs is ascribed by Adamnan to his prophetic power (*Vita*, ii, 15).

l. 383. His four ways of interpreting scripture, according to the gloss in LU, were the historical, spiritual, moral, and anagogical. This well-known division is explained in a homily in the *Leabhar Breac* on the Epiphany.[4]

l. 385. The *rosualt* is perhaps the *walrus*, but more probably a *whale*. If the sea cast one up on the shore, it was counted an omen. A similar explanation of its significance is given in the *Dinnsenchas* on Mag Murisce (*Book of Leinster*, p. 167β and elsewhere), and ascribed, as here, to Columba.[5] In Adamnan's *Vita* (i. xix) there is a story of how the saint foretold the appearance of Tiree of a "cetus mirae et immensae magnitudinis."

l. 392. It is tolerably plain that the words 'among schools of scripture' belong to the preceding fragment, to which they are attached in LU. This record of Columba's skill in astronomical calculations harmonises curiously with the semi-scientific language of part of the *Altus Prosator*.

l. 397. It is evident that the last two lines of the gloss belong to the next fragment, and should come after l. 400.

l. 400. The LU copy explains the relevance of the verses in the marginal note: "it may be *rian* [not *Rhine*] that it ought to be, ut

---

[1] *Hibernica minora* (Anecd. Oxon, 1894).
[2] Cf. *Felire of Oengus* (ed. Stokes), p. cxliv.
[3] *Early Scottish Worship*, p. 22.
[4] See Atkinson, *Passions and Homilies*, p. 468.
[5] See *Rev. Celt.*, i. 258.

dixit Find U Baiscne &c." The verses on "Winter's Approach" are introduced to illustrate the use of *rian*, but are difficult to translate. Dr. Sigerson[1] has given a free rendering which is worth citing, as he has tried to keep the metre of the original:

> "List my lay: oxen roar;
> Winter chides, Summer's o'er,
> Sinks the sun, cold winds rise,
> Moans assail, ocean cries.
>
> Ferns flush red, change hides all,
> Changing now, grey geese call,
> Wild wings cringe, cold with rime,
> Drear, most drear, ice-frost time."

Find, the descendant of Baiscne, is no less a personage than the giant Finn Mac Cumhaill, who seems to have added the art of poetry to his other accomplishments. According to the Four Masters he was slain in 283 A.D. But see below p. 236.

l. 419. Here verses 114-117 come in, as in LU and in YBL.

l. 451. The hospitality of the monastery of Iona is frequently mentioned by Adamnan. See Reeves' *Adamnan*, p. 345 and ll. 468, 574, *infra*.

l. 463. We have here a tradition, that Saturday, as well as Sunday, was observed at Iona as a festival. This is not hinted at by Adamnan (see *Vita Columbae* iii. 12); but, as Mr. Warren has observed,[2] the ranking of Saturday with Feasts of Martyrs in a rubric in the *Bangor Antiphonary*, would suggest a similar practice. This would be inconsistent with the practice of the Roman Church, but not with that of the East and the majority of Western Churches in the time of Columba.[3]

l. 463. The first words of this line seem to relate to St. Columba's voice; and they constitute a distinct fragment of the Amra in LU. See ll. 89-94.

l. 473. "The blind man" is, of course, Dallan mac Forgaill, the author of the Amra.

l. 474. The piece of the Amra contained in the *Leabhar Breac* (B) begins at this point.

l. 476. This fragment is not intelligible to us.

l. 486. In B and LU a new section begins here. "De prudentia eius et lectione et sapientia"; or, more correctly in YBL: "De sapientia et prudentia illius," for there is no mention of the saints *reading* in what follows.

l. 489. *Quia apud Finnianum euangelium legit*. It is probable that this Finnian was St. Finnian of Moville (d. 576); the statement of the text is confirmed by the opening words of Adamnan's second book, viz.: "Alio in tempore, cum uir uenerandus in Scotia apud sanctum Findbarrum episcopum, adhuc iuuenis sapientiam Sacrae Scripturae addiscens commaneret, &c." See p. 145 *supra*.

l. 495. Reeves has drawn up in his *Adamnan* (pp. 276-298) a long

---

[1] *Bards of the Gael and Gall*, p. 116.
[2] *Antiphonary of Bangor*, ii. p. xxiv   See *Dict. of Chr. Ant.* ii. 1825.

list of churches in Ireland and Scotland associated with the name of Columba.

l. 496. The word *cometaid* or 'guardian' apparently glossed in T: *or, to whom he counts*.

l. 526. The pedigree is this (as given in the *Book of Leinster*, 347β): Columba was the son of Feidlimid, son of Fergus, son of Conall Gulban, son of Neill of the Nine Hostages, son of Eochaid Muighmedan, son of Muiredach Tirech, son of Fiacaid Srabtini, son of Cairpre Lifechair, son of Cormac, son of Art the Solitary, son of Conn of the Hundred Battles, son of Feidlimid Rechtmair. He is here called "the son of the descendant of Conn." See ll. 604, 675.

l. 539. 'Credulous chariot' does not convey any meaning; but we must leave it so. The gloss on *fri conuail* in T, viz. *fri coluain* we cannot translate.

l. 545. This is again unintelligible to us; the 'king's son' is, of course, Columba.

l. 554. The allusion is to the saint's penitence for his share in the battle of Cuil Dremne. See above p. 140.

l. 555. A new section begins here in LU, YBL, and the Stowe MS. with the heading "De commendatione laudis eius a regi nepotum Neill." There is no Latin title in B, but a capital letter marks the beginning of the section.

The glossator's explanation of the appearance of Aed's name in the eulogy is instructive. A 'cumal' was a standard of value frequently mentioned in the Brehon Laws as the equivalent of three cows.

l. 566. Conall was the king of British Dalriata. See p. 141 above.

l. 568. See the note on l. 256. The 'High King of Toi' is Gartnaid.

l. 579. It is not an unfair inference from this gloss, that the glossator knew nothing precise about the meaning of *udbud*.

Cenel Conaill is Tirconnell, or Donegal, of which territory the O'Donnells afterwards were over-lords. This great clan were the descendants of Conall Gulban (d. 464), who was Columba's great-grandfather.

l. 588. The tradition amounts to this, that Columba had some knowledge of Greek. See G. T. Stokes' essay on "the knowledge of Greek in Ireland between A.D. 500 and 900." (*Proc. R.I.A.* 3rd ser. ii. 2 p. 187), for the evidence as to the extent to which that language was known to the Celtic monks.

The LU copy of the Amra is deficient after this point.

l. 603. See on l. 526.

l. 608. That is, according to the glossator, he did not commit any injury which would render him liable to the penalty of death; not very high praise, according to modern ways of thinking. But it is quite possible that the glossator did not understand his text.

l. 611. In the Stowe MS., as well as in T, what follows is marked off by a large initial letter; but there is no indication that it forms a separate section in the other MSS.

l. 611. *Cond, i.e.*, Conn of the Hundred Battles. See l. 603. From his prowess the northern half of Ireland was sometimes called 'Conn's Half'; whence it would seem that the glossator understands l. 611 to refer to the grief that was felt in the North of Ireland when Columba went away to Iona.

l. 620. All that the glossator is sure of is that the words *ecce aer* have reference to the restoration of sight to Dallan mac Forgaill (see l. 45), which is probably accurate.

l. 625. The piece *Pilip apstail* printed in vol. i. p. 185, of which a translation is given above at p. 83, is found in the Stowe MS. as part of the glossator's note on this fragment; the first stanza of it is also cited in YBL. It is introduced in connexion with the word *alliath*; the melodiousness of Columba's voice is compared to the sweet singing of the birds in the Enchanted Island.

l. 633. The word *incoisni* is glossed in T: *i.e. thing* (?)

l. 660. In the Stowe MS., a new section begins here, entitled "De consummatione laudis eius poetae."

The words "quia post mortem pretium laudis datum est caeco" have reference to the restoration of sight to Dallan mac Forgaill after Columba's death. See l. 45.

l. 670. Here the note ll. 58–60 comes in.

l. 675. The descent of Columba on his mother's side was as follows. Her name was Ethne, and she was the daughter of Dimma, son of Noe, son of Echin, son of Cairpre, who was descended from Cathair Mor, king of Ireland, who was son of Feidlimid the All Wise. See on l. 526.

ll. 85–88 come in here in the other MSS.

THE PRAYER OF ST. ADAMNAN.

This piece, in the form in which it has come down to us, is very similar to the *Amra* as regards its fragmentary character and its consequent obscurity. It follows the *Amra* in T, in the Stowe MS. C 3, 2, in the Yellow Book of Lecan (YBL), and in Rawl. B. 502. It is plainly a very ancient devotional piece, but there is not large scope for intelligent comment; the glossators do not seem to have made much of it.

At the top of fol. 28b, col. 2 (the last page of T in its original form), a late hand has written the letters of the alphabet. Then follows a ✠, and then a piece seemingly of prose, but so much rubbed that it is impossible to decipher. It is difficult even to determine the language in which it was written: we have only succeeded in reading two or three words, viz. *retia . . . in pollicem . . . sed*. It was probably written at a later date than the preceding matter; and the ink is of a different colour.

THE PEDIGREE OF ST. MOBI.

This pedigree is written at the foot of fol. 28b, col. 2. Mobi, of whom a legend is told above (p. 28) in the Preface to the *Noli Pater*, was abbot of Glasnevin and died of the *prima mortalitas* in the year 544, according to the Annals of Ulster. His pedigree is also given in the *Book of Leinster* (fol. 352, col. 7), in the *Leabhar Breac* (fol. 21, col. 2, and p. 97), and in the *Book of Lecan* (fol. 45 *a b*).

Cairpre, who appears in it, is Cairpre Lifechair, son of Cormac mac Art.

We have met with the epithet *clarinech* or 'flat-faced' above in Broccan's hymn, l. 84. It is applied in the *Book of Ballymote* to a poet called Gilla Modubhda[1]; and in the *Book of Fenagh*[2] to Congall, one of the legendary kings. It is used in the Irish Tales to express the dead level of uniformity produced by snow covering the face of a country.

THE HYMN OF ST. PHILIP.

This hymn is written in T on one of three fragments of vellum inserted at the end of the book. It is evidently intended as an additional note on l. 624 of the *Amra*, for in the Stowe MS. (C. 3. 2) it forms part of the gloss on that passage. The first verse is also cited at the same point in YBL.

Lines 49 to end are not found in the Stowe copy, and have been added by a later hand in T.

MISCELLANEA.

p. 84. (a) This note is apparently set down in connexion with the verses quoted at l. 400 of the *Amra*, and ascribed to one Finn. The LU text explains that this was Finn mac Cumhaill; but our commentator gives him another pedigree. He is Finn, the father of Conchobar of the Red Eyebrows (who was king of Ireland about the beginning of our era), father of MogCorb (who was slain at Breenmore, in Westmeath), father of Cu-Corb.

(b) and (c) are too fragmentary to identify; but they may both be from some account of the battle of Rosnaree. The details of the arming of Conchobhar fit in with the legible words in (c).[3]

(d) This is an additional note on the word *mortlaid*, which occurs at l. 24 of St. Sanctan's hymn.

(e) Of this scrap we can make nothing.

THE RELEASE OF SCANDLAN MOR.

This account of the Release of Scandlan Mor has been added by a scribe to explain the somewhat obscure references to that episode found in the T copy of the *Amra* (see pp. 54, 55, above). The story is also told in the Edinburgh copy of the old Irish Life,[4] as also in the

---

[1] See McCarthy, *Todd Lect.* iii. p. 409.   [2] Ed. Kelly, p. 33.
[3] See Hogan, *Todd Lect.* iv. 81.
[4] It is printed in Stokes' *Book of Lismore*, p. 309 f.

Leabhar Breac (p. 238), and (in a brief form) in LU. According to the tale, Aed refused Columba's petition, whereupon the saint declared that Scandlan would be free before morning, and would assist him to remove his shoes on entering the chancel for the night offices of prayer. Columba was treated with insolence by Aed's elder son Conall, who was urged on by the queen-mother, but with courtesy by the younger son Domnall, who was blessed accordingly.[1] The queen then mocked the saint, addressing him as a 'crane-cleric.' This has been explained as said in allusion to Columba's tall stature (*alta proceritas* in Adamnan's phrase); but it would appear that *coir-cleric* was a term of contempt applied to degraded ecclesiastics, and so it seems more probable that the use of it by the queen conveyed a taunting reference to the circumstances under which Columba left Ireland in his penitence for the battle of Cuil Dremne. *Coir*, however, also means a crane or heron; and so the saint retorts it, declaring that the queen and her handmaid who accompanied her should for ever hover in the form of cranes by the banks of the river Roe, a threat which was firmly believed to have been fulfilled. Columba then withdrew across Ciannachta,[2] and Ui mac Carthaind,[3] over Loch Foyle to his Black Church in Derry (according to the usual account). That night a storm came upon the place of Scandlan's imprisonment, and he was miraculously carried in the air to the Ferry over Loch Foyle. He was conveyed across by Cumine, a relative of Columba, who appears to have been present when the saint was reviled by the queen, but who was on bad terms with him for some reason. Scandlan arrived, as Columba had foretold, just in time to remove Columba's shoes for nocturns[4]; but was so distracted with thirst after the tortures of his imprisonment that he could say nothing at first but 'Drink, drink.' Baithin having satisfied his needs, Scandlan interceded for Cumine and made his peace with Columba.

Scandlan was then dismissed by Columba to his kingdom of Ossory; and inasmuch as he feared the journey, he was given the saint's pastoral staff for protection. This he brought to the monastery of Durrow (one of Columba's foundations in the King's County), where he handed it to the abbot Laisren mac Feradach, afterwards the third abbot of Iona.

The words with which Columba entrusted the staff to Scandlan, "Take my staff with thee in thy hand, &c.," are the opening words of a poem on the subject in Laud. 615.[5]

The words at the end of the piece "Dundelga, good the gold place," are also a fragment of some poem.

---

[1] Compare the reference to Domnall's connection with Columba in the Preface to the hymn of St. Cummain the Tall (p. 10, *supra*).
[2] The region between Coleraine and Derry.
[3] The barony of Tirkeeran in co. Derry.
[4] This is an interesting allusion to the practice of removing the shoes before entering the chancel of a church. Cf. Warren, *Liturgy of Ante Nicene Church*, p. 224.
[5] The gloss on *fo dinraidh* in l. 9 means *under the shelter of the door it ought to be*.

The Death of St. Columba.

This memorandum records the announcement of Columba's death to Dallan, the blind bard. In the Prologue to the *Amra* (p. 56 above), it is told that the eulogy was not to be finished until the tidings of the saint's death had been brought by a rider on a piebald horse.

The end of the note is taken up with the circumstances of the Assembly of Druim Cetta, which have already been explained. Like the preceding fragment, this was intended as a note on the *Amra*, probably on l. 211.

The Five Divisions of Munster.

There is a late paper copy of this poem in the O'Longan manuscript of the Royal Irish Academy $\left(\frac{23}{\text{E. 16}} \text{ p. 319}\right)$; but the text differs considerably from that of T, and we have not ventured to fill up the lacunae by its means. The piece is headed in that MS. "It is not known who wrote this lay"; but the last quatrain ascribes the composition to Breasal O'Tracy. However, in l. 26 of T we have plainly *Thasaig* not *Trasaig*.

The Five Divisions of Munster in early times were the following, as given by Keating and other authorities:—

(1) *Thomond*, or North Munster, extending from Cuchulaind's Leap to Slige Dala of the Horses. Cuchulaind's Leap is now Loop Head, at the mouth of the Shannon; Cuchulaind was fabled to have leaped across at this point. Slige Dala of the Horses is the great road of Ossory leading to Tara. The northern boundary of Thomond was Slieve Aughty, a range of hills on the confines of Galway and Clare; and the southern was Slieve Phelim (properly, *Elim*) in the co. Limerick.

(2) *Ormond*, or East Munster, extending as far as O'Bric's Island, near Bonmahon on the Waterford coast; Cnawhill (now Cleghile), near the town of Tipperary, being another boundary.

(3) *Mid Munster*, from Cleghile to Luachair (now Slieve Lougher in Kerry) in one direction; and from Slieve Phelim to Slieve Cain or Slieve Reagh in the co. Limerick in another.

(4) *Desmond*, or South Munster, from Slieve Cain to the sea; and

(5) *West Munster*, from Slieve Lougher in Kerry to the sea, and from Glenn-na-Ruachta (Glenarought) to the Shannon.

The etymological glosses written on the fragment which contains this poem (see vol. i, p. 190), on *adnacul* and *eclais*, respectively refer to the use of these words in l. 8 of the *Lorica S. Patricii*, and in l. 186 of Broccan's hymn. See notes *in loc.*

In Praise of Hymnody.

This and the following hymn on the Magi are written on the blank initial page (fol. 1 r°.) of F in a late hand, quite distinct from the writing of the body of the book.

Neither piece has been printed before as the writing is hard to read; but they do not seem to be of much importance.

We have not succeeded in identifying the work ascribed to S. Jerome, on the "Medicine of the Soul"; but, indeed, the whole piece seems to be imaginative. There was no Pope of the name of Clement in Jerome's lifetime. The tone of the fragment is very like that of the piece by Niceta, Bishop of Remesiana, entitled *De bono Psalmodiae*.[1]

Hymn on the Three Kings.

There is a late paper copy of this hymn on the Magi and the Star in the Royal Irish Academy paper MS. classed $\frac{23}{G.\ 23}$ p. 307; we have not thought it worth while to append a collation.

The hymn does not seem to have been printed before; it is, in some places, difficult to read, and we have been obliged to leave blank spaces, as the text of the R.I.A. MS. does not always agree with that of F.

Lines 33–40 do not appear in the paper MS.; they are evidently of the nature of an appendix and did not belong to the original hymn which ended at l. 32.

Benedicite.

For this piece we have collated the manuscripts, A and Σ with F, as they exhibit the same peculiar type of text. The Latin texts of *Benedicite* fall into two groups, viz.: (i) that of Western Breviaries generally, the text of the Vulgate (which corresponds with the true LXX version). The refrain is *laudate et superexaltate*, &c. This is the text followed by our English Book of Common Prayer. (ii) The text of the O.L. version of Theodotion's Greek. If the verses in (i) be numbered consecutively 1 to 32, the text of (ii) may be thus represented: 1, 3, 2, 4–10, 15, 16, 11, the verse *Benedicite pruina et niues*, &c., 17–20, 22, 21, 23–32. The refrain after each verse here is *hymnum dicite et superexaltate*, &c. This is the text found in the *Westminster Missal*,[2] and, with an interchange of place between verses 27 and 26, in our Irish MSS. FAΣ. The repetition of the refrain *ymnum dicite et superexaltate eum in secula* suggests affinity (as Mr. Warren has pointed out[3]) with Eastern usage; and the addition of *domini* in ll. 7, 9–29, in F and Σ (not in A) is also a curious feature.

[1] Printed by Dom Morin in the *Revue Bénédictine* for September, 1897.
[2] Ed. Dr. Wickham Legg, (i, 127).
[3] *Antiphonary of Bangor*, II. xxiii.

It will be observed that in the case of this canticle the place of the *Gloria* is taken by the words (ll. 36, 37): *Benedicamus patrem et filium et spiritum sanctum dominum; ymnum dicamus et superexaltemus eum in secula.* The usual additional clause or antiphon in Western Breviaries, viz.: *Benedictus es domine in firmamento caeli, et laudabilis et gloriosus et superexaltatus in secula* is wanting in our Irish MSS. F seems to be singular in adding l. 38. The appended prayer *Te enim omnipotens*, &c., is given in A as one of a number of collects which may be used after *Benedicite.* There is nothing similar in Σ.

In both East and West this canticle was used at Lauds; but it is not easy to determine its special position in the monastic offices of the Celtic Church. Mr. Warren concludes (*l.c.*) that it was said at Mattins on Saturdays and Sundays. The F Preface[1] gives no direct information, but the context in which it is found in B is noteworthy. At p. 97 of that MS., i.e., on the lower margin of the page of the *Felire of Oengus* which deals with the Saints of October, we find in order (a) the Preface to *Benedicite*; (b) the words *Christe lux eis* ✠; (c) the Preface to *Magnificat* (see vol. i. p. 53); (d) the Preface to *Gloria in Excelsis* (vol. i. p. 49). Now (b) plainly represents the Compline hymn *Christe qui lux es et dies* which is our No. 44, and follows *Benedicite* in F, being itself in that MS. followed by the *Gloria in Excelsis*. The juxtaposition of *Benedicite, Christe qui lux es*, and *Gloria in Excelsis*, in both B and F is remarkable, and perhaps indicates that they were used at the same office. Now of both the latter pieces the Irish Prefaces note "at night it is due to be sung"; and this would lead us to conclude that *Benedicite* was also in use at one of the offices corresponding in the Celtic Church to Compline. There is a rhyming *oratio* prefixed to *Benedicite* in Σ² which affords some confirmation of this view:—

> Deus altissime rex angelorum
> deus laus omnium elimentorum
> deus gloria et exultatio sanctorum
> custodi animas seruorum tuorum
> qui regnas in sæcula sæculorum. amen.

The fourth line of this would be especially suitable for a prayer on retiring to rest.

[1] This has been printed by Stokes in *Rev. Celtique*, vi. 264.
[2] It is worth while to note here the contents of Σ. Foll. 5r°–35v° are taken up with Pss. i–l; then follow the lines quoted above; then come *Benedicite, Canticum Issaiae*, and *Canticum Ezechiae*. We next have Pss. li–c (foll. 39r°–69v°), followed by the lines:

. . . deo gratias ago . . .
deus quem exercitus canet angelorum
quemque ecclessiæ laudat sanctorum
quem spiritus ymminizat uniuersorum
miserere obsecro omnium seruorum tuorum
qui regnas in sæcula sæculorum. amen.

Canticum Annæ, Canticum Mariæ sororis Moysi, and *Canticum Ambacuc* follow, and then Pss. ci–cl (foll. 72r°–99r°), with the words added *finit. amen. finit.* Then we have:

Te dominum de coelis laudamus
Teque omnium regem regum rogamus
Tibi uni et trino in quem speramus
cum excelsis angelis imnum cantamus.
per dominum nostrum et reliqua.

After these lines comes, without title, the *Canticum Moysi* (Deut. xxxii). Foll. 4v°, 38v° and 71v°, are occupied with full page illustrations: and foll. 4r°, 38r° and 101v° are blank.

It needs not to be added that *Magnificat*, associated in the notes cited from B with *Benedicite, Christe qui lux es*, and *Gloria in Excelsis*, was used at Vespers in the West, and was appointed for Lauds in the Greek Church.

The Hymn *Christe qui lux es*.

The tradition of the Irish Preface that this well-known hymn was composed by Ambrose is a venerable one, as Hincmar in the year 857 distinctly names him as the author.[1] But his Benedictine editors refuse to allow the hymn to be by Ambrose, and Mone (*Hymni medii aeui*, i. p. 92) holds that it cannot be older than the seventh century. It exists in countless manuscripts, and was in use in many parts of Europe as a Compline hymn so early as the ninth century.[2] There is nothing specifically Celtic about it, and it is not worth while to collate the texts.

Mone prints ll. 3, 4, thus:—

> Lucifer lucem proferens
> uitam beatam tribue.

He points out that the application of the title *Lucifer* to Christ is a mark of antiquity; He is πηγὴ φωσφόρον.

The hymn has been translated into English a dozen times (see Julian's *Dict. of Hymnology*, p. 227), and is one of the most familiar hymns in use at Evensong in our churches.

The Hymn *Christi patris in dextera*.

We have found this hymn nowhere save in F, where it follows the *Gloria in excelsis*. It has been recently printed by Dreves in his *Analecta Hymni medii aeui*, xix. 236; following him, we have entitled it "De SS. Petro et Paulo." The rhyming system on which it is constructed is Celtic (see p. xxiii), and it is very probably a native hymn of the Irish Church. The monastery in which the manuscript F was written may have been dedicated to St. Peter and St. Paul, such a dedication being common in Ireland as in England. Thus the great abbey church of Glendalough was "SS. Petri et Pauli"; there was a monastery with the same dedication at Armagh[2]; and on Saint's Island in Lough Derg the Augustinian priory of St. Peter and St. Paul was on the site of an old foundation. Another abbey of the same name was founded by St. Tighernach, afterwards Bishop of Clones, in the sixth century.

ll. 21, 22. "talenta euangelica sancta non sine ussura" recall the words used of St. Patrick in the hymn of St. Sechnall (ll. 17, 18): "Electa Christi *talenta* uendit *euangelica* quae Hibernas inter gentes *cum usuris* exigit."

In l. 30 *bradium* is evidently a blunder for *brabium* = βραβεῖον. See Phil. iii. 14 "ad *brauium* supernae *uocationis* Dei."

---

[1] Migne, P.L. cxxv. 591.　　[2] See Baeumer, *Gesch. des Breviers*, p. 329.　　[3] See p. 5 above.

l. 43) " per sanctorum suffragia apostolorum fortia " seems to be an imitation of l. 37 of the hymn of St. Cummain the Tall, "*sanctorum . . . ualida . . . suffragia.*

CANTEMUS DOMINO GLORIOSE.

As in the case of *Benedicite* we have collated A and Σ with F for this canticle. Its position in Σ is described on p. 240 n. above. The text exhibited is noteworthy; Mr. Warren has compared it with the Vulgate and with certain O. L. authorities in *Antiph. of Bangor*, II. xxxi.

It seems probable that in the Celtic Church it was used in the Mattin offices; for the evidence as to usage see Warren, *l.c.*, p. 42.

The *collectio* at the end in F appears in A as one of a number of prayers which are prescribed *super Canticum*.

In the last line of the Preface, *mulieribus* is, doubtless, a scribe's blunder for *muliebris*.

QUICUNQUE VULT.

The Irish Preface to the *Quicunque* has been printed with a translation by Stokes in *Rev. Celtique*, vi. 265; it is evident that the author of it confused the Athanasian with the Nicene Creed. As we have pointed out in our Introduction (vol. i. p. xiv), it had been read by Ussher, who quotes part of it.[1]

The *Quicunque* was well-known in Ireland, and several early manuscripts of it, written by Irish scribes, are extant; in particular there is one of the eighth century in the Ambrosian Library at Milan (O. 212 *sup.*), and there are ninth century copies at St. Gall. We have remarked above (p. 155) that the first stanza of the *Altus Prosator* seems to be based upon it, as the writer of the B Preface to that hymn observed. There is an Irish version of the *Quicunque* preserved in a paper manuscript belonging to the Royal Irish Academy classed $\frac{23}{M. 45}$; and one of the Homilies in the *Leabhar Breac* (fol. 257a) plainly implies a knowledge of its teaching.[2]

The antiphon *Te iure* after the *Gloria* in F (ll. 73, 74) is interesting; we may compare the rubrical direction found in the *Crede Michi*[3]: "Ad primam et ad alias horas omnia fiant sicut in ceteris diebus preter antiphonam super psalmum (*Quicunque uult saluus esse*) que erit (*Te iure*)."

THE LORICA OF GILDAS.

This curious piece has been often printed; but we have thought it desirable to add it to the hymns contained in these volumes, although

[1] Works. vii. 100. [2] See Hogan, *Todd Lectures*, vi. p. 30.
[3] See Wordsworth, *Tracts of Clement Maydestone*, p. 63.

it is not found in either of our two principal manuscripts, as it illustrates many points which have been discussed in the preceding pages.

In 1853, Mone printed the hymn from the MS. which we have called Δ; our record of its readings is derived from a transcript by Zimmer.[1]

In 1855, Daniel printed it[2] from a Vienna MS. (No. 11,857) of the sixteenth century, the text of which so closely resembles that of Δ, that we have not thought it necessary to record its readings.

In 1860, Stokes printed it[3] from B, with the Irish glosses which that MS. contains.

In 1864, Cockayne printed it[4] from C, adding the Anglo-Saxon glosses there found, and also recording some variants of the MS. which we call ψ.

The next step was the publication in 1889 of the hymn by Birch from N, in which manuscript it immediately follows the *Oratio S. Johannis Euangelistae* (our No. 17). The variants of ψ are given in this edition.[5]

We have presented above (vol. i. p. 206) the text of B, with the variants of CNΔψ, having collated afresh BCN. We do not give either the Irish glosses of B or the Anglo-Saxon glosses of Cψ; they can be read in the pages of Stokes and Cockayne.

The Latinity of the *Lorica Gildae* has been much studied of late years in connection with the *Hisperica Famina*, which it strikingly resembles. This has already been incidentally mentioned in our discussion of the *Altus Prosator* (p. 143 above); and we need only repeat that the date of both the *Lorica* and the *Hisperica Famina* is generally assigned to the latter half of the sixth century. With this well agrees the tradition of the B Preface which states that the author of the *Lorica* was one Gillas, and that the hymn was introduced into Ireland by Laidcenn, son of Baeth the Victorious. Now Laidcenn died, according to the Irish Annals, in the year 661; and thus *Gillas* may well be the famous Gildas who died cir. 570. It is not improbable, indeed, that *mortalitas huius anni* of ll. 5, 6, may enable us to fix the year of the composition of the piece; for this seems to have been the Yellow Plague (see p. 114 above), which first ravaged Britain in 547. It will be observed that the titles in CN and the colophon in Δ speak of Laidcenn as the author; but if he first made the hymn popular, it is easy to understand why his name became associated with it. The strange vocabulary of the piece requires larger treatment than we have space for here; many references to treatises on the subject, in addition to the works we have already mentioned, will be found in an article by Zimmer published in 1895.[6] On the metre see p. xxi above.

It will be seen that the Lorica is naturally divided into three parts, the introductory invocation of the Trinity[7] being followed by an

---

[1] See vol. i. p. xv.　[2] *Thesaurus*, iv. 364.　[3] *Irish Glosses*, p. 133.
[4] *Leechdoms, Wortcunning, and Starcraft of Early England*, i. lxviii.
[5] *Book of Nunnaminster*, p. 91.
[6] *Nachrichten des K. Gesellschaft der Wissenschaften zu Göttingen* (1895), Heft 2. Mr. F. Jenkinson has kindly supplied us with this reference.
[7] See above, p. 211.

invocation of heavenly powers, and the rest of the piece being taken up with an enumeration, in the most minute detail, of the various members of the human body.[1] A similar, though less elaborate, enumeration is found in a collect in the Basle Psalter (P), and another in the *Ordo Baptismi* in the Stowe Missal (S).[2] And the unpublished Lorica of Mugron cited above (p. 212) begins thus:

"The Cross of Christ upon this cheek, upon this ear, . . .
The Cross of Christ upon this eye, upon this nose,
The Cross of Christ upon this mouth, upon this tongue, upon this throat,
The Cross of Christ upon this back, the Cross of Christ upon this side,
✦   ✦   ✦   ✦
The Cross of Christ upon my hands, from my shoulders to my palms,
The Cross of Christ upon my hips, the cross of Christ upon my hair."

A still closer parallel to the text before us is afforded by the *Lorica of Leyden*, lately published (with a facsimile of the MS.) by V. H. Friedel.[3] This begins with the invocation *Domine exaudi*, &c., and then proceeds to enumerate the various parts of the body, exactly in the style of the *Lorica Gildae*, the Latinity being of the same curious kind. Angels and archangels and the powers of heaven and earth are then invoked, each clause ending with the words *ut euacuatis cor. N. pro amore meo*. The final invocation is *adiuro uos matheus. marcus. lucas. et iohannes*.[4]

Mr. Birch in his *Book of Nunnaminster* has given other illustrations of this practice of praying for protection for the several parts of the body.[5] At p. 29 he cites a collect from the MS. we call D; and at p. 128 he gives an interesting parallel from the *Canones editi sub Edgaro rege* (printed in Wilkins' *Concilia*, i. 230), viz., "Confiteor omnia corporis mei peccata cutis et carnis et ossis et neruorum et renum et cartilaginum et linguae et labiorum et faucium et dentium et comae et medullae et rei cuiusque mollis uel durae, humidae uel siccae," &c. Yet another example is found in the *Lorica Columbae*, beginning "Sciath Dé," which is contained in the *Leabhar na hUidhre* and in other manuscripts. And, finally, in the *Book of the Dean of Lismore* (ed. W. F. Skene), at p. 159, is printed an ancient Gaelic poem, which, beginning with an invocation of the Trinity, proceeds to ask protection for the several parts of the human frame.[6]

---

[1] Compare the glosses printed among the works of Hraban Maur in Migne, P.L. cxii. 1575.
[2] See Warren, *Liturgy and Ritual of the Celtic Church*, pp. 186, 207.
[3] *Zeitschrift fur Celtische Philologie*, II. i. p. 64 (1898).
[4] See above, p. 173.
[5] Mone finds this Celtic love of detail illustrated in the delicacy and minuteness of the illuminated scrolls and borders in the more elaborately executed Irish manuscripts, such as the Book of Kells: "dieses specialitairen ist demnach ein nationaler Zug," he says in his notes on the *Lorica Gildae* (*Hymni Latini*, i. 369).
[6] There is a word in l. 5 of the B Preface which we cannot read; it looks like *ols*. The similarity of the phraseology here, in which the benefits of recitation of the *Lorica* are described, to the words of the B Preface to the *Altus* (vol. I. p. 64, l. 39) should be observed.

INDICES.

I.
OF PERSONAL NAMES.

II.
OF PLACES AND TRIBES.

LONDON:
HARRISON AND SONS, PRINTERS IN ORDINARY TO HER MAJESTY,
ST. MARTIN'S LANE.

ERRATA.

Vol. ii. p. xxxiii. for 'thes Irishe' read 'these Irish.'

Vol. ii. p. 50. After l. 32 of the Lorica of St. Patrick, insert l. 33 "Power of God to uphold me," and alter accordingly the numbering of all the lines which follow.

I. INDEX OF PERSONAL NAMES.

Abgar, k. of Edessa, 30, 111, 173, 174.
Adamnan, St., 9th abbot of Iona (d. Sept. 23, 704). His birth, 117; parentage, 122; holds Synod of Uisnech, 20, 134; praises hymn of Oengus mac Tipraite, xviii, 20; his law, 16, 122; *Canons* of, 122; verse ascribed to him, 17, 123; his *Prayer*, 81, 139, 235; his *Vita Columbae*, 109, 113, 122, 123, 135, 163, 164, 170, 226, 228, 231, 233 etc.; *Second Vision* of, 105, 106, 127, 133.
Adhna, 230.
Aed (?), 84, 87.
Aed mac Ainmerech, k. of Ireland (572-599), 10, 23, 24, 27, 28, 37, 140, 171; his name inserted in *Amra*, 75, 234; at Assembly of Druim Cetta, 53, 55, 224, 225; treaty with Aedan mac Gabrain, 54, 226; refuses to release Scandlan, 85, 237.
Aed mac Neill, *see* Loegbaire.
Aed, bishop of Sletty (d. Feb. 7, 699), 176.
Aed Slane, son of Diarmait mac Cerbaill, succeeded Aed mac Ainmerech (d. 604), 12, 38, 114.
Aedan mac Gabrain, k. of Scotland (574-606), 23, 24, 54, 55, 85, 140, 224, 226.
Aiduus, *see* Aed, of Sletty.
Ailbe, St., of Emly (d. Sept. 12, 541), 127.
Ailell mac Dunlainge, k. of Leinster (d. 526), 40, 196, 200.
Aileran, St., lector of Clonard (d. Dec. 29, 664), 12, 114.
Ailgel, 82.
Amargen, one of the sons of Milesius, 184.
Amatorex, bp. of Auxerre, (?) 180.
Aphrodisius, 129.
Arelius, *i.e.* Melchior, 129.
Arenus, *i.e.* Jaspar, 129.
Aristodemus, 29.
Art, the Solitary, son of Conn of the Hundred Battles, 77, 234.
Artchorp, 82.
Assal, 58.
Assicus, *see* Tassach.
Athrae, 82.
Axal, Columba's guardian angel, 65, 66, 71, 231.

Baeth the Victorious, 243.
Bairche, 183.
Baithin, 2nd abbot of Iona (d. June 9, 600), 23, 67, 85, 232, 237.
Balthasar, 128, 129.
Bartholomew, St., 52, 222.
Basil, St., the Great (d. Jan. 1, 379), 67, 232.
Benen, or Benignus, bp. of Armagh (d. Nov. 9, 468), 49.
Bernard of Clairvaux, St., 216.
Bern, 6.
Bevan, 82.

INDEX OF PERSONAL NAMES.

Bile, son of Bregon, 183.
Bite, one of Patrick's artificers, 185.
Blaithmac, son of Aed Slane, 12, 114.
Blathnait, Brigid's cook, 196.
Breasal O'Tracy, 238.
Breccan, 188.
Bregan, grandfather of Fiacc of Sletty. *See* Todd, *Book of Hymns*, p. 291.
Bregdolb, 82.
Bregon, 183.
Brendan, St., of Clonfert (*d.* May 16, 577). The hymn *Brigit bé bithmaith* ascribed to him, 38, 188; his voyage, and subsequent visit to Brigid, 38, 196; his powerful voice, 228.
Bresal, 82.
Brian Borumha, k. of Ireland (*d.* 1014), 227.
Brig, 6.
Brigid, St., of Kildare (*d.* Feb. 1, 523). Her parentage, 38; hymns in her honour, *Christus in nostra*, xxix, 8; *Brigit bé bithmaith*, xxxiii, 37ff, 187ff; *Ni car Brigit*, l, 37, 40ff, 189ff; *Phœbi diem*, 223; her patronage invoked, 16, 45, 117, 205; equally honoured with Patrick, 39, 189; compared to B.V.M., 39, 40, 46, 107, 190, 223; her character, 40, 168, 188, 190; her miracles, 8, 38, 41-45, 194-204; her "ordination," 41, 192, 193; her Rule, 191; her artist Condlaed, 44, 185, 204; Brendan visits her, 38, 196; verses ascribed to her, 59 (?), 194, 195.
Brittus, 177.
Broicsech, Brigid's mother, 38.
Broccan, St., the Squinting (*d.* Sept. 17, 650), the panegyrist of Brigid 37, 40, 188, 189.
Brolchan, 221.
Bruide mac Maelcon, k. of the Picts (*d.* 584), 230; his gift of Iona to Columba, 24, 141.
Buan, of Dal Araide, 3, 178.

Cairpre Lifechair, k. of Ireland, (*d.* 284) son of Cormac mac Art, 82, 234, 236.
Cairpre Niafer, killed at battle of Rossnaree, a descendant of Cathair Mor, 80, 235.
Calpurn, Patrick's father, 3, 32, 177, 186.
Canice, St., or Kenneth (*d.* Oct. 11, 600), 98, 141.
Carell, 226.
Cassian, 67, 170, 171, 232.
Cathair Mor, k. of Ireland (*circa* 174), 31, 80, 175, 235.
Cathbath, 59.
Celestine, Pope (422-432), 3, 7, 177, 180.
Ciannan, 178, 179.
Ciaran, St., of Clonmacnoise (*d.* Sept. 9, 547), xxvi, 141, 218, 220.
Ciaran, St., of Saighir (*d.* March 5, *circa* 551), 218.
Cinnenum, a sister of Patrick, 177.
Cinnfaela, father of Scandlan Mor, 54, 55, 226.
Cirine, *i.e.* Jerome.
Clement, Pope (?), 89, 239.
Cobthach, k. of Ireland, 58, 229.
Coemgen, *see* Kevin.
Cogitosus, the biographer of Brigid (*d. circa* 670), l.ff. 189, 195-204.
Colman, Ela, St. (*d.* Sept. 26, 610), 6, 98.
Colman mac Comgellain, one of the Irish Dalriads (*d.* 625); his decision accepted by the Scotch and Irish at Druim Cetta, 56, 226.

INDEX OF PERSONAL NAMES

Colman mac Lenine, St., of Cloyne (d. Nov. 24, 600 ?), 58, 228.
Colman mac Murchon, St. (d. 731 ?), xv, xxiv, xxv, 19, 132, 133, 211.
Colman mac Ui Cluasaig, St., lector in Cork (d. 661 ?), 12, 13, 114, 117, 121.
Colman Mor, defeated at battle of Cull Feda, 38, 68.
Colptha, one of the sons of Milesius, 184.
Columba, *see* Colum Cille.
Columbanus, St., Abbot of Luxeuil and Bobbio (d. Nov. 21, 615), 101, 138.
Colum Cille, St., first Abbot of Iona (b. 521, d. June 9, 597); one of the three patrons of Ireland, 16, 117; of royal descent, 140; his father's pedigree, 53, 234; his mother's, 80, 235; his original name, 122; where baptized, 122; his teachers, 28, 72, 145; Derry granted him, 28, 171; his "Black Church" there, 23, 57, 140, 228; other churches, 20, 73, 108; not a bishop, 108; the three battles which he caused, 23, 24, 68, 140; Iona granted him, 24, 141; mission to the Picts, 63, 76, 230; recommends Cummain to Domnall (?), 10, 109; attends Assembly of Druim Cetta, 53, 55; three reasons for doing so, 55, 85, 224; releases Scandlan Mor, 57, 85, 226, 237; gives him his staff to carry to Durrow, 86, 237; receives presents from Gregory, 23, 141; his miraculous visits to Rome, 231; and to heaven, 62, 132; guardian angel, 65, 66, 71, 76, 231; his hymns, the *Altus*, 23ff, 142ff; criticised by Gregory, 25, 141; its metre, xxvi, 26; indulgence for its recitation, 26, 142, 169; *In te Christe*, xxiii, 27, 169; *Adiutor laborantium*, 23, 141; *Noli Pater*, indulgenced, 28; when recited, 171; *Alto et Ineffabili*, 218; *Brigit bé bithmaith* ascribed to him, 37, 188; also other Irish verses, 10, 28, 55, 56; *Amra* composed in his honour, 53ff, 223ff; indulgenced, 56, 59; Columba's stature, 237; his voice, 57, 66, 71, 77, 235; character, 71, 72; pride, 67, 232; hospitality, 76, 233; asceticism, 63, 64, 65, 70, 74; learning, 64, 232; knowledge of Greek, 76, 234; of natural science, 67, 68, 161; death, 57, 62, 65, 87, 238; grief caused thereby, 61, 77, 79, 229; his relics translated to Down, 57, 66, 232.
Comgall, St., of Bangor (d. May 10, 602), 24, 68, 141.
Conall, son of Aed mac Ainmerech, 237.
Conall Cernach of the Red Branch, 97.
Conall Gulban, brother of Loegaire, son of Neill, (d. 464), 53, 234.
Conall, k. of British Dalriata (d. 574), 76, 86, 141, 234.
Conchess, Patrick's mother, 3, 177.
Conchobar, or Conor, mac Nessa, k. of Ulster, the conqueror at Rossnaree, 59, 84, 236.
Conchobar Abratruad, k. of Ireland, 84, 236.
Condlaed, bp. of Kildare, Brigid's "artist," 44, 45, 185, 204.
Congall Clarinech, a legendary k. of Ireland, 236.
Conn of the Hundred Battles, k. of Ireland (177–212), 74, 77, 226, 234.
Conor, *see* Conchobar.
Constantine, 92.
Cormac mac Art, k. of Ireland (254–277), 54, 55, 60, 82, 102, 226, 230, 234, 236.
Cothraige, one of Patrick's names, 3, 4, 7, 32, 177, 178.
Craiptine, the first legendary harper, 57, 227.
Crebriu, daughter of Glerand, 180.
Crimthan, the original name of Columba, 121, 122.
Cuchuimne, St. (d. Oct. 7, 746 ?), xvi, xxiv, xxv, 17, 123.
Cuchulaind, the hero of Rossnaree, 84, 229, 238.
Cu Corb, 84, 236.
Cumine, son of Feradach, 85, 86, 237.
Cummain, the Fair, St., 7th abbot of Iona (d. Feb. 24, 668), 108, 123.

INDEX OF PERSONAL NAMES.

Cummain, the Tall, St., bp. of Clonfert (*d.* Nov. 12, 661), xix, 9, 10, 108, 109, 111, 114, 237, 242.
Cummean, author of a *Penitentiale* and of a letter on Paschal question (*cir.* 634), 108, 123.

Dabog, 168.
Daire Barrach, 31.
Dallan mac Forgaill, high poet of Ireland (*d.* Jan. 29, 594?), author of the *Amra*, 53-56, 59, 223-238.
Dallbronach, Brigid's maternal grandfather, 38, 190.
Darerca, Patrick's sister, 3, 96, 113, 177, 193.
Darerca, *see* Moninna.
Demal, Columba's demon, 231.
Deman, 55, 226.
Dermot, *see* Diarmait.
Diarmait mac Cerbaill, k. of Ireland (544-565), 23, 24, 38, 68, 140.
Diarmait, son of Aed Slane and grandson of preceding, 12, 114.
Diarmait, the lover of Grainne, 230.
Diarmait, coarb of Patrick, son of German (*circa* 848), 117, 121.
Dimma, maternal grandfather of Columba, 57, 80, 235.
Dionysius, 92.
Domitian, 29.
Domlech, 230.
Domnall, son of Aed mac Ainmerech, 10, 58, 109, 237.
Donn, one of the sons of Milesius, 183, 184.
Drust, a Pictish king, 11.
Drustice, daughter of preceding, 11, 113.
Dubthach mac Ui Lugair, high poet of Ireland, 31.
Dubthach, Brigid's master, 192, 197.
Dubthach, a scribe, 130.

Eber, one of the sons of Milesius, 183, 184.
Echach, 8.
Echin, 235.
Emer, 33, 183.
Eochaid Muighmedan, k. of Ireland, father of Neill of the Nine Hostages, 234.
Eochaid Righ Eigheas, *i.e.* Dallan mac Forgaill, q.v.
Eochaid Ua Flannucain, a poet (*d.* 1003), 4, 7, 98. See vol. i. p. xiv.
Eogan, son of Neill, 85, 86.
Eogan, son of Olioll olom, k. of Munster, 109.
Ephraem Syrus, 174.
Erca, 31.
Erimon, one of the sons of Milesius, 33, 181, 183, 184.
Essu, one of Patrick's artificers, 185.
Etarnel, *see* Nel.
Ethne, Columba's mother, 57, 80, 235.
Eugenius of Toledo, 98.

Falcus, *i.e.* Phocas, q.v.
Fechin, St., of Fore (*d.* Jan. 20, 664), 12, 113.
Feidlimid, Columba's father, 53, 77, 234.
Feidlimid Rechtmair, k. of Ireland, father of Conn of the Hundred Battles, 234.
Feidlimid, the All-Wise, father of Cathair Mor, 80, 235.
Fenius Farsa, 183, 184.

INDEX OF PERSONAL NAMES.

Feradach, son of Muiredach, 85.
Feradach, father of Laisren, q.v., 86.
Feradach Find Fechtnach, k. of Ireland, 84.
Ferchertne, poet, 59, 227, 229, 230.
Ferdomnach, scribe of *Book of Armagh* (fl. 807), 97.
Ferdomnach, Abbot of Kells (d. 1008), 56, 227.
Fergus, Columba's paternal grandfather, 53, 234.
Fergus, 68.
Ferin, 177.
Fiacaid Srabtini, k. of Ireland (*circa* 297), 234.
Finee, St., of Sletty (d. Oct. 12, *sub. fin. saec.* V.). His pedigree, 175; receives tonsure from Patrick, 31; reputed author of *Christus in nostra*, 8, 107; of *Ninine's Prayer*, 36; and of the hymn *Génair Patruic*, 31-35, 96, 104, 175; date of this hymn, 176; quotation from it, 7.
Fiachna, k. of West Munster, father of St. Cummain the Tall, 9, 10, 109.
Fiachra Gairrine, father of preceding, 10.
Fiad, 202.
Fincholl, 62, 230.
Find, *see* Finn.
Findabair, 203.
Finn mac Cumhaill, or Find U Baiscne, hero and poet (d. 283), 69, 233, 236.
Finn, father of Conchobar Abratruad, poet, 84, 236.
Finnian, St., of Clonard (d. Dec. 12, 548), 229.
Finnian, St., of Moville (d. Sept. 10, 579), 11, 72, 112, 113, 145, 233.
Flann, mother of St. Cummain the Tall, 9, 10, 109.
Forgall, father (?) of Dallan, 53, 55.
Fotaid, *see* Potitus.
Frigidianus, St., of Lucca (*commem.* Mar. 18, fl. 570), 113.
Froech, 203.

Galgalad, *i.e.* Jaspar, 129.
Gartnaid, k. of the Picts, 230, 234.
Gerald, St., of Mayo (d. Mar. 13, 732?), 114.
German, father of Diarmait, bp. of Armagh, 121.
German, St., of Auxerre (d. July 31, 448). Patrick studied with him, 32, 178, 180; received the name Magonius from him, 3, 7, 177.
Gildas, St. (d. cir. 570); his *Lorica*, xxi, 143, 211, 243.
Gilla Modubbda, a poet, 236.
Gillas, *see* Gildas.
Glerand, 180.
Goedel Glas, 183, 184.
Gorianas, 4.
Gorniad, 177.
Grainne, daughter of Cormac mac Art, 60, 230.

Hencret, 177.
Herimon, *see* Erimon.
Hilary, St., of Arles (d. May 5, 449), 125, 126.
Hilary, St., of Poitiers (d. Jan. 13, 368), author of the piece *Hymnum dicat*, 18, 125, 126, 128; its metre, xi, xii, xiv; when recited, 127; other hymns of his 97, 126, 136.
Hraban, St., of St. Maur (d. Feb. 4, 856), known in Ireland, 106, 112, 137; reproduces the *Altus* of Columba, 145-149, 155; and *In te Christe*, 170.

INDEX OF PERSONAL NAMES.

Iaspar, 128, 129.
Idnae, 82.
Ignatius, St., of Antioch (*com.* Feb. 1, *d.* 110?), 14, 119.
Ioseph, foster-father of Christ, 14, 118.
Ir, one of the sons of Milesius, 183.
Ita, St., of Killeedy (*d.* Jan. 15, 569), 9, 108.
Iulianus Pomerius (*fl. cir.* 500), 142, 143, 145.
Iustin II, Emperor (565-578), 24.
Iustinian I, Emperor (527-565), 24.

Kenneth, *see* Canice.
Kevin, St., of Glendalough (*d.* June 3, 618), 6, 41, 193, 194, 218.

Labraid Loingsech Lorcc, victor at Dinn-rig (*fl. cir.* 550 B.C.), 57, 58, 227, 229.
Laidcenn, son of Baeth the Victorious (*d.* Jan. 12, 661), 243.
Laisren mac Feradach, 3rd Abbot of Iona (600-605), formerly of Durrow, 86, 237.
Lasrian, *see* Molaise.
Lenine, 58.
Leo, 177.
Lesru, daughter of Glerand, 180.
Liamain, sister of Patrick, 96, 177.
Linne, *see* Tinne.
Loegaire mac Neill, k. of Ireland (428-463), 3, 4, 31, 33, 40, 49, 208.
Loingsech mac Oengusa, k. of Ireland (695-704), 17, 123.
Lonan, St., of Trevet, son of Talmach, 11.
Loran, *see* Ronan.
Lucat-Mael, a druid, 181.
Lucru, a druid, 181.
Lugaid mac Loegaire, k. of Ireland (483-507), 31, 40, 189.
Lugaid, a champion of Leinster, 44, 202.
Lugnae Trinog, 82.
Lupait, sister of Patrick, 3, 177, 178.

Mac Caille, St., bp. of Croghan, brother to Bp. Mel (*com.* Apr. 25), 41, 192, 193.
Macculasrius, *see* Molaise.
Mac Midrui, a druid, 194.
Madian, *i.e.* Matthias, 52, 110, 111, 222.
Mael Brigte ua Mael Uanaig, scribe (*fl.* 1139), 129.
Mael Choba, k. of Ulster (612-615), 55, 226.
Maelcon, father of Bruide, 24, 141.
Mael-fith, 168.
Mael Isu ua Brolchain (*d.* Jan. 16, 1086?), 52, 221.
Mael Sechnall, 60.
Mael Suthain, scribe and confessor to Brian Borumha (*d.* 1009), 56, 227.
Mael-tuile, 168.
Maen, *see* Labraid.
Magonius, one of Patrick's names, 3, 7, 177.
Malgalath, *i.e.* Melchior, 129.
Mancend, *see* Moinenn.
Manchan, St., of Liath (*d.* Jan. 24, 664), 12, 114.
Marcianus Capella (*saec.* v.), 166.
Martin, a disciple of Patrick, 135.
Martin, St., of Tours (*d.* Nov. 11, 397), hymn in his honour, xvii, 20, 134;

well known in Ireland, 113, 134, 135; churches dedicated to him, 134, 135; appears in vision to Adamnan, 20; accounted uncle of Patrick, 134, 177; a prayer of his, 116.
Matoc, brother to Bp. Sanctan (*com.* Apr. 25), 47.
Maurice, Emperor (582–602), 23, 140.
Maxim, 177.
Mel, bp. of Ardagh, son of Darerca (*d.* Feb. 6, 488), 192, 193.
Melchisar, *i.e.* Melchior, 128, 129.
Melchon, *see* Maelcon.
Mercud, 177.
Meugan, St. (*cir.* 500), 112.
Michael, St., the Archangel (Sept. 29), 178, 184; hymn in his honour, xv, 19, 133; popular in Ireland, 133; invocation of him, 134.
Miled, or Milesius, of Spain, 114, 181, 183, 186.
Miliuc (or Milchu) mac Ua Bain, Patrick's master in Antrim, chief of Dal Araide (*fl.* 390), 3, 4, 7, 32, 178.
Mobi, St., of Glasnevin, the Flatfaced, *alias* Berchan (*d.* Oct. 12, 544); his pedigree, 82, 235, 236; his death, 28, 236; teacher of Columba, 171.
Mochta, St., of Louth (*d.* Mar. 24, 535), 225.
Mog Corb, k. of Ireland, 84, 236.
Moinenn, St., of Clonfert (*d.* Mar. 1, 570), 112.
Molaise, St., of Devenish (*d.* Sept. 12, 563), 220, 221.
Molaise, St., of Inismurray (*comm.* Aug. 12, *fl.* 561) 140, 220.
Molaise, St., of Leighlin (*d.* Apr. 18, 638), 220.
Mongan, 228.
Moninna, St., of Slieve Gullion (*d.* July 6, 518), 187.
Morand, 62, 230.
Moriath, of Morca, 57, 227.
Mugint, St. (*sæc.* v.?), 11, 112, 113.
Mugron, 30th Abbot of Iona (964–980), 117, 121.
Mugron, author of a *Lorica*, 212, 244.
Muirchu Maccu Mactheni (*sæc.* vii), 101, 104, 105, 176, 181, 182, 185, 209.
Muiredach, son of Eogan mac Neill, 85.
Muiredach Tirech, 234.
Murchu of Connaught, 19.
Mureth, 202.
Muric, 177.

Natfraich, Brigid's lector, 193, 199, 200.
Natfraich, father of St. Molaise of Devenish, 220.
Neidhe, one of the Two Sages, 230.
Neill of the Nine Hostages, k. of Ireland (379–405), 53, 61, 77, 81, 87, 140, 168, 188, 230, 234.
Nel, 183, 184.
Nene, 180.
Nennio, *see* Moinenn.
Nera, son of Fincholl, 62, 230.
Nera, son of Morand (*fl.* 14), 62, 230.
Nia, a poet (?), 202.
Niceta, bp. of Remesiana (392–414), author of *Te Deum*, 22, 138, 139, 239.
Nicetius, bp. of Treves (527–566), 138.
Ninian, St. (*d.* Sept. 16, 432?), 113.
Ninine, or Nine Ecis, a poet (*sæc.* vi?), 36, 187.
Ninnid Purehand, son of Eochaid (*sæc.* vi?), 8, 107.
Noe, son of Echin, 57, 80, 235.

Ocmus, Patrick's maternal grandfather, 177.
Odisse, a deacon, Patrick's paternal great grandfather, 32, 177.
O'Domnal mac Dabog, 168.
Oengus mac Tipraite, St. (d. 745), xvii, xviii, 20, 134, 135.
Oric, 177.
Ota, 177.
Otide, *see* Potitus.

Palladius, mission to Ireland, 180, 187.
Partholon, *see* Bartholomew.
Patifarsat, *see* Balthasar.
Patrick, St., of Armagh (d. Mar. 17, 493?), Patron of Ireland, 16, 39, 117, 121, 189; his birthplace, 3, 32, 176, 177; his ancestry, 3, 32, 177; his kindred, 3, 96, 113, 134, 135, 177; baptism, 4; captured in boyhood, 3, 177; sold to Milchu, 3, 32, 178; his four names, 3, 7, 32, 98, 100, 177, 178; prediction to Milchu, 4; encouraged by Angel Victor, 32, 178; his deliverance, 179; baptizes Ciannan, 179; studies with Germanus, 32, 179, 180; call of children of Fochlad, 32, 106, 180; refused ordination by Celestine, 180; finds the Baculus Jesu, 180, 181; ordained, when sixty, by Amatorex, 180; druids foretold his coming, 181; concealed it from Loegaire, 33; his preaching, 36; for sixty years, 34; at Saul, 33, 183; miracles, 33, 96; asceticism, 33; devotions, 33, 104, 182; Sechnall's hymn in his honour, 3ff, 96ff; its use, 97; its indulgence, 6, 34, 120; quarrel with Sechnall and reconciliation, 5; sends Sechnall to Rome for relics; Fiacc's metrical life of him, 31, 176; tonsures Fiacc, 31; baptizes Dubthach; his feats at Tara Hill, 31, 49, 208, 209; his *Lorica*, 49ff 208ff.; its structure, lvii, 211; its indulgence, 49; its use, 97, 210; his leper, 199; desires to go to Armagh, 34, 184; Primacy to Armagh, 34, 185; his "four petitions," 33, 34, 97, 105, 176; receives his last communion, 34, 185; death, 34; light for a year thereafter, 34, 185; the angels' requiem, 35; his burial place, 184; his relics, 186, 222; the "other" Patrick, 35, 186; confusion with Palladius, 186; invocation of him, 113, 187; hymn *Ecce fulget* in his praise, 222; special honours paid his memory, 97, 210; his "law," his *Confessio* and *Letter to Coroticus*, 96; used O.L version of Scripture, 145.
Pelagius, heretic (d. cir. 440), 179.
Pharaoh, 115, 116, 183.
Philip, St., the Apostle, 52, 83, 84, 110, 235, 236.
Philip, the Commentator (d. 455), 160, 161, 166.
Phocas, Emperor (602-610), 23, 140.
Piran, *see* Ciaran, St., of Saighir.
Pledi, *i.e.* Palladius (?), 180.
Potitus, Patrick's paternal grandfather, 3, 32, 177.
Probus, author of the *Quinta Vita* of Patrick (*saec.* x ?), 177.
Prosper, St., of Aquitaine (*saec.* v), 142, 143, 144, 145.

Restitutus, Sechnall's father, 3, 4, 96.
Rioc, St., of Inisbofin in Loch Ree (*saec.* vi ?), also called Darerca's son (?) 11, 113.
Rodincus, St., of Beaulieu (d. Sept. 17, 680), 132.
Ronan, Adamnan's father, 122.
Roncend, *see* Condlaed.
Ronnat, Adamnan's mother, 122.
Ross mac Finn, poet, 227.
Rossa Rig-bude, k. of Ulster (fl. cir. 250), 183.
Rovin, St., *see* Rodincus.

Sanctan, St., of Killdaleas (*com.* May 9), 47, 48, 206, 236.
Sanicis, *see* Balthasar.
Sannan, deacon, Patrick's brother, 177.
Sárbile, *see* Moninna.
Scandlan Mor, prince of Ossory, son of Cinnfaela (*fl.* 575), 54, 55, 85, 86, 224, 226, 236, 237.
Scotta, daughter of Pharaoh, 183.
Sechmall, 135.
Sechnall, St., or Secundinus, of Dunshaughlin (*d.* Nov. 27, 448). His parentage, 3, 4, 7, 96; quarrel with Patrick and reconciliation, 5; goes to Rome, 5; his hymn in praise of Patrick, 4, 96ff, 176, 182, 185, 241; its metre, xiii, xiv, 97; its indulgence, 6, 7, 97, 98, 120.
Sechtmaide, a pirate chieftain, "king of the Britons," 3, 177. Keating identifies him with Neill of the Nine Hostages.
Secundinus, *see* Sechnall.
Sedulius, junior (*saec.* ix ?), 105.
Segetius, priest, appointed Patrick's companion by Germanus, 180.
Seghine, 5th abbot of Iona (*d.* Aug. 12, 652), 108.
Senan, St., of Scattery Island (*com.* Mar. 8, *fl.* 544), 225.
Sen Patrick, of Glastonbury, 186.
Sincerna, *see* Balthasar.
Sixtus III, Pope (432-441), 180.
Succat, one of Patrick's names, 3, 7, 32, 177.
Suibne mac Colman Moir (*d.* 600), 38.
Sulpicius Severus (*d. cir.* 415), 134, 135.

Talmach, St., perhaps a disciple of St. Brendan (*d.* Feb. 26, *saec.* vi ?), 11, 113.
Tassaig, 88, 238.
Tassach, Patrick's artificer, bp. of Raholp (*com.* Apr. 14), 34, 185.
Tea, wife of Erimon, 181.
Thaddaeus, 30, 52, 111, 174, 175.
Theodosius II, Emperor of the East (408-450), 180.
Tighernach, St., bp. of Clones (*d.* Apr. 4, 548), 241.
Tighernach, annalist (*saec.* xi), 141.
Tigris, Patrick's sister, 177.
Tinne, Adamnan's grandfather, 122.
Tirechan, bp. (*com.* July 3, *saec.* vii), 177.

Ultan, St., of Ardbreccan (*d.* Sept. 4, 656), tutor of Broccan, 189; collected Brigid's miracles, 8, 40; hymn *Christus in nostra*, 8, 107, 223; its metre, xxix, xxx; hymn *Brigit bé bithmaith*, 38, 188, 197; its metre, xxxiii; poem in praise of him, 107.

Valens, Emperor (364-378), 18, 125.
Valentinian I, Emperor (364-375), 18, 125.
Victor, Patrick's angel, 32, 34, 97, 178, 179, 184.

II. Index of Places and Tribes.

Abernethy, 230, 231.
Ader, *see* Gadder.
Africa, 83.
Aghaboe, 141.
Ail Clúade, *i.e.* Dumbarton, 3, 176, 177.
Airiud Boinne, near Clonard, 195.
Alanensis insula, 180. Stokes (*Trip. Life*, 302, 420) suggests *Arelatensis*, *i.e.* Arles.
Alban, *see* Scotland.
Alene, 202.
Alps, 18.
Altissiodorum, *i.e.* Auxerre, 179, 180.
Amalgada, the district of Tirawley (Tir Amalgaid), co. Mayo, 181.
Arad Cliach, *i.e.* Kilteely in co. Limerick, 194.
Ardagh, in co. Longford, 192.
Ardbreccan, in co. Meath, 8, 38, 40, 107.
Arcal, the valley of the Braid in co. Antrim, 178.
Ard mac n-Odrain, in Inishowen, 85.
Ardmurcher, in co. Meath, 134.
Argyle, 224.
Armagh, 5, 34, 96, 184, 185.
Armorica, 3, 96, 177, 179.
Arnon, Mount, 180. The locality intended is doubtful; *see* Todd's *St. Patrick*, 323, 337.
Ath Feni, in West Meath, 53, 56.

Ballymartin, near Belfast, 134.
Banba, an ancient name of Ireland, 186.
Bannauenta, near Daventry, 176.
Belach Feda, *see* Cuil Feda.
Benna Boirche, the Mourne mountains, in co. Down, 33, 183.
Bishops' Hill, on the borders of co. Kildare and co. Wicklow, 195.
Blasantia, *i.e.* Placentia (?), 37, 188, 191.
Blathnat, or Moel-blatha, a flat stone at the monastery at Iona, 23, 141.
Bonmahon, co. Waterford, 238.
Breg, Bregia, a district including Meath, Westmeath, part of Dublin and part of Louth, 199, 203.
Breifne of Connaught, equivalent to co. Leitrim and co. Cavan, 53, 55, 225.
Bri, or Bri Cobthaig Coil, a place in Bregia, 43, 199.
Druiden Da Choca, *i.e.* Breenmore in Westmeath, 84, 236.
Burgundy, 179.

Cahir Ultan, 107.
Caille Fochlad, *see* Fochlad.
Cambray, 106.
Candida Casa, in Galloway, 113.
Carburys, The, 57, 80.

INDEX OF PLACES AND TRIBES.

Cell Ciannain, near Monasterboice, 178.
Cell Culind, *i.e.* Old Kilcullen in co. Kildare, 200.
Cell Fine, perhaps Killeen Cormaic near Dunlavin, 180.
Cell Fionend, 198.
Cell Forcland, west of the R. Moy in co. Mayo, 180.
Cenell Conaill, *i.e.* Tirconnell or Donegal, 76, 121, 122, 234.
Chechtraige Slecht, 53.
Ciannachta, now Keenaght, between Coleraine and Derry, 85, 237.
Ciarraige Luachra, in co. Kerry, 186.
Clocthech, in co. Kildare, 200.
Clonard, 24, 47, 141, 195.
Clonfert, 108, 188.
Cloyne, 228.
Cluaide, *i.e.* Clyde, *see* Ail Cluade.
Cluain Corcaige, in Offaly, 198.
Cluain Fota Baitan Aba, *i.e.* Clonfad in co. Westmeath, 20, 134.
Cluain Moiscna, near Fartullagh in co. Westmeath, 197.
Cluain Mor Moedoc, *i.e.* Clonmore in co. Carlow, 40, 189.
Cnawhill, now Cleghile near Tipperary, 88, 238.
Coleraine, *see* Cuil Rathin.
Conaille Muirthemne, or co. Louth, 3, 97, 178.
Conn's Half, the northern portion of Ireland, 184, 201, 235.
Conry, in Meath, 134.
Cooladrummon, *see* Cuil Dremne.
Corccan Ochaide (?), 64.
Cork, 9, 12, 114.
Corryvreckan, the channel between Rathlin Island and the mainland, 37, 188.
Corthe Snama, "pillar of swimming," near Loch Foyle, 85. See *Felire of Oengus*, p. clx.
Cruach, *i.e.* Croagh Patrick in co. Mayo, 7, 99.
Cruachan Bri Ele, *i.e.* Croghan in King's co., 192.
Cuchulaind's Leap, now Loop Head, 88, 238.
Cuil Dremne, near Sligo, 23, 24, 68, 140, 168, 234, 237.
Cuil Feda, near Clonard, 24, 68, 141.
Cuil Rathin, now Coleraine, 24, 68, 140.
Curragh of Kildare, 45, 196, 198, 199.

Daire Calcaig, now Derry, 10, 23, 28, 73, 109, 140, 171, 228, 237.
Dal Araide, including co. Down, and S. of co. Antrim, 3, 4, 24, 97, 178, 183.
Dal Conchobair, in S. of Bregia, 38.
Dal Osraide, 85.
Dal-riata, now the Route, co. Antrim, 54, 55, 56, 85, 86, 141, 224, 226, 234.
Darinis, near Youghal, 123.
Daventry, 176, 177.
Derry, *see* Daire Calcaig.
Desert Dallan, in Raphoe, 235.
Desert Martin, in Derry, 134.
Desmond, or South Munster, 238.
Devenish, in Lough Erne, 220, 221.
Dinn-rig, now Ballyknockan Fort on the Barrow, near Leighlin Bridge, 58, 227, 229.
Domnach Mor, in Kildare, 195, 196.
Domnach Sechnaill, now Dunshaughlin in co. Meath, 3, 4, 96.
Downpatrick, *see* Dun Lethglasse.
Druim Cetta, near Newtownlimavady, in co. Derry, 53, 55, 58, 67, 85, 122, 224, 225, 226, 231, 238.

LIBER HYMN. II.

INDEX OF PLACES AND TRIBES.

Druim-Lias, now Drumlease, co. Leitrim, 59.
Drumalban, between Argyleshire and Perthshire, 179.
Drumblade, in Aberdeenshire, 127.
Duma Gobla, near Sletty, Queen's co., 31.
Dumbarton, 176.
Dundelga, i.e. Dundalk, 86, 237.
Dun Lethglasse, now Downpatrick, 34, 57, 66, 184, 185, 222, 228.
Dun na n-Airbed, in Meath, 53, 56.
Durrow, see Ross Grencha.

Eder, see Gadder.
Edessa, 30, 111, 173, 174.
Egypt, 116, 129, 183.
Elca, an ancient name of Ireland, 186.
Elpa, Mount, 179, see vol. i, p. 13.
Emania, the royal fort of Ulster, near Armagh, 34, 230.
Emly, 127.
Eoganacht, of Loch Lein, the tribe of Eogan Mor of Munster, 9, 109.
Ephesus, 29.
Eriu, an ancient name of Ireland, 34, 186.
Ethiopia, 131.
Etna, Mount, 161.
Euphrates, 30.

Faichnech, Bog of, now Boughna Bog, 192.
Fail, an ancient name of Ireland, 186.
Fene, see Ath Feni.
Fettar, in Shetland, 127.
Fingal, N. of Dublin, 203.
Fir Telech, now Fartullagh, in co. Westmeath, 192, 197.
Fochlad, near Killala, in co. Mayo, 32, 180, 181.
Fordun, in Kincardineshire, 180, 181.
Fore, in Westmeath, 12, 114.
Forraig Rath, in co. Kildare (?), 200.
Fortuatha, of Leinster, co. Wicklow, 180, 181.
Fotharta Tire, in co. Wexford (?), 200.
Fotla, an ancient name of Ireland, 186.
France, 19.
Franks, 177.
Futerna, probably Whitherne, in Galloway, 11, 113.

Gaba, i.e. Gibeah, 15, 120.
Gabder, see Gadder.
Gadder, Tower of, 21, 128, 135.
Gaels, 3, 58, 184, 186.
Gall-gaels, i.e. "Dano-Irish," 54. They lived along the west coast of Scotland. See *Martyrology of Gorman*, p. 312.
Galls, 58.
Gibeon, 34.
Glasnevin, near Dublin, 171, 236.
Glastonbury, 186, 187.
Glendalough, co. Wicklow, 41, 193.
Glenn Dian, in West Munster, 88.
Glenn-na-Ruachta, now Glenarought, in West Munster, 238.
Greeks, 25, 76.

INDEX OF PLACES AND TRIBES.

Her-cluaide, *see* Ail Cluade.
Hi or Hy, *i.e.* Iona, 23, 24, 27, 54, 57, 66, 73, 108, 109, 121, 122, 135, 140, 141, 225, 230, 233, 235, 237.

Ibar of Cinntracht, *i.e.* Newry, in co. Down, 53, 55, 87, 97, 225.
Ictian Sea, *i.e.* the British Channel, 19, 132, 177, 191.
Inber Boinne, also called Inber Colptha, the mouth of the Boyne, 178.
Inber Colptha, *see* Inber Boinne.
Inber Mara, perhaps the Straits of Gibraltar, 191.
India, 61, 131.
Inis Boffin, off the coast of Mayo, 64, 231.
Inis Cleire, off the coast of Cork, 114.
Inis Eidbeand (?) 83.
Inishowen, at the western side of Loch Foyle, 85.
Inis Matoc, perhaps in the Lake of Temple Port, co. Leitrim, 47, 206.
Inis Murray, off the coast of Sligo, 140, 220.
Iona, *see* Hi.
Irarus, now Oris in co. Westmeath, 53, 225.
Ita's Cell, now Killeedy, in co. Limerick, 9, 108.

Kilcummin, in co. Mayo, 108.
Kildallan, 225.
Kildare, 38, 45, 191, 195-201, 203.
Killdaleas, 206.
Kilmacrenan, 122.
Kilmartin, 134.

Lamlash, 220.
Letha, *i.e.* Letavia or Armorica, *i.e.* Brittany, 3, 4, 32, 96, 177, 179.
Letha, *i.e.* Latium or Italy, 44, 179, 204.
Leth Cuinn, *see* Conn's Half.
Liath, now Lemanaghan in King's co., 114.
Licc Brendan, apparently in Kildare, 196.
Liffey, R., 196, 197, 199.
Loch Foyle, 85.
Loch Lein, the largest lake at Killarney, 9, 109.
Loch Lemnachta, in Kildare, 196.
Loch Owel, in Westmeath, 227.
Lombards, 3, 4, 7, 96.
Luachair, now Slieve Lougher in Kerry, 88, 238.

Mag Coil, in Fingal, 44, 203.
Mag Fea, in the barony of Forth, co. Carlow, 43, 201.
Mag Fenamain, in co. Limerick, 194.
Mag Inis, now Lecale, co. Down, 185.
Mag Lorha, in Bregia. Stokes (*Gorman*, pp. 319, 320) suggests that it is Moylagh in co. Meath.
Mag Murisce, in co. Mayo, 232.
Mag Slecht, near Ballymagauran in co. Cavan, 55, 225.
Mag Soile, apparently in co. Down, 185.
Maisten, now Mullaghmast, in co. Kildare, 200, 201.
Masraige, a district in Westmeath, 53, 55, 225.
Mog-Nuadat, now Maynooth in co. Dublin, 58, 228.
Monasterboice, in co. Louth, 178.
Mons Gargani, 18, 125.
Mons Iouis, 19, 125.
Morca, 57, 227.

Moville, near Strangford Lough, 11, 112, 132, 145, 233.
Moy R., in co. Mayo, 180.
Munster, 9, 88, 184, 238.

Nemthur, 32. See pp. 176, 177, for a discussion of its situation.
Nicaea, 92.

O'Bric's Island, on the coast of co. Waterford, 88, 238.
Offaly, in co. Kildare, 192, 197, 198, 202.
Ormond, 88, 238.
Osraige, *i.e.* Ossory, 54, 55, 141, 237, 238.

Placentia, *see* Blassantia.
Plea (?), 41, 191.
Portus Iccius, near Boulogne, 132.

Raholp, in co. Down, 185.
Rath Cathair, near Kildare, 196.
Rath Derthaige, in Offaly, 197.
Rathlin Island, off the coast of co. Antrim, 188.
Ratismace, 60.
Remesiana, 138, 139.
Rhine, R., 69, 232.
Ri Cuind, in co. Kildare (?), 200.
Rodan's Island, 19, 132.
Rome, 5, 22, 23, 37, 89, 204.
Ross Dela, now Rossdala, in co. Westmeath, 186, 187.
Ross Grencha, now Durrow, in King's co., 86, 237.
Ross na Ferta, in Kildare, 200.
Ross na Ree, on the R. Boyne, 236.
Ross Torathair, near Coleraine, 24, 68.

Sanna, *see* Susanna.
Saul, in co. Down, 183, 184.
Scecha, in co. Kildare, near Killeen Cormaic, 204.
Scirit, now Skerry, in co. Antrim, 178.
Scotland, or Alban, 16, 23, 24, 54, 55, 57, 63, 75, 85, 86, 122, 179.
Scythia, 183.
Shinar, 91, 183.
Sidh Femin, in co. Tipperary, 230.
Slan, a fountain at Saul, 33, 183.
Slane, Hill of, near Tara, 208.
Slemish, in co. Antrim, 3, 97, 178.
Slemish, in co. Kerry, 186.
Sletty, in Queen's co., 8, 31, 36, 175, 176.
Slieve Aughty, between co. Galway and co. Clare, 88, 238.
Slieve Bloom, on the borders of King's co. and Queen's co., 40, 189.
Slieve Cain, in co. Limerick, 88, 238.
Slieve Elim, *see* Slieve Phelim.
Slieve Gullion, in co. Armagh, 187.
Slieve Lougher, *see* Luachair.
Slieve Phelim, properly Slieve Elim, in co. Limerick, 88, 238.
Slieve Reagh, in co. Limerick, 238.
Slige Assail, the great road dividing Meath, 56, 227.
Slige Dala, the great road of Ossory, 88, 238.
Spain, 186.

Suidhe Adamnain, now Syonan, in Westmeath, 134.
Susanna, or Sanna, perhaps Soissons or Sens, 18, 135.

Tai, the river Tay, 63, 76, 230, 234.
Tara, in Meath, 31, 33, 34, 49, 122, 176, 181, 184, 208, 238.
Tech Duinn, an island in Kenmare Bay, 184.
Tech na Romanach, now Tigroney, in co. Wicklow, 180.
Temhair, *see* Tara.
Temple Kieran, in Meath, 218.
Temple Martin, (a) near Bandon, (b) near Kilkenny, 134.
Temple Michael, 133.
Thomond, or North Munster, 88, 238.
Tig Lommain, in co. Westmeath, 56, 227.
Tirawley, *see* Amalgada.
Tirconnell, or Donegal, 234.
Tiree, an island off Mull, 232.
Tir Lugdach, in barony of Kilmacrenan, co. Donegal, 121, 122.
Tir na bennact, "Land of the Benediction," near Clonard, 195.
Toi, *see* Tai.
Tory Island, off the Donegal coast, 141.
Treoit, now Trevet, in co. Meath, 11.
Tuaim Tenma, *i.e.* Dinnrig, q.v., 58, 229.
Tulach Dubglaisse, now Temple Douglas, near Letterkenny, in co. Donegal, 121, 122.
Turbi, in Bregia, N. of Dublin (?), 193.
Tyrrhene Sea, adjoining W. coast of Italy, 19, 32, 132, 180.

Uachtur Gabra, "in the plain of Leinster," 43, 201.
Ui Bard, 4, 7.
Ui Barrchi, now the barony of Slievemargy, Queen's co., 31.
Ui Briuin Cualand, partly in co. Dublin and partly in co. Wicklow, 195.
Ui Ceinselaig, in co. Wexford, 200, 201.
Ui Cerbaill, 203.
Ui Cluasaig, 12.
Ui Culduib, 204.
Ui Domnaill, 140, 234.
Ui Enna (?), 180.
Ui Garrchon, in co. Wicklow, near Glenealy, 180.
Ui Loscain, 201.
Ui Lugair, 31.
Ui mac Carthaind, the region between Coleraine and Derry, 85, 237.
Ui Muredaig, in co. Kildare, 201.
Ui Neill, *i.e.* the southern O'Neills occupying a territory in Meath, 192.
Uisnech, the reputed centre of Ireland, now Usnagh, in Westmeath, 20, 134.
Ui Tigernan, in Meath, 53.
Ulstermen, 68, 84, 87.
Ur of the Chaldees, 15, 115, 119.

Whitherne, *see* Futerna.

www.ingramcontent.com/pod-product-compliance
Lightning Source LLC
Chambersburg PA
CBHW030117240426
43673CB00041B/1307